Skillful Coping

C000116863

For fifty years Hubert L. Dreyfus has addressed an astonishing range of issues in the fields of phenomenology, existentialism, cognitive science, and the philosophical study of mind. Dreyfus has inspired a whole generation of philosophers as he has creatively drawn on and clearly articulated the seminal works of thinkers like Kierkegaard, Husserl, Heidegger, Merleau-Ponty, and Foucault. This volume presents a selection of Dreyfus's most influential essays on mind and action.

The book begins with a model of skillful engaged human action, which informs much of Dreyfus's philosophy, and was developed in collaboration with Stuart Dreyfus. The volume then presents articles developing a critique of the representational model of the mind in analytical philosophy of mind and mainstream cognitive science. Dreyfus argues that representational models of mind offer an impoverished and distorting account of human engagement with the world. The chapters show this by addressing issues in philosophy of mind and the cognitive sciences through phenomenology.

Skillful Coping

Essays on the Phenomenology of Everyday Perception and Action

Hubert L. Dreyfus

EDITED BY
Mark A. Wrathall

OXFORD
UNIVERSITY PRESS

OXFORD
UNIVERSITY PRESS

Great Clarendon Street, Oxford, OX2 6DP,
United Kingdom

Oxford University Press is a department of the University of Oxford.
It furthers the University's objective of excellence in research, scholarship,
and education by publishing worldwide. Oxford is a registered trade mark of
Oxford University Press in the UK and in certain other countries

Published in the United States of America by Oxford University Press
198 Madison Avenue, New York, NY 10016, United States of America

British Library Cataloguing in Publication Data
Data available

Library of Congress Cataloging in Publication Data
Data available

ISBN 978–0–19–965470–3 (Hbk.)
ISBN 978–0–19–877729–8 (Pbk.)

Credits

Chapter 1 originally published in Carl Mitcham and Alois Huning, eds, *Philosophy and Technology II: Information Technology and Computers in Theory and Practice*, Boston Studies in the Philosophy of Science Series (D. Reidel, 1985). Reprinted with kind permission from Stuart Dreyfus and Springer Science+Business Media B.V.

Chapter 2 originally published in L. Embree, ed., *Life-World and Consciousness* (Northwestern University Press, 1970). Reprinted by permission of Northwestern University Press.

Chapter 3 originally published in *Social Research*, vol. 60, no. 1 (Spring 1993). Reprinted by permission of *Social Research*.

Chapter 4 originally published as the introduction to Samuel Todes's *Body and World*, MIT Press (April 2001). Reprinted by permission of Piotr Hoffman and MIT Press.

Chapter 5 originally published in *Proceedings and Addresses of the American Philosophical Association*, vol. 79, issue 2 (November 2005).

Chapter 6 originally published in *The Review of Metaphysics* (September 1980). Reprinted by permission of *The Review of Metaphysics*.

Chapter 7 originally published in *Philosophical Topics*, ed. Mark A. Wrathall and Hubert L. Dreyfus, vol. 27, no. 2, Fall 1999 (2001). Reprinted by permission of *Philosophical Topics*.

Chapter 8 originally published in Alexandre Métraux and Bernhard Waldenfels, eds, *Leibhaftige Vernunft* (Fink Verlag, 1986). Reprinted by permission of Hubert L. Dreyfus.

Chapter 9 originally published in James Ogilvy, ed., *Revisioning Philosophy* (State University of New York Press, 1992). Reprinted by permission of SUNY Press.

Chapter 10 originally published in *Daedalus* (Winter 1988). Reprinted by permission. © 1988 by the American Academy of Arts and Sciences.

Chapter 11 originally published in Taylor Carman and Mark Hansen, eds, *The Cambridge Companion to Merleau-Ponty* (Cambridge: Cambridge University Press, 2004). Reprinted by permission of Cambridge University Press.

Chapter 12 originally published in *Philosophical Psychology* (Routledge), vol. 20, no. 2 (April 2007), 247–68. Reprinted by permission of Taylor & Francis.

Acknowledgments

This project simply would not have been possible without Genevieve Dreyfus. I can't thank her enough for her encouragement and generous assistance with every aspect of the process of editing this volume. Also deserving of thanks are Christian Pillsbury, Will Swanson, Kevin Gin, Patrick Londen, Patrick Ryan, and Justin White for their participation in a reading group devoted to Bert's work during compilation and preparation of this manuscript for publication.

M.A.W.

Contents

Part IV. Embodied Coping and Artificial Intelligence

Introduction

Hubert Dreyfus and the Phenomenology
of Human Intelligence

Mark A. Wrathall

A central aim of Hubert Dreyfus's work is to offer an account of the nature of
human understanding that can do full justice to our ability to cope intelligently
with the world. In advancing this aim, Dreyfus has found it necessary to develop
an account of human nature that is at odds with many of the background
assumptions of the Western philosophical tradition. Of the mainstream way of
thinking about intelligence, Dreyfus writes:

> During the past two thousand years, the importance of objectivity; the belief that actions
> are governed by fixed values; the notion that skills can be formalized; and in general that
> one can have a theory of practical activity, have gradually exerted their influence in
> psychology and in social science. People have begun to think of themselves as objects
> able to fit into the inflexible calculations of disembodied machines: machines for which
> the human form-of-life must be analyzed into meaningless facts, rather than a field of
> concern organized by sensory-motor skills. Our risk is not the advent of superintelligent
> computers, but of subintelligent human beings.[1]

As this passage makes clear, Dreyfus's inquiry into human understanding opens out
into broad existential questions about the good life, and world-historical questions
about nihilism and our technological age. These themes will be a central concern in
volume 2 of these collected papers. In this volume, however, the essays are primarily
concerned with setting up the alternative account of human understanding and
intelligence that Dreyfus advances, and tracing out the implications this account
has for epistemology, philosophy of mind and psychology, philosophy of action,
philosophy of the social sciences, cognitive science, and ethics.

---

[1] Hubert L. Dreyfus, *What Computers Still Can't Do* (Cambridge, MA: MIT Press, 1992), 280.

In his published works, Dreyfus tends (rather too modestly, in my opinion) to attribute his insights to other philosophers—primarily Heidegger and Merleau-Ponty. But his account of skillful coping offers an original account of human understanding in several important respects. In particular, Dreyfus's account of *skillful coping* as the paradigm of human action is something that is, at best, implicit in his philosophical antecedents. Dreyfus has elaborated that account into a rich phenomenology of a variety of levels of skill, each of which illuminates a different mode of world disclosure and different normative standards. As a result, Dreyfus's engagement with analytic philosophy of mind and action, with theory in the human sciences, and with artificial intelligence research, is in no way a simple or straightforward application of the work of others to new domains. At the same time, Dreyfus's engagement with these different disciplines has allowed him to develop and refine the phenomenology of human under-standing that he has inherited from the existential-phenomenological tradition.

* * *

To set the stage for the papers that follow, I'd like to sketch out in very broad strokes two competing ways of thinking about human intelligence: the traditional approach that Dreyfus critiques, and the phenomenologically based model that Dreyfus advances. A central element of intelligence, an element common to both models, is purposiveness—the ability to achieve one's aims in response to changing circumstances and starting from a variety of different situations.

Traditional or mainstream approaches to human intelligence are premised on what Dreyfus has dubbed "the epistemological view of the mind":

the epistemological conception of mind is roughly that the mind consists of a set of ideas, analogous to images or descriptions, that represent the outside world and may correspond or fail to correspond to what is actually out there in the world. The mind is a set of representations, and through these representations the person knows and relates to the world. (Chapter 8)

This picture of the mind encourages us to think of purposive action as a bodily movement that is guided or directed by some psychological or mental state. Intentional actions, on this view, are bodily movements which are caused by a prior intention to make those bodily movements in order to perform the action. The intention, in turn, is caused by some conjunction of desires directed at some end, and beliefs about what actions will satisfy those desires.

This traditional approach to thinking about our place as intelligent beings in the world rests on three important and interrelated assumptions. First, there is an assumption that a clear distinction can be drawn between an agent and the world within which the agent acts. The world is generally thought of as a more or less determinate collection of objects which causally impinge on the agent. The agent is taken as roughly co-extensive with a body, and the mental economy of the agent is in some sense contained in the agent's head. Second, the explanatory grounds of action are thought to be internal to the agent—to lie within the economy of mental events and states that produce the bodily movements. This is not to deny that those mental events and states are causally impacted by events in the world, but rather that without the mediation of the mind, the causal impingements from the world cannot themselves cause the responding bodily movements to be actions. The action must trace its foundation as an action to some state or event internal to the agent—a representation, for example, of the conditions of satisfaction of the action. Finally, consummate action—action at its best—is thought to result from deliberation, understood as the assessment and weighing of reasons in order to determine which course of action is the most rational way to pursue the purposive ends of the agent.

The key move in Dreyfus's analysis of intelligent or purposive comportment is to take skillful bodily activity—"skillful coping," in Dreyfus's words—as the consummate form of human intelligence: "This alternative conception of man and his ability to behave intelligently," as Dreyfus notes, "is really an analysis of the way man's skillful bodily activity…generates the human world."[2] So rather than starting from cognition as the primary locus of intelligence, and *building out* to an account of action, Dreyfus starts with the premise that skillful activity itself is the consummate form and foundation of human intelligence, and derives an account of cognition from coping.

When I am engaged in skillful coping—"in the flow," as we say—my ability to stay in the flow depends not on a deliberative assessment of competing desires and motivations, but rather on the world drawing me into and sustaining me in a single clear course of action—the one which will allow me to maintain a sure-footed stance. This view does not require the mediation of mental or psychological states. Rather, through learning and practice, I become attuned to the world in such a way that the situation itself presents to me "reasons" for action that immediately draw on my body, soliciting a response: "past experience is projected back into the perceptual world of the learner and shows up as affordances or solicitations to further action" (Chapter 11).

All it takes to disrupt a fluid immersion in skillful activity is to consider and assess alternate possibilities for action. Thus, skillful coping is sustained, not by the weighing and examining of beliefs, desires, and reasons, but by the withdrawal of deliberative activity and the silencing of reasons. Competitors for my attention recede, leaving me to respond without distraction to the flow of solicitations that arise in response to my bodily movements—movements

---

[2] Dreyfus, *What Computers Still Can't Do*, 280.

which themselves are drawn out of me by the solicitations of the world. Dreyfus likes to quote Merleau-Ponty on this point, according to whom the agent's "projects polarize the world, bringing magically to view a host of signs which guide action, as notices in a museum guide the visitor."[3] But skillful coping, Dreyfus points out, is not some rare and exotic category of human behavior—it is instead simultaneously the highest and most basic form of engagement with the world. Each of us is expert at a host of everyday activities that sustain everything we do—we know how to stand in a crowded room, how to drive a car, how to check out of a grocery store, how to carry on a conversation, and so on. So skillful coping is something with which each of us is familiar, and thus we can readily consult it in assessing the assumptions about human intelligence made by the model of deliberative action.

Dreyfus argues that the phenomenon of fluid coping, taken as the paradigm of intelligent action, gives us good reason to reject the background assumptions of the traditional model of human intelligence. In the place of these traditional presuppositions, we get:

(1) a rejection of the "common sense" distinction between mind and world.

Dreyfus advances "an alternative model of the mind's relation to reality" or, more precisely, a model that "do[es] not refer to the mind at all. Rather...the whole human being is related to the world. Indeed, even 'relation' is misleading, since it suggests the coming together of two separate entities—human being and world—whereas...mind and world [are] inseparable" (Chapter 8). Naturally, we can still distinguish between a particular person and the world, but the person is not primarily individuated by the outer contours of a particular occurrent body. Rather, an individual is a particular style of projecting into the world—a projection that 'generates the human world' because it is from our skillful, passionate, involved engagement with our setting that solicitations can arise and function as grounds for our actions. (Of course, this style involves a body, but much else as well.)

It follows that:

(2) the explanatory grounds of intelligent activity lie as much in the world as in the agent.

Dreyfus notes: "I can't be skillfully coping, say, dribbling a basketball, unless I am responding to the actual object" (Chapter 4). The point is not the trivial one that actions that involve objects can't be executed without those objects. The point is

---

[3] Maurice Merleau-Ponty, *Phenomenology of Perception*, tr. Colin Smith (New York: Humanities Press, 1962), 112.

rather that skillful movements are guided by the particular significances that are sedimented into the relevant features of the situation. Even the best mime doesn't precisely reproduce the movements of skillfully dribbling a basketball, for instance, because the very specific form and texture of the basketball and the surface of the ground (among other things) guide the shape and position and movement of our hands. Dreyfus notes, "in our most basic way of being—i.e., as skillful copers—we are not minds at all but one with the world.... [T]he inner–outer distinction becomes problematic. There's no easily askable question about where the absorbed coping is—in me or in the world" (Chapter 12).

Finally,

> (3) from the perspective of the paradigm of fluid coping, the need to delib-
> eratively weigh reasons, assess beliefs, evaluate desires and so on, far from
> being the distinguishing feature of intelligence, typically arises in cases of a
> breakdown in our understanding:
>
>> when a master has to deliberate . . . it's because there has been some sort of disturb-
>> ance that has disrupted her intuitive response. Perhaps the situation is so unusual
>> that no immediate response is called forth. Or several responses are solicited with
>> equal pull. (Chapter 5)

Of course, such cognitive activities do manifest human intelligence—reasoning can contribute to achieving our purposive ends. But these activities are left behind when fluid coping is possible.

The assumptions that support the model of deliberative action are so ingrained in the ways we talk about and describe action that they are taken as self-evident, commonsensical. To loosen their hold on us, Dreyfus returns repeatedly to a description of the process of skill acquisition. According to the model of deliberative action that we have outlined, degrees of expertise or skillfulness are reduced simply to the ease, rapidity, and intuitiveness with which someone can perform an action. But the expert's actions are not regarded as fundamentally different from the actions of a beginner or a merely competent performer—for the beginner and virtuoso alike, the situation is articulated in the same way and the action is performed according to the same rules and governed by the same standards of assessment. But the phenomenology of skill acquisition, as Dreyfus demonstrates, shows that agents who possess different levels of skill are, in a very real sense, engaged in different kinds of activities.

Dreyfus developed his account of skill acquisition in collaboration with Stuart Dreyfus.[4] The initial focus was on modeling what it is like for an adult to learn a

---

[4] See Chapter 1, this volume. Some version of the "skills model" or the "phenomenology of skill acquisition" is presented in Chapters 5, 9, and 11. See also "Could Anything Be More Intelligible than Everyday Intelligibility?", in volume 2.

new skill. In studying such learning contexts, the brothers Dreyfus noticed that learners advance through five distinct levels of skillfulness—the "novice," the "advanced beginner," "competence," "proficiency," and "expertness"—as they gradually are weaned from a dependence on using rules and deliberating on aims and strategies, and start responding more intuitively to the solicitations of the environment (Chapter 1). As the Dreyfuses noted, learning works slightly differently in different contexts—for example, a child acquires skillfulness in social norms and conventional behavior (like distance standing or language use) differently than an adult acquires a new skill. It makes a difference to learning to have a knowledgeable coach guiding the learning, rather than having to acquire everything on one's own through a process of trial and error. And different skills present importantly different dimensions that impact the learning process. For instance, learning to play a musical instrument involves a kind of bodily engagement with a dynamic situation that is absent in learning to philosophize. Different skills are subject in different ways to the existence of social norms that govern the appropriate and inappropriate ways to do things—skills of ethics and etiquette, for example, are much more concerned with social proprieties than skills of carpentry. And Dreyfus does not hold that one necessarily progresses serially through each of the stages in order to arrive at the highest level of skillfulness. In certain domains and under certain circumstances, it might be possible to skip stages altogether. As a result, there is no single model of skill acquisition that could account for all the variety of ways we learn to act skillfully.

But the basic skills model is sufficient to illuminate how action actually bears a different structure at each of the different levels of expertise. For instance, on the traditional model, the same rules govern the actions of the beginner and the expert alike. Learning is thus thought of as coming to understand the rules which govern behavior—of beginning with an acquaintance with specific cases and learning through experience to abstract out of those specific cases general rules which are followed in all skillful action. But the phenomenology of skill acquisition shows that learning in fact moves in the other direction—from abstract rules to the recognition of particular cases. By the time one becomes an expert in a domain, one has an intuitive ability to recognize and respond to highly particularized situations and, unlike the beginner, is in no sense applying rules at all. The deliberative model of purposive action, it turns out, describes at best the way that a merely competent performer interacts with the world. A true expert acts in a way that is too flexible and sensitive to the specificities of the concrete situation to be governed by rules and guided by mental representations.

If agents at different levels of skill are, in an important sense, involved in different types of action, we should be able to describe the structure of these different modes of action. The phenomenology of skill acquisition suggests that more and less skillful actions differ from one another in terms of:

- the different sorts of elements to which the agent responds;
- the different means the agent employs for guiding or governing his or her response to the features of the world;
- different ways of determining the successful performance of an action.

Let's address each of these things in turn.

The Elements to Which an Agent Responds

Dreyfus sees the world at its most basic level as a rich and fine-grained structure of functionality relationships. What we normally encounter is not a desk, and certainly not an object with properties of shape, dimension, color, hardness, and so on. What we first encounter is an affordance—a "for sitting at and writing on." As Dreyfus puts it, the world is made up of "for-whats," not "whats" (Chapter 12). The world presents to the agent a fluctuating pull of solicitations as the affordances of the world draw her into action. The more skillful the agent is, the more fluidly she is able to respond to these solicitations. And that means that the world immediately shows up for the skillful agent as drawing her to perform the optimal action.

Higher levels of skillfulness are thus marked by the ability to discriminate and experience the particular solicitations offered by the concrete setting of action in a maximally refined way—that is, as drawing out of us movements which are more nuanced, more precisely tailored to fluidly deal with the demands of the current situation. Lower levels of skillfulness could be said to perceptually decompose the world, uncovering objects in cruder, more simplistic ways. At the lowest, most deliberative level of skillfulness, the agent is taught to discriminate features in a maximally decontextualized way. A learner driver, for instance, is taught to shift gears when the needle on the tachometer points to a certain number. To discern such decontextualized elements, one need only to be able to recognize numbers and find one of a few positions for the gear shifter. An advanced learner acquires a more nuanced skill—the ability to recognize the significance things have in their context or situation. So rather than relying on the maximally decontextualized skill of reading numbers off a gauge, for instance, an advanced learner driver learns to recognize the significance that the sound of an engine has in different contexts. An advanced learner can pick up that an engine straining while driving up a steep hill sounds different than an engine racing while accelerating on a highway.

As one becomes more practiced in dealing with things, the environment no longer shows up as composed out of objects with discriminable properties. Instead, one's discriminatory capacities are enriched so that one can immediately discern affordances—that is, the opportunities and possibilities for action that a particular setting offers us. Which affordances show up, of course, are relative to the perspective or stance one adopts on the situation. If a soccer player adopts a defense posture—perhaps because she is trying to protect a lead—different areas of the pitch will draw her attention than if she is trying to score an equalizing goal. As one gains experience with taking up different perspectives on a situation, one acquires the skill to discriminate which stances are most likely to lead to success in a given type of situation. The result will be that one acquires the skill for immediately discriminating different meaningful types of situations. A situation will acquire a "look"—it will show up, say, as the kind of situation that will reward a more defensive style of play, prompting one to change one's stance or perspective. Ultimately, as one gets used to recognizing situations, taking up an appropriate perspective, and responding to affordances for action, one gets so attuned that one no longer identifies affordances or situations as such. Instead, we find ourselves taken up immediately into what Merleau-Ponty describes as "the dialectic of milieu and action."[5] One copes most fluidly and skillfully when one allows oneself to be drawn into action by the environmental solicitations which, in turn, respond to one's response.

Means of Action Guidance and Governance

Corresponding to the different features in the world to which an agent is capable of responding are different modes of governing one's actions.

Maximally decontextualized features do not, in and of themselves, offer us any guidance in knowing how to respond. The mere fact that the needle points to the number 3 on the tachometer, or that the engine is loud and racing, tells me nothing about what I ought to do. If the beginner's bodily movements are to be anything more than a random response to these facts, he needs some rule to tell him how to get reliably and predictably from this situation to a desired outcome. Thus, a beginner's movements are purposive to the degree that they are guided by a rule or a maxim that gives him an understanding of the relationship between situations, actions, and outcomes.

[5] Maurice Merleau-Ponty, *The Structure of Behavior*, tr. A. L. Fisher (2nd edn; Boston: Beacon Press, 1966), 169.

To see an affordance, in contrast to a decontextualized feature, is simultaneously to see what I can do, how I could respond. When I see a door as an affordance, for instance, I don't just see a large rectangular object, but I see a means of egress or ingress. But the affordance doesn't tell me whether I *should* respond to the possibility for action. And the emergence of the affordances depends, in the first place, on my taking up a particular stance on the situation. Thus, to come to see objects as affordances might require deliberation and a considerable amount of experimentation on my part, as I try to work out which perspectives to take up so that the situation can show me the most efficacious path to my desired end, and which of the many possible affordances I ought to respond to. The deliberation engaged in at this level is an *involved* kind of deliberation, an experimental or counterfactual form of reasoning (if I take up this perspective, then this will happen; if I respond to this affordance, then the situation will change in this way). This deliberation might at times appeal to the rules and maxims that structure a rule-following response. But with an ability to discriminate the various possibilities and risks afforded by a particular situation in a more and more subtle and nuanced way, the rules and maxims increasingly constrain rather than facilitate response. The more experienced one is at deliberation, and the more one is dispositionally attuned to the situation, the more intuitively one will recognize the relative advantages and disadvantages of each alternative perspective and decision.

Finally, in the very moment that one perceives solicitations, one is simultaneously drawn into motion. The solicited agent no longer needs to deliberately initiate and guide her actions. Her role rather becomes one of monitoring and governing an ongoing course of action by an intuitive feel or sense of greater and lesser tension, ease, or flow. The more experienced and expert an agent is in a domain, the more types of cases she will be able to deal with intuitively, and the fewer occasions there will be where she needs to deliberate about which features are the important ones to which she should respond. Nor will she need to deliberate about how to proceed or what perspective she should take on the situation. If an expert or master does need to deliberate, she doesn't reason in a detached, rule-governed way (the way a beginner would). Instead, her deliberation is grounded in intuition. She stays engaged and involved in the situation, reflecting on the appropriateness of her intuitive responses, or looking for previously ignored subtleties that, once noticed, make a particular action "intuitively compelling."

Thus, we can distinguish several different ways in which agents guide their actions, by: (1) the application of rules and maxims; (2) deliberation and experimentation; and (3) a feeling of greater or lesser tension.

Ways of Determining Success

Analysis of skill acquisition brings out an important feature of our pre-philo-sophical way of thinking about action—namely, that the success or failure of an action is not simply a matter of achieving a certain goal, but rather of achieving the goal in the right way. We don't consider someone a successful driver, for instance, just because he drives to the place he wants to go, if in the process he drives randomly and unpredictably, causing other drivers to have accidents along the way. So the outcome needs to be achieved by exercising an appropriate kind of guidance control over the action. But as we've seen, there are different ways in which an action can be guided. There are correspondingly different ways in which the success of an action can be determined. And, in fact, the success or failure of the action can to some degree swing free of the realization of the desired outcome inherent in the activity. We consider a beginning player of chess to succeed, for instance, if she accurately follows the strategic rules she has been taught, even if she loses the game. Conversely, we would not consider her genuinely successful if she haphazardly and accidentally won a game while ignoring the rules and maxims of good play.

As an agent becomes more skillful at performing a task, success is increasingly a matter of intuitively picking up and responding to the meanings the situation offers, and doing so in such a way that one achieves what Dreyfus calls a "maximal grip" or the "optimal coping point" for dealing with a situation. As Dreyfus explains:

once an expert has learned to cope successfully, at each stage in a sequential, goal-directed activity, either he senses that he is doing as well as possible at that stage, or he senses a tension that tells him he is deviating from an optimal gestalt and feels drawn to make a next move that, thanks to his previous learning, is likely to be accompanied by less tension. (Chapter 11)

For Dreyfus, this kind of success condition is actually more fundamental than success in achieving the aims of the activity as it is conventionally understood. Thus, Dreyfus does not rank levels of skillfulness in terms of how reliably one's actions succeed by conventional standards. That is to say, possessing the highest level of skill for Dreyfus is not like a chess or tennis ranking, where the higher ranked player will predictably and reliably beat lower ranked players. Since the levels of skill really name different ways of disclosing and responding to the world, it's entirely possible on Dreyfus's account that an expert at tennis is a "worse" player than someone who is merely competent or proficient—"worse," that is, when judged in terms of winning or losing tennis games. Dreyfus explains:

when Stuart (Dreyfus) and I describe how one can become an expert, let us say, in tennis, chess, driving or whatever, that *could* mean becoming very good at driving or playing tennis or chess. But that is not what it means when Stuart and I say it. It means that you become able to respond intuitively in a way which is appropriate to the situation. But you might have learned tennis in such a way that you chop at the ball, and you may have become an expert at playing tennis without a forehand stroke. That means you will never play very good tennis, but you will be able, given your limitations, to respond intuitively with the best possible chop. So we just need to distinguish two senses of expertise.[6]

In other words, expertise as Dreyfus understands it is an ability to discern and respond fluidly to the solicitations of the situation. Dreyfus continues:

you could do that while being a bad driver or a bad tennis player. My favorite example of this is that if you were a stunt driver you might well be a very bad driver in the everyday world, if you like to drive fast and want to see how well you can make the car spin around in a circle when you put on the brakes, and so forth. You could do that with intensity, you could do that intuitively, you could do that on the basis of a lot of experience. You would be valuable in Hollywood, but you would be a disaster on the highway. The point is that Stuart and I are interested in a certain attitude; experts have to be intuitive, committed, involved and open—and that is going to be the case even if they do whatever they do in a way they are not supposed to do it, so that they don't win in chess, they don't win in tennis and so forth. We are much more interested in the attitude. Of course it is important that the people who are best in these fields, that do win in chess or tennis, do have this attitude. You can't be an expert, in the sense of being the best, without having this attitude that we are talking about, but you can have this attitude and still not be the best. In either case, you can learn a skill like chess by playing lots of games, and perhaps imitating a coach. You don't have to be integrated into the traditional practices of a community.[7]

So at the level of rule following, success is governed by the facility with which one identifies the features and aspects that are relevant to execution of the rule or maxim, and by one's accuracy and reliability in applying the rules and maxims to those features and aspects. At the level of deliberation, success is governed by one's ability to take up the right perspective for disclosing the affordances of the situation, and then deciding which affordances to respond to in order to be led to the goal that guides the activity. It is at this level that success is most clearly governed by the achievement of one's aims. At the level of fluid coping, however, success is a matter of being responsive to solicitations in such a way that one can approximate the optimal gestalt for continuing to fluidly respond to the situation, no matter what contingencies occur.

---

[6] Hubert Dreyfus, 'Teaching between Skill and Philosophy by a Philosopher of Skills', *Journal of Nordic Educational Research* (2000), 107–16.

[7] Dreyfus, "Teaching between Skill and Philosophy".

But an important feature of Dreyfus's view is the recognition that there is no single "optimal gestalt." And Dreyfus has accordingly distinguished between three kinds of expertise, each of which has its optimum determined in a different way. There are, in other words, different ideals for fluid coping. For what I'll call the "conventional expert," an optimal gestalt is the one in which the solicitations one picks up and responds to are those which also lead one to succeed by conventional standards. The tension that guides the conventional expert's action is an intuitive feeling for what is socially appropriate or inappropriate under the circumstances. For the "cultural master" or *phronimos*, the optimal gestalt is the one that allows the agent to disclose new possibilities for continuing the social practice in the face of conflict. The cultural master's responsiveness to solicitations is one that has been shaped by a sensitivity to the meaning of the practice as a whole. Finally, for the "radical innovator" or "world-discloser,"[8] the optimal gestalt is the one in which those solicitations stand out that will lead to a whole new way of understanding and experiencing the world. The radical innovator is able to do this because she has shaped her receptivity to solicitations by fostering marginal practices, and thus feels constantly drawn to act in a way that will open up new forms of intelligibility and new possibilities for action.

* * *

Taking our lead from Dreyfus's phenomenology of skill acquisition, we can summarize the analysis of different forms of action as in Table 1. The natural course of development in skill acquisition tracks closely the ascent from rule following to fluid coping. On Dreyfus's view, this fact helps us to recognize that these levels fall naturally into a hierarchical order of higher and lower forms of activity. The more intuitively we respond to the world, and the more fine-grained discriminations we can recognize in the situation, the better the world is disclosed to us. In acquiring a skill, then, we can rightly regard the levels of skillful action as stages that one passes through as one gradually acquires command of a domain. But this can be misleading in a couple of respects. First, it is important to emphasize that Dreyfus believes that human beings always acquire new skills on the foundation of a pre-existing expertise—that human action, at its most basic level, already involves expert coping with the world. Skill acquisition enriches and develops one's expertise with the world as one learns to discriminate and respond to situations that were not evident or well-articulated before. But one is never confronted with a bare world of decontextualized features, and one never relies wholly on rules for dealing with those features. Instead, even our ability to discern

---

[8] See "Could Anything Be More Intelligible than Everyday Intelligibility?", in volume 2 of these collected papers.

Table 1. Types of skillful action

	Elements responded to:	Action governed by:	Success determined by:
Rule following (novices and advanced beginners)	maximally decontextualized features, situational aspects	application of rules and maxims	accuracy in identifying features and aspects, precision in applying rules and maxims
Deliberation (competence and proficiency)	affordances (perspectival opportunities, risks, expectations, possibilities), meaningful types of situation	deliberation and experimentation	taking up the right perspective, responding to the right affordances
Skillful Coping			
Conventional expert	solicitations that lead to a conventionally accepted outcome	feeling of greater or lesser tension	degree to which one achieves a maximal grip/approximation to an optimal gestalt
Mastery	solicitations that lead to the meaning of the practice/world as a whole	feeling of greater or lesser tension	disclosing new possibilities for continuing the practice in the face of conflict
Radical innovation	solicitations that are articulated by marginal practices	feeling of greater or lesser tension	disclosing a new world

decontextualized features depends on our discerning and responding to a rich background of the solicitations that guide our everyday activity (navigating the home and workplace, preparing food and eating, and so on).

Second, the hierarchy that Dreyfus recognizes is not a function of which level of skillfulness most reliably succeeds in achieving publicly shared and communicable aims or goals. In fact, because it is disclosing a new practice, Dreyfus's very highest level of skillfulness, radical innovation, will quite possibly look like a failure when judged according to the standards of the practice that is being transformed and transcended. What makes the higher levels *higher*, then, is the way that they manifest more fully what is essential to our being as human beings: namely, that we are world disclosers. An expert does this by disclosing the world in its most basic form—that is, as a richly articulated whole of significations. A master does this in an even more original way by clarifying the style that organizes and makes that world a coherent and intelligible whole. And the radical innovator does this yet more profoundly by showing that new worlds are possible. So while it may be true, by and large, that someone who has achieved a higher level of skillfulness will be regarded as having a kind of virtuosity to which those at a lower level often aspire, this is not determinative of skillfulness in any straightforward way. Conversely, one's ability to attain the very highest levels of skillfulness might in some cases actually be hindered by having achieved a lower level of skill. Radical innovation might be limited by virtuosity in a domain (innovative rock musicians, for instance, are rarely the most expert guitar players or the best singers).

Overview of this Volume

The essays in this volume trace out the philosophical significance of giving priority to the paradigm of skillful coping over the paradigm of deliberative action. The first chapter, "From Socrates to Expert Systems: The Limits of Calculative Rationality," sets out Dreyfus's account of skill acquisition. This account underwrites his critique of the Western philosophical focus on rule-based modes of understanding.

The essays in Part II of this volume focus on the implications of his critique of rule-based models of understanding for issues surrounding intentionality and the philosophy of mind. Chapter 2 argues that even rules and rule-governed cognitive states depend on a bodily set, "an actualization of a particular habit or skill...a skill which, indeed, I cannot entertain apart from its actualization in a given activity of anticipating." Dreyfus begins this essay with an exegetical problem in the interpretation of Husserl—the debate over the meaning of the "perceptual noema." The interpretive debate points, however, to an important philosophical problem: the problem of how fulfillment of intentions is possible in perception. Being is given to us perceptually, Dreyfus argues, through a particular embodied skill or set for dealing with the world. A skill is a bodily set, given concreteness in a particular worldly setting, and only by means of such a set do we gain access to the "thickness" of existence. For instance, objects with other sides, Dreyfus argues, are given when "I am here and now actually set to explore them." Thus, I am neither a transcendental ego nor a "being-at-the-world," but a being in the world, an embodied subject. By locating our understanding of the world in bodily skills instead of mental noemata, Dreyfus argues, we don't have to give up on generality. These skills are "aspatial and atemporal, like the noema. The same skill can be actualized in many different situations." But they do not have ideal, abstractable meanings, and "cannot be entertained apart from some particular activation." And they are not objects either in the field of experience; they are "the means *through which* we refer to and unify the objects of experience." A phenomenology of skills thus overthrows the distinctions that philosophers have traditionally relied upon in explaining experience—distinctions between mind and body, meaning and sign, form and matter—because these distinctions cannot do justice to the way that skills consist in an actual anticipation of and response to particular presentations: "the moral is that, once one has used gestalt considerations to deny the traditional metaphysical dichotomies of matter/form, linguistic sign/meaning, and physical/mental in perception, as Gurwitsch has, one cannot find a stable stopping place until one has overthrown the body/consciousness dichotomy as well. Thus one arrives at an existential phenomenology of embodied being-in-the-world."

While Dreyfus, in Chapter 2, argued for the priority of a doing subject over a knowing subject, he eventually comes to reject altogether the usefulness of a notion of subjectivity. In Chapter 3, he argues that, in understanding human being, "the real issue concerns two opposed accounts of intentionality." Heidegger's significance, Dreyfus claims, lies in his recognition of "a kind of intentionality that does not involve intentional content at all. He wants to show that *neither* practical activity *nor* contemplative knowing can be understood as a relation between a self-sufficient subject with its intentional content and an independent object." For Dreyfus's Heidegger, everyday activity is intentional without self-referential content. Self-referential content only arises in cases of disturbance.

Thus, Dreyfus rejects any account that builds a mind/world distinction into the logic of action, even in the minimal form of the distinction between the experience of acting (mind) and the bodily movement that accompanies that experience (world). Of course, I do experience myself as the source of activity, but this is not the same as experiencing my intention as causing my movement (that only happens in deliberate action). Instead, an experience of action is "the experience of a steady flow of skillful activity in response to one's sense of the environment. Part of that experience is a sense that when one's situation deviates from some optimal body/environment relationship, one's motion takes one closer to that optimal form and thereby relieves the 'tension' of the deviation." Because in ordinary fluid action, there is not even a notional distinction between the experience of action and the movement, it follows that there is no way to experience oneself as causing the movement. Experience is rather of our bodily movements being drawn out by the situation into which we are absorbed.

On Dreyfus's account, then, we are capable of acting purposively without entertaining a purpose, and we are involved in guiding our movements without needing to represent to ourselves a goal. Of course, as agents we are not simply causally driven to move. First of all, fluid coping involves a kind of awareness. In particular, I sense that I could stop the movement and that I am cooperating in it.

Fluid coping is also adaptable, and alters itself in response to the dynamic particular situation in which it finds itself. And finally, in cases of disturbance, we can switch to a deliberate form of intentionality, where one has "a sense of effort with the condition of satisfaction that my effort causes the appropriate goal-directed movements." Our ordinary activities, Dreyfus concludes, are made possible by a background ability to "accommodate" ourselves to a world as we are "constantly adjusting to our situation." This most basic form of intentionality is being-in-the-world, absorption in an equipmental whole. This is genuinely a kind of intentional activity—we can succeed or fail to maintain ourselves in a situation. But it is not self-referential. Maintaining our stance in the world is not a goal that guides action.

Dreyfus's account of originary or background intentionality is further developed in Chapter 4. Drawing on Samuel Todes's account of poise, and Merleau-Ponty's account of motor intentionality, Dreyfus explores the sense in which "successful ongoing coping is...itself a kind of knowledge" that grounds conceptual representations. But understanding the nature of this grounding relationship is anything but straightforward. This chapter offers a sketch of "the stages by which the body turns the objects of practical perception into objects of thought."

Chapter 5 continues Dreyfus's inquiry into the relationship between conceptuality and the world that is "always already organized in terms of our bodies and [practical] interests." Here, Dreyfus argues that the world is fundamentally articulated into affordances which must withdraw from the foreground in order to guide our actions. The failure of cognitivism as an understanding of human intelligence, Dreyfus concludes, is that it founders on the problem of relevance—of knowing which facts are relevant to our action. But the phenomenology of fluid coping shows that the world is already organized in terms of our bodies and interests and is permeated by relevance. The world is thus not initially given to us to think. Rather than directing our actions by prior intentions, we are drawn to achieve a maximal grip on the world:

As we cope, we experience ourselves to be getting a better or worse grip on the situation. Such coping has *satisfaction conditions* but it does not have success *conditions*. Rather, it has what one might call *conditions of improvement*. Its satisfaction conditions are normative rather than descriptive. True to the phenomenon of affordance and response, plus the tendency to achieve maximal grip, Merleau-Ponty is led to introduce, between the space of causes and the space of reasons, what one might call *the space of motivations*.

The features of the world may have motivational content, even if they are not thinkable. Indeed, we may not even be capable of becoming aware of the features of the world which are moving us. This pushes Dreyfus, in the end, toward a "switch over" account of the relationship between fluid coping and thought—that is, a view according to which there is no smooth progression between practical affordances and conceptual contents. Rather, deliberative action produces a radical transformation of the situation that tends to cover up the practical affordances of the world. "What makes us [humans] special," Dreyfus concludes, "isn't that, unlike animals, we can *respond directly* to the conceptual structure of our environment; it's that, unlike animals, we can *transform* our unthinking nonconceptual engagement, and thereby encounter new, thinkable, structures."

The essays in Part III develop the implications of Dreyfus's phenomenology of fluid coping for various issues in the human sciences. Chapter 6 argues that the human sciences are distinguished from the natural sciences as a result of the way that human understanding is essentially founded in an embodied familiarity with the world. As a result, Dreyfus explains, there is an essential difference between theoretical and practical holism. According to theoretical holism, there are no neutral, uninterpreted data, and no testing of individual sentences against the data. Instead, a theory needs to be tested as a whole. Even if such a holism obtains with respect to the natural sciences (thus complicating our ability to compare and test competing discourses), it is a mistake to think that this kind of holism exhausts the holism involved in human domains. A theoretical holism, after all, presupposes that the background against which particular sentences get their meaning can be accounted for as a system of *beliefs* (albeit a system in which the meaning of each belief is determined by its relationship to other beliefs). But, as we've seen, it is a mistake to think that all human understanding is theoretical in this way. Practical understanding is holistic in a different way: "everyday coping with things and people" involves meanings that depend upon specific contexts and occur against a background of shared practices that we are capable of acquiring without forming beliefs and learning rules. We have skills that "embody a whole cultural interpretation of what it means to be a human being, what a material object is, and, in general, what counts as real." This background cannot be spelled out in a theory, Dreyfus argues, because (1) it is too pervasive to be an object of analysis, and (2) the practices involve habits and customs that are embodied in skills. As we've seen in previous chapters, these skills cannot be accounted for as a belief system, a system of rules, or formalized procedures. Instead, they can be understood only by getting a footing in the background practices.

Practical and theoretical forms of holism look similar because, among other things, each leads to a kind of nondeterminacy. But theoretical holism allows for the existence of objective facts, although it recognizes that there are an indeterminate number of alternative ways of making sense of the facts. For a theoretical holism, individual meanings aren't important in their own right. Instead, they are theoretical posits, introduced to keep track of features relevant to the theory as a whole. Practical holism, by contrast, has no facts—the background being interpreted isn't *about* anything or a representation of anything. It is an expression of human being. What makes one interpretation better than another, then, isn't the degree to which it accords with the facts. It is better because either (*a*) it makes the interpreter more flexible and open to dialogues with other interpretations of what it is to be human (*à la* the early Heidegger, Gadamer, and Habermas), or (*b*) it focuses and makes sense of more of what is at issue in a current cultural self-interpretation (*à la* the later Heidegger).

Recognition of the practical holism that marks the human domain shows us that a holistic background is not merely the condition of doing science (as in the natural sciences). It is itself what is to be investigated. It can't be bracketed out of the inquiry. And it can't be accounted for once and for all. So human sciences are, at their best, revolutionary. In any functioning field in the human sciences, there will be an ongoing fight over which elements of the background are most significant. Whenever a human science accepts a particular orthodoxy, it means that scientists will have given up on an important feature of human existence— that human understanding always involves a contingent self-interpretation. Denying this leads to nihilism. Thus there is an important cultural and political issue at stake in the practice of the human sciences. A genuine conflict of interpretations helps reveal to us "the cultural commitments we cannot help sharing because they make us what we are." The chapter closes by arguing that mistaking practical holism for theoretical holism encourages a nihilistic approach to the interpretation of theories in the human sciences. Recognizing practical holism for what it is, on the other hand, opens up possibilities for more firmly grounding our practices in the meaningful differences that organize our world.

Chapter 7 argues that the paradigm of deliberative action distorts our understanding both of human action and of the constitution of the social domain. The phenomenology of skillful coping, Dreyfus argues, demonstrates that action does not need an intention with success conditions as its direct cause. Even when an intention is responsible for initiating the action, this intention can be a mere occasion that allows absorbed coping to take over. Once we switch into absorbed coping, the intention can drop out of the picture as we are guided by the solicitations of the world. Moreover, since the skillful body is constantly moving toward an equilibrium with its setting, coping can be initiated without the formation of an intention. Thus, Dreyfus concludes, "absorbed coping is the background condition of the possibility of all forms of comportment." After reviewing and developing his critique of the Husserlian and Searlean models of intentionality, Dreyfus turns to the problem of the constitution of the social domain. Here, Dreyfus critiques the tendency to treat the entities within the social domain as if they are constituted by the assignment of certain functions or significance to meaningless facts. We've learned from the phenomenology of absorbed coping that we don't encounter a meaningless world, but rather a meaningful setting of affordances and solicitations. Institutional and social facts, more generally, are instituted on the basis of social norms into which we are introduced as we learn to participate in social practices. "To do justice to the unique character of absorbed coping and social norms," Dreyfus argues, "we should adopt a richer ontology than the Cartesian one of minds and nature." In doing so, we will recognize that the worlds we inhabit have "a kind of being that is neither natural nor constituted, but is produced by the embodied intentionality that is always already present in the world of involved, active, social beings."

Chapter 8 explores the purportedly mental nature of human understanding by examining the problem of psychopathologies. If embodied being in the world is the proper locus for human understanding, what are the implications for thinking about the mind? Psychopathologies can no longer be reduced to a problem in the way our representations "mediate between subject and object." Instead of a "depth psychology," which tries to "help[] the patient to uncover the hidden contents and to reintegrate them into his overall mental system," Dreyfus and Wakefield propose a "breadth psychology" which sees pathologies in terms of the way "the whole human being is related to the world." Inappropriate modes of response come to be "sedimented into [the patient's] posture and other body sets" in a way that distorts his or her ability to maintain a fluid and successful course of engagement with the world.

Chapter 9 shows how the phenomenology of skill acquisition might be "a step towards righting a wrong to involvement, intuition, and care that traditional philosophy, by passing over skillful coping, has maintained for 2,500 years." In ethics, one finds the same intellectualist prejudice that dominates philosophy of mind and action—namely, the privileging of acts of judgment, and detached critical modes of reasoning over intuitive, involved actions and perceptions. Theorists of morality then fall into the by-now-familiar mistake of reading the deliberative structure involved in judgment and reasoning "back into our account of everyday coping." But "most of our everyday ethical comportment consists in unreflective, egoless responses to the current interpersonal situation." So, the brothers Dreyfus ask, "Why not begin on the level of this spontaneous coping?" Doing so calls into question the "traditional Western and male belief in the superiority of critical detachment to intuitive involvement."

The chapters in Part III illuminate in manifold ways how our human, embodied form of understanding the world resists being captured in cognitivist, conceptual, and rule-bound theories. The chapters in Part IV present a series of sustained efforts to understand a special case of this general problem in the way theoreticians approach human beings: namely, the case of modeling cognition and intelligence.

Chapter 10 contrasts two fundamentally different approaches to the creation of an artificial intelligence. On the "making a mind" approach, human understanding is grasped in terms of the manipulation of mental symbols that offer a formal representation of the world. The program of artificial intelligence, built on this approach, was motivated by the idea that brains and computers, while different in structure and mechanism, have a common functional description: both are devices that manipulate symbols by means of formal rules. This approach to intelligence was thus inherently atomistic and reductivist: "AI can be thought of as the attempt to find the primitive elements and logical relations in the subject (man or computer) that mirror the primitive objects and their relations that make up the world." And human understanding is thus ultimately taken to consist in having a *theory*, where "a theory formulates the relationships among objective, *context-free* elements (simples, primitives, features, attributes, factors, data points, cues, etc.) in terms of abstract principles (covering laws, rules, programs, etc.)." This approach also tended to treat human understanding as a static system, since the aim was to program a computer with the present ability to do some discrete task.

The "modeling the brain" approach to artificial intelligence, by contrast, takes learning as the paradigm for intelligence and treats understanding as an inherently dynamic system. Artificial intelligence programs that adopted this approach took as our most essential traits whatever it is that allows us to evolve the ability to deal with our environment. The construction of an artificial intelligence on this approach is inspired by the neurosciences rather than philosophical theories, and attempts to artificially simulate the interactions of neurons. This approach is thus inherently holistic and gestaltist, as it seeks to imbue an artificial system with the ability to discriminate relevant patterns in the environment, rather than to manipulate representations in the system itself.

In the history of twentieth-century artificial intelligence, Dreyfus argues, the "making a mind" approach triumphed over the "modeling the brain" approach, largely because of certain "philosophical assumptions" or "quasi-religious philosophical prejudices"—precisely the assumptions and prejudices, it turns out, which also lie behind the deliberative model of human understanding. But the attempt to atomistically reduce human understanding ran aground on the problem of relevance: "The analysis of everyday situations into facts and rules (which is where most traditional philosophers and AI researchers think theory must begin) is itself only meaningful in some context and for some purpose. Thus, the elements chosen already reflect the goals and purposes for which they are carved out. When we try to find the ultimate context-free, purpose-free elements, as we must if we are going to find the primitive symbols to feed a computer, we are in effect trying to free aspects of our experience of just that pragmatic organization which makes it possible to use them intelligently in coping with everyday problems."

This failure of this classical form of AI, Dreyfus argues, offers some support for his phenomenology of embodied skillful coping: "If background understanding is indeed a skill and if skills are based on whole patterns and not on rules, we would expect symbolic representations to fail to capture our commonsense understanding," as, indeed, they did.

This failure has encouraged researchers to revisit the other approach, and it is worth spelling out the philosophical implications of an effort to ground human understanding in a holistic, multilayered neural network. If such a model of the brain succeeds, it will force us to give up the conviction that "the only way to produce intelligent behavior is to mirror the world with a formal theory in the mind." We will also have to give up "the more basic intuition at the source of philosophy that there must be a theory of every aspect of reality—that is, there must be elements and principles in terms of which one can account for the intelligibility of any domain."

The result would be a fundamentally anti-representationalist account of understanding which coheres well with Dreyfus's view, for it will acknowledge that our most basic form of understanding does not consist in using rules and principles to relate representational elements. At the same time, Dreyfus warns in this chapter that "building an interactive net sufficiently similar to the one our brain has evolved may be just too hard." Human embodied understanding develops under very specific conditions. These include the structure of the human body itself, as well as human needs, desires, emotions, vulnerabilities, and so on. Humans, Dreyfus points out, are "much more holistic than neural nets. Intelligence has to be motivated by purposes in the organism and goals picked up by the organism from an ongoing culture. If the minimum unity of analysis is that of a whole organism geared into a whole cultural world, neural nets as well as symbolically programmed computers still have a very long way to go."

This insight is further developed and pursued in the concluding chapters of the volume. Chapter 11 tackles the problem of explaining how human behavior can manifest understanding without recourse to mental representations of the skill domain or of conditions of satisfaction. Dreyfus argues that representational accounts cannot do justice to the "flexibility, transferability, and situational sensitivity of skills." One enormous hurdle that representationalist accounts need to overcome is explaining "how the organism could possibly use features of the current situation to determine which rule or concept should be applied. There are just too many features, so the selection of the relevant features requires that one has already subsumed the situation under the relevant concept." Attention to the phenomenology of expertise shows, however, that experts don't need to use rules or concepts like this. Rather, in fluid coping, the world is "polarized" in such a way that the relevant features of the situation offer themselves to view. Action, Dreyfus argues, is guided by a sensitivity to "conditions of improvement" rather than a representation of "conditions of satisfaction."

Chapter 12, finally, develops the ontological implications of the fundamental nature of fluid coping for our engagement with the world. "*For the user*," Dreyfus observes, "equipment is a solicitation to act, not an entity with a function feature." These solicitations make up the situation on the basis of which we sometimes step back from our involved engagement with the world and disclose entities. But "when we are pressing into possibilities, there is no experience of an *entity* doing the soliciting; just the solicitation." Human understanding thus involves an "intentional arc," a feedback loop in which our actions and projections are drawn out of us by the meaningful features of the world and, in turn, alter the way the world shows up as soliciting us. The phenomenology of skillful coping should inform the way we set about modeling human intelligence and, Dreyfus argues, coheres well with Walter Freeman's account of the brain as a "nonlinear dynamical system."

PART I

The Phenomenology of Skills

1

From Socrates to Expert Systems
The Limits of Calculative Rationality (1985)

Hubert L. Dreyfus and Stuart E. Dreyfus

For the past quarter of a century researchers in Artificial Intelligence (AI) have been trying without success to write programs which will enable computers to exhibit general intelligence like Hal in *2001*. Now out of this work has recently emerged a new field called knowledge engineering, which by limiting its goals has applied this research in ways that actually work in the real world. The result is the so-called expert system which has been the subject of recent cover stories in *Business Week* and Edward Feigenbaum's book *The Fifth Generation: Artificial Intelligence and Japan's Computer Challenge to the World*.[1] The occasion for this new interest in machine intelligence is no specific new accomplishment but rather a much publicized competition with Japan to build a new generation of computers, with built-in expertise. This is the so-called fifth generation. (The first four generations were computers whose components were vacuum tubes, transistors, chips, and large-scale integrated chips.) According to a *Newsweek* headline: "Japan and the United States are rushing to produce a new generation of machines that can very nearly think."

Feigenbaum, one of the original developers of expert systems, who stands to profit greatly from this competition, spells out the goal.

In the kind of intelligent system envisioned by the designers of the Fifth Generation, speed and processing power will be increased dramatically; but more important, the machines will have reasoning power: they will automatically engineer vast amounts of knowledge to serve whatever purpose humans propose, from medical diagnosis to product design, from management decisions to education.[2]

---

[1] Edward Feigenbaum and Pamela McCorduck, *The Fifth Generation: Artificial Intelligence and Japan's Computer Challenge to the World* (Reading, MA: Addison-Wesley, 1983), 56.
[2] Feigenbaum and McCorduck, *The Fifth Generation*, 56.

What the knowledge engineers claim to have discovered is that, in areas which are cut off from everyday common sense and social intercourse, all a machine needs in order to behave like an expert are some general rules and lots of very specific knowledge. As Feigenbaum puts it:

The first group of artificial intelligence researchers . . . was persuaded that certain great, underlying principles characterized all intelligent behavior. . . .

In part, they were correct. . . . [Such strategies] include searching for a solution (and using "rules of good guessing" to cut down the search space); generating and testing (does this work? no; try something else); reasoning backward from a desired goal; and the like.

These strategies are necessary, but not sufficient, for intelligent behavior. The other ingredient is knowledge—specialized knowledge, and lots of it. . . . No matter how natively bright you are, you cannot be a credible medical diagnostician without a great deal of specific knowledge about diseases, their manifestations, and the human body.[3]

This specialized knowledge is of two types:

The first type is the facts of the domain—the widely shared knowledge . . . that is written in textbooks and journals of the field, or that forms the basis of a professor's lectures in a classroom. Equally important to the practice of the field is the second type of knowledge called *heuristic knowledge*, which is the knowledge of good practice and good judgement in a field. It is experiential knowledge, the "art of good guessing" that a human expert acquires over years of work.[4]

Using all three kinds of knowledge Feigenbaum developed a program called DENDRAL which is an expert in the isolated domain of spectrograph analysis. It takes the data generated by a mass spectrograph and deduces from this data the molecular structure of the compound being analyzed. Another program, MYCIN, takes the results of blood tests such as the number of red cells, white cells, sugar in the blood, etc. and comes up with a diagnosis of which blood disease is responsible for this condition. It even gives an estimate of the reliability of its own diagnosis. In their narrow areas, such programs are almost as good as the experts.

And is not this success just what one would expect? If we agree with Feigenbaum that: "almost all the thinking that professionals do is done by reasoning,"[5] we can see that once computers are used for reasoning and not just computation they should be as good or better than we are at following rules for deducing conclusions from a host of facts. So we would expect that if the rules which an expert has acquired from years of experience could be extracted and programmed,

---

[3] Feigenbaum and McCorduck, *The Fifth Generation*, 38.
[4] Feigenbaum and McCorduck, *The Fifth Generation*, 76–7.
[5] Feigenbaum and McCorduck, *The Fifth Generation*, 18.

the resulting program would exhibit expertise. Again Feigenbaum puts the point very clearly:

[T]he matters that set experts apart from beginners, are symbolic, inferential, and rooted in experiential knowledge. Human experts have acquired their expertise not only from explicit knowledge found in textbooks and lectures, but also from experience: by doing things again and again, failing, succeeding... getting a feel for a problem, learning when to go by the book and when to break the rules. They therefore build up a repertory of working rules of thumb, or "heuristics," that, combined with book knowledge, make them expert practitioners.[6]

Since each expert already has a repertory of rules in his mind, all the expert system builder need do is get the rules out and program them into a computer.

This view is not new. In fact, it goes back to the beginning of Western culture when the first philosopher, Socrates, stalked around Athens looking for experts in order to draw out and test their rules. In one of his earliest dialogues, *Euthyphro*, Plato tells us of such an encounter between Socrates and Euthyphro, a religious prophet and so an expert on pious behavior. Socrates asks Euthyphro to tell him how to recognize piety: "I want to know what is characteristic of piety... to use as a standard whereby to judge your actions and those of other men." But instead of revealing his piety-recognizing heuristic, Euthyphro does just what every expert does when cornered by Socrates. He gives him examples from his field of expertise: in this case situations in the past in which men and gods have done things which everyone considers pious. Socrates persists throughout the dialogue in demanding that Euthyphro tell him his rules, but although Euthyphro claims he knows how to tell pious acts from impious ones, he will not state the rules which generate his judgments.

Plato admired Socrates and sympathized with his problem. So he developed an account of what caused the difficulty. Experts had once known the rules they use, Plato said, but then they had forgotten them. The role of the philosopher was to help people remember the principles on which they act. Knowledge engineers would now say that the rules the experts use have been put in a part of their mental computers where they work automatically.

When we learned how to tie our shoes, we had to think very hard about the steps involved... Now that we've tied many shoes over our lifetime, that knowledge is "compiled," to use the computing term for it; it no longer needs our conscious attention.[7]

---

[6] Feigenbaum and McCorduck, *The Fifth Generation*, 64.
[7] Feigenbaum and McCorduck, *The Fifth Generation*, 55.

On this Platonic view the rules are there functioning in the expert's mind whether he is conscious of them or not. How else could we account for the fact that he can perform the task?

Now 2,000 years later, thanks to Feigenbaum and his colleagues, we have a new name for what Socrates and Plato were doing:

[W]e are able to be more precise... and with this increased precision has come a new term, *knowledge acquisition research.*[8]

But although philosophers and even the man in the street have become convinced that expertise consists in applying sophisticated heuristics to masses of facts, there are few available rules. As Feigenbaum explains:

[A]n expert's knowledge is often ill-specified or incomplete because the expert himself doesn't always know exactly what it is he knows about his domain.[9]

So the knowledge engineer has to help him recollect what he once knew.

[An expert's] knowledge is currently acquired in a very painstaking way; individual computer scientists work with individual experts to explicate the expert's heuristics—to mine those jewels of knowledge out of their heads one by one... the problem of knowledge acquisition is the critical bottleneck in artificial intelligence.[10]

When Feigenbaum suggests to an expert the rules the expert seems to be using he gets a Euthyphro-like response. "That's true, but if you see enough patients/rocks/chip designs/instrument readings, you see that it isn't true after all."[11] And Feigenbaum comments with Socratic annoyance: "At this point, knowledge threatens to become ten thousand special cases."[12]

There are also other hints of trouble. Ever since the inception of Artificial Intelligence, researchers have been trying to produce artificial experts by programming the computer to follow the rules used by masters in various domains. Yet, although computers are faster and more accurate than people in applying rules, master-level performance has remained out of reach. Arthur Samuel's work is typical. In 1947, when electronic computers were just being developed, Samuel, then at IBM, decided to write a checker-playing program. Samuel did not try to make a machine play checkers by brute force calculation of all chains of moves clear to the end. He calculated that if you tried to look to the end of the game with the fastest computer you could possibly build, subject to the speed of light, it

---

[8] Feigenbaum and McCorduck, *The Fifth Generation*, 79.
[9] Feigenbaum and McCorduck, *The Fifth Generation*, 85.
[10] Feigenbaum and McCorduck, *The Fifth Generation*, 79–80.
[11] Feigenbaum and McCorduck, *The Fifth Generation*, 82.
[12] Feigenbaum and McCorduck, *The Fifth Generation*, 82.

would take 10 followed by 21 zeros centuries to make the first move. So he tried to elicit heuristic rules from checker masters and program a computer to follow these rules. When the rules the experts came up with did not produce master play, Samuel became the first and almost the only AI researcher to make a learning program. He programmed a computer to vary the weights used in the rules, such as the trade-off between center control and loss of a piece, and to retain the weights that worked best. After playing a great many games with itself the program could beat Samuel, which shows that in some sense computers can do more than they are programmed to do. But the program still could not beat the sort of experts whose heuristic rules were the heart of the program.

The checkers program is not only the first and one of the best experts ever built, but it is also a perfect example of the way fact turns into fiction in AI. The checkers program once beat a state checkers champion. From then on AI literature cites the checkers program as a noteworthy success. One often reads that it plays at such a high level that only the world champion can beat it. Feigenbaum, for example, reports that "by 1961 [Samuel's program] played championship checkers, and it learned and improved with each game."[13] Even the usually reliable *Handbook of Artificial Intelligence* states as a fact that "today's programs play championship-level checkers."[14] In fact, Samuel said in a recent interview at Stanford University, where he is a retired professor, that the program did once defeat a state champion but the champion "turned around and defeated the program in six mail games." According to Samuel, after 35 years of effort, "the program is quite capable of beating any amateur player and can give better players a good contest." It is clearly no champion. Samuel is still bringing in expert players for help but he "fears he may be reaching the point of diminishing returns." This does not lead him to question the view that the masters the program cannot beat are using heuristic rules; rather, like Socrates and Feigenbaum, Samuel thinks that the experts are poor at recollecting their compiled heuristics: "the experts do not know enough about the mental processes involved in playing the game."[15]

The same story is repeated in every area of expertise, even in areas unlike checkers where expertise requires the storage of large numbers of facts, which should give an advantage to the computer. In each area where there are experts with years of experience the computer can do better than the beginner, and can

[13] Feigenbaum and McCorduck, *The Fifth Generation*, 179.

[14] Avron Barr and Edward A. Feigenbaum, *The Handbook of Artificial Intelligence* (Los Altos, CA: Wm. Kaufmann, 1981), i. 7.

[15] These quotations are taken from an interview with Arthur Samuel, released by the Stanford University News Office, 28 Apr. 1983.

even exhibit useful competence, but it cannot rival the very experts whose facts and supposed heuristics it is processing with incredible speed and unerring accuracy.

In the face of this impasse it was necessary, in spite of the authority and influence of Plato and 2,000 years of philosophy, for us to take a fresh look at what a skill is and what the expert acquires when he achieves expertise. One must be prepared to abandon the traditional view that a beginner starts with specific cases and, as he becomes more proficient, abstracts and interiorizes more and more sophisticated rules. It might turn out that skill acquisition moves in just the opposite direction: from abstract rules to particular cases. Since we all have many areas in which we are experts, we have the necessary data, so let's look and see how adults learn new skills.

Stage 1: Novice

Normally, the instruction process begins with the instructor decomposing the task environment into context-free features which the beginner can recognize without benefit of experience. The beginner is then given rules for determining actions on the basis of these features, like a computer following a program. The beginning student wants to do a good job, but lacking any coherent sense of the overall task, he judges his performance mainly by how well he follows his learned rules. After he has acquired more than just a few rules, so much concentration is required during the exercise of his skill that his capacity to talk or listen to advice is severely limited.

For purposes of illustration, we shall consider two variations: a bodily or motor skill and an intellectual skill. The reader wishing to see real-life examples of the process we shall outline should consult Patricia Benner's *From Novice to Expert: Excellence and Power in Clinical Nursing Practice*.[16] The student automobile driver learns to recognize such interpretation-free features as speed (indicated by his speedometer) and distance (as estimated by a previously acquired skill). Safe following distances are defined in terms of speed; conditions that allow safe entry into traffic are defined in terms of speed and distance of oncoming traffic; timing of shifts of gear is specified in terms of speed, etc. These rules ignore context. They do not refer to traffic density or anticipated stops.

The novice chess player learns a numerical value for each type of piece regardless of its position, and the rule: "always exchange if the total value of

[16] Patricia Benner, *From Novice to Expert: Excellence and Power in Clinical Nursing Practice* (Reading, MA: Addison-Wesley, 1984).

pieces captured exceeds the value of pieces lost." He also learns that, when no advantageous exchanges can be found, center control should be sought, and he is given a rule defining center squares and one for calculating extent of control. Most beginners are notoriously slow players, as they attempt to remember all these rules and their priorities.

Stage 2: Advanced Beginner

As the novice gains experience actually coping with real situations, he begins to note, or an instructor points out, perspicuous examples of meaningful additional components of the situation. After seeing a sufficient number of examples, the student learns to recognize them. Instructional maxims now can refer to these new *situational aspects* recognized on the basis of experience, as well as to the objectively defined *non-situational features* recognizable by the novice. The advanced beginner confronts his environment, seeks out features and aspects, and determines his actions by applying rules. He shares the novice's minimal concern with quality of performance, instead focusing on quality of rule following. The advanced beginner's performance, while improved, remains slow, uncoordinated, and laborious.

The advanced beginner driver uses (situational) engine sounds as well as (non-situational) speed in his gear-shifting rules, and observes demeanor as well as position and velocity to anticipate behavior of pedestrians or other drivers. He learns to distinguish the behavior of the distracted or drunken driver from that of the impatient but alert one. No number of words can serve the function of a few choice examples in learning this distinction. Engine sounds cannot be adequately captured by words, and no list of objective facts about a particular pedestrian enables one to predict his behavior in a crosswalk as well as can the driver who has observed many pedestrians crossing streets under a variety of conditions. Already at this level one leaves features and rules and turns to learning by prototype, now being explored by researchers such as Eleanor Rosch at Berkeley and Susan Block at MIT.

With experience, the chess beginner learns to recognize over-extended positions and how to avoid them. Similarly, he begins to recognize such situational aspects of positions as a weakened king's side or a strong pawn structure despite the lack of precise and universally valid definitional rules.

Stage 3: Competence

With increasing experience, the number of features and aspects to be taken account of becomes overwhelming. To cope with this information explosion, the performer learns, or is taught, to adopt a hierarchical view of decision-making. By first choosing a plan, goal, or perspective which organizes the situation and by then examining only the small set of features and aspects that he has learned are the most important given that plan, the performer can simplify and improve his performance.

Choosing a plan, a goal, or perspective is no simple matter for the competent performer. It is not an objective procedure, like the feature recognition of the novice. Nor is the choice avoidable. While the advanced beginner can get along with recognizing and using a particular situational aspect until a sufficient number of examples makes identification easy and sure, to perform competently *requires* choosing an organizing goal or perspective. Furthermore, the choice of perspective crucially affects behavior in a way that any one particular aspect rarely does.

This combination of necessity and uncertainty introduces an important new type of relationship between the performer and his environment. The novice and the advanced beginner applying rules and maxims feel little or no responsibility for the outcome of their acts. If they have made no mistakes, an unfortunate outcome is viewed as the result of inadequately specified elements or rules. The competent performer, on the other hand, after wrestling with the question of a choice of perspective or goal, feels responsible for, and thus emotionally involved in, the result of his choice. An outcome that is clearly successful is deeply satisfying and leaves a vivid memory of the situation encountered as seen from the goal or perspective finally chosen. Disasters, likewise, are not easily forgotten.

Remembered whole situations differ in one important respect from remembered aspects. The mental image of an aspect is flat in the sense that no parts stand out as salient. A whole situation, on the other hand, since it is the result of a chosen plan or perspective, has a "three-dimensional" quality. Certain elements stand out as more or less important with respect to the plan, while other irrelevant elements are forgotten. Moreover, the competent performer, gripped by the situation that his decision has produced, experiences and therefore remembers the situation not only in terms of foreground and background elements but also in terms of senses of opportunity, risk, expectation, threat, etc. These gripping, holistic memories cannot guide the behavior of the competent performer since he fails to make contact with them when he reflects on problematic situations as a detached observer, and holds to a view of himself as a computer following better and better rules. As we shall soon see, however, if he does let them take over, these memories become the basis of the competent performer's next advance in skill.

A competent driver beginning a trip decides, perhaps, that he is in a hurry. He then selects a route with attention to distance and time, ignores scenic beauty, and as he drives, he chooses his maneuvers with little concern for passenger comfort or for courtesy. He follows more closely than normal, enters traffic more daringly, occasionally violates a law. He feels elated when decisions work out and no police car appears, and shaken by near accidents and traffic tickets. (Beginners, on the other hand, can perpetrate chaos around them with total unconcern.)

The class A chess player, here classed as competent, may decide after studying a position that his opponent has weakened his king's defenses so that an attack against the king is a viable goal. If the attack is chosen, features involving weaknesses in his own position created by his attack are ignored, as are losses of pieces inessential to the attack. Removal of pieces defending the enemy king becomes salient. Successful plans induce euphoria and mistakes are felt in the pit of the stomach.

In both of these cases, we find a common pattern: detached planning, conscious assessment of elements that are salient with respect to the plan, and analytical rule-guided choice of action, followed by an emotionally involved experience of the outcome.

Stage 4: Proficiency

Considerable experience at the level of competency sets the stage for yet further skill enhancement. Having experienced many situations, chosen plans in each, and having obtained vivid, involved demonstrations of the adequacy or inadequacy of the plan, the performer sees his current situation as similar to a previous one and so spontaneously sees an appropriate plan. Involved in the world of the skill, the performer "notices," or "is struck by," a certain plan, goal, or perspective. No longer is the spell of involvement broken by detached conscious planning.

There will, of course, be breakdowns of this "seeing," when, due perhaps to insufficient experience in a certain type of situation or to more than one possible plan presenting itself, the performer will need to take a detached look at his situation. But between these breakdowns, the proficient performer will experience longer and longer intervals of continuous, intuitive understanding.

Since there are generally far fewer "ways of seeing" than "ways of acting," after understanding without conscious effort what is going on, the proficient performer will still have to think about what to do. During this thinking, elements that present themselves as salient are assessed and combined by rule to produce decisions about how best to manipulate the environment. The spell of involvement in the world of the activity will thus temporarily be broken.

On the basis of prior experience, a proficient driver approaching a curve on a rainy day may sense that he is traveling too fast. He then consciously decides whether to apply the brakes, remove his foot from the accelerator, or merely to reduce pressure on the accelerator.

The proficient chess player, who is classed a master, can recognize a large repertoire of types of positions. Recognizing almost immediately and without conscious effort the sense of a position, he sets about calculating the move that best achieves his goal. He may, for example, know that he should attack, but he must deliberate about how best to do so.

Stage 5: Expertise

The proficient performer, immersed in the world of his skillful activity, sees what needs to be done, but *decides* how to do it. For the expert, not only situational understandings spring to mind, but also associated appropriate actions. The expert performer, except of course during moments of breakdown, understands, acts, and learns from results without any conscious awareness of the process. What transparently *must* be done *is* done. We usually do not make conscious deliberative decisions when we walk, talk, ride a bicycle, drive, or carry on most social activities. An expert's skill has become so much a part of him that he need be no more aware of it than he is of his own body.

We have seen that experience-based similarity recognition produces the deep situational understanding of the proficient performer. No new insight is needed to explain the mental processes of the expert. With enough experience with a variety of situations, all seen from the same perspective or with the same goal in mind, but requiring different tactical decisions, the mind of the proficient performer seems gradually to decompose this class of situations into subclasses, each member of which shares not only the same goal or perspective, but also the same decision, action, or tactic. At this point, a situation, when seen as similar to members of this class, is not only thereby understood but simultaneously the associated decision, action, or tactic presents itself.

The number of classes of recognizable situations, built up on the basis of experience, must be immense. It has been estimated that a master chess player can distinguish roughly 50,000 types of positions. Automobile driving probably involves a similar number of typical situations. We doubtless store far more typical situations in our memories than words in our vocabularies. Consequently these reference situations, unlike the situational elements learned by the advanced beginner, bear no names and, in fact, defy complete verbal description.

The expert chess player, classed as an international master or grandmaster, in most situations experiences a compelling sense of the issue and the best move. Excellent chess players can play at the rate of 5–10 seconds a move and even faster without any serious degradation in performance. At this speed they must depend almost entirely on intuition and hardly at all on analysis and comparison of alternatives. We recently performed an experiment in which an international master, Julio Kaplan, was required rapidly to add numbers presented to him audibly at the rate of about one number per second while at the same time playing five-second-a-move chess against a slightly weaker, but master level, player. Even with his analytical mind completely occupied by adding numbers, Kaplan more than held his own against the master in a series of games. Deprived of the time necessary to see problems or construct plans, Kaplan still produced fluid and coordinated play.

The expert driver, generally without any awareness, not only knows by feel and familiarity when an action such as slowing is required, but he generally knows how to perform the act without evaluating and comparing alternatives. He shifts gears when appropriate with no conscious awareness of his acts. Most drivers have experienced the disconcerting breakdown that occurs when suddenly one reflects on the gear shifting process and tries to decide what to do. Suddenly the smooth, almost automatic, sequence of actions that results from the performer's involved immersion in the world of his skill is disrupted, and the performer sees himself, just as does the competent performer, as the manipulator of a complex mechanism. He detachedly calculates his actions even more poorly than does the competent performer since he has forgotten many of the guiding rules that he knew and used when competent, and his performance suddenly becomes halting, uncertain, and even inappropriate.

It seems that a beginner makes inferences using rules and facts just like a heuristically programmed computer, but that with talent and a great deal of involved experience the beginner develops into an expert who intuitively sees what to do without applying rules. Of course, a description of skilled behavior can never be taken as conclusive evidence as to what is going on in the mind or in the brain. It is always possible that what is going on is some unconscious process using more and more sophisticated rules. But our description of skill acquisition counters the traditional prejudice that expertise necessarily involves inference.

Given our account of the five stages of skill acquisition, we can understand why the knowledge engineers from Socrates, to Samuel, to Feigenbaum have had such trouble getting the expert to articulate the rules he is using. The expert is simply not following any rules! He is doing just what Feigenbaum feared he might be doing—recognizing thousands of special cases. This in turn explains why expert systems are never as good as experts. If one asks the experts for rules one will, in effect, force the expert to regress to the level of a beginner and state the rules he still remembers but no longer uses. If one programs these rules on a computer one can use the speed and accuracy of the computer and its ability to store and access millions of facts to outdo a human beginner using the same rules. But no amount of rules and facts can capture the understanding an expert has when he has stored his experience of the actual outcomes of tens of thousands of situations.

The knowledge engineer might still say that in spite of appearances the mind and brain *must* be reasoning—making millions of rapid and accurate inferences like a computer. After all the brain is not "wonder tissue" and how else could it work? But there are other models for what might be going on in the hardware. The capacity of experts to store in memory tens of thousands of typical situations and rapidly and effortlessly to see the present situation as similar to one of these apparently without resorting to time-consuming feature detection and matching, suggests that the brain does not work like a heuristically programmed digital computer applying rules to bits of information. Rather it suggests, as some neurophysiologists already believe, that the brain, at times at least, works holographically, superimposing the records of whole situations and measuring their similarity. Dr Karl Pribram, a Stanford neurophysiologist who has spent the last decade studying holographic memory, explicitly notes the implication of this sort of process for expertise. When asked in an interview whether holograms would allow a person to make decisions spontaneously in very complex environments, he replied, "Decisions fall out as the holographic correlations are performed. One doesn't have to think things through...a step at a time. One takes the whole constellation of a situation, correlates it, and out of that correlation emerges the correct response."[17]

We can now understand why, in a recent article in *Science*, two expert systems builders, Richard Duda and Edward Shortliffe, who assume rather cautiously but without evidence that "experts seem to employ rule-like associations to solve routine problems quickly,"[18] are, nonetheless, finally forced by the phenomenon to conclude:

[17] Daniel Coleman, "Holographic Memory: An Interview with Karl Pribram", *Psychology Today*, 12/9 (Feb. 1979), 80.
[18] Richard O. Duda and Edward H. Shortliffe, "Expert Systems Research", *Science*, 220/4594 (15 Apr. 1983), 266.

The identification and encoding of knowledge is one of the most complex and arduous tasks encountered in the construction of an expert system...Even when an adequate knowledge representation formalism has been developed, experts often have difficulty expressing their knowledge in that form.[19]

We should not be surprised that, in the area of medicine, for example, we find doctors concluding that:

The optimistic expectation of 20 years ago that computer technology would also come to play an important part in clinical decisions has not been realized, and there are few if any situations in which computers are being routinely used to assist in either medical diagnosis or the choice of therapy.[20]

In general, based on this model, our prediction is that in any domain in which judgments improve with experience, no system based upon heuristics will consistently do as well as experienced experts, even if they were the informants who provided the heuristic rules. Since there already seem to be many exceptions to our prediction, we will now deal with each alleged exception in turn.

To begin with there is a system developed at MIT called MACSYMA, for doing certain manipulations required in calculus. MACSYMA began as a *heuristic* system. It has evolved, however, into an *algorithmic* system, using procedures guaranteed to work which involve so much calculation people would never use them, so the fact that, as far as we can find out, MACSYMA now outperforms all experts in its field, does not constitute an exception to our hypothesis.

Next there are expert systems that are indeed heuristic, and which perform better than anyone in the field. This happens when there are no experts at the particular task such systems perform. This is certainly the case with the very impressive R1 developed at Digital Equipment Corporation to decide how to combine components of VAX computers to meet customers' needs. Configuring VAXes is a new problem and the relevant facts, viz., performance characteristics of components, are rapidly changing. Thus, no one has had time to develop the repertoire of typical cases necessary for expertise. This is also the case with spectrograph analysis. Duda notes that "For the molecular families covered by [its] empirical rules, [DENDRAL] is said to surpass even expert chemists in speed and accuracy."[21] But expert chemists need not be expert spectrograph interpreters. Before DENDRAL, chemists did their own spectrograph analysis,

[19] Duda and Shortliffe, "Expert Systems Research", 265.
[20] G. Octo Barnett, "The Computer and Clinical Judgment", *New England Journal of Medicine*, 307/8 (19 Aug. 1982), 493.
[21] Richard O. Duda and John G. Gashnig, "Knowledge-Based Expert Systems Come of Age", *Byte* (Sept. 1981), 254.

but it was not their main work so no one chemist needed to have dealt with sufficient cases to become an expert. Thus it would be no surprise if DENDRAL outperforms all comers.

Chess seems an obvious exception to our prediction, since chess programs have already achieved master ratings. The chess story is complicated and stimulating. Programs that play chess are among the earliest examples of expert systems. The first such program was written in the 1950s and by the early 1960s fairly sophisticated programs had been developed. The programs naturally included the facts of the chess world (i.e. the rules of the game) and also heuristics elicited from strong players.

Master players, in checking out each plausible move that springs to mind, generally consider one to three plausible opponent responses, followed by one to three moves of their own; etc. Quite frequently, only one move looks plausible at each step. After looking ahead a varying number of moves depending on the situation, the terminal position of each sequence is assessed based on its similarity to positions previously encountered. In positions where the best initial move is not obvious, about one hundred terminal positions will typically be examined. This thinking ahead generally confirms that the initial move intuitively seen as the most plausible is indeed best, although there are occasional exceptions.

To imitate players, the program designers attempted to elicit from the masters heuristic rules that could be used to generate a limited number of plausible moves at each step, and evaluation rules that could be used to assess the worth of the roughly one hundred terminal positions. Since masters are not aware of following any rules, the rules that they suggested did not work well and the programs played at a marginally competent level.

As computers grew faster in the 1970s, chess programming strategy changed. In 1973, a program was developed at Northwestern University by David Slate and Larry Atkin which rapidly searched *every* legal initial move, every legal response etc. to a depth determined by the position and the computer's speed, generally about three moves for each player. The roughly one million terminal positions in the look-ahead were still evaluated by rules. Plausible-move-generation heuristics were discarded, the program looked less like an expert system, and quality of play greatly improved. By 1983, using these largely brute-force procedures and the latest, most powerful computer (the Cray X-MP, capable of examining about ten million terminal positions in choosing each move), a program called Cray-Blitz became world computer chess champion and achieved a master rating based on a tournament against other computers which already had chess ratings.

Such programs, however, have an Achilles heel. While they are perfect tacticians when there are many captures and checks and a decisive outcome can be found within the computer's foreseeable future (now about four moves ahead for each player), computers lack any sense of chess strategy. Fairly good players who understand this fact can direct the game into long-range strategic channels and can thereby defeat the computer, even though these players have a somewhat lower chess rating than the machine has achieved based on play against other machines and humans who do not know and exploit this strategic blindness. The ratings held by computers and reported in the press accurately reflect their performance against other computers and human players who do not know or exploit the computer's weakness, but greatly overstate their skill level when play is strategic.

A Scottish International Master chess player, David Levy, who is a computer enthusiast—and chairman of a company called Intelligent Software in London—is ranked as roughly the thousandth best player in the world, bet about $4,000 in 1968 that no computer could defeat him by 1978. He collected, by beating the best computer program at that time 3.5 games to 1.5 games in a five-game match. He was, however, impressed by the machine's performance and the bet was increased and extended until 1984, with Levy quite uncertain about the outcome. When the 1984 match approached and the Cray-Blitz program had just achieved a master-level score in winning the world computer championship, Levy decided to modify his usual style of play so as maximally to exploit the computer's strategic blindness. Not only did he defeat the computer decisively, four games to zero, but, more importantly, he lost his long-held optimism about computer play. As he confessed to the *Los Angeles Times* of 12 May 1984,

During the last few years I had come to believe more and more that it was possible for programs, within a decade, to play very strong grandmaster chess. But having played the thing now, my feeling is that a human world chess champion losing to a computer program in a serious match is a lot further away than I thought. Most people working on computer chess are working on the wrong lines. If more chess programmers studied the way human chess masters think and tried to emulate that to some extent, then I think they might get further.

Levy summed up his recent match by saying "The nature of the struggle was such that the program didn't understand what was going on."[22] Clearly, when confronting a player who knows its weakness, Cray-Blitz is not a master-level chess player.

We could not agree more strongly with Levy's suggestion that researchers give up current methods and attempt to imitate what people do. But since strong,

[22] Dembart Lee, "Man Is Still Master: King of Chess Computers Humbled by Wily Human", *Los Angeles Times*, 12 May 1984.

experienced, chess players use the holistic similarity recognition described in the highest of our five levels of skill, imitating people would mean duplicating that pattern recognition process rather than returning to the typical expert system approach. Since similarity for a strong chess player means similar "fields of force" such as interrelated threats, hopes, fears, and strengths, not similarity of the location of pieces on the board, and since no one can describe such fields, there is little prospect of duplicating human performance in the foreseeable future.

The only remaining game program that appears to challenge our prediction is Hans Berliner's backgammon program, BKG 9.8. There is no doubt that the program used heuristic rules obtained from masters to beat the world champion in a seven-game series. But backgammon is a game involving a large element of chance, and Berliner himself is quite frank in saying that his program "did get the better of the dice rolls" and could not consistently perform at championship level. He concludes:

The program did not make the best play in eight out of 73 non-forced situations... An expert would not have made most of the errors the program made, but they could be exploited only a small percent of the time.... My program plays at the Class A, or advanced intermediate, level.[23]

These cases are clearly not counterexamples to our claim. Neither is a recent SRI contender named PROSPECTOR, a program which uses rules derived from expert geologists to locate mineral deposits. Millions of viewers heard about PROSPECTOR on the CBS Evening News in September 1983. A special Dan Rather Report called "The Computers are Coming" showed first a computer and then a mountain (Mount Tolman) as Rather authoritatively intoned: "This computer digested facts and figures on mineral deposits, then predicted that the metal molybdenum would be found at this mountain in the Pacific Northwest. It was." Such a feat, if true, would indeed be impressive. Viewers must have felt that we were foolish when, later in the same program, we were shown asserting that, using current AI methods, computers would never become intelligent. (While we explained and defended this claim during an hour-long taped interview with CBS, all of this was necessarily omitted during the five-minute segment on computers that was aired.) In reality, the PROSPECTOR program was given information concerning prior drilling on Mount Tolman where a field of molybdenum *had already been found*. The expert system then mapped out undrilled portions of that field, and subsequent drilling showed it to be basically

---

[23] Hans Berliner, "Computer Backgammon", *Scientific American* (June 1980), 64–72.

correct about where molybdenum did and did not exist.[24] Unfortunately, economic-grade molybdenum was not found in the previously unmapped area; drilling disclosed the ore to be too deep to be worth mining. These facts do not justify the conclusion that the program can outperform experts. So far there are no further data comparing experts' predictions with those of the system.

This leaves MYCIN, mentioned earlier, INTERNIST-I, a program for diagnosis in internal medicine, and PUFF, an expert system for diagnosis of lung disorders, as the only programs that we know of which meet all the requirements for a test of our hypothesis. They are each based exclusively on heuristic rules extracted from experts, and their performance has been compared with that of experts in the field.

Let us take MYCIN first. A systematic evaluation of MYCIN was reported in the *Journal of the American Medical Association*. MYCIN was given data concerning actual meningitis cases and asked to prescribe drug therapy. Its prescriptions were evaluated by a panel of eight infectious disease specialists who had published clinical reports dealing with the management of meningitis. These experts rated as acceptable 70 percent of MYCIN's recommended therapies.[25]

The evidence concerning INTERNIST-I is even more detailed. In fact, according to the *New England Journal of Medicine*, which published an evaluation of the program, "[the] systematic evaluation of the model's performance is virtually unique in the field of medical applications of artificial intelligence."[26] INTERNIST-I is described as follows:

From its inception, INTERNIST-I has addressed the problem of diagnosis within the broad context of general internal medicine. Given a patient's initial history, results of a physical examination, or laboratory findings, INTERNIST-I was designed to aid the physician with the patient's work-up in order to make multiple and complex diagnoses.

---

[24] See *Byte* (Sept. 1981), 262, caption under figure. The CBS News report is not the only sensationalized and inaccurate report on PROSPECTOR spread by the mass media. The 9 July 1984 issue of *Business Week* reports in its cover story, "Artificial Intelligence: It's Here": "Geologists were convinced as far back as World War I that a rich deposit of molybdenum ore was buried deep under Mount Tolman in eastern Washington. But after digging dozens of small mines and drilling hundreds of test borings, they were still hunting for the elusive metal 60 years later. Then, just a couple of years ago, miners hit pay dirt. They finally found the ore because they were guided not by a geologist wielding his rock hammer, but by a computer located hundreds of miles to the south in Menlo Park, California."

[25] Victor L. Yu et al., "Antimicrobial Selection by a Computer", *Journal of the American Medical Association* 242/12 (21 Sept. 1979), 1279.

[26] Randolph A. Miller, Harry E. Pople Jr., and Jack D. Myers, "INTERNIST-I, an Experimental Computer-Based Diagnostic Consultant for General Internal Medicine", *New England Journal of Medicine*, 307/8 (19 Aug. 1982), 494.

The capabilities of the system derive from its extensive knowledge base and from heuristic computer programs that can construct and resolve differential diagnoses.[27]

The program was run on 19 cases, each with several diseases, so that there were 43 correct diagnoses in all, and its diagnoses were compared with those of clinicians at Massachusetts General Hospital and with case discussants. Diagnoses were counted as correct when confirmed by pathologists. The result was:

[O]f 43 anatomically verified diagnoses, INTERNIST-I failed to make a total of 18, whereas the clinicians failed to make 15 such diagnoses and the discussants missed only eight.[28]

The evaluators found that:

The experienced clinician is vastly superior to INTERNIST-I in the ability to consider the relative severity and independence of the different manifestations of disease and to understand the temporal evolution of the disease process.[29]

Dr G. Octo Barnett, in his editorial comment on the evaluation, wisely concludes:

Perhaps the most exciting experimental evaluation of INTERNIST-I would be the demonstration that a productive collaboration is possible between man and computer—that clinical diagnosis in real situations can be improved by combining the medical judgment of the clinician with the statistical and computational power of a computer model and a large base of stored medical information.[30]

PUFF is an excellent example of an expert system doing a useful job without being an expert. PUFF was written to perform pulmonary function test interpretations. One sample measurement is the patient's Total Lung Capacity (TLC), that is, the volume of air in the lungs at maximum inspiration. If the TLC for a patient is high, this indicates the presence of Obstructive Airway Disease. The interpretation and final diagnoses is a summary of this kind of reasoning about the combinations of measurements taken in the lung test. PUFF's principal task is to interpret such a set of pulmonary function test results, producing a set of interpretation statements and a diagnosis for each patient.

Using 30 heuristic rules extracted from an expert, Dr Robert Fallat, PUFF agrees with Dr Fallat in 75–85 percent of the cases. Why it does as well as the expert it models in only 75–85 percent of the cases is a mystery if one believes, as Robert MacNeil put it on the MacNeil-Lehrer television news, that researchers "discovered that Dr Fallat used some 30 rules based on his clinical expertise to diagnose whether patients have obstructive airway disease." Of course, the

---

[27] Miller et al., "INTERNIST-I", 468.
[29] Miller et al., "INTERNIST-I", 494.
[28] Miller et al., "INTERNIST-I", 473.
[30] Miller et al., "INTERNIST-I", 494.

machine's limited ability makes perfect sense if Dr Fallat does not in fact follow these 30 rules or any others. But in any case, PUFF does well enough to be a valuable aid. As Dr Fallat puts it:

There's a lot of what we do, including our thinking and our expertise, which is routine, and which doesn't require any special human effort to do. And that kind of stuff should be taken over by computers. And to the extent that 75% of what I do is routine and which all of us would agree on, why not let the computer do it and then I can have fun working with the other 25%.[31]

Feigenbaum himself admits in one surprisingly honest passage that expert systems are very different from experts:

Part of learning to be an expert is to understand not merely the letter of the rule but its spirit.... [The expert] knows when to break the rules, he understands what is relevant to his task and what isn't... Expert systems do not yet understand these things.[32]

But because of his philosophical commitment to the rationality of expertise and thus to underlying unconscious heuristic rules, Feigenbaum does not see how devastating this admission is.

Once one gives up the assumption that experts must be making inferences and admits the role of involvement and intuition in the acquisition and application of skills, one will have no reason to cling to the heuristic program as a model of human intellectual operations. Feigenbaum's claim that "we have the opportunity at this moment to do a new version of Diderot's *Encyclopedia*, a gathering up of all knowledge—not just the academic kind, but the informal, experiential, heuristic kind,"[33] as well as his boast that thanks to Knowledge Information Processing Systems (KIPS) we will soon have "access to machine intelligence—faster, deeper, better than human intelligence,"[34] can both be seen as a late stage of Socratic thinking, with no rational or empirical basis. In this light those who claim we must begin a crash program to compete with the Japanese Fifth Generation Intelligent Computers can be seen to be false prophets blinded by these Socratic assumptions and personal ambition—while Euthyphro, the expert on piety, who kept giving Socrates examples instead of rules, turns out to have been a true prophet after all.

[31] The MacNeil-Lehrer Report on Artificial Intelligence, 22 Apr. 1983.
[32] Feigenbaum and McCorduck, *The Fifth Generation*, 184–5.
[33] Feigenbaum and McCorduck, *The Fifth Generation*, 229.
[34] Feigenbaum and McCorduck, *The Fifth Generation*, 236.

PART II

Intentionality and Mind

2

The Perceptual Noema

Gurwitsch's Crucial Contribution (1972)

Everyone who has studied Husserl's *Ideas* would agree that the notion of the noema is central to Husserl's theory of consciousness and, in particular, that the notion of the perceptual noema is central to the Husserlian theory of perception. This should be no surprise, since for Husserl intentionality is the defining feature of consciousness, and intentionality is defined in terms of the necessary correlation of noesis and noema. What is surprising is that running through the commentaries on Husserl's theory of consciousness there is a fundamental disagreement as to what Husserl has in mind when he speaks of the perceptual noema. Moreover, this division seems to go completely unnoticed.

The opposition is obscured by the tendency of all interpreters to explain the noema in terms of a set of synonyms proposed by Husserl himself. Thus all would readily agree that the perceptual noema is the intentional correlate of perceptual consciousness: it is neither a (*real*) physical object, nor a (*reell*) momentary act of consciousness, but rather a meaning, an ideal entity correlated with every act of perception, whether the object intended in that act exists or not.

Two interpreters, however, have undertaken the task of translating Husserl's technical vocabulary into other terms and in so doing have unwittingly revealed a systematic ambiguity running through the whole constellation of noema terminology. Crudely put, Dagfinn Føllesdal interprets the perceptual noema as a concept, while Aron Gurwitsch takes it to be a percept.

Føllesdal traces the development of the perceptual noema back to Husserl's adoption of Frege's distinction of sense and reference. According to Føllesdal the perceptual noema is an "abstract entity"[1] "in virtue of which an act of perception is directed toward its object."[2] The noema itself is never sensuously given but is "entertained" in a special act of reflection called the phenomenological reduction.

---

[1] Dagfinn Føllesdal, "Husserl's Notion of the Noema", *Journal of Philosophy*, 66/20 (1969), 684.
[2] Føllesdal, "Husserl's Notion", 682.

Gurwitsch, on the other hand, while recognizing the Fregean filiation of the concept, has attempted to explicate Husserl's notion of the perceptual noema in terms of the findings of Gestalt theory. Thus for Gurwitsch the perceptual noema is a concrete sensuous appearance, through which the object of perception is presented: "We interpret the perceptual noema ... as a Gestalt-contexture whose constituents are what is given in a direct sense experience."[3] This noema is not, in a strict sense, perceived, since only a physical object can be perceived. It is, however, perceptually given and can be thematized in a special act of attending to the perceptual object—Gurwitsch's version of the phenomenological reduction.

Føllesdal's reading is recent and claims to do nothing more than explicate the Husserlian texts, so it has not given rise to a school of interpretation.[4] Gurwitsch's version, however, dating from 1929 and proposing to "advance and to develop further rather than merely expound"[5] Husserl's view, has had a broad influence. The Gurwitschian interpretation of the noema is taken for granted in the works of Cairns,[6] Schutz,[7] Boehm,[8] and Fink,[9] to emerge transformed into a criticism of Husserl in the writings of Merleau-Ponty.

The ambiguity revealed by these interpretations so consistently contaminates the terms Husserl uses to explain his noema that it has so far proven impossible to decide definitively which of these two interpretations is correct.[10] In any case,

---

[3] Aron Gurwitsch, "The Phenomenology of Perception: Perceptual Implications", in James Edie (ed.), *An Invitation to Phenomenology* (Chicago: Quadrangle Books, 1965), 23.

[4] It is, however, shared by such influential thinkers as Jacques Derrida and Maurice Merleau-Ponty.

[5] Aron Gurwitsch, *Studies in Phenomenology and Psychology* (Evanston, IL: Northwestern University Press, 1966), p. xv.

[6] See Dorton Cairns, "An Approach to Phenomenology", in Marvin Farber (ed.), *Philosophical Essays in Memory of Edmund Husserl* (Cambridge, MA: Harvard University Press, 1968), 9: "The 'object per se' (or object simpliciter) and 'intentional object' are names for one and the same object only attended in different ways."

[7] Alfred Schutz, *Collected Papers* (The Hague: Martinus Nijhoff, 1962), i. 107–8, first identifies the noema with the intentional object, "the noema itself, the intentional object perceived," and then identifies the intentional object with the percept: "The intentional object of my perceiving is a specific mixture of colors and shapes in a special perspective."

[8] Cf. n. 63.   [9] Cf. n. 63.

[10] The most serious attempt to settle the question is Føllesdal's "Husserl's Notion." Føllesdal's theses 8, 9, 10, and 11 are implicitly directed against Gurwitsch's view. Føllesdal wants to establish that the noema is indeed a conceptual entity, which cannot be perceived. Once these two possible interpretations of "noema" are distinguished, however, the evidence for theses 8, 9, 10, and 11 turns out either to assume dogmatically what Føllesdal is trying to establish or to be infected with the very ambiguity these theses are meant to clear up.

Thesis 8. Noemata are abstract entities. Evidence: Husserl says: "The tree in nature is by no means the perceived tree as such. The real tree can burn ... ," etc. But Gurwitsch and all those who believe that the noema is a sort of ostensible object—an appearance, as Gurwitsch calls it—would agree that this entity does not have the properties of a physical object but rather has the special properties of a

that decision is more important for the historian of philosophy than for the phenomenologist. What is important for us is to work out the conception of consciousness and of phenomenology which follows from each view and then to decide which interpretation fits the phenomena.

In keeping with this goal, the first section of this chapter, although incidentally marshaling evidence that the Føllesdal interpretation of the noema is more consistent with Husserl's development, is mainly meant to bring out the stark contrast between two possible antecedents of the noema. This contrast then enables us in the following section to understand Gurwitsch's interpretation of

view of the object. Moreover, both schools would agree that the noema is not a temporal event, since it can be the object of an indefinite number of temporally indexed acts.

Thesis 9 is more decisive. Here Føllesdal contends that noemata are not perceived through the senses. If this could be shown, then the ambiguity would be definitely cleared up, for Gurwitsch does clearly contend that the perceptual noema is sensuously given. Unfortunately, Føllesdal's argument that "Thesis 9 is an immediate consequence of Thesis 8," that, since the noema is abstract, it cannot be perceived, begs the question at hand. Nor does it help to base the argument on Husserl's claim that "all visible objects can be experienced only through perspectives" and conclude, as Føllesdal does, that, "since noemata are not experienced through perspectives, they are not visible." For, from the above, it might equally well follow that they are not perceptual objects, which is just what Gurwitsch contends.

At this point, Føllesdal introduces as evidence a quotation from an unpublished manuscript in which Husserl does indeed say that "the *Sinn* is not perceived"; but, as Føllesdal remarks, here Husserl is talking about the *Sinn* and not directly about the perceptual noema. Gurwitsch would presumably agree that the *Sinn* is indeed not perceived, for Husserl himself calls the *Sinn* an abstract component in the perceptual noema. (It must be abstract, for it is what is held in common by a perceptual noema, a memory noema, an image noema, etc., of the same object, seen from the same perspective, etc.)

Thesis 10, that noemata are known through a special kind of reflection, is also critical, but critically ambiguous. Noemata are indeed known through a special reflection; but whether this is *a* special reflection on a conceptual entity, or whether it is a special way of regarding a perceptual object so as to describe only what is given in a particular act of perception, is unclear. Each interpretation could cite in its favor Husserl's claim that "the reflecting judgment is directed toward the Sinn, and hence not toward that which is the object of the nonreflecting judgment." But for Føllesdal this means that the noema is given only in a special act of abstract reflection turned away from the object presented and toward the sense we give that presentation, whereas for Gurwitsch the noema is the object of perception itself attended to in a special way so as to notice exactly what is presented.

Thesis 11, that phenomenological reflection can be iterated, if established, would be decisive, provided it could be shown that by iteration Husserl means that *the same sort* of reflection can be repeated at higher levels. For if the noema were an abstract entity, we could indeed reflect on the higher-order noemata involved in reflecting on the first-order noema without changing our mode of reflection, whereas if the noema were a percept singled out by reflection, the mode of reflection involved could not be iterated. Unfortunately, in the passage quoted by Føllesdal, Husserl says only that the meaning used on one level can always be made an object of reflection on a higher level, not that this higher-level entity has to be the same sort of entity revealed on the first level. This leaves open the possibility, compatible with Gurwitsch's account, that, after noticing the perceptual presentation, the phenomenologist could reflect on the abstract entity by means of which he intended the first-order percept, etc.

the noema as an attempt to fill a fundamental gap in Husserl's system and, incidentally, it enables us also to marshal evidence that this is not what Husserl could or did propose. Then in the final section we will be in a position to see how Gurwitsch's radical and original interpretation of the perceptual noema, if frankly and consistently read back into Husserl's thought, would lead to a total transformation of Husserl's project for doing transcendental phenomenology.

Husserl's Conceptualization of Perception—the Noema as Interpretive Sense

All Husserl interpreters agree that the perceptual noema, introduced by Husserl in *Ideas*, represents a generalization of Husserl's theory of meaning to perception. To understand the noema, then, we must follow this process of generalization.

In the First Logical Investigation, Husserl begins by distinguishing the physical manifestations of linguistic expressions (noises, marks on paper, etc.) from the acts of consciousness which give them meaning. Then, turning to an analysis of the meaning-conferring acts, Husserl notes that such acts are always correlated with a meaning or sense. It is by virtue of this sense that an expression intends or means an object, regardless of whether the object aimed at is actually present in a fulfilling intuition. Since the meaning does not depend on the existence of anything beyond the act itself, Husserl calls the meaning the content of the act. This ideal content, Husserl declares, does not belong to the real world of changing objects or even to our stream of consciousness, since this too belongs to the "temporal sphere." Rather, "meanings constitute... a class of concepts in the sense of 'universal objects.'"[11]

Husserl's analysis of linguistic expressions in terms of meaning-giving act, ideal meaning, and fulfilling intuition exactly parallels the distinction between idea, sense, and reference in Frege's article "On Sense and Reference."[12] This is no coincidence. Husserl's first book, *The Philosophy of Arithmetic*, was criticized by Frege for being too psychologistic, i.e. for "a blurring of the distinction between image and concept, between imagination and thought." Images, Frege had argued, are psychic events confined to each man's mind, whereas "it is quite otherwise for thoughts; one and the same thought can be grasped by many men."[13]

---

[11] Edmund Husserl, *Logical Investigations*, tr. J. N. Findlay (New York: Humanities Press, 1970a), i. 330.
[12] Gottlob Frege, *Translations from the Philosophical Writings of Gottlob Frege* (Oxford: Blackwell, 1960), 59.
[13] Frege, *Translations*, 79.

Husserl simply accepted and applied Frege's distinctions:

The essence of meaning is seen by us, not in the meaning-conferring experience, but in its "content," the single, self-identical intentional unity set over against the dispersed multiplicity of actual and possible experiences of speakers and thinkers.[14]

The only change Husserl made in Frege's analysis was terminological. Husserl proposes to use "object" (*Gegenstand*) for "reference" (*Bedeutung*), and "meaning" and "sense" (*Bedeutung* and *Sinn*) interchangeably for "sense" (*Sinn*), since this is closer to German usage, and "it is agreeable to have parallel, interchangeable terms in the case of this concept, particularly since the sense of the term 'meaning' is itself to be investigated."[15] The meaning of "Sinn" (or "Bedeutung") and its function in knowledge and experience becomes henceforth the subject of all of Husserl's work, and our task will be to follow the generalization of meaning in its transfer to the field of perception.

To begin with, Husserl notes with approval Brentano's dictum that: "In perception something is perceived, in imagination, something imagined, in a statement, something stated, in love, something loved…etc.,"[16] and he follows his teacher in taking the "intentional relation…to be the essential feature of 'psychical phenomena' or 'acts.'"[17] He then appeals to his Fregean theory of meaning to argue that every act is at least correlated with a sense. He admits that in our ordinary everyday attitude we have before our mind the reference, not the sense, of our acts; but, he holds, the sense is always present, and we can make it explicit as an object of study if we turn from a straightforward to a reflective attitude.

Instead of becoming lost in the performance of acts built intricately on one another, and instead of (as it were) naïvely positing the existence of the objects…we must rather practise "reflection," i.e., make these acts themselves, and their immanent meaning-content, our objects.[18]

This method of reflection, which turns the intentional correlate of an act into an object, is not a method invented by the phenomenologist. Although it is an unnatural (*wider natürlich*) orientation for the active involved individual, it is

---

[14] Husserl, *Logical Investigations*, i. 327.

[15] Husserl, *Logical Investigations*, i. 292. In the light of Husserl's explicit attribution of this distinction to Frege here, it is misleading of Gurwitsch to claim that "the distinction between *meanings as ideal units* and *mental states as real psychological events* (acts), through which meanings are apprehended and actualized, is one of the most momentous and most consequential achievements for which modern philosophy is indebted to Husserl" (Aron Gurwitsch, *The Field of Consciousness* (Pittsburgh: Duquesne University Press, 1964), 177 n.). The most that can be claimed is that Husserl was the first to realize the import of this Fregean distinction.

[16] Husserl, *Logical Investigations*, ii. 554.   [17] Husserl, *Logical Investigations*, ii. 555.

[18] Husserl, *Logical Investigations*, i. 254–5.

perfectly natural for the reflective thinker and has from the beginning been practiced by logicians.

If we perform the act and live in it, as it were, we naturally refer to its object and not to its meaning. If, e.g., we make a statement, we judge about the thing it concerns, and not about the statement's meaning, about the judgment in the logical sense. This latter first becomes objective to us in a reflex act of thought, in which we not only look back on the statement just made, but carry out the abstraction (the Ideation) demanded. This logical reflection is not an act that takes place only under exceptional, artificial conditions: it is a normal component of *logical* thinking.[19]

In this logical reflection we become aware of what we do not ordinarily notice, viz., that, when we are thinking of, wishing for, or passing judgment on objects or states of affairs, there is a thought, a wish, or a judgment involved. Between our thinking and the object or reference of our thinking lies the sense, which, as Frege puts it, "is indeed no longer subjective like the idea, but is yet not the object itself."[20] Frege uses a suggestive analogy to show the role of these objective meanings in conception.

Somebody observes the Moon through a telescope. I compare the Moon itself to the reference; it is the object of the observation, mediated by the real image projected by the object glass in the interior of the telescope, and by the retinal image of the observer. The former I compare to the sense, the latter is like the idea or experience. The optical image in the telescope is indeed one-sided and dependent upon the standpoint of observation; but it is still objective, inasmuch as it can be used by several observers.[21]

The real image in the telescope is not normally what is observed. If it could be observed by the observer changing his position and looking at it through some instrument which itself involved a real image, the situation would be analogous to what the phenomenologist or logician is doing. The phenomenologist can at will, through an act of reflection, change the intentional correlate of his act into an object of a second-order act. He can think of the thought rather than the object he is thinking about, and he then becomes aware that the thought was present all along. He can also reflect on the second-order thought by which his attention was directed to the first-order thought, etc. On reflection we can thus discover something thought in each act of thinking, something wished in each wishing, something judged in each judging, etc., whether the objects of these thoughts, wishes, and judgments exist or not. Even though we are not ordinarily reflectively aware of this fact, it is nonetheless reflected in our grammar, which treats the objects thought of, wished for, judged about, etc., as *indirect* objects, suggesting

---

[19] Husserl, *Logical Investigations*, i. 332.   [20] Frege, *Translations*, 60.
[21] Frege, *Translations*, 60.

thereby that the proximate object is the thought, the judgment, the wish. A signifying act can thus be said to have its own intermediary object, the sense, whether it is confirmed by a filling act or not, i.e. whether or not it corresponds to any real object or state of affairs.

Thus, the intentionalist thesis that every act has a correlate is saved, at least for the signifying acts such as thinking, judging, etc. But what about perception, the filling act par excellence, by means of which the signifying acts are confirmed? In perception, is something always perceived?

To save the intentionalist thesis that all acts always have objects, Husserl must generalize his Fregean threefold analysis of signifying acts to perceptual or, more generally, to filling acts. He must exhibit a perceptual sense as correlate of the perceptual act, to correspond to the conceptual sense we have seen to be correlated with each signifying act. And he must show why we can speak of the sense as "what is perceived" in every act of perception.

Husserl's defense is not convincing. He plausibly holds that

> We distinguish, in a perceptual _statement_, as in every statement, between _content_ and _object_; by the "content" we understand the self-identical meaning that the hearer can grasp even if he is not a percipient.[22]

He then goes on to claim without further argument that when a sense-fulfilling _act_ has an object, "object" can mean one of two things: on the one hand, it can mean the reference or, _"more properly"_ it can mean "the object's ideal correlate in the acts of meaning-fulfillment... _the fulfilling sense (erfüllende Sinn)._"[23] Yet we are not told how we know there is such a fulfilling sense or why it is properly called the object of the act. Rather, Husserl seems to expect us to accept this fulfilling sense on the basis of a parallel with the way linguistic sense-conferring acts are always correlated with a conferred meaning.

> The ideal conception of the act which _confers meaning_ yields us the Idea of the _intending meaning_, just as the ideal conception of the correlative essence of the act which _fulfills meaning_ yields the fulfilling meaning, likewise _qua_ Idea. This is the _identical content_ which, in perception, pertains to the totality of possible acts of perception which intended the same object perceptually, and intend it actually as the same object. This content is therefore the ideal correlate of this _single_ object, which may, for the rest, be completely imaginary.[24]

But what is this identical content which belongs to all perceptual acts which intend the same object regardless of whether that object exists? So far this is by no

---

[22] Husserl, _Logical Investigations_, i. 290. (Underlining is mine.)

[23] Husserl, _Logical Investigations_, i. 290. (Underlining is mine.)

[24] Husserl, _Logical Investigations_, i. 291. Note that Husserl says that this ideal entity is a _correlate_ of the object, as would be expected of the meaning in the Frege-Føllesdal interpretation, not an _aspect_ of the object (a member of a family which makes up the object), as in Gurwitsch's account.

means clear. Husserl is aware that "the application of the terms 'meaning' and 'sense' not merely to the content of the meaning-intention... but also to the content of meaning-fulfillment, engenders a most unwelcome ambiguity."[25]

Indeed, there is trouble here; for while signifying acts can be viewed as opaque (to adopt Russell's terminology) and thus always correlated with a sense, fulfilling acts, by virtue of their function of presenting the state of affairs itself, can never be construed as referentially opaque in ordinary discourse.[26] An example will help to highlight this difference. Suppose that, unknown to me, my neighbor, whom I see every day, is a murderer. Suppose further that each day I spend some time thinking about this neighbor, judging his actions, admiring him, etc. At his trial I could honestly testify that I had not for a moment thought about a murderer, judged him, admired him, etc. But to say that, up to the moment of his conviction, I had never *seen* a murderer would be outright perjury. For, seeing my neighbor, I had seen a murderer whether I knew it or not. A fulfilling act seems to go directly to its object. This difference in function between signifying and fulfilling acts is so fundamental that it remains to be shown that there is any fulfilling sense at all.

* * *

Before he can legitimately introduce the fulfilling sense as an intentional correlate, Husserl must extend his discussion of intentional experience beyond the discussion of signifying acts which is his focus in the first of the *Logical Investigations*. In the Fifth and Sixth Investigations Husserl undertakes this

---

[25] Husserl, *Logical Investigations*, i. 291.

[26] This is argued in greater detail in my doctoral dissertation: Hubert L. Dreyfus, "Husserl's Phenomenology of Perception: From Transcendental to Existential Phenomenology" (Harvard University, 1963).

Chisholm's argument concerning perception words in Roderick Chisholm, *Perceiving: A Philosophical Study* (Ithaca, NY: Cornell University Press, 1957), 172, might appear to present a counterargument to the claim that fulfilling acts must be construed as transparent. In his chapter on "intentional inexistence" Chisholm gives a definition of intentionality which equates intentionality with Frege's indirect reference or what we have been calling "referential opacity." Chisholm then tries to argue, following Brentano, that all psychic acts are intentional. "When we use perception words propositionally, our sentences display the... above marks of intentionality," he claims (p. 172). This propositional use might seem to contradict our conclusion that in ordinary usage the act context of perception words is transparent. Chisholm's argument is simple: "I may see that John is the man in the corner, and John may be someone who is ill; but I do not now see that John is someone who is ill." What this shows is merely that sentences involving "see that" display intentionality as defined by Chisholm. But Chisholm does not claim that "see" in this propositional sense is used perceptually. Rather, it could be replaced by "realize" or "take it to be the case that." If we use "see" in a way that is strictly perceptual, the sentence becomes: "I may see John in the corner, and John may be someone who is ill." In which case I *do* see someone who is ill. The intentionality, in Chisholm's sense of the term, vanishes. This shift is instructive. It shows that if we could construe perceiving as "taking" or "seeing" something to be the case, rather than simply seeing something, the intentionalist thesis could be saved. This seems to be precisely Husserl's move in generalizing his theory of meaning to perception.

generalization. The Fifth Investigation studies the essential relation of *all* acts to their ideal content, and the Sixth studies the relation of signifying acts to fulfilling acts and that of fulfilling acts to their objects.

According to Husserl, when we perform an act of perception, we are directly aware of a perceptual object. Since the perceptual act is a fulfilling act, we can be sure that its object must have two characteristics: it must be recognized as fulfilling a certain signifying intention, and it must be sensuously given, for "a signitive intention merely points to its object, an intuitive intention gives it 'presence,' in the pregnant sense of the word."[27] Thus the perceptual act, in order to fulfill its function, must coordinate two components: an act which intends a certain object as having certain characteristics, and an act which presents the object, thereby fulfilling or failing to fulfill this intention. Perception is veridical if we can adjust these two acts so that their meanings coincide and there emerges a unity of coincidence (*Deckung*) between what is taken and what is given.

In other words, the thing which, from the point of view of our acts is phenomenologically described as fulfillment, will also, from the point of view of the two objects involved in it, the intuited object, on the one hand, and the thought object, on the other, be expressly styled "experience of identity," "consciousness of identity," or "act of identification." A more or less complete *identity is the objective datum which corresponds to the act of fulfillment*, which "appears in it." This means that, not only signification and intuition, but also their mutual adequation, their union of fulfillment, can be called an act, since it has its own peculiar intentional correlate, an objective something to which it is "directed."[28]

If the intentionalist thesis is to hold for all acts, we must be able to exhibit the intentional content of each of these acts. We must show that each component act has an ideal correlate which it retains, whether there is a corresponding perceptual object or not.

It is relatively easy to identify the intentional correlate of the signifying component. The signifying act is the act which intends the object as having certain characteristics. Husserl calls its intentional correlate the matter of the act.[29] "Since

---

[27] Husserl, *Logical Investigations*, ii. 728.   [28] Husserl, *Logical Investigations*, ii. 696.

[29] Husserl, *Logical Investigations*, ii. 589. "The matter must be *that element in an act which first gives it reference to an object, and reference so wholly definite that it not merely fixes the object meant in a general way, but also the precise way in which it is meant.*" It is the matter through which the act attains its object "exactly as it is intended." Like a meaning, the matter is a "universal object" which conveys as completely as possible what specific determinations we take the object to have. Husserl thus calls the matter an "abstract form" (*abstracter Form*). It is confusing to the reader that what corresponds to the form of the object should be called its matter, but Husserl presumably uses this term because of the capacity of the matter to take on various "qualities," i.e., to be affirmed, denied, doubted, etc. Perhaps it is helpful in fixing in mind the way Husserl is using "matter" to think of it as the "subject matter" of the act. For matter in the more traditional sense Husserl uses the German *Stoff* or, in *Ideas*, the Greek *hylê*.

the matter...fixes the *sense* in which the representative content is interpreted (*aufgefasst*), we may also speak of the interpretive sense (*Auffassungssinn*)."[30] The act of taking, we have seen, like any conceptual act, can be directed toward an object whether or not there is any such object. I can, for example, mistakenly take a dust particle on the lens of my telescope to be a planet, which I take to be the planet Venus. In such cases, even if there is no such object as I take there to be, the act of taking has nonetheless its intentional content, its interpretive sense.

It would seem we could treat the other act component of perception in the same fashion. The intuitive act, too, must have its intentional correlate, which determines that it is an intuition of this object rather than another. If the intuitive act did not have such content, we could never tell whether our anticipations had been fulfilled. The content of the intuitive act must tell us, as completely as possible, the determinations of the object being intuited. Then, in the case of successful perception, the intentional contents of the signifying and the intuitive acts will correspond and can be identified.

If at this point, however, we define the intentional correlate of the intuitive act, on a strict analogy with the intentional content of the signifying act, as an abstractable component of the intuitive act which determines what sort of object is being intuited and which can itself then be either empty or fulfilled, we run into difficulty. The intuitive act will indeed have its own intentional content, which is independent of whether this content is fulfilled or not, but only at the cost of ceasing to be a fulfilling act. And we will have to seek again for an act which can supply the filling.

Let us review the steps by which we have arrived at this impasse: first of all, in the First Logical Investigation acts were divided into signifying and fulfilling acts. Then the perceptual act, which one would suppose to be a fulfilling act par excellence, was in turn analyzed into *its* signifying and intuitive components. Now the intuitive component of the perceptual act itself has turned out to have an intentional content or signifying component. Thus a regress develops in which sense coincides with sense indefinitely. At each stage we arrive at a fulfilling meaning for an intending meaning, but at no stage does the fulfilling meaning imply a sensuous filling. How are we to end this regress of meaning superimposed on meaning and account for our knowledge of the world?

If we wish to preserve the notion of fulfilling acts which corresponds to our experience of perceiving objects and thus arrive at the end of this regress, so that knowledge is seen to be possible, we must introduce an incarnate meaning, a meaning which is not abstractable from the intuitive content which it informs.

---

[30] Husserl, *Logical Investigations*, ii. 741.

This would mean that, although the signifying act and the intentional correlate of the signifying act are unaffected by the existence or nonexistence of the object of that act, the intentional correlate of the intuitive act would be dependent upon there being something to intuit.

To distinguish this incarnate meaning from the interpretive sense (*Auffassungssinn*), the intentional content of the signifying act which is independent of the existence of the object of the act, i.e. which can be entertained whether the object exists or not, we could call the intentional content of the intuitive act the intuitive sense (*Anschauungssinn*). This intuitive sense would be an entirely new sort of sense whose existence would be essentially inseparable from the intuitive content of the object whose sense it was. Perception would then be described as the coincidence of the interpretive sense with the intuitive sense.

This would be a complex and convincing theory of perception. It would call attention to the fact that perception is not a purely passive presentational act in which something is merely given, or a pure act of taking in which nothing is given, but that it involves both an act of interpretation, which can be dealt with on the model of conceptual acts, and an intuitive act, which must be analyzed in a unique way.

This may be the view which Husserl eventually adopts,[31] but it is not the position he holds in the *Logical Investigations*. In this work there is no mention of the intuitive sense, nor could there be, for Husserl has no way of generalizing his Fregean conception of a nonspatial, nontemporal, universal, abstract sense to cover a *concrete* "form" which is *inseparable* from the sensuous content it organizes.[32]

Lacking an *Anschauungssinn*, Husserl is constrained to make the most of this position while at the same time admitting its limitations, viz., that what is left

---

[31] Husserl notes in the *Lectures on Internal Time-Consciousness* that "not every constitution has the *Inhalt-Auffassung* schema" (p. 5), which is tantamount to admitting that not all structures can be understood in terms of the imposition of *separable* meanings. In Edmund Husserl, *Erfahrung und Urteil* (Hamburg: Claassen & Govert, 1948), Husserl expresses the same reservation from the other side by distinguishing a "pure or original passivity" from a "secondary passivity" which is the passivity of habit: "Every active grasping of an object presupposes that it is given beforehand. The objects of receptivity with their associative structure are given beforehand in an original passivity. Grasping these structures is the lowest form of activity, the mere reception of the originally passive pre-constituted sense (*Sinne*)" (p. 300). The important thing to note in this passage is that there is a form of constitution which was never active and which is not the imposing of sense on some prior senseless data. This suggests that at its lowest level constitution is not the bringing to bear of a form on a distinct material—i.e. not *Sinngebung*—but that from the start the material has a certain form.

[32] Husserl does once refer to a perceptual sense (*Wahrnehmungsinn*) and tells us that "the homogeneous unity of the perceptual sense pervades the total representation" (Husserl, *Logical Investigations*, ii. 807), but he does not elaborate on this notion and never employs it again in *Logical Investigations*.

unclear is precisely the relation of the sense of the fulfilling act to the fulfillment itself. Husserl acknowledges this failure in the following difficult passage:

In our First Investigation (§14) we opposed "fulfilling sense" to meaning (or fulfilling meaning to intending meaning) by pointing to the fact that, in fulfillment, the object is "given" intuitively in the same way in which the mere meaning means it. We then took the ideally conceived element which thus coincides with the meaning to be the *fulfilling* sense and said that, through this coincidence, the merely significant intention (or expression) achieved relation to the intuitive object (expressed this and just this object).

This entails, to employ conceptual formations later introduced, that the fulfilling sense is interpreted as the intentional essence of the completely and adequately fulfilling act.

This conceptual formation is entirely correct and suffices for the purpose of pinning down the entirely general aspects of the situation where a signitive intention achieves relation to its intuitively presented object: it expresses the important insight that the semantic essence of the signitive (or expressive) act reappears *identically* in corresponding intuitive acts, despite phenomenological differences on either side, and that the living unity of identification realizes this coincidence itself, and so realizes the relation of the expression to what it expresses. On the other hand, it is clear, in virtue precisely of this identity, that the "fulfilling sense" carries no implication of fullness, that it *does not accordingly include the total content of the intuitive act, to the extent that this is relevant for the theory of knowledge.*[33]

This difficulty is serious but not surprising. Since Husserl's whole conception of phenomenological reflection is based on the claim that one can isolate the intentional correlate, he must necessarily fail to account for the interpenetration of sense and sensuous presentation, which alone would account for knowledge.

Husserl's commitment to the separation of form and matter and his consequent inability to deal with incarnate meaning is already present in his original linguistic model. Husserl speaks only of the act of giving meaning to meaningless sounds or marks and of the meaning given. He assumes that perceptual appearance of the marks is unaffected by the meaning thus superimposed. "While what constitutes the object's appearing remains unchanged, the intentional character of the experience alters."[34] When sounds become linguistically meaningful, however, they do not remain unaffected. A sentence in an unfamiliar language is heard as an uninterrupted torrent, whereas the same sounds in a familiar language are grouped into words and silences. Thus one would expect a *fourfold* distinction: marks or sounds, act of giving meaning, meaning given, and new perceptual entity, the meaningful expression. In *Ideas*, §124, Husserl again raises this question. There he first makes his usual distinction between the marks or sounds and the meaning given: "Let us start from the familiar distinction between the sensory, the so to speak bodily aspect of expression, and its non-sensory

---

[33] Husserl, *Logical Investigations*, ii. 743–4.   [34] Husserl, *Logical Investigations*, ii. 283.

THE PERCEPTUAL NOEMA 59

'mental' aspect."[35] Then, having assumed the traditional distinctions between body and mind, sensory and nonsensory, he postpones indefinitely any discussion of the problem raised by the union of sensory and sense in the meaningful expression:

> There is no need for us to enter more closely into the discussion of... the way of uniting the two aspects, though we clearly have title-headings here indicated for phenomenological problems that are not unimportant.[36]

Likewise in *Ideas* Husserl touches on the epistemological problem of uniting apprehension and intuition, only to drop it. He introduces the needed *Anschauungssinn*, "the meaning in its intentional *fullness*," and he equates this notion with the "very important concept of *appearance*."[37] He even remarks that "In a phenomenology of external intuitions... concepts such as the ones here set out stand in the center of scientific inquiry."[38] But he drops this concept after one paragraph, never to take it up again; and in the margin of his own copy of *Ideas* he wrote, after "Meaning in the mode of its filling" (*Der Sinn im Modus seiner Fülle*): "This concept so grasped is untenable" (*Dieser Begriff so gefasst ist nicht haltbar*).[39] It seems that Husserl saw the need in a phenomenology of perception for an *Anschauungssinn*, an intuitive sense; but he also saw that, according to his fundamental assumption that sense can be separated from filling in every act, he could not allow such a notion.

Thus strict adherence to the form/matter, mind/body dichotomy dictates the future development of Husserl's phenomenology away from a phenomenology of perception. For if even in perception one must always separate the act of meaning from the act of intuition which fills that meaning, it follows that one can have an account of the interpretive sense (*Auffassungssinn*) but no account of the corresponding intuitive sense (*Anschauungssinn*). One can have an account of what the mind takes the object to be but no account of our bodily interaction with the object in perceiving it.

To save the generality of his conception of intentionality, Husserl must, therefore, abandon an account of outer intuition. He must treat perception as

---

[35] Edmund Husserl, *Ideen zu einer Reinen Phänomenologje und Phänomenologischen Philosophie* (Husserliana, 3; The Hague: Martinus Nijhoff, 1950), 303–4 (my translation). Jacques Derrida cites this passage in his article, "La Forme et le vouloir-dire", *Revue Internationale de Philosophie*, 81 (1967), 284, and follows it with the following interesting footnote: "Ces précautions avaient été prises et longuement justifiées dans les *Recherches*. Bien entendu, ces justifications, pour être démonstratives, ne s'en tenaient pas moins à l'intérieur d'oppositions métaphysiques traditionnelles (âme/corps, psychique/physique, vivant/non-vivant, intentionnalité/non-intentionnalité, forme/matière, signifié/signifiant, intelligible/sensible, idéalité/empiricité, etc.)."

[36] Husserl, *Ideen* (1950), 303–4.   [37] Husserl, *Ideen* (1950), 325.
[38] Husserl, *Ideen* (1950), 325.   [39] Husserl, *Ideen* (1950), 385.

referentially opaque and confine himself to what we take there to be rather than what there is. He can study the conditions of the *possibility* of evidence, confirmation, etc., but never its *actuality*.

After fourteen years of meditation, Husserl made a virtue of this necessity. Phenomenology is henceforth presented as transcendental phenomenology: a theory of how objects are taken or intended but not how they are given or presented—a study of a field of meanings which are entertained independently of whether empirical objects actually exist (although, of course, I must *take* them to exist). Thus, it is only one consistent step from Husserl's admission in the *Logical Investigations* that his phenomenology does not provide a theory of knowledge to the bracketing of existence in *Ideas*. And it is only one step—albeit a very dubious one—from normal logical reflection directed toward the ideal correlates of referentially opaque *conceptual acts* to a special kind of reflection, the phenomenological reduction, in which Husserl claims to abstract the meanings of the referentially transparent *act of perception* as well.

Gurwitsch's Incarnation of Perception: The Noema as Intuitive Sense

Aron Gurwitsch seems to have sensed the one-sidedness of Husserl's phenomenology of perception and sought to supplement Husserl's account of what is intended or taken in perception with an account of what is presented or given. He found that the Gestalt psychologists were already at work describing "whatever is given to consciousness just as it presents itself in its phenomenal nature"[40] and set as the goal of his doctoral dissertation "to further certain phenomenological problems with the help of Gestalt-theoretical theses."[41]

According to the Gestalt psychologists and Gurwitsch, what is presented in perception is an incarnate form.

... the internal organization of the percept reveals itself as unity by Gestalt-coherence ... : a system of functional significances, interdependent and determining each other ... ; there is no unifying principle in addition to the matters unified.[42]

Gurwitsch introduces this perceptual gestalt, "the sense of what is experienced," as a development of what Husserl means by the *Anschauungssinn*. "The term 'sense' does not refer to the meaning of the 'sign': 'Sense' is to be understood

---

[40] "Phenomenology of Thematics and of the Pure Ego: Studies of the Relation between Gestalt Theory and Phenomenology", in Gurwitsch, *Studies in Phenomenology and Psychology*, 193.

[41] Gurwitsch, *Studies in Phenomenology*, 177.

[42] Gurwitsch, *Field of Consciousness*, 277–8.

here as when Husserl (*Ideen*, I, p. 274) speaks of the sense of an intuition (*Anschauungssinn*)."[43] Identifying this intuitive sense with the perceptual noema, Gurwitsch then tells us that:

On the basis of this interpretation of the perceptual noema, it is possible to account for the phenomenon of fulfillment of a merely signifying act by a corresponding perception. Fulfillment occurs when an object intended in a merely signifying mode, e.g., by means of a meaning in the narrower sense, also appears in the mode of self-presentation.[44]

This introduction of an intuitive sense (*Anschauungssinn*) which could coincide with and fulfill an interpretive sense (*Auffassungssinn*) would indeed, if coherent, complete Husserl's phenomenology of perception. Whether it is coherent and whether it is compatible with the rest of Husserl's system, however, requires further investigation.

An evaluation of Gurwitsch's contribution turns on his interpretation of the perceptual noema. By "noema" Husserl means the intentional correlate of any act. It follows that the *perceptual* noema must be a perceptual sense, the intentional correlate of an act of perception. But this is ambiguous: is the perceptual sense (*Wahrnehmungssinn*) to be understood as the interpretive sense (*Auffassungssinn*) or as the intuitive sense (*Anschauungssinn*)?

Husserl introduces the noema in a way which does little to clear up this ambiguity:

In all cases the manifold data of the really inherent noetic content...corresponds to the manifold data in a correlative noematic content, or in short, in the noema—a term which we will constantly use from now on.

  Perception, for example, has its Noema—at the most basic level its perceptual sense (*Wahrnehmungssinn*), that is, the perceived as such.[45]

Gurwitsch, however, without seeming to notice the ambiguity, opts for the intuitive sense and takes this occasion to identify Husserl's perceptual noema with his own notion of a percept or perceptual gestalt.

Following the dismissal of the constancy hypothesis, the percept has to *be* considered as a homogeneous unit, though internally articulated and structured. It has to be taken at face value; as that which it presents itself to be through the given act of perception and through that act alone; as it appears to the perceiving subject's consciousness; as it is meant and intended (the term "meaning" understood in a properly broadened and enlarged sense) in that privileged mode of meaning and intending which is perceptual presentation. In other

---

[43] "Gestalt Theory and Phenomenology", in Gurwitsch, *Studies in Phenomenology and Psychology*, 191.

[44] Gurwitsch, *Field of Consciousness*, 180–1.   [45] Husserl, *Ideen* (1950), i. 219.

words, the percept as it is conceived after the constancy hypothesis has been dismissed proves to be what we called the *perceptum qua perceptum*, the *perceptual noema*.[46]

But Husserl never says that the perceptual noema is perceptually presented. To support his interpretation, Gurwitsch must take an indirect line. Husserl does say that the phenomenological reduction reveals noemata:

In this phenomenological orientation we can and must pose the essential questions: What is this "perceived as such"? What are the essential moments of this perceptual Noema?[47]

And the phenomenological reduction does seem to be a technique for describing what appears exactly as it appears: "We can obtain the answer to the above question by pure openness to what is essentially given; we can describe 'what appears as such' in complete evidence."[48] It seems that Husserl must be advocating an exact description of appearances. And this is what Gurwitsch takes him to mean when he writes:

Understood in this way, the procedure of Gestalt theory, in taking the psychic purely descriptively and disregarding all constructions, has the same significance and methodical function for psychology as the transcendental reduction has for phenomenology. Objects in the normal sense of the word fall away, and noemata alone are left over; the world as *it really is* is bracketed, the world as *it looks* remains.[49]

Or, in the same vein:

As in the natural attitude, so under the phenomenological reduction, there still corresponds to an act of perception a perceptual noema or perceptual meaning, namely, the "perceived as such," the perceived object as appearing in a certain manner of presentation.[50]

Gurwitsch takes the "perceived as such" quite naturally as a restriction to what is purely perceived, free from any admixture of what for other reasons we might believe is present. But before we can accept this seemingly self-evident reading, we must determine what Husserl means by the phrase "the perceived as such"— indeed, what he means by the phrase "as such" in general. Husserl does sometimes use "as such" in the restrictive sense, as when, in *Ideas*, he speaks of "the sensuous appearance, i.e., the appearing object as such,"[51] or, in the psychology lectures, when he speaks of restricting our description to "the perceived as such,

---

[46] "The Phenomenological and the Psychological Approach to Consciousness", in Gurwitsch, *Studies in Phenomenology and Psychology*, 104.

[47] Husserl, *Ideen* (1950), i. 241.   [48] Husserl, *Ideen* (1950), i. 241.

[49] "Gestalt Theory and Phenomenology", in Gurwitsch, *Studies in Phenomenology and Psychology*, 194.

[50] Gurwitsch, *Field of Consciousness*, 182.   [51] Husserl, *Ideen* (1950), i. 128.

purely in the subjective mode of being given."[52] But Husserl also has a special use of "as such" which he uses in connection not just with perception but with any conscious act. In continuing the passage introducing the perceptual noema, he relates "the perceived as such" to other sorts of "as such" entities:

Perception, for example, has its Noema, at the most basic level, its perceptual sense, that is, the perceived as such. Similarly, recollection has its remembered as such precisely as it is "meant" and "consciously known" in it; again, the judging has the judged as such, the pleasing the pleasant as such, etc. We must everywhere take the noematic correlate, which (in a very extended meaning of the term) is here referred to as "sense" precisely as it lies "immanent" in the experience of perception, of judgment, of liking, and so forth.[53]

This complete quotation is less tractable to the Gurwitschian reading. The judgmental noema, the judged as such, immanent in the experience of judging, would seem to be the intentional correlate of the act of judging. It is *what* is judged, i.e. the judgment, as distinguished from what is judged *about*, the state of affairs, and also as distinguished from the object judged about taken exactly as it is judged to be. Correlatively, the perceptual noema, the perceived as such, would seem to be the intentional correlate of the act of perceiving, which directs the act to the object perceived, in just the way it is perceived, rather than being the object of perception exactly as it is given, as Gurwitsch contends.

Husserl himself points out in *Ideas*[54] that the "matter" of the *Logical Investigations* has its "noematic parallel" in the "noematic nucleus" ("Every noema has a 'content,' namely, a 'meaning' through which it relates to 'its' object") and implies that the "intentional essence" of the *Logical Investigations* (the matter plus the quality of the act) has its parallel in the full noema. ("If we recall our earlier analysis, we find the full noesis related to the full noema as its intentional and full What.")

For Husserl, then, the perceptual noema, like the intentional essence of a perceptual act, is a meaning *by virtue of which we refer to perceptual objects. It is what is intended* in perception in the same way that the judgment is *what is judged* in making a judgment. Gurwitsch agrees with Husserl that the noema is "what is intended," but his interest in Gestalt theory leads him to conclude that the noema is "the object *as* it is intended"[55] rather than the What of the intending. Thus, Gurwitsch collapses the object *as referred to* with the *reference to* the object.

This results in a characteristic confusion in each of Gurwitsch's many definitions of the perceptual noema. Already in his doctoral dissertation we are

[52] Edmund Husserl, *Phänomenologische Psychologie* (Husserliana, 9; The Hague: Martinus Nijhoff, 1962), 159.

[53] Husserl, *Ideen* (1950), i. 219.   [54] Husserl, *Ideen* (1950), i. 316, 317.

[55] Aron Gurwitsch, "Husserl in Perspective", *Phenomenology and Existentialism* (Baltimore, MD: Johns Hopkins University Press, 1967), 45.

told: *"the sense of consciousness directed toward the theme*... the noema of the theme...forms the subject matter of investigation of a noematically oriented phenomenology."[56] Yet, only a few lines later, the theme is defined as "that which is *given* to consciousness, precisely just as and only to the extent to which it is given," and we are told that "a phenomenology of the theme is a noematic analysis."[57] Here Gurwitsch refers first to *the sense of the act of intending the theme* as the noema and then identifies the noema with *the theme as given*. In 1966 we still find the same conflation of the What of the act of referring with what is referred to (exactly *as* it is referred to) when Gurwitsch introduces the noema as "an object as *intended* and *presenting* itself under a certain aspect."[58]

All this confusion arises because Husserl chooses to call the What in our intending rather than what is intended "the perceived as such." Why does Husserl use such misleading terminology? Why use "the perceived as such" to denote precisely that element in perception which is not perceptually presented? To understand, if not to pardon, such usage we must remember that Husserl first became concerned with "sense" and "referential opacity" through his analysis of linguistic expressions. The basic phenomenon to be analyzed in this connection is that expressions have meanings and that the meanings may refer to objective states of affairs. In this connection, "the meant" is quite naturally used to refer to the meaning of the expression rather than the objective state of affairs. As Husserl notes:

The terms "meaning"...and all similar terms harbour such powerful equivocations that our intention, even if expressed most carefully, still can promote misunderstanding.... Each expression not merely says something, but says it *of* something: it not only has a meaning, but refers to certain *objects*.... And, if we distinguish between "content" and object in respect of such "presentations," one's distinction means the same as the distinction between what is meant or said, on the one hand, and what is spoken of, by means of the expression, on the other.[59]

Moreover, since "relation to an actually given objective correlate, which fulfills the meaning intention, is *not* essential to an expression,"[60] it seems plausible to say that what is "really expressed" is the meaning rather than the object meant.

We note that there are two things that can be said to be expressed in the realized relation to the object. We have, on the one hand, the *object itself*, and the object as meant in this or

---

[56] "Gestalt Theory and Phenomenology", in Gurwitsch, *Studies in Phenomenology and Psychology*, 183 (my italics).

[57] Gurwitsch, *Studies in Phenomenology and Psychology*, 183 (my italics).

[58] Aron Gurwitsch, "Towards a Theory of Intentionality", *Philosophy and Phenomenological Research*, 27 (1970).

[59] Husserl, *Logical Investigations*, i. 287.   [60] Husserl, *Logical Investigations*, i. 290.

that manner. On the other hand, and *more properly*, we have the object's ideal correlate in the acts of meaning-fulfillment which constitute it, the fulfilling sense.[61]

So, to clear up the ambiguity of the phrase "what is meant," Husserl quite naturally chooses to call the object "what is meant" and to call the sense of the expression "the meant as such," i.e. what is purely and essentially meant. Likewise, in an act of judging the judgment can be said to be what is essentially judged, and therefore it can be called "the judged as such." (Although here it is no longer quite natural to say that what is judged in an act of judging is the judgment rather than the object judged about.)

The use of "as such" to refer to the intentional correlate gets more and more obscure as we move further from Husserl's linguistic home base. Only in some technical sense of "essential" is "what is essentially remembered" the memory rather than the object recalled. Moreover, although the question "What is he seeing (or finding pleasant)?" may allow two possible responses—the *description of the object* and *an indication of* the object itself—the perceiver's way of intending the object could hardly be said to be what is essentially seen, the seen as such, since it is not seen, nor could a description of what I take an enjoyed object to be be called the essentially pleasant, the pleasant as such, since the description is not enjoyed at all.

Yet this counterintuitive use of "as such" is exactly what Husserl has in mind. For it is Husserl's basic point, which first becomes explicit in *Ideas*, that *all* acts can be understood on his linguistic model; that "the noema is nothing but a generalization of the notion of meaning to the total realm of acts."[62] This means that all acts can be understood as ways of making sense of our experience by giving a meaning to meaningless data. For Husserl, judging, remembering, perceiving, and enjoying are all forms of meaning-giving, and all have their correlative meaning whether the object exists or not. Just as in the case of the meaning of a linguistic expression—the judgment, the memory, the perceptual sense, and the sense of the pleasurable are what is essential. Thus for Husserl it is natural, even necessary, to speak of these meanings as the judged as such, the remembered as such, the perceived as such, and the pleasant as such, no matter how forced this may sound.

---

[61] Husserl, *Logical Investigations*, i. 290 (my underlining). Note that Husserl here clearly distinguishes the fulfilling sense from the object as meant. He would therefore not identify the fulfilling sense with the noema, as he seems to do in *Ideas*, if, as Gurwitsch contends, the noema is the object as meant.

[62] Edmund Husserl, *Ideen zur einer Reinen Phänomenologie und Phänomenologischen Philosophie*, iii. *Die Phänomenologie und die Fundamente der Wissenschaften*, ed. Marly Biemel (Husserliana, 5; The Hague, Netherlands: Martinus Nijhoff, 1971), 89.

The difficulty revealed in Husserl's need to construct such bizarre terminology and the difficulty his interpreters find in understanding it are a measure of the difficulty of the phenomenological reduction, which generalizes referential opacity beyond the sphere of its everyday application, extending it to all, even filling, acts.

Presented with the expression "the perceived as such" with no explanation, as in *Ideas*, the reader is in a quandary. Since, in the natural attitude, perception is experienced as going directly to its object, there is no genuine ambiguity, not even a trumped-up ambiguity, in the expression "what is perceived" which the qualifier "as such" could serve to clear up. Consequently, counter to Husserl's intention, the "as such" which focuses our attention on what is *essentially* perceived or enjoyed, far from leading us to reflect on what the object is *taken* to be, seems to focus our attention on the object exactly as it is given.[63]

To make matters worse, Husserl seems to introduce the transcendental reduction as just such a way of concentrating on appearances:

> In this phenomenological orientation we can and must pose the essential questions: What is this "perceived as such"? What are the essential moments of this perceptual Noema? We can obtain the answer to the above questions by pure openness to what is essentially *given*; we can describe "what appears as such" faithfully and in perfect self-evidence.[64]

And in his "Critical Study of Husserl's *Nachwort*" Gurwitsch understood Husserl in just this way: "Under the phenomenological *epochê* we deal with thing-phenomena, with 'things' just as they appear, and within the limits in which they appear."[65]

But such a reading, which would turn phenomenological analysis into a sophisticated analysis of what is sensuously given, ignores the fact that these

---

[63] There does seem to be one passage in all the published writing of Husserl which backs up this interpretation of the perceived as such as the directly perceived—a passage from *The Crisis of European Sciences*, Husserl's last and, in that sense, most authoritative work: "At any given time the thing presents itself to me through a nucleus of 'original presence' (which *denotes the continual subjective character of the actual perceived as such*) as well as through its inner and outer horizon" (Edmund Husserl, *The Crisis of European Sciences and Transcendental Phenomenology* (Evanston, IL: Northwestern University Press, 1970b), 165). If one looks up the textual comments on this passage in the Louvain edition, however, one finds that the parenthetical comment which equates the perceived as such with the sensuous original presence is an interpolation by Eugen Fink, Husserl's last assistant. Rudolf Boehm, the editor of several volumes of Husserl's collected works, also follows the Gurwitschian reading: "Die Sache ist eben die, dass Husserl bemerken musste, dass das Noema, was zunächst ein blosses Abstraktions bzw. Reduktionsprodukt der Phänomenologie, ein *phänomenologisch* allein absolut Gegebenes scheinen konnte, sich als eine durchaus *phänomenale Realität* aufweisen liess, am Ende gar als *das* phänomenal Gegebene in der 'Realität.' 'In Wirklichkeit' tritt, was das Warhnehmungsnoema heisst, als das auf, was Husserl ein 'Phantom' nennt" (personal correspondence, 27 Jan., 1963).

[64] Husserl, *Ideen* (1950), 221.

[65] Gurwitsch, *Studies in Phenomenology and Psychology*, 109.

remarks immediately follow the passage where Husserl introduces the noema as "a meaning (in a very extended sense)" which "lies 'immanent' in experiences of perception, judgment, enjoyment, etc.," and which can be "given in really pure intuition."[66] In line with Husserl's generalization of his linguistic model to all acts, this would suggest that the noema is the interpretive sense, and the givenness in question is the result of a special act of reflection.

Gurwitsch, on the other hand, after identifying the noema with what is given in perception, goes on to identify the perceptual noema with Husserl's notion of perceptual adumbration.

The noema at large being defined as that which is meant as such, the perceptual noema must, accordingly, be determined as the "perceived as such." It turns out to be the perceived thing, just as it presents itself through a concrete act of perception—namely, as appearing from a certain side, in a certain perspective, orientation, etc. In this sense all *manners of appearance and presentation* which we mentioned above in connection with the adumbrational theory of perception are to be considered as *perceptual noemata*.[67]

And once having identified the noema with a perceptual adumbration, and still guided by the notion that the noema is what is essentially perceived, Gurwitsch sees no problem in also identifying the noema with an appearance. He even finds a shred of textual evidence in the isolated passage where Husserl defines appearance as the meaning in the mode of its filling. Citing this passage, Gurwitsch concludes:

Discussing perception of material things, Husserl frequently uses the term "appearance" (*Erscheinung*), and even the term "image" (*Bild*) occasionally. Both these terms are taken by Husserl as synonymous with the term perceptual noema.[68]

Husserl, however, never says that "appearance," as meaning plus filling, is synonymous with "noema." In fact, he finds this notion of appearance untenable and never uses the term appearance in this way except in this one passage. He does, however, frequently use the term appearance in its normal sense as synonymous with perceptual adumbration—the way the object presents itself from a particular point of view. But Gurwitsch cannot cite *this* use of appearance in defense of his view, since Husserl never identifies appearance in the sense of adumbration with the noema and never refers to adumbrations as meanings.

Indeed, it is hard to determine what Gurwitsch could have in mind when he says that an appearance is a perceptual *sense*. An appearance, as Gurwitsch uses

[66] Husserl, *Ideen* (1950), 221.

[67] "Contribution to the Phenomenological Theory of Perception", in Gurwitsch, *Studies in Phenomenology and Psychology*, 341.

[68] Gurwitsch, *Field of Consciousness*, 183.

the term, is not a specific temporal appearing, a sense datum, since Gurwitsch makes it quite clear that what distinguishes the noema or perceptual sense from a noesis or psychological event is that the same noema can occur again and again, but neither is it an ideal, abstractable entity like the interpretive sense, since in a perceptual gestalt "a separation between *hylê* and *morphê* is not even abstractly possible."[69]

Perhaps Gurwitsch's perceptual sense might be best thought of as the look of an object, which is *distinguishable* but not *separable* from the object which has that look or appearance, Gurwitsch uses the example of a melody to argue that "What is immediately given, the phenomenological primal material, is given only as articulated and structured."[70] "It is only at its place within an organized structure [such as a melody] that a sensuous item becomes what it is in a given case."[71] This suggests that, although a melody cannot be entertained independently of some sequence of notes, still the melody is a distinguishable organized structure which can be embodied or actualized in various sequences. Thus it could be thought of as a recurring ideal structure, a meaning in an extended sense, which could be actualized in a series of illustrations.[72] Gurwitsch, however, does not make this point. In his concern with rejecting Husserl's *hylê/morphê* distinction, he is led to the opposite extreme of *identifying* the distinguishable if not abstractable gestalt with its specific embodiments. He does once suggest that the noema is a distinguishable form in speaking of its "actualization,"[73] but his general tendency, as expressed in his identification of the perceptual noema with a perceptual adumbration, is to think of the noema as a specific illustrative appearance, like a specific performance of a melody.

The noema, then, according to Gurwitsch, turns out to be a very special sort of entity, which is neither an act of experiencing nor a material object.

Each time that we open our eyes, we experience an act of perception, which, once it is past, can never recur.... Meanwhile, we perceive not only the same house *qua* physical thing but are also confronted with the same thing as presenting itself to us under the same aspect; briefly, we are faced with the same house perceived as such. The latter being

---

[69] "Gestalt Theory and Phenomenology", in Gurwitsch, *Studies in Phenomenology and Psychology*, 257.

[70] Gurwitsch, *Studies in Phenomenology and Psychology*, 256.

[71] Gurwitsch, *Studies in Phenomenology and Psychology*, 256.

[72] I am indebted to Samuel Todes for pointing out this possible interpretation of Gurwitsch's noema, as well as for his phenomenology of the differences between conception and perception: Samuel Todes, "Comparative Phenomenology of Perception and Imagination", *Journal of Existentialism* (Spring and Fall 1966), which influenced the overall approach of this essay.

[73] "Phenomenological Theory of Perception", in Gurwitsch, *Studies in Phenomenology and Psychology*, 349.

neither the physical house nor an act of consciousness, we have to recognize the perceived *qua* perceived as a special and specific entity—"perceptual noema" is the technical term which Husserl uses.[74]

Such an entity, which can be repeatedly experienced but which is not physically real, can, perhaps, best be understood as a perspectival view of an object. A view from a mountaintop, for example, is not a physical object, but it is not a temporal experience either, since it can be presented to the same viewer again and again and can also be presented to others.

This seems to be what Gurwitsch has in mind, but such an understanding of the noema is hard to reconcile with Husserl's assertion that the noema is a meaning. Gurwitsch would, however, argue that there are two senses of meaning: one, the linguistic sort, in which the sense can be separated from the reference, and the other—meaning in an extended sense—which still involves reference but only the reference of the sensuous aspects of a gestalt organization to other hidden aspects. In this extended sense the meaning *is* the referring of the aspects and so is inseparable from them. Gurwitsch quotes with approval Merleau-Ponty's observation that "the sense is incorporated and incarnated in the very appearances themselves."[75]

Gurwitsch argues that such an incarnate meaning

proves to be on a par with noematic correlates of any intentional act. It is an ideal unit with neither spatial nor temporal determinations, uninvolved in any causal relation; it pertains to the realm of meanings in the enlarged sense, a realm within which meanings in the more narrow or proper sense form a special domain.[76]

But a perspectival view is far from what Husserl has in mind when he speaks of the perceptual noema as a sense. The perspectival view is indeed not in *objective* space and time, and it does not entail the existence of any material object; but as a sensuous perceptual presentation it has apparent extension (it fills a greater or smaller portion of the visual field), and it has its own sort of duration (it comes into existence and it ceases to exist at a specific moment in history). Husserl nowhere attributes these sorts of spatiotemporal indices even to meanings in his extended sense. Husserl's extended use seems rather to be the widening of meaning from the linguistically expressible meanings treated in the *Logical Investigations* to the interpretive senses correlated with all acts.

Originally [the words *bedeuten* and *Bedeutung*] were exclusively related to the sphere of language and expression. It is, however, unavoidable, and at the same time an important

---

[74] "The Kantian and Husserlian Conceptions of Consciousness", in Gurwitsch, *Studies in Phenomenology and Psychology*, 155.

[75] Gurwitsch, *Field of Consciousness*, 296.   [76] Gurwitsch, *Field of Consciousness*, 181.

advance in knowledge, to broaden the meanings of these words so that they may be applied to the whole noetico-noematic sphere, therefore to all acts, whether these are interwoven with expressions or not.[77]

Moreover, for Husserl the noema is a special sort of meaning. Every noesis is *correlated* with a noema *through which* it intends its object. Thus the noema is not present (even marginally) to ordinary involved consciousness; rather it is presented only in that special act of reflection which Husserl calls the phenomenological reduction. Gurwitsch, however, since he identifies sense and appearance, is led to the view that "a conscious act is an act of awareness, *presenting* to the subject who experiences it a sense, an ideal atemporal unity."[78] But the passage in *Cartesian Meditations* which Gurwitsch cites to back up this statement—"Each cogito ... means something or other and bears in itself, in this manner peculiar to the meant, its particular cogitatum"[79]—makes no such claim. Rather, it suggests, as we have seen, that Husserl thinks of the meaning as what is essentially meant in the act and thus *contained* in it rather than *presented to* it.

In following out the logic of his identification of the noema with a percept and thus of his identification of the interpretive sense with the intuitive sense and both with the perceptual adumbration, Gurwitsch is ultimately led to adopt the view that objects literally consist of noemata. This is a view which nowhere appears in Husserl's works and which, indeed, explicitly contradicts the views of the master. Husserl does say that the object is the set of its actual and possible perceptual presentations. As Gurwitsch puts it:

The thing cannot be perceived except in one or the other manner of adumbrational presentation. It is nothing besides, or in addition to, the multiplicity of those presentations through all of which it appears in its identity. Consequently, the thing perceived proves to be the group, more precisely put, the systematically organized totality of adumbrational presentations.[80]

But since Husserl never identified the adumbrations with the perceptual sense, he would never conclude with Gurwitsch that "the perceptual senses are united into systems which are the real perceptual things."[81] This mixture of faithfulness to Husserl (in continuing to hold that the noema is a meaning) and radical

[77] Husserl, *Ideen* (1950), i. 304.

[78] "On the Intentionality of Consciousness", in Gurwitsch, *Studies in Phenomenology and Psychology*, 138.

[79] Edmund Husserl, *Cartesian Meditations*, tr. Dorion Cairns (The Hague: Martinus Nijhoff, 1960), 33.

[80] Gurwitsch, "Husserl in Perspective", 81.

[81] "On the Intentionality of Consciousness", in Gurwitsch, *Studies in Phenomenology and Psychology*, 139.

innovation (in holding objects to *be* systems of noemata) poses a fundamental problem in interpreting Gurwitsch's phenomenology of perception. If the noema is interpreted as an atemporal, aspatial, nonsensuous, abstractable, ideal entity in Husserl's sense, there is no way to understand how a system of such entities could ever be said to *be* a perceptual object. But if we take the noema as a specific illustration of such an abstract entity—a sensuous perceptual presentation—from which objects could be made up, there is no way to understand how this percept can be said to be ideal in Husserl's understanding of the term.

These difficulties cast doubt on Gurwitsch's contribution to a phenomenology of perception. They also obscure his otherwise outstanding Husserl interpretation. Still, whether Gurwitsch holds that the noema is the structure of a percept or whether it is the percept itself, and regardless of the merits of his attempt to find support for this new interpretation of Husserl's work, one thing is clear: Gurwitsch has raised the question of how to understand the fulfilling sense and has provided an account of the perceptual noema which makes it incarnate in the sensuous perceptual presentation. By refusing to separate the sense from the filling, he has, almost in spite of himself, recognized the special referential transparency of perception. Such a modification of Husserl's attempt to treat perception as referentially opaque is an important step in faithfulness to the phenomenon, even if, as we shall see, it requires greater and greater unfaithfulness to Husserl.

From Transcendental to Existential Phenomenology

Whether Gurwitsch holds that the perceptual noema is an ideal form, distinguishable from the presentations which illustrate it, or whether, as his words suggest, he holds that the noema is a perceptual presentation itself, one thing is certain: he rejects the view, essential to Husserl's whole project, that the noema is separable from its filling. And once Gurwitsch breaks with Husserl on this point, he is committed to more far-reaching changes in the Husserlian system than he seems prepared to admit.

We have seen that Gurwitsch himself draws the important conclusion from his gestalt analyses that one must reject Husserl's distinction between *morphê* and *hylê*, between meaning and filling. He also recognizes that this change, plus careful attention to the phenomena, leads to a rejection of the Husserlian notion of a disembodied, detached, transcendental ego capable of creating these ideal meanings and imposing them on the sensuous manifold.[82]

[82] "A Non-Egological Conception of Consciousness", in Gurwitsch, *Studies in Phenomenology and Psychology*, 287–300.

But at this point Gurwitsch stops short of drawing the further conclusions that his radical break with Husserl's traditional preconceptions entails. To begin with, if the gestalt analysis of perception is correct, and the intuitive sense is inseparable from its filling, the transcendental reduction, as modified by Gurwitsch, will have to be given up. For, if the phenomenologist describes the perceptual object exactly as it is *given*, he will have to admit that it is given as *"bodily present"* with hidden aspects—in short, as existing. If he tries to bracket that existence and claim that what is given is only a perspectival presentation of an object, which *implies* other possible *appearances* but does not entail the *copresence* of these other *concealed aspects*, he will not be faithful to the phenomenon.[83] Thus Gurwitsch, who agrees with Husserl that in the natural attitude the perceptual object is experienced as "bodily present," contradicts himself when he says, in claiming phenomenological validity for his phenomenalism:

On strictly phenomenological grounds, there is no justification for distinguishing the thing itself from a systematically concatenated group of perceptual noemata, all intrinsically referring to, and by virtue of their mutual references, qualifying, one another.[84]

It seems that a faithful description of the given and a bracketing of existence, as Gurwitsch understands bracketing, are incompatible.

Husserl does not have this problem. His version of the reduction abstracts the meaning or intending of the objects and the meanings correlated with these intentional acts without concern for the existence or bodily presence of the objects, except as that too is meant or intended.[85] Gurwitsch, however, does not have this way out. Having denied the *hylê/morphê* distinction and the transcendental ego in his commitment to the incarnate sense, and having thus redefined the reduction as a way of noticing the way the object is given, exactly as it is given, Gurwitsch has no way of shifting the object of investigation so as to

---

[83] Roderick Firth, who tries to reconcile the results of Gestalt psychology and traditional epistemology in his article, "Sense Data and the Percept Theory", *Mind*, 58/232 (1949), 434–65, develops a view similar to Gurwitsch's. He also defines the material object as a system of appearances, or ostensible objects, but he remains truer to the phenomenon. He remarks that "the ostensible object is not ostensibly ostensible," and he therefore introduces an epistemological (as opposed to phenomenological) point of view. Only from the epistemological point of view can we say that, since the material object may be illusory, we know that it has no hidden aspects even though it *presents itself* as having them. This approach has its own difficulties. Cf. Dreyfus, "Husserl's Phenomenology of Perception".

[84] Gurwitsch, *Field of Consciousness*, 301.

[85] This way out has its problems, too. Even if we grant the dubious claim that in the perception of ordinary objects the interpretive sense can be entertained as an abstractable entity, it does not follow—it perhaps does not even make sense to hold—that the meaning of preobjective experience, on the one hand, and the world, on the other, can be entertained in the same way. See my doctoral dissertation (cited in n. 27).

avoid the embarrassing fact that existence or thickness is itself phenomenologic-ally presented. He can only redefine existence, giving a phenomenalist account of perceptual thickness as an infinitely open system of thin appearances. But this is tantamount to admitting that the originally given bodily presence can never be recovered from his supposedly neutral phenomenological analysis.

If, following Gurwitsch, we deny the separation of meaning and sensuous content in perception and thus no longer accept Husserl's account of the inter-pretive sense as an ideal, abstractable meaning imposed by a transcendental ego, we will need some new account of the object's "thickness." If the hidden sides of the object are given as *copresent*, we will need an account of how the subject can be *present with* the object. Therefore, we will have to return to some account of the role of the subject—a role which Gurwitsch wants to reject.

Gurwitsch gets into difficulty with bodily presence because he is forced to stop halfway in his incarnation of perception. He concludes that, since in perception there is no act of meaning-giving whose meaning is abstractable from its sensu-ous filling, there is no act of meaning-giving at all. He is thus led to *replace* an analysis of the way objects of experience are *taken* with an analysis of the way they are *given* and to reinterpret the activity of the subject—the noesis—as simply the experiencing of the presented gestalts.

[F]or intentional analysis the ultimate fact and datum is the sense or meaning itself as a structured whole. This necessitates a redefinition of the conceptions of noesis and intentionality. By the term "noesis" we can no longer denote an organizing and appre-hending function.... [86]
The only distinction is between the noeses as temporal psychological events and the noemata as atemporal ideal entities pertaining to the realm of sense and meaning. [87]

Having thus eliminated the subject giving meaning to his experience and the meaning he gives, no way remains for Gurwitsch to complete his phenomenology of perception by giving an account of the incarnation of the interpretive sense which parallels his account of the incarnation of the intuitive sense.

Yet the elements of such an account are already required in Gurwitsch's gestalt analysis. Gurwitsch analyzes the experience of a sequence of notes making up a melody, to point out how the notes have the value they have only within the organized perceptual structure, which itself does not exist apart from the notes. As Gurwitsch sees it, indeed, it follows that the organization of the notes, the melody itself, cannot be entertained apart from some illustrative embodiment

---

[86] "Gestalt Theory and Phenomenology", in Gurwitsch, *Studies in Phenomenology and Psychology*, 257.
[87] Gurwitsch, *Studies in Phenomenology and Psychology*, p. xxiii.

and thus cannot be imposed by a transcendental subject on otherwise neutral notes. Still, to have a melodic organization, the notes must be *taken as* a melody: a subject must *give* them this organization by anticipating the subsequent notes as a continuation of an ongoing melody. Gurwitsch has no philosophic account of this taking. It would seem appropriate, however, following through the implications of his analysis, to think of the interpretive sense as a bodily set, an actualization of a particular habit or skill acquired in becoming acquainted with this piece of music—a skill which, indeed, I cannot entertain apart from its actualization in a given activity of anticipating this particular sequence of notes.

In perception such a body set would be correlated with the experience of the "thickness" of objects. I not only take it that objects have other sides; I am here and now actually set to explore them. So the other sides are not experienced as *possible* experiences implied by the present *appearance;* they are experienced as *actually present* but concealed aspects of the present *object* soliciting further exploration. As a perceiving subject I am therefore not a monadic transcendental ego with the world in me, but neither am I just a field open to a stream of appearances—a being-at-the-world.[88] I am a situated subject, set to explore objects, whose concealed aspects are copresent to me because I am copresent to them. Only an embodied subject allows such presence.

Our habits or skills for coping with objects are aspatial and atemporal, like the noema. The same skill can be actualized in many different situations. But unlike Husserl's conceptualized noema, skills are not ideal, abstractable meanings. They cannot be entertained apart from some particular activation. However, when actualized, an incarnate meaning or interpretive sense can mesh with a particular perceptual illustration of an intuitive sense, thereby producing a successful act of perception. Since these perceptual skills, like noemata, are the means *through which* we refer to and unify the objects of experience, they cannot be treated as another object in the field of experience. Gurwitsch again mistakes the noema (this time the incarnate interpretive sense) for a presentation when he argues against Merleau-Ponty that the body must be just another object for

---

[88] In his most recent paper, Gurwitsch writes: "[T]he insight that in our perceptual life we are directly and immediately at the things and at the world, far from being due to the subsequent emergence of existentialist philosophy, must be seen as a consequence following from Husserl's theory of the intentionality of consciousness, especially perceptual consciousness" Aron Gurwitsch, "Perceptual Coherence as the Foundation of the Judgement of Predication", in Aron Gurwitsch and Lester Embree (eds), *Phenomenology and the Theory of Science* (Evanston, IL: Northwestern University Press, 1974), 243. It is doubtful that Husserl, with his conceptualization of perception and his transcendental ego as monad, ever allowed for being-at-the-world. Gurwitsch's account, however, like Sartre's, does, indeed, allow being-at-the-world, *but it allows for nothing more.* Such an account does not arrive at the existential phenomenology of being-in-the-world, in a situation, together with objects.

consciousness.[89] The kinesthetic body may be such an object, but not the skillful body as percipient.

Now we can see more fully why neither Husserl's nor Gurwitsch's transcendental reduction can be carried out. For Husserl the reduction was that special and detached reflection which the phenomenologist could undertake as transcendental ego in order to entertain meanings apart from their sensuous filling. Gurwitsch, as we have noted, once he had criticized Husserl's form/matter separation and had identified the noema and the perceptual presentation, could not understand the reduction in this way. He had to reinterpret the transcendental reduction as a way of noticing a special realm of being, viz., consciousness in its transcendental function as "the universal medium of access to, and...the fountain and origin of, whatever exists."[90] To do this, he had to reinterpret perceptual objects as a system of appearances so as to understand their existence in terms of their "equivalent of consciousness."[91] But, as we have now seen, there is no such field of pure disembodied appearances. There is only the embodied subject coming to grips with embodied objects. Given the referential transparency of perception, any bracketing of existence, even Gurwitsch's attenuated version, is incompatible with an accurate phenomenological description.

The moral is that, once one has used gestalt considerations to deny the traditional metaphysical dichotomies of matter/form, linguistic sign/meaning, and physical/mental in perception, as Gurwitsch has, one cannot find a stable stopping place until one has overthrown the body/consciousness dichotomy as well. Thus one arrives at an existential phenomenology of embodied being-in-the-world. Throughout his works, Gurwitsch has resisted this conclusion. He has valiantly attempted to read back his incarnation of the intuitive sense into Husserl's account of the noema, as if the gestalt considerations he was the first to appreciate could be introduced into a somewhat patched-up transcendental phenomenology.

It was left to Merleau-Ponty, who learned so much from Gurwitsch, to take the radical steps necessitated by Gurwitsch's suppressed originality: to deny the feasibility of the transcendental reduction and to incarnate the interpretive as well as the intuitive sense. To Gurwitsch goes the honor of having prepared the decisive step from transcendental to existential phenomenology; to Merleau-Ponty, the credit for actually taking the step by facing and resolving the problems raised by Gurwitsch's insight.

---

[89] "Bodily phenomena may be resorted to only as experienced bodily phenomena, that is, phenomena such as they appear and present themselves through our specific awareness of them" (Gurwitsch, *Field of Consciousness*, 305).

[90] Gurwitsch, *Studies in Phenomenology and Psychology*, p. xxiv.

[91] Gurwitsch, *Field of Consciousness*, 288.

3

Heidegger's Critique of the Husserl/Searle Account of Intentionality (1993)

In *Being and Time*, Heidegger seeks to undermine the Cartesian tradition of the priority of knowledge over practice.[1] At first it looks as if Heidegger seeks simply to invert this tradition by arguing that detached contemplation is a privative modification of everyday involvement. More specifically, he seems to be saying that the detached, meaning-giving, *knowing* subject, still at the center of Husserlian phenomenology, must be replaced by an involved, meaning-giving, *doing* subject. But if one simply inverts the tradition, one risks being misunderstood and reappropriated, and, indeed, Dagfinn Føllesdal, the best interpreter of Husserl's phenomenology, has been led to underestimate Heidegger's originality on just this point. In an article on the role of action in Husserl and Heidegger, Føllesdal interprets Heidegger as holding that Husserl and the tradition overemphasized detached contemplation, and he agrees with what he takes to be Heidegger's claim that practical activity is the basic way subjects give meaning to objects:

It has commonly been held that practical activity presupposes theoretical understanding of the world...Heidegger rejects this. He regards our practical ways of dealing with the world as more basic than the theoretical....This idea of Heidegger's that...human activity plays a role in our constitution of the world, and his analyses of how this happens, I regard...as Heidegger's main contribution to philosophy.[2]

---

[1] Some of the ideas in this chapter were first expressed in Jerry Wakefield and Hubert L. Dreyfus, "Action and the First Person", in Ernest LePore and Robert Van Gulick (eds), *John Searle and his Critics* (Cambridge: Basil Blackwell, 1990), 259–70.

[2] Dagfinn Føllesdal, "Husserl and Heidegger on the Role of Actions in the Constitution of the World", in E. Saarinen et al. (eds), *Essays in Honour of Jaakko Hintikka* (Dordrecht: D. Reidel, 1979), 371. A similar trivializing reduction of Heidegger's work to a practical variation on Husserl's is assumed by Mark Okrent: "[A]s soon as one realizes that, for Heidegger, intentionality is always practical rather than cognitive and that the primary form of intending is doing something for a purpose rather than being conscious of something, the structural analogies between the argument

Føllesdal reports that "after he came to Freiburg in 1916...Husserl clearly became more and more aware that our practical activity is an important part of our relation to the world."[3] He then tries to determine who deserves credit for this new interest in the phenomenology of practical activity. "It is possible that Husserl influenced Heidegger in this 'practical' direction," he notes. "However, it is also possible," he admits, "that it was Husserl who was influenced in this direction through his discussion with the younger Heidegger."[4]

Once one sees the depth of Heidegger's difference from Husserl on this issue, however, one sees that the question of influence is irrelevant. Much more is at stake than the relation of practice to theory. The real issue concerns two opposed accounts of intentionality. As used by Franz Brentano and then Husserl, "intentionality" names the fact that mental states like perceiving, believing, desiring, fearing, doubting, etc. are always about something, i.e. directed at something under some description, whether the extramental object exists or not. The mental property that makes this directedness possible is called the representational or intentional content of the mental state. By focusing his discussion on the primacy of the intentional content of action over the intentional content of thought, Føllesdal misses Heidegger's radical claim that an account of intentionality in terms of mental content presupposes but overlooks a more fundamental sort of intentionality—a kind of intentionality that does not involve intentional content at all. Heidegger does not merely claim that practical activity is primary; he wants to show that *neither* practical activity *nor* contemplative knowing can be understood as a relation between a self-sufficient subject with its intentional content and an independent object.

What Føllesdal assumes and Heidegger opposes is the traditional representational view of practice. To this day philosophers such as John Searle and Donald Davidson, who do not agree on much else, agree that action must be explained in terms of mental states with intentional content. Heidegger's attempt to break out of the philosophical tradition is focused in his attempt to get beyond the subject/object distinction that such views presuppose. In a lecture in 1929 he says, "My essential intention is to first pose the problem [of the subject/object relation] and work it out in such a way that the essentials of the entire Western tradition will be concentrated in the simplicity of a basic problem."[5] The basic

---

strategies of Husserl and Heidegger become apparent": *Heidegger's Pragmatism* (Ithaca, NY: Cornell University Press, 1988), 10.

   [3] Føllesdal, "Husserl and Heidegger", 372.   [4] Føllesdal, "Husserl and Heidegger", 376.
   [5] Martin Heidegger, *The Metaphysical Foundation of Logic* (Bloomington, IN: Indiana University Press, 1984), 132.

problem is not which kind of intentionality—theoretical or practical—is more fundamental, but what sort of experience makes both kinds of intentionality possible.

Husserl defined phenomenology as the study of the intentional content remaining in the mind after the bracketing of the world, i.e. after the phenomenological reduction. Jerry Fodor calls such an approach to the mind "methodological solipsism." Heidegger opposes the claim underlying this method—the claim that a person's relation to the world and the things in it must always be mediated by intentional content, so that one can perform a reduction that separates the mind and its content from the world. As he puts it:

The usual conception of intentionality ... misconstrues the structure of the self-directedness-toward, the intention. This misinterpretation lies in an *erroneous subjectivizing* of intentionality ... The idea of a subject which has intentional experiences ... encapsulated within itself is an absurdity which misconstrues the basic ontological structure of the being that we ourselves are.[6]

This makes Heidegger sound like what would now be called an externalist. It is as if he were claiming that mental states get their intentional content by way of some connection with the external world. But as we shall see, Heidegger's view is more radical. He wants to introduce a kind of intentionality that avoids the notion of mental content altogether.

Before we can fully appreciate Heidegger's project and decide whether he succeeds, we have to sharpen as much as possible the intentionalistic theory of mind he opposes. Just how is the subject/object distinction supposed to be built into all ways of relating to the world whether they be knowing or acting? Since Heidegger focuses on action as the area in which it is easiest to see that our experience need not involve a mind/world split, I too will concentrate on action. But since Husserl never worked out a theory of action, I will turn to the work of John Searle, who defends an intentionalist account of action of the sort Heidegger opposes. I will therefore first spell out Searle's formulation of the way the mind/world split is supposedly built into the experience of acting, and then present Heidegger's phenomenological critique. (Where Searle agrees with Donald Davidson I will also remind the reader of Davidson's view.)

It is generally agreed that our commonsense concepts of perception and action are causal concepts. Paul Grice showed that our concept of perception is that of a

---

[6] Martin Heidegger, *Basic Problems of Phenomenology*, tr. Albert Hofstadter (Bloomington, IN: Indiana University Press, 1982), 63–4.

perceptual experience caused in the right way by the object perceived.[7] In the parallel case of acting, Searle and Davidson argue that our concept of an action is likewise causal. An action is a bodily movement which is understood as having been caused in the right way by something mental. Davidson thinks that, for a movement to count as caused in the right way, it must be interpreted as caused by brain states token identical with the beliefs and desires that count as reasons for the action. Davidson gives an account that requires attributing something like a prior intention. Searle denies this requirement, since actions can be spontaneous, but suggests that two other conditions must be met before a bodily motion qualifies as an action. *First*, a representation of the goal of the action must exist throughout the motion and must play a continuing causal role in shaping the action. Searle calls this continuing representation of the goal the "intention in action," thus differentiating it from the "prior intention" which corresponds to the initial representation of the goal of the action prior to the initiation of motion. *Second*, Searle maintains that the subject must experience the causal connection between the intention in action and the bodily movement continuously. Indeed, according to Searle, the experience of acting is just the experience of the bodily movement being caused by the intention in action.

Note that in his account of action, as elsewhere in his account of intentionality, Searle attempts a unique integration of logical conditions and phenomenological description. The standard analysis of action is "bodily motion caused by a reason." Searle incorporates a phenomenological analog of this analysis into his account of action by maintaining that the experience of an action must include a direct experience of the causal relation between the intention in action and the bodily motion. He argues that both the prior intention and the intention in action are causally self-referential. They both include in their conditions of satisfaction the requirement that the intention to bring about a goal cause the goal-directed action. Thus an action is a bodily movement experienced as caused by my intention to perform it.

In his attempt to overthrow the subject/object account, Heidegger seeks to show (1) that intentionality without the experience of self-referential content is characteristic of the unimpeded mode of everyday activity, whereas Husserl's (and Searle's) mentalistic intentionality is a derivative mode that occurs only when there is some disturbance, and (2) that both these modes of intentionality presuppose being-in-the-world, a more fundamental form of intentionality that Heidegger calls originary transcendence, and that he claims is the condition of

---

[7] Paul Grice, "The Causal Theory of Perception", in Robert Swartz (ed.), *Perceiving, Sensing, and Knowing* (New York: Anchor Books, 1965).

the possibility of both active and contemplative intentionality. In his lecture course the year *Being and Time* was published, he refers to this double task (when he speaks of Dasein he is speaking of human beings):

The task of bringing to light Dasein's existential constitution leads first of all to the twofold task, intrinsically one, of interpreting more radically the phenomena of intentionality and transcendence. With this task...we run up against a central problem that has remained unknown to all previous philosophy.

It will turn out that intentionality is founded in Dasein's transcendence and is possible solely for this reason—that transcendence cannot conversely be explained in terms of intentionality.[8]

Heidegger's Account of Primordial Intentionality

In using Searle's account as a stand-in for Husserl's, I will highlight two aspects of Searle's view that Husserl presumably would have shared, both of which Heidegger rejects.[9] Searle points out that the experience of acting is phenomenologically distinguishable from the experience of being acted upon. I can have the experience of acting even if I am deluded—for example, paralyzed—and the bodily movement I take it I am causing is in fact not taking place. Conversely, if electrodes are applied to my brain, my body can be caused to move without my having an experience of acting. It follows from these considerations that the experience of acting and the bodily movement it causes belong to two totally separate domains. Thus, according to Searle, the distinction between mind and world, what Husserl and Heidegger would call the distinction between subject and object, is built directly into the logic of acting:

[J]ust as the case of seeing the table involves two related components, an Intentional component (the visual experience) and the conditions of satisfaction of that component (the presence and features of the table), so the act of raising my arm involves two components, an Intentional component (the experience of acting) and the conditions of satisfaction of that component (the movement of my arm).[10]

Heidegger questions phenomenological claims of the sort that accompany Searle's analysis of the logic of perception and action. He denies *first* that the

---

[8] Heidegger, *Basic Problems of Phenomenology,* 162.

[9] This is not to say that Searle was influenced by Husserl, nor that their accounts of the intentionality of perception and action are identical. Searle's account of the logical role of causality and thus of the necessary self-referentiality of the intentional content of the experience involved in perception and action is not found in Husserl.

[10] John R. Searle, *Intentionality: An Essay in the Philosophy of Mind* (Cambridge: Cambridge University Press, 1983), 88.

experience of acting must be an experience of my causing the action, and *second* that the experience of acting must *represent the conditions of satisfaction* of the action.[11]

Searle begins his account of intentions in action by pointing out that we always seem to know during an action that we are acting—at least in the sense that we experience ourselves as the source of our activity rather than as being passively moved about. Heidegger would agree, but he would point out that only in *deliberate* action is the experience of acting an experience of one's intention in action causing one's movement. In everyday absorbed coping, the experience of acting is instead the experience of a steady flow of skillful activity in response to one's sense of the environment. Part of that experience is a sense that when one's situation deviates from some optimal body/environment relationship, one's motion takes one closer to that optimal form and thereby relieves the "tension" of the deviation. As Maurice Merleau-Ponty would put it, one's body is solicited by the situation to get into the right relation to it. When everyday coping is going well, one experiences something like what athletes call flow, or playing out of their heads. One's activity is completely geared into the demands of the situation. One does not distinguish one's experience of acting from one's ongoing activity, and therefore one has no self-referential experience of oneself as causing that activity.

Aron Gurwitsch, a student of Husserl's, yet a perceptive reader of Heidegger, gives, in his interpretation of *Being and Time*, an excellent account of this nonintentionalistic, i.e. nonself-referential, awareness:

[W]hat is imposed on us to do is not determined by us as someone standing outside the situation simply looking on at it; what occurs and is imposed are rather prescribed by the situation and its own structure; and we do more and greater justice to it the more we let ourselves be guided by it, i.e., the less reserved we are in immersing ourselves in it and subordinating ourselves to it. We find ourselves in a situation and are interwoven with it, encompassed by it, indeed just "absorbed" into it.[12]

To get the phenomenon in focus, we can consider a Merleau-Pontyan example such as a tennis swing. (Since Merleau-Ponty attended Gurwitsch's lectures explaining Heidegger's account of comportment in terms of gestalt perception,

---

[11] Searle could give up his phenomenological claims and stick to the logical conditions of perception and action, viz., that they both must in some way be able to succeed or fail, and that action must be something we do, not what is done to us (and perception vice versa). But as long as he accepts the causal theory, he accepts the existence of the terms between which the causal relation holds, viz., physical events and mental experiences, and it is ultimately this ontology that Heidegger is challenging.

[12] Aron Gurwitsch, *Human Encounters in the Social World* (Pittsburgh: Duquesne University Press, 1979), 67.

there may well be a direct line of influence here.) If one is a beginner or is off one's form, one might find oneself making an effort to keep one's eye on the ball, keep the racket perpendicular to the court, hit the ball squarely, etc. But if one is expert at the game and things are going well, what is experienced is more like one's arm going up and its being drawn to the appropriate position, the racket forming the appropriate angle with the court—an angle we need not even be aware of—all this so as to complete the gestalt made up of the court, one's running opponent, and the oncoming ball.

The phenomenon, then, requires us to modify Searle's taxonomy as presented in his book, *Intentionality*.[13] *Action* does, as Searle claims, have a world-to-mind direction of fit—our actions bring the world into line with what we would want if we thought about it—but, contrary to Searle's account, *the experience of acting* has a *world-to-mind* direction of causation also. We experience the situation as drawing the action out of us.

Searle applies to perception the same analysis he applies to action. His example is seeing a flower:

The seeing consists of two components, the visual experience and the flower, where the presence of (and features of) the flower cause the visual experience and the visual experience has the presence and features of the flower as the rest of its conditions of satisfaction. The content of the visual experience is that there is a flower there and it is self-referential in the sense that, unless the fact that there is a flower there causes this experience, the conditions of satisfaction do not obtain, i.e., I do not actually see that there is a flower there, nor do I see the flower.[14]

But just as skillful absorption does not involve an experience of acting separate from an action that it causes, so perception does not involve a subjective visual experience separate from and caused by its object. A nonmentalistic phenomenology of perception that parallels Heidegger's phenomenology of absorbed action is found in Maurice Merleau-Ponty's *Phenomenology of Perception*. There, Merleau-Ponty describes the experience of perceiving as the experience of our openness to the world:

The child lives in a world which he unhesitatingly believes is accessible to all around him. He has no awareness of himself or of others as private subjectivities. . . . For him men are empty heads turned towards one single, self-evident world where everything takes place. . . . It must be the case . . . that the unsophisticated thinking of our earliest years remains as an indispensable acquisition underlying that of maturity, if there is to be for the adult one single intersubjective world.[15]

[13] Searle, *Intentionality*, 95.   [14] Searle, *Intentionality*, 95.
[15] Maurice Merleau-Ponty, *The Phenomenology of Perception* (London: Routledge & Kegan Paul, 1979), 355.

While the image of an empty head gets at the phenomenological truth of direct realism, it is misleading in another respect. In perception we do not experience ourselves as passive receivers. By turning my attention to something I experience myself as enabling it to show up. Moreover, I can zoom in on it and reveal it in greater and greater detail. In the activity of looking I feel I am responsible for what I see. Thus *looking as experienced* has a mind-to-world direction of causation.

Common sense maintains an unstable mixture of a first-person and a third-person—an internal and an external—account of perception and action. A *private* experience causes or is caused by something in the *public* world. This ontologically unstable idea is expressed in our everyday concepts of perception and action. There then seem to be two possible positions for making the concepts consistent. Davidson accepts objective causation *of* brain states in the case of perception and *by* brain states in the case of action, and treats the first-person experience as a matter of attribution. Searle starts from the first-person experience and builds the third-person causal account into the intentional content of the experience. Thus both are led to distort the phenomena. Merleau-Ponty speaks of "the prejudice of common sense," and Heidegger warns:

> The most dangerous and stubborn prejudices relative to the understanding of intentionality are not the explicit ones in the form of philosophical theories but the implicit ones that arise from the natural apprehension and interpretation of things by... everyday "good sense." These latter misinterpretations are exactly the ones that are least noticeable and hardest to repulse.[16]

Phenomenology rejects common sense in the name of the phenomena of everyday involved perception and action.

Heidegger's second point amounts to a rejection of Searle's claim that the intentional content of the experience of acting is a representation of the action's conditions of satisfaction, viz., a representation of my bringing about the state of affairs I am trying to achieve. But phenomenological examination shows that in a wide variety of situations human beings relate to the world in an organized purposive manner without the constant accompaniment of a representational state which specifies what the action is aimed at accomplishing. Examples are skillful activity like playing tennis; habitual activity like driving to the office or brushing one's teeth; casual unthinking activity like rolling over in bed or making gestures while one is speaking; and spontaneous activity such as fidgeting and drumming one's fingers during a dull lecture. In all these cases of action it is possible to be without any representation of what one is doing as one performs

---

[16] Heidegger, *Basic Problems of Phenomenology*, 59.

the action. Indeed, at times one is actually surprised when the action is accomplished, as when one's thoughts are interrupted by one's arrival at the office. We should try to impress on ourselves what a huge amount of our lives—working, getting around, talking, eating, driving, etc.—is spent in this immediate coping mode, and what a small part is spent in the deliberate, purposeful, subject/object mode, which is, of course, the mode we tend to notice, and which has therefore formed our commonsense concepts and been studied in detail by philosophers.

From Aristotle's discussion of the practical syllogism to recent accounts of action such as Davidson's, philosophers have held that we must explain action as caused by the attempt to achieve some goal. According to Searle, even when there is no prior setting of a goal, as when I jump up and pace about the room, I must have in mind what I am doing. According to Heidegger, however, skillful coping does not require a mental representation of its goal at all. It can be *purposive* without the agent entertaining a *purpose*. Heidegger would like basketball player Larry Bird's description of the experience of the complex purposive act of passing the ball in the midst of a game:

[A lot of the] things I do on the court are just reactions to situations. . . . A lot of times, I've passed the basketball and not realized I've passed it until a moment or so later.[17]

We can return to Merleau-Ponty's account of action to understand this experience. Remember the gestalt account of the experience of an expert tennis stroke. If one is expert at tennis and things are going well, what is experienced is one's arm going up and its being drawn to the appropriate position so as to complete the gestalt made up of the court, one's running opponent, and the oncoming ball. We not only feel that our motion was caused by the perceived conditions, but also that it was caused in such a way that it is constrained to reduce a sense of deviation from some satisfactory gestalt. Now we can add that *the nature of that satisfactory gestalt is in no way represented.*

To help convince us that the representation of the final gestalt need play no role in achieving the result, Merleau-Ponty uses the analogy of a soap bubble. The bubble starts as a deformed film. The bits of soap just respond to local forces according to laws which happen to work so as to dispose the entire system to end up as a sphere, but the spherical result does not play a causal role in producing the bubble. The same holds for the final gestalt of body and racket (although, unlike the bubble, the actor has a sense that he is cooperating in the movement and could stop it at will). Indeed, I cannot represent how I am turning my racket

---

[17] Quoted in Lee Daniel Levine, *Bird: The Making of an American Sports Legend* (New York: McGraw-Hill, 1988).

since I do not know what I do when I return the ball. I may once have been told to hold my racket perpendicular to the court, and I may have succeeded in doing so, but now experience has sculpted my swing to the situation in a far more subtle and appropriate way than I could have achieved as a beginner following this rule.

An even more striking case, where the goal the body is to achieve is not available to the actor as something to aim at, will make the point clear. Instructor pilots teach beginning pilots a rule for determining the order in which to scan their instruments—a rule the instructor pilots were taught and, as far as they know, still use. At one point, however, Air Force psychologists studied the eye movements of the instructors during simulated flight and found, to everyone's surprise, that the instructor pilots were not following the rule they were teaching; in fact, their eye movements varied from situation to situation and did not seem to follow any rule at all. The instructor pilots had no idea of the way they were scanning their instruments and so could not have represented to themselves what they were doing.

Searle's response to such objections is that only the broader action of winning a tennis point or finding out how everything is going by scanning the instruments is intentional, and it is this goal that is represented in the intentional content of the intention in action. Searle points out that an expert skier does not have to form a separate intention to shift his weight from one ski to the other or to execute each turn. He just intends to ski down the mountain. This is a safe response since the intentionalist can, indeed, always find a level at which the actor is trying to achieve something, and the experience of acting can be defined as the experience of causing my body to bring about that end.

There is no doubt something right about this response, but something troubling about it too. The tennis player might well be trying to win a point, but what he or she is doing seems to be much more fine-grained. For example, expert tennis players learn to rush the net and slam the ball behind their opponent, and go on doing so whether they are aware of doing so or not. Of course, as Searle points out, they are also winning a point, winning the set, getting exercise, moving air molecules, using energy, etc. How do we determine what they are really doing? Searle has an answer which seems right: Ask the agent. He argues that there must be goal-awareness in action, since, if one is stopped and questioned even while acting in a nondeliberate way, one can say what one is doing. This, Searle concludes, shows that even in nondeliberate activity our movements are being guided by a self-referential intention in action which represents our goal. But the agent in our tennis example might well just say if asked that he was playing tennis. We could, of course, then restate our question, insisting that he tell us what he was doing *right then*. But then he might answer he was trying to win a point, or he might equally well say that he was rushing the net, or, like Larry Bird, he might say he was so absorbed he does not know what he was doing. The point is that if we are to trust what the agent says he is doing, as Searle says we should, what the agent is doing need not be the same as the conscious intention that initiated the flow of activity. So it seems we have no reason to deny that these are units of activity that count as what the agent is doing but whose conditions of satisfaction are not represented by the agent.

Heidegger has an alternative account of our ability to say what we are doing, not based on the inspection of an internal mental state. Comportment is not simply an undifferentiated flow. One can make sense of it as having a direction and recognizable chunks—"toward-whichs" is Heidegger's nonintentionalistic term for these end-points we use in making sense of a flow of directed activity. For example, I leave home, drive to work, park, enter my office building, open my office door, enter my office, sit down at my desk, and begin working. These are all action segments defined by their toward-whichs. We thus make sense of our own comportment, and the comportment of others in terms of a directedness toward the sort of long-range and proximal ends that are sometimes our explicit goals. That is why, if asked what we or others are in the process of doing, we always have an answer. But this fact should not mislead us into postulating mental intentions in action. There is no evidence that our shared social segmentation of flows of activity into intelligible subunits is in the mind of the person who is absorbed in the activity. Heidegger notes explicitly that it is a mistake to think of the toward-which as the *goal* of the activity, i.e. as the condition of satisfaction the actor has in mind: "The awaiting of the 'towards-which' is neither a considering of the 'goal' nor an expectation of the impending finishing of the work to be produced."[18]

The phenomenon of purposive action without a purpose is not limited to bodily activity. It occurs in all areas of skillful coping, including intellectual coping. Many instances of apparently complex problem solving which seem to implement a long-range strategy, as, for example, a masterful move in chess, may be best understood as direct responses to familiar perceptual gestalts. After years of seeing chess games unfold, a chess grandmaster can, simply by responding to the patterns on the chess board, play master-level chess while his deliberate, analytic mind is absorbed in something else.[19] Such play, based as it is on previous attention to thousands of actual and book games, incorporates a

---

[18] Martin Heidegger, *Being and Time*, tr. John Macquarrie and Edward Robinson (New York: Harper & Row, 1962), 405.
[19] For a full discussion of this phenomenon, see Hubert L. Dreyfus and Stuart Dreyfus, *Mind over Machine* (New York: Free Press, 1988).

tradition which determines the appropriate response to each situation and therefore makes possible long-range, strategic, purposive play without the player needing to have in mind any plan or purpose at all.[20]

Notice that explaining Heidegger's objections to Husserl and Searle I have had to speak of *activity* rather than *action*. Heidegger might well grant Husserl and Searle that their intentionalistic account reflects our commonsense concept of *action*. He is not, however, trying to explicate our commonsense concept, but to make a place for a sort of activity that has been overlooked both by common sense and a fortiori by the philosophical tradition. Indeed, Heidegger holds that the commonsense concept of action covers up our most basic mode of involvement in the world. He therefore introduces his own term, *Verhalten*, translated "comportment," for the way human beings normally cope. Heidegger uses "comportment" to refer to our directed activity, precisely because the term has no mentalistic overtones. But he claims that comportment, nonetheless, exhibits intentionality.

Husserlian intentionality is often called "aboutness," because mental content is directed toward an object under an aspect. Heidegger's more primordial intentionality is also appropriately called aboutness, but in this case it is not the *mind* which is thinking about something, but the *embodied person* going about his or her business. This active aboutness, like the kind described by Husserl, is directed toward things under aspects. I can be transparently coping in such a way as to use my desk in order to write on, or to read at, or to keep things in. Thus, depending on what I am about, i.e. upon the "toward-which" of my activity, I reveal the desk under different aspects. So Heidegger can say: "*Comportments* have the structure of directing-oneself-toward, of being-directed-toward.... [P]henomenology calls this structure *intentionality*."[21] But, as we have seen, for Heidegger "comportment" denotes not merely acts of consciousness, but human activity in general. Thus, intentionality is attributed not to consciousness but to Dasein:

Because the usual separation between a subject with its immanent sphere and an object with its transcendent sphere—because, in general, the distinction between an inner and an outer is constructive and continually gives occasion for further constructions, we shall in the future no longer speak of a subject, of a subjective sphere, but shall understand the being to whom intentional comportments belong as *Dasein*, and indeed in such a way that

[20] Pierre Bourdieu, influenced as he is by Merleau-Ponty, has seen the same phenomenon: "The conditionings associated with a particular class of conditions of existence produce habitus, systems of durable, transposable dispositions, structured structures predisposed to function as structuring structures, that is, as principles which generate and organize practices and representations that can be objectively adapted to their outcomes *without presupposing a conscious aiming at ends*" Bourdieu, *The Logic of Practice* (Stanford, CA: Stanford University Press, 1980), 53; my italics.

[21] Heidegger, *Basic Problems of Phenomenology*, 58; first italics mine.

it is precisely with the aid of *intentional comportment*, properly understood, that we attempt to characterize suitably the being of Dasein.[22]

Heidegger's understanding of Dasein's comportment enables him to contrast his view with that of the tradition. He explains why in the tradition knowledge was mistakenly taken as basic, and why even action was interpreted as a kind of knowledge:

The previous concept of intentionality proves to be a restricted conception ... [B]ecause of this restriction, intentionality is conceived primarily as "taking as" [as meaning-giving]. ... Thus every act of directing oneself toward something receives the characteristic of knowing, for example, in Husserl.[23]

The point is that for Husserl (and Føllesdal and Searle too) intentionality always amounts to *my taking* something *as* something, taking it under some aspect. So whether I take what I am seeing as a house, or take what I am doing to be reaching for the salt, I am performing the same sort of mental act. One way to see this is to note that, according to Husserl and Searle, there must always be an ego doing the taking. I must represent to myself that my bodily movement is meant to bring about a specific state of affairs. The gestalt account of purposive action, however, shows that one can dispense with this active meaning-giving and still respond to the situation under one aspect or another. This is why Heidegger, Gurwitsch, Sartre, and Merleau-Ponty each criticized Husserl's egological conception of consciousness.

Lest it appear that Heidegger's account of our everyday dealings, denying as it does a self-referential experience of acting, is committed to interpreting involved activity as zombie-like behavior, we can in summary see that skillful coping differs in at least three ways from mindless, mechanical behavior:

1. *Skillful coping is a mode of awareness.* Heidegger actually uses the term *experience (Erfahrung)*, but this experience can be characterized only as openness. It is not a mental, inner, private event (*Erlebnis*, Husserl's term), aware of itself as separate from, and directed toward, things in the world.
2. *Comportment is adaptable and copes with the situation in a variety of ways.* In ongoing coping one responds to things on the basis of vast past experience of what has happened in previous situations, or, more exactly, one's behavior manifests dispositions that have been shaped by a vast amount of previous dealings, so that in most cases when we exercise these dispositions everything works without interruption.

---

[22] Heidegger, *Basic Problems of Phenomenology*, 64.
[23] Heidegger, *Metaphysical Foundation of Logic*, 134.

3. *If the going gets difficult we pay attention and so switch to deliberate subject/ object intentionality.* One then has a sense of effort with the condition of satisfaction that my effort causes the appropriate goal-directed movements. Such representations certainly have a place in the overall explanation of how it is that we manage to act in a wide range of situations. Indeed, when the situation is new or especially complex, manipulation of representations seems to be the primary way we have of carefully considering our options and orienting ourselves.

Being-in-the-World as Originary Intentionality

Having argued so far that much of our everyday activity does not involve a mental state whose intentional content represents its conditions of satisfaction, but rather involves an open responsiveness to a gestalt, Heidegger next argues that all human activity, whether absorbed or deliberate, requires a background orienting that makes directed activity possible.

So far we have seen that in nondeliberate activities we experience ourselves only as an open responsiveness to what solicits our activity. Heidegger now adds that such unthinking activity provides the nonsalient *background*, both for specific acts of ongoing coping and for deliberately focusing on what is unusual or difficult. The basic idea is that for a particular person to be directed toward a particular piece of equipment, whether using it, perceiving it, or whatever, there must be a correlation between that person's general capacity for skillful coping and the interconnected equipmental whole in which the thing has a place. For example, when I enter a room I normally cope with whatever is there. What enables me to do this is not a set of beliefs about rooms, nor a rule for dealing with rooms in general and what they contain; it is a sense of how rooms normally behave, a skill for dealing with them, that I have developed by crawling and walking around many rooms. Such familiarity involves not only acting but also not acting. In dealing with rooms I am skilled at not coping with the dust, unless I am a janitor, and not paying attention to whether the windows are opened or closed, unless it is hot, in which case I know how to do what is appropriate. My competence for dealing with rooms determines both what I will cope with by using it, and what I will cope with by ignoring it, while being ready to use it should the appropriate occasion arise.

Here Heidegger's account sounds deceptively similar to the appeal to the background introduced by Searle in his account of intentionality,[24] but in fact

---

[24] See Searle, *Intentionality*, ch. 5.

it is quite different. Searle, like Heidegger, holds that the background of intentionality involves "abilities," "capacities," and "practices," but he insists that these are not a kind of intentionality, but rather the nonintentional conditions that make intentional action possible. For Heidegger, on the contrary, the sort of background familiarity that functions when I take in a room as a whole and deal with what is in it is neither a set of specific goal-directed actions nor merely a capacity that must be activated by a self-referential intentional state. Rather, what Heidegger calls *the background* consists in a continual intentional activity that he calls *ontological transcendence*.

In an early lecture, Heidegger describes this transcendence as "the background of ... primary familiarity, which itself is not conscious and intended but is rather present in [an] unprominent way."[25] In *Being and Time* he speaks of "[T]hat familiarity in accordance with which Dasein ... 'knows its way about' (*sich "auskennt"*) in its public environment."[26] In *Basic Problems* he calls it the "sight of practical *circumspection* ... our practical everyday orientation." This familiarity has a crucial function:

Circumspection oriented to the presence of what is of concern provides each setting-to-work, procuring, and performing with the way to work it out, the means to carry it out, the right occasion, and the appropriate time. This sight of circumspection is the skilled possibility of concerned discovering.[27]

On analogy with the ways our eyes are always accommodating to the light, we might call this background activity "accommodation." It is the way we are constantly adjusting to our situation. Heidegger has no specific term for this most basic activity. It is so pervasive and constant that he simply calls it being-in-the-world: "Being-in-the-world ... amounts to a non-thematic circumspective absorption in ... an equipmental whole."[28]

In response, then, to Husserl and Searle, Heidegger points out that, whenever we are revealing entities by using or contemplating them, we must simultaneously be exercising a general skilled grasp of our circumstances. It is this background orienting that makes everyday coping possible. Thus even if we normally experienced acting as an effort directed toward achieving some goal (which Heidegger does not find in his normal coping experience), there would still be good reason to deny that goal-directed action was the only kind of intentional activity.

---

[25] Martin Heidegger, *The History of the Concept of Time* (Bloomington, IN: Indiana University Press, 1985), 189.

[26] Heidegger, *Being and Time*, 405.   [27] Heidegger, *History of the Concept of Time*, 274.

[28] Heidegger, *Being and Time*, 107.

Just as in ordinary cases of coping, Dasein is absorbed in its activity in such a way that its experience does not have any self-referential intentional content, so, in general, Dasein is absorbed in the background coping that discloses the world as familiar in such a way that there is no separation between Dasein's disclosing comportment and the world disclosed. Heidegger tells us: "[W]e define [concerned being-in-the-world] as *absorption* in the world, being drawn in by it."[29]

Self and world belong together in the single entity, Dasein. Self and world are not two entities, like subject and object... but self and world are the basic determination of Dasein itself in the unity of the structure of being-in-the-world.[30]

Or, even more directly, "Dasein... is nothing but... concerned absorption in the world."[31]

Our general background coping, our familiarity with the world, what Heidegger calls originary transcendence, turns out to be what Heidegger means by our understanding of being.

That wherein Dasein already understands itself... is always something with which it is primordially familiar. This familiarity with the world... goes to make up Dasein's understanding of being.[32]

And Heidegger is explicit that this understanding of being is more basic than either practice or theory.

In whatever way we conceive of knowing, it is... a comportment toward beings.... But all practical-technical commerce with beings is also a comportment toward beings.... In all comportment toward beings—whether it is specifically cognitive, which is most frequently called theoretical, or whether it is practical-technical—an understanding of being is already involved. For a being can be encountered by us *as* a being only in the light of the understanding of being.[33]

It is the discovery of the primacy of this understanding of being, not of the primacy of practical activity, that Heidegger rightly holds to be his unique contribution to Western philosophy.

---

[29] Heidegger, *History of the Concept of Time*, 196.
[30] Heidegger, *Basic Problems of Phenomenology*, 297.
[31] Heidegger, *Basic Problems of Phenomenology*, 197.
[32] Heidegger, *Being and Time*, 119.
[33] Heidegger, *Basic Problems of Phenomenology*, 275.

4

Todes's Account of Nonconceptual Perceptual Knowledge and its Relation to Thought (2001)

Are there two fundamentally different ways we make sense of the world, or does all understanding consist in using concepts to think about things? The philosophical tradition has generally assumed—or, in the case of Kant, argued persuasively—that there is only one kind of intelligibility, the unified understanding we have of things when we make judgments that objectify our experience by bringing it under concepts. But there have always been others—painters, writers, historians, linguists, philosophers in the romantic tradition, Wittgensteinians, and existential phenomenologists—who have felt that there is another kind of intelligibility that gets us in touch with reality besides the conceptual kind elaborated by Kant.

Samuel Todes enters this debate by opposing the intelligibility of conception and perception. He sums up his project as follows:

Kant [does justice] neither to the claims of conceptual imagination nor to the claims of perception. My solution is to show that there are two levels of objective experience: the ground floor of perceptually objective experience; and the upper storey of imaginatively objective experience.... I attempt to show *that* the imaginative objectivity of theoretical knowledge presupposes a pre-imaginative, perceptual form of objectivity, by showing just *how* this is so.[1]

Todes proposes to show further that, just as Kant summed up his argument for the unity and comprehensiveness of our theoretical understanding by systematizing the forms of detached, conceptual judgment in his Table of Categories, one can systematize the forms of practical perceptual judgment in a parallel Table of *Perceptual* Categories.

---

[1] Samuel Todes, *Body and World* (Cambridge, MA: MIT Press, 2001), 100. All subsequent parenthetical pages references in this chapter are to *Body and World.*

In attempting to help Kant out by supplying the categories of perceptual judgment he sought in vain, Todes's work seems *timeless*. But it turns out to be *timely* too. Donald Davidson holds that the only philosophical relevance of perception is that it causes us to have beliefs and other attitudes that are directed toward the world. John McDowell, in *Mind and World,* answers that we can say at least this much—that, for perception to enter into the space of reasons, it must have conceptual content "all the way out":

> To avoid making it unintelligible how the deliverances of sensibility can stand in ground-ing relations to paradigmatic exercises of the understanding such as judgments and beliefs...we must insist that the understanding is already inextricably implicated in the deliverances of sensibility themselves. Experiences are impressions made by the world on our senses, products of receptivity; but those impressions themselves already have con-ceptual content.[2]

Neither Davidson nor McDowell tries to describe perceptual objects as they are in themselves and how they become the objects of thought. By calling attention to the structure of nonconceptual, practical perception and showing how its judg-ments can be transformed into the judgments of detached thought, Todes is able to provide a framework in which to explain how the content of perception, while not itself conceptual, can provide the basis for conception. Thus, Todes's *Body and World* can be read as a significant anticipatory response to McDowell's *Mind and World.*

Todes's account of the nature of nonconceptual content builds on the work of Maurice Merleau-Ponty. Merleau-Ponty claims that, in perceiving things, I sense that they could be more clearly perceived and my body is drawn to get a firmer grip on them:

> My body is geared to the world when my perception offers me a spectacle as varied and as clearly articulated as possible, and when my motor intentions, as they unfold, receive from the world the responses they anticipate. This maximum distinctness in perception and action defines a perceptual ground, a basis of my life, a general milieu for the coexistence of my body and the world.[3]

In Todes's terms, our perception of the things around us is a response to our dissatisfaction with our lostness in the world. We make ourselves at home in the world by moving so as to organize a stable spatiotemporal field in which we use our skills to make determinate the determinable objects that appear in that field. The skills we acquire then feed back into the perceptual world, which becomes

---

[2] John McDowell, *Mind and World* (Cambridge, MA: Harvard University Press, 1994), 46.
[3] Merleau-Ponty, *Phenomenology of Perception,* 49–50.

more and more determinate as we learn to make more refined discriminations and have more reliable anticipations. Merleau-Ponty calls this feedback phenomenon the *intentional arc.*

To explain how perception hides its essential indeterminacy, Todes introduces a phenomenological account of need. A *need*, whether for getting a maximal grip or for something more specific, is at first experienced as an indeterminate deprivation, not a simple absence. This distinction, according to Todes, is the difference between *perceptual negation* as a positive lack that calls for a response, and *logical negation* as the absence of something specific that might have been present. In moving to meet a need, the perceiver makes both the need and the object that satisfies that need sufficiently determinate so that the need is satisfied. The perceiver then understands the object as the determinate object that was needed all along. As Todes puts it:

> The retroactive determination of needs by their being met covers up the fact that they first become determinate by being met. The meeting of a need first fixes it; but it is fixed retroactively as having been that determinate need all along. (178)

Thus, although perception is temporal, moving from lack to satisfaction and from indeterminacy to relative determination, after the act is completed, the dissatisfaction and the objects of perception that satisfied it are experienced as having all along been determinate.

A similar tendency to read back into everyday coping the result of a transformation of that coping takes place in our experience of acting. When Todes describes our absorbed, skillful coping, he is clear that in coping we are not *trying* to achieve a goal that can be described apart from our activity, as John Searle, for example, claims.[4] Absorbed coping does not require that the agent's movements be governed by a representation of the action's success conditions. Todes agrees with Merleau-Ponty that, in absorbed coping, the agent's body is led to move so as to reduce a sense of deviation from a satisfactory gestalt without the agent being able to represent what that satisfactory gestalt will be like in advance of achieving it.

Merleau-Ponty calls the embodied coping that is directed toward objects but that has no propositional success conditions *motor intentionality.* Todes calls this nonconceptual, ongoing coping *poise.*[5] He notes that "the primary form of

---

[4] Searle, *Intentionality*, 90.

[5] "Poise," which usually describes a static stance, is a rather misleading term for the way skilled perceivers move successfully to lower the tension produced in them by the indeterminacy or disequilibrium in their perceptual field. The reader must always keep in mind that, for Todes, poise is a characteristic of skillful *activity.*

directed action is an intention of the *body*.... This intention of the active body is *poise* in dealing with the things and persons around us" (65). Todes, however, goes further than Merleau-Ponty in that he not only, like Merleau-Ponty, distinguishes the *expected success conditions* of willful trying from the ongoing *satisfaction of the anticipations* of poised perception; he adds that the continuing activity of ongoing coping gives us *perceptual knowledge* of the things with which we are coping.

> My response to an anticipated object reveals to me directly, merely by virtue of its existence, not merely the self-produced movements of my own body by which I make that response, but also, and equally immediately, that thing in respect to which I have been able to make the response. This is not true if I construe the primary form of directed action on the model of an act of will...so that I must await the effect of actions to see whether they coincide with my previously definite intentions....Poise does not, when successful, "coincide" or "agree" with its later "effects," as does will with its achievement.... The success of poise is not in its *execution*, but in its very *existence*, by which the body is, to begin with, knowingly in touch with the objects around it. As soon as I am poised in my circumstances, I know...something about those objects to which I am doing something with my body. (65–6)

For example, I can't be skillfully coping, say, dribbling a basketball, unless I am responding to the actual object. Successful ongoing coping is thus itself a kind of knowledge.[6]

Trying to achieve *conditions of satisfaction* only occurs when the flow of ongoing coping is somehow disturbed.

> When I act in an effective, poised way, it is not merely that what I was trying to do is in *agreement with* what I (distinguishably) did do. Rather...there were no two things to compare, but only the *perfect fit* of me-in-my circumstances...It is only in failure of response, and loss of poise, that a distinction appears between what I was trying to do and what I did. (70)

What happens in the conversion of absorbed coping to willful trying will be a helpful guide in understanding what happens in perception when the nonconceptual is converted into the conceptual. When my nonconceptual coping skill fails, and I have to make an effort to bring about what my skill should have effortlessly accomplished, it seems that, since I am trying to achieve the same end toward which my skill was directed, I must have been trying to achieve that goal all along. But, on careful reflection, it should be clear that trying does not simply make explicit *a willful effort* to achieve a goal—both of which were already there but unnoticed. If a doorknob sticks and I have to make an effort to turn it, that

---

[6] Merleau-Ponty sees this phenomenon but doesn't draw out the epistemological consequences.

does not show that I had been *trying* to turn it all along—that my movements have been caused by my entertaining those success conditions—anymore than it shows that I *believed* that turning the doorknob would enable me to open the door or that I *expected* the door to open, even though I did, indeed, *anticipate* its opening in that my body was set to walk through it. The transformation from nonconceptual, absorbed coping to attentive action introduces a new element: the conceptual representation of my goal.[7]

A further, more fundamental, dependence of the conceptual on the nonconceptual arises from the way both absorbed coping and attentive trying are dependent on the spatiotemporal field produced by the body. That field is produced by the way the body's specific structure constrains and enables its coping skills. To make his case that, in structuring the spatiotemporal field, the body plays a fundamental unifying role in *all* human experience, Todes goes beyond Merleau-Ponty's account of the body as a pure "I can" that responds to the world's solicitations. He describes in detail how the structure of the active body produces our unified experience of space and time. Since the body moves forward more effectively than backwards, it opens a *horizontal field* that organizes experience into what can be coped with directly, what can be reached with effort, and what is over the perceptual horizon. Furthermore, the front/back asymmetry of the active body—the fact that it can cope well only with what is in front of it—organizes the temporal field. In everyday coping, what has yet to be faced is experienced as in the future, what is currently being faced and dealt with makes up the pragmatic present, and what already has been faced and is behind us is experienced as both spatially and temporally past. Todes concludes: "Thus through movement we do not merely notice but produce the spatiotemporal field around us, our circumstantial field, the field in which things appear to us" (49).[8]

Because perceptual objects can be experienced only in a spatiotemporal field, they can never be given as fully determinate. Rather, a perceptual object has a front and a back and an inside and an outside, so that any particular experience of such an object "perceptually implies"[9] hidden aspects soliciting further exploration and determination. For example, what I take to be a house seen from the

---

[7] For details, see Hubert L. Dreyfus, "A Merleau-Pontian Critique of Husserl's and Searle's Representationalist Accounts of Action", *Proceedings of the Aristotelian Society* (2000).

[8] Although the structure of the spatiotemporal field depends on the structure of the lived body, Todes is no idealist. In Introduction II, in Todes, *Body and World*, pp. xxviii–xlvi, Piotr Hoffman shows how the fundamental phenomenon of balance, which is so close to us that no previous phenomenologist has described it, enables Todes to avoid the antirealism that threatens the philosophies of both Heidegger and Merleau-Ponty.

[9] Aron Gurwitsch coined this expression. Todes uses the term on p. 196.

front *looks* like a *house* not a *facade*. *It is not* as if I see what looks like a house front and I then *infer* that it has a back and inside. In confronting what I take to be a house, my body is solicited to go around it, while, if I take it that I am seeing a facade, I embody no such readiness. In the second case, the facade consequently looks thin and seems to hide empty terrain behind it, whereas a house looks thick and as if it conceals rooms to be discovered upon further exploration. Thus one has nonconceptual perceptual "beliefs" about perceptual objects; for example, one of my "beliefs," in seeing a *house*, is my being set to walk through the front door. The intentional content of such a perceptual belief is in the motor intentionality of my bodily set, that is, in the way I am prepared to act and do act if nothing intervenes.[10]

According to Todes, we also make perceptual *inferences* and form perceptual *judgments*. To take another example, on the basis of past experience with similar boxes, one might mistakenly see a belted box as heavy, with the "perceptual implication" that lifting it would require an effort. A "perceptual inference" would then normally lead me to be set to use more force than necessary to pick it up. My readiness to use such force would be a mistaken "perceptual judgment." Philosophers generally agree with Aristotle and Kant that, in making a judgment, we subsume a particular under a general concept. In a *perceptual judgment*, however, although our set to lift the object is similar to our set for lifting other heavy objects, we bring to bear a *specific* body-set—in the example, a set to lift this particular heavy object in this particular situation. Indeed, one cannot specify the perceiver's practical knowledge of an object independent of the perceiver's actual disposition to cope with it.[11]

McDowell proposes as a test for *conceptual* content that its objects must be reidentifiable.[12] To determine whether the content of perceptual attitudes is an alternative and irreducible kind of content, we must therefore ask: Does the

---

[10] The indeterminacy of perceptual objects and their dependence on various situational and bodily capacities is argued for in detail in Sean D. Kelly, "The Non-Conceptual Content of Perceptual Experience: Situation Dependence and Fine-ness of Grain", *Philosophy and Phenomenological Research*, 62/3 (May 2001), with a response by Christopher Peacocke.

[11] I owe this way of putting the point to Sean Kelly, "What Do We See (When We Do)?", *Philosophical Topics*, 27/2 (Fall/Winter 1999).

[12] McDowell, *Mind and World*, 57. "We can ensure that what we have in view is genuinely recognizable as a conceptual capacity if we insist that the very same capacity to embrace a color in mind can in principle persist beyond the duration of the experience itself." McDowell doesn't speak of "reidentification." However, Sean Kelly argues that McDowell's "recognitional capacity" gives rise to a reidentification criterion. The reidentification criterion states that, for a subject to possess a concept of an object or property *x*, the subject must be able consistently to reidentify a given object or property as falling under that concept if it does. See Sean D. Kelly, "Demonstrative Concepts and Experience", *Philosophical Review*, 110/3 (2001), 397–420.

content of motor intentionality pass the reidentification test? It is crucial, in answering this question, to realize that, as Todes points out, when objects are made determinate by skillful coping, it is our whole, unified body that gets a grip on the whole unified object in a specific unified context:

In the last analysis...we can have an object in perception only by our whole perceptual field and all its contents being sensed as centered in the felt unity of our active body. (206)

We can now anticipate that Todes will seek to show that, just as practical perception involves its own sort of implications, beliefs, judgments, and know-ledge, it has its own nonconceptual form of reidentification. In thought, I can reidentify an object as the same object in a wide variety of possible contexts. So, for example, I recognize a chair by subsuming it under the general concept chair and can then reidentify it in any context as long as I retain that concept. In practical perception, on the contrary, my "reidentification" does not depend on the intellectual act of *recognizing* that this is the same object I have encountered in other situations; it consists simply in my coping with the object in a way that is *in fact* similar to the way I have coped with it on other occasions.

I may, for example, have a body-set to deal with a particular chair in my office, and, while that particular body-set is in fact similar to my set for dealing with other chairs, and with this chair on other occasions, I don't experience this chair *as* similar to other chairs or *as* identical with the one I sat on yesterday. I am simply disposed to sit on this chair, in this situation, in this stiff or relaxed or seductive way. I perceptually *identify* the chair I am about to sit on as my office chair simply by being set to sit on it in the way I usually sit on my office chair. I don't *reidentify* it as a chair that I could encounter in other possible contexts. Indeed, while I can *conceptually reidentify* the chair in my office as an instance of a type of chair and as having certain characteristics that would enable me to recognize it even on the street, my *perceptual identification* of the chair in my office is so concrete, contextual, and tied to my current disposition to cope with it that it does not follow that I could reidentify it in other possible contexts.

Just as the body-set involved in the practical perception of an object is too responsive to the specific external context to ensure reidentification in other contexts, the body-set for coping with the whole object makes it impossible to isolate the various characteristics of the object from their internal context as characteristics of that specific object. The characteristics of a perceptual object are, therefore, not experienced as *isolable features* that could be features of other possible objects, but, rather, as the *aspects* of that particular object. Todes points out that we always perceive aspects *of an object*.

Merleau-Ponty makes the same point when he says: "It is impossible to understand perception as the imputation of a certain significance to certain sensible signs, since the most immediate sensible texture of these signs cannot be described without referring to the object they signify." In this connection he speaks of seeing the woolly-blueness of a carpet.[13] That is, given the perceiver's current coping capacities (which are based on skills formed in prior experiences with this carpet or similar ones), the carpet looks to be a blue rich with perceptual implications, as one's body is set to feel the carpet's particular flexibility, weight, warmth, fuzziness, etc. On the basis of other past experiences and their correlated body-set, a block of ice would presumably look slick-hard-cold-blue. In general, the experience of any characteristic of an object of practical perception is tied to the perceiver's holistic body-set. Thus, the aspects of the objects of practical perception, such as the woolly-warm-flexible-blueness of this carpet, are so contextually determined that they cannot be seen as the features of other possible objects and so could not be reidentified in a different object. Yet the perceiver's anticipations are determinate enough to have conditions of satisfaction. That is, the perceiver anticipates the experience of this warm-flexible-blue carpet. It follows that the intentional content by means of which the aspects of perceptual objects are perceived must be nonconceptual.

But that leaves us with a troubling question: If perception is, indeed, holistic and nonconceptual all the way in, how are we able to entertain propositional beliefs about isolable perceptual objects and their isolable properties, and, more generally, how are we able to make judgments on the basis of perceptual experience?

The objects of thought must be context-free, as must be the perceived properties of such objects, but it is important to see that just as in absorbed coping there is neither an act of trying nor a representation of a goal, so in practical perception, when I am transparently coping, I do not encounter context-independent objects or reidentifiable *properties* or *features* of the object I am perceiving. But if the context-free and thus reidentifiable objects and properties that thought takes up are neither perceptual objects nor aspects of perceptual objects, how do the objects of practical perception become the objects of abstract thought?

---

[13] Maurice Merleau-Ponty, "The Film and the New Psychology", *Sense and Nonsense* (Chicago: Northwestern University Press, 1964), 51. Merleau-Ponty develops this gestalt account of the "synasthesia" of perception in Merleau-Ponty, *Phenomenology of Perception* (see esp. 229 and 313) and in Merleau-Ponty, "Cézanne's Doubt". There he says: "Cézanne said that one could see the velvetiness, the hardness, the softness, and even the odor of objects. My perception is therefore not a sum of visual, tactile, and audible givens: I perceive in a total way with my whole being; I grasp a unique structure of the thing, a unique way of being, which speaks to all my senses at once" (50).

According to Todes, the transformation of *contextually determined perceptual* objects with *integrated aspects* into *decontextualized conceptual* objects with *isolable features* takes place in two stages. To begin with, the spectatorial attitude, by deactivating one's bodily set to cope, transforms the integrated *aspects* of the perceptual object into a set of isolable *qualities*. In his book, Todes explicitly excludes a treatment of this transformation of the embodied, involved attitude into the disembodied, spectatorial attitude, but he does describe the genesis of the spectatorial attitude and the transformation it brings about in an article included as appendix II.[14] There, Todes points out that practical perception takes place in three stages:

(1) In the first stage we prepare ourselves to perceive an object by getting into a proper position or attitude in respect to it.
(2) Having prepared ourselves to perceive it, we next ready the object to be perceived. This is done by "getting at" the object in some essentially preliminary, tentative, and easily reversible way that allows us to test, with comparatively light consequences, the desirability of going on to perceive the object fully.
(3) In the third stage we finally perceive the object.

Todes then claims that, when we inhibit stage three, we transform practical perception so as to produce sensuous abstractions. "In...cases of skillfully inhibited perception...one becomes aware of *qualities* rather than things" (274).

Thus, the contemplative subject no longer experiences perceptual objects through their integrated aspects, but rather experiences collections of qualities. However, since they still experience themselves as in the world, spectators still experience objects in a shared context with other objects, and so as *stable* collections of *stable* qualities.[15] Such objects and qualities are precisely the reidentifiable elements required by thought.

In the spectatorial attitude, if I come across the same quality in several objects, I can reidentify it as the one I saw before. It is as if one held a painter's color chart up to Merleau-Ponty's woolly-blue carpet and found that the carpet's color

---

[14] Samuel J. Todes, "Sensuous Abstraction and the Abstract Sense of Reality", in James M. Edie (ed.), *New Essays in Phenomenology* (Chicago: Quadrangle Books, 1969), 19, 20.

[15] If the spectator were to assume an even more detached attitude, from outside the world, so to speak, as an impressionist painter does, the object would be isolated from the context it shares with other objects. Then, the object's qualities would lose their perceptual constancy. What one would then see is captured by Monet's paintings of the Rouen cathedral at various times of day. The painter shows how the cathedral's purely spectatorially perceived color-qualities change with changes in the color of the illumination.

matched color chip #29, which was not woolly at all, and, indeed, also matched the tangy-blue of blue berries and the icy-blue of ice. But such conceptual content is still not in the space of reasons.

Thinking about objects requires more than simply being able to reidentify their properties. Much of our thinking concerns *possible* objects in *possible* situations that need never in fact occur. So Todes next explains how our imagination enables us to understand the products of spectatorial decomposition as *possible* objects with *possible* properties. Once we contemplate an object so that our unified and unifying body is no longer involved, our imagination enables us to conjure up the object in various possible contexts, and to imagine the qualities we have disengaged as the qualities of other possible objects. That is, we can imagine the object we are contemplating as a *type* of object that could be encountered and reidentified on other occasions, and we can conceive of it as having a set of reidentifiable features each of which could be a feature of other objects.

Such imaginative representations nonetheless depend on our embodied involvement. For

only by reference to a character-of-this-world, as distinct from objects-in-this-world, can we have any ground for holding such imaginative verbal beliefs about, or undertaking such imaginative purposive action in respect to, objects not in our perceptual field. For such long-range suppositions and purposes pre-suppose that the concrete as well as formal kinds of order self-evidently manifest to us within our perceptual field (in virtue of our centrally habit-forming active body), generally hold also in the apparently placeless regions beyond our perceptual horizon—merely in virtue of the fact that these regions are also regions in the same world as the perceptually present region.[16] (135)

Thanks to our disengagement and our imagination, the object of perception is transformed from an *actually existing* object into a *possible* object about which we can form hypotheses and on the basis of which we can make inferences; that is, we have turned the perceptual object into an object of thought. And just as when we abandon absorbed coping and act attentively, it seems that we have been trying to achieve a goal all along, and when we make our needs determinate by satisfying them, we seem to have had those determinate needs all along, so when we abandon practical perception for the detached, imaginative attitude in which we think and do philosophy, it seems that the objects of practical perception must have been objects of thought all along.

---

[16] This important qualification is part of Todes's argument that, although neither of the two modes of intelligibility he distinguishes can be reduced to the other, embodied perception is more basic than disembodied thought. I cannot, however, deal with this important issue within the space of this chapter.

Once the stages by which the body turns the objects of practical perception into objects of thought have been covered up by detached philosophical reflection, McDowell, like Kant, can conceive of only two alternatives: either perception is so radically nonconceptual as to be totally outside the space of reasons and therefore blind, or, if it is to enable us to form beliefs and make inferences, it must be as conceptual as thought itself. McDowell, therefore, can understand perception as the result of a causal, mechanical interaction of the physical body and the world, but he holds that what one receives in perception must be directly available for forming judgments and so must be permeated by conceptual content. There is no place in such a view for the body's motor intentionality and for the perceptual objects that it reveals. But, as we have now seen, Todes shows how, thanks to our bodily dispositions, perceptual objects are articulated without being *conceptually* articulated. Conceptual articulation is then accomplished by means of a detached, spectatorial perception that can transform perceptual articulations into decontextualized qualities, so that these qualities, in turn, can be represented as possible features of possible objects by the imagination, and thus serve as material for conceptual thought.

Todes concludes:

Phenomenological analyses have shown that perception and imagination are radically different. We have two irreducibly *different ways* of experiencing things: by anticipating them, and by immediate production of them. Neither capacity is derivable from the other. Yet we are *not* bound to understand one in terms of the other. We can pass back and forth between them as modes of understanding. Together with our two radically different ways of experiencing things, we have two basic modes of worldly understanding: we have… *two sets of categories* of matters of fact. (201)

We have seen that the embodied subject is able to meet its factual needs by developing more and more refined skills for coping with the various determinable objects that show up in its spatiotemporal field. We have also seen that the perceiver's nonconceptual readiness to cope with the world and the things in it exhibits the perceptual equivalents of belief, inference, and judgment. Finally, we have seen that, for ongoing coping to take place at all, it must be continually succeeding in getting a grip on its object. Todes, therefore, claims that the perceiver has *practical objective knowledge* of the world and the objects in it. He sums up this crucial claim as follows:

We perceive always *that* something is so. "I see a chair," implies "I see that there is a chair."… Perceptual determinations make sense only in the context of a judgment. (217)

This may sound at first like a concession to McDowell's claim that in order to enter the space of reasons perception must be conceptual, but we must remember that, for Todes, perceptual knowledge is the result of a movement from need to satisfaction. Successfully coping with an object "justifies" the "judgment that" there is, in fact, an object that satisfies and retroactively makes determinate the need that motivated the coping. For example, as I enter my office, I "judge" that coping with this as yet indeterminate object as a chair will give me a grip on my circumstances. That is, I am set to exercise my specific skill for sitting on this chair in these circumstances. "I see that there is a chair" means, where practical perception is concerned, that I successfully sit on it.

Todes assumes, with McDowell, that Kant has worked out the kind of intelligibility characteristic of thought. Todes wants to show that perception, like thought, reveals the world as it is and, as a mode of intelligibility, has a parallel structure to the structure that Kant worked out for thought. So Todes sets out to "deduce" a Table of the Twelve Categories of *Perceptual* Knowledge. He reasons as follows:

A perceptual judgment is an argument. . . . We have, in addition, found the primary form of this argument. It is a three-stage motivational argument: from our ineluctable unity of need that prompts all our activity, through our consequent finding of some unity of object, to a concluding unity of satisfaction derived from this object. All perceptual sense makes sense in the context of this argument. To determine the fundamental quantities, qualities, relation to an object, and modalities that characterize perception, we need merely to ask these four questions about each of the three stages of perceptual knowledge, in what we now see to be their phenomeno-*logical* order. (217–18)

Given current interest in the body in philosophy and in so many other domains both in the English-speaking world and on the Continent, we now have a context for appreciating Todes's achievement. Indeed, Todes's original account of the role of the body in disclosing a spatiotemporal field in which practical perception is directed by need and reaches satisfaction by means of nonconceptual skillful coping, as well as his account of how our capacity for disembodied observation and our conceptual imagination make possible the compatibility of perception and thought, appear so in step with contemporary concerns that his book reads as if it were a response to the most recent development in both analytic and continental philosophy.

5

Overcoming the Myth
of the Mental

How Philosophers Can Profit from the
Phenomenology of Everyday Expertise (2005)

Back in 1950, while a physics major at Harvard, I wandered into C. I. Lewis's epistemology course.[1] There, Lewis was confidently expounding the need for an indubitable Given to ground knowledge, and he was explaining where that ground was to be found. I was so impressed that I immediately switched majors from ungrounded physics to grounded philosophy.

For a decade after that, I hung around Harvard writing my dissertation on ostensible objects—the last vestige of the indubitable Given. During that time, no one at Harvard seemed to have noticed that Wilfrid Sellars had denounced the Myth of the Given, and that he and his colleagues were hard at work, not on a rock-solid foundation for knowledge, but on articulating the conceptual structure of our grasp of reality. Sellars's decision to abandon the old Cartesian problem of indubitable grounding has clearly paid off. While Lewis is now read, if at all, as a dead end, Sellars's research program is flourishing. John McDowell, for example, has replaced Lewis's phenomenalist account of perceptual objects with an influential account of perception as giving us direct access to reality.

But, although almost everyone now agrees that knowledge doesn't require an unshakeable foundation, many questions remain. Can we accept McDowell's

[1] I would like to thank Stuart Dreyfus for his contribution to my understanding of skill and of neural networks. I am especially indebted to Sean Kelly, Joe Rouse, Charles Taylor, and Mark Wrathall, for important suggestions, as well as to Corbin Collins, William Blattner, Taylor Carman, Dagfinn Føllesdal, Beatrice Han, Alva Noe, David Cerbone, Rick Canedo, John Schwenkler, Martin Stokhof, John Haugeland, Ted Schatzki, Iain Thomson, Dan Turner, and Charles Spinoza for their helpful comments on earlier versions of this chapter.

Sellarsian claim that perception is conceptual "all the way out,"[2] thereby denying the more basic perceptual capacities we seem to share with prelinguistic infants and higher animals? More generally, can philosophers successfully describe the conceptual upper floors of the edifice of knowledge while ignoring the embodied coping going on on the ground floor; in effect, declaring that human experience is upper stories all the way down?

In this chapter, I'd like to convince you that we shouldn't leave the conceptual component of our lives hanging in midair and suggest how philosophers who want to understand knowledge and action can profit from a phenomenological analysis of the nonconceptual embodied coping skills we share with animals and infants.

1. The Failure of Cognitivism

One promising proposal for understanding human intelligence, while bypassing the body and, indeed, experience altogether, seems to have run its course. In the mid-twentieth century, philosophers, linguists, psychologists, and computer scientists joined in proposing a new discipline called Cognitive Science that promised to work out how the logical manipulation of formal, symbolic representations enabled minds and suitably programmed computers to behave intelligently. Marvin Minsky, head of MIT's Artificial Intelligence Laboratory, declared in a 1968 press release for Stanley Kubrick's movie *2001* that "in 30 years we should have machines whose intelligence is comparable to man's."[3] Hilary Putnam and I were both teaching at MIT during that optimistic functionalist era, and I remember Hilary asking me earnestly over coffee when I would admit to being a Turing machine.

In the early 1970s, however, Minsky's AI lab ran into an unexpected problem. Computers couldn't comprehend the simple stories understood by 4-year-olds.[4] Minsky suggested that giving the computer the requisite commonsense knowledge would merely require representing a few million facts. But it seemed to me that the real problem wasn't storing and organizing millions of facts; it was knowing which facts were relevant.

One version of this relevance problem is called the frame problem. If the computer has a representation of the current state of the world and something changes, how does the computer determine which of the represented facts stay

[2] McDowell, *Mind and World*, 67.
[3] MGM press release for *2001: A Space Odyssey*, 1968, cited on Michael Krasny's KQED Forum.
[4] For details, see Dreyfus, *What Computers Still Can't Do*, 27–62.

the same, and which representations have to be updated? Minsky suggested that to avoid the frame problem AI programmers could use descriptions of typical situations like going to a birthday party to list and organize the relevant facts. I was influenced by a computer science student who had taken my phenomenology course, who suggested a structure of essential features and default assignments, which, like Husserl, he called a "frame."

But a system of frames isn't *in* a situation, so how, I wondered, could the computer determine which of the millions of facts in its database were relevant for recognizing the relevant frame? It seemed to me obvious that any AI program using frames to solve the story-understanding problem by organizing millions of facts was going to be caught in a regress, and that, therefore, the project was hopeless. And, indeed, Minsky has recently acknowledged in *Wired Magazine* that AI has been brain dead since the early 1970s when it encountered the problem of commonsense knowledge.[5]

Jerry Fodor nails the point with characteristic clarity: "The problem," he writes,

is to get the structure of an entire belief system to bear on individual occasions of belief fixation. We have, to put it bluntly, no computational formalisms that show us how to do this, and we have no idea how such formalisms might be developed.... If someone—a Dreyfus, for example—were to ask us why we should even suppose that the digital computer is a plausible mechanism for the simulation of global cognitive processes, the answering silence would be deafening.[6]

2. The Phenomenological Alternative

How, then, do *we* manage to organize the vast array of facts that supposedly make up commonsense knowledge so that we can retrieve just those facts that are relevant in the current situation? The answer is: "We can't manage it any more than a computer can, but fortunately we don't have to." Only if we stand back from our engaged situation in the world and represent things from a detached theoretical perspective do we confront the frame problem. That is, if you strip away relevance and start with context-free facts, you can't get relevance back. Happily, however, we are, as Martin Heidegger and Maurice Merleau-Ponty put it, *always already* in a world that is organized in terms of our bodies and interests and thus permeated by relevance.

As I said in *What Computers Can't Do*: "[T]he meaningful objects ... among which we live are not a *model* of the world stored in our mind or brain; *they are*

---

[5] *Wired Magazine*, 11/08 (Aug. 2003).

[6] Jerry A. Fodor, *The Modularity of Mind* (Cambridge, MA: Bradford/MIT Press, 1983), 128–9.

the world itself."[7] So, for us embodied agents, keeping track of changes in relevance is not the intractable problem it was for Symbolic AI. Recently, Rodney Brooks, Minsky's successor as director of MIT's AI Lab, has adopted the slogan "the best model of the world is the world itself," and he gives me credit for "being right [back in 1972] that the way in which people operate in the world is intimately coupled to the existence of their body."[8] He now says, looking back at the frame problem:

And why could my simulated robot handle it? Because it was using the world as its own model. It never referred to an internal description of the world that would quickly get out of date if anything in the real world moved.[9]

But Brooks's robots respond only to *fixed features* of the environment. That is, his robots don't feed back into their world what they have learned by acting in it. Such ant-like "animats," as he calls them, lack what Merleau-Ponty calls an intentional arc—the way our successful coping continually enriches the way things in the world show up. Our experience of finding our way around in a city, for example, is sedimented in how that city *looks* to us so that we see new opportunities for action. Brooks's animats, it turns out, finesse rather than solve the frame problem.

It seems that our everyday coping can't be understood in terms of symbolic representations, as Minsky's intellectualist approach assumed, nor in terms of responses caused by fixed features of the environment, as in the empiricist approach of Brooks. We need to consider the possibility that embodied beings like us take as input energy from the physical universe and process it in such a way as to open them to a world organized in terms of their needs, interests, and bodily capacities without their *minds* needing to impose a meaning on a meaningless Given, as Minsky's frames require, nor their *brains* converting the stimulus input into reflex responses, as in Brooks's animats.

Fortunately, there are models of how the embodied brain could provide a causal basis for the intentional arc without doing any symbolic information processing and without instantiating a causal chain from input to response. For example, Walter Freeman, a founding figure in neuroscience and the first to take seriously the idea of the brain as a nonlinear dynamical system, has worked out an account of how the brain of an active animal can, in effect, categorize inputs

[7] Dreyfus, *What Computers Still Can't Do*, 265–6.
[8] Rodney A. Brooks, *Flesh and Machines: How Robots Will Change Us* (New York: Vintage Books, 2002), 168.
[9] Brooks, *Flesh and Machines*, 42.

significant to the organism by forming an attractor landscape.[10] Freeman's model exhibits a kind of top-down governing causality. As the organism responds to what is significant to it, the overall pattern of attractor activity "enslaves" the activity of the individual neurons the way a storm enslaves the individual raindrops. Freeman considers the philosophy underlying his work close to Merleau-Ponty's, and, indeed, Merleau-Ponty seems to anticipate an attractor account when he says:

It is necessary only to accept the fact that the physico-chemical actions of which the organism is in a certain manner composed, instead of unfolding in parallel and independent sequences, are constituted...in relatively stable "vortices."[11]

Time will tell whether Freeman's Merleau-Pontyan model is on the right track for explaining the functioning of the brain; meanwhile, the job of phenomenologists is to get clear concerning the phenomena that need to be explained.

3. Are Perception and Action Conceptual?

In his book *Mind and World,* John McDowell champions a seemingly similar view to Merleau-Ponty's when he says: "An experiencing and acting subject is...herself embodied, substantially present in the world that she experiences and acts on."[12] And he sounds as if he is channeling Heidegger when he speaks of "our unproblematic openness to the world"[13] and how "we find ourselves always already engaged with the world."[14] Like these existential phenomenologists, McDowell makes the bold claim that "this is a framework for reflection that really stands a chance of making traditional philosophy obsolete."[15] But, unlike the existential phenomenologists, McDowell goes on to speak of this engagement in the world as a "*conceptual* activity."[16]

To suggest how impingements received from nature can be conceptual through and through without the mind imposing meaning on a meaningless Given, McDowell introduces an account of Aristotle's idea of second nature:

Human beings are...initiated into...the space of reasons by ethical upbringing, which instills the appropriate shape into their lives. The resulting habits of thought and action are second nature.[17]

---

[10] See Walter J. Freeman, *How the Brain Makes up its Mind* (New York: Columbia University Press, 2001).

[11] Merleau-Ponty, *Structure of Behavior*, 153.   [12] McDowell, *Mind and World*, 111.

[13] McDowell, *Mind and World*, 155.   [14] McDowell, *Mind and World*, 134.

[15] McDowell, *Mind and World*, 111.   [16] McDowell, *Mind and World*, 111 (my italics).

[17] McDowell, *Mind and World*, 84.

McDowell then generalizes Aristotle's account of the production of second nature:

Imposing a specific shape on the practical intellect is a particular case of a general phenomenon: initiation into conceptual capacities, which include responsiveness to other rational demands besides those of ethics.[18]

The phenomenon McDowell has in mind is clearest in *phronesis,* usually translated "practical wisdom." He tells us:

"Practical wisdom" is the right sort of thing to serve as a model for the understanding, the faculty that enables us to recognize and create the kind of intelligibility that is a matter of placement in the space of reasons.[19]

McDowell concludes that, given our second nature, we can "see ourselves as animals whose natural being is permeated with rationality."[20] Thanks to our inculcation into our culture, we become sensitive to reasons, which then influence our "habits of thought and action."[21]

One can easily accept that in *learning* to be wise we learn to follow general reasons as guides to acting appropriately. But it does not follow that, once we have gotten past the learning phase, these *reasons* in the form of habits still *influence* our wise actions. Indeed, a phenomenological reading suggests that Aristotle's account of phronesis is actually a counterexample to McDowell's conceptualism.

Heidegger, like McDowell, is interested in Aristotle's account of phronesis as a paradigm case of human perception and action, but he has a decidedly different take on it from McDowell's emphasis on the role of reasons. Heidegger describes phronesis as a kind of understanding that makes possible an immediate response to the full concrete situation:

[The *phronimos*]...is determined by his situation in the largest sense....The circumstances, the givens, the times and the people vary. The meaning of the action...varies as well...It is precisely the achievement of *phronesis* to disclose the [individual] as acting *now* in the *full* situation within which he acts.[22]

Of course, there will be problematic cases of conflicting goods where the *phronimos* does not see immediately what must be done. Thus, Aristotle says the *phronimos* must be able to deliberate well.[23] But, according to Heidegger, most of

---

[18] McDowell, *Mind and World,* 84.   [19] McDowell, *Mind and World,* 79.
[20] McDowell, *Mind and World,* 85.   [21] McDowell, *Mind and World,* 84.
[22] Martin Heidegger, *Plato's Sophist,* tr. Richard Rojcewicz and André Schuwer (Bloomington, IN: Indiana University Press, 1997), 101 (my italics).
[23] Aristotle, *The Ethics of Aristotle,* tr. J. A. K. Thomson (Harmondsworth: Penguin, 1955), 180 (1141b10). Charles Taylor has suggested that, even when the *phronimos* does deliberate, "his actions will be 'post' or 'ultra' conceptual, because his training has opened him to situations with refined

our ethical life consists in simply *seeing* the appropriate thing to do and responding without deliberation, as when we help a blind person cross the street or when, after years of experience, we unreflectively balance, case by case, the demands of our professional and personal lives. As Aristotle says: "*Phronesis*... involves knowledge of the ultimate particular thing, which cannot be attained by systematic knowledge but only by 'perception.'"[24]

Heidegger thus claims that Aristotle's account of phronesis does not assume, as McDowell does, that, ethical expertise can be conceptually articulated. On the contrary, phronesis shows that socialization can produce a kind of master whose actions do not rely on habits based on reasons to guide him. Indeed, thanks to socialization, a person's perceptions and actions at their best would be so responsive to the specific situation that they could not be captured in general concepts.

Relative to such specificity, all reasons advanced to justify an action could only be retroactive rationalizations. McDowell seems to agree when he notes, "I construe Aristotle's discussion of deliberation as aimed at the reconstruction of reasons for action not necessarily thought out in advance."[25] But speaking of a reconstruction, rather than a construction, of reasons suggests that these reasons must have been implicit all along, whereas, for Heidegger, the *phronimos*'s actions are not in the space of reasons at all. As Heidegger sums it up: "In [phronesis] there is accomplished something like a pure perceiving, one that no longer falls within the domain of logos."[26]

McDowell, however, would no doubt reply that there couldn't be any such logos-free pure perception. So, in taking perception out of the space of reasons, Heidegger can only be imposing on Aristotle a version of the Myth of the Given. Heidegger could counter, however, that in assuming that all intelligibility, even perception and skillful coping, *must be, at least implicitly, conceptual*—in effect, that intuitions without concepts must be blind, and that there must be a maxim behind every action[27]—Sellars and McDowell join Kant in endorsing what we might call the Myth of the Mental.

---

meanings that he can sense and respond to, way beyond his ability to articulate them conceptually" (personal communication).

[24] Aristotle, *The Ethics*, 182 (1142a25); translation slightly modified.

[25] John McDowell, "Virtue and Reason", *Mind, Value, and Reality* (Cambridge, MA: Harvard University Press, 1998), 66.

[26] Heidegger, *Plato's Sophist*, 112. For specific mention of the "non-conceptually understandable," see Heidegger, *Basic Problems of Phenomenology*, 309.

[27] McDowell notes: "Kant says... 'intuitions without concepts are blind'. Similarly... movements of limbs without concepts are mere happenings, not expressions of agency." McDowell, *Mind and World*, 89.

Merleau-Ponty makes a similar point playing off the intellectualist against the empiricist. For the intellectualist, "judgment is everywhere pure sensation is not, which is to say everywhere."[28] For McDowell, *mind* is everywhere that the pure *given* is not, which is to say, "all the way out." Precisely because the myth of the pure Given is dead, we must understand our experience as conceptually permeated through and through. Thus, like a vulture, the Myth of the Mental feeds off the carcass of the Myth of the Given.

4. What is Expertise?

McDowell and Heidegger both agree with Aristotle that practical wisdom is a kind of expertise acquired as second nature. So I suggest that to decide who is right as to whether skilled perception and action must be permeated by conceptual rationality we turn to the phenomena and take a look at how one becomes an expert in any domain, and at what capacities an expert thereby acquires.

While infants acquire skills by imitation and trial and error, in our formal instruction we start with rules. The rules, however, seem to give way to more flexible responses as we become skilled. We should therefore be suspicious of the cognitivist assumption that as we become experts our rules become unconscious. Indeed, our experience suggests that rules are like training wheels. We may need such aids when learning to ride a bicycle, but we must eventually set them aside if we are to become skilled cyclists. To assume that the rules we once consciously followed become unconscious is like assuming that, when we finally learn to ride a bike, the training wheels that were required for us to be able to ride in the first place must have become invisible. The actual phenomenon suggests that to become experts we must switch from detached rule following to a more involved and situation-specific way of coping.

Indeed, if learners feel that they can act only if they have reasons to guide them, this attitude will stunt their skill acquisition. A study of student nurses, for example, showed that those who remained detached and followed rules never progressed beyond competence, while only those who became emotionally involved and took to heart their successes and failures developed into experts.[29] This finding suggests that, if something goes wrong, the way to achieve expertise is to resist a disinterested, objective examination of the problem and the temptation to formulate sophisticated rules to prevent it from happening again, and,

[28] Merleau-Ponty, *Phenomenology of Perception*, 34.
[29] Patricia A. Benner, Cristine A. Tanner, and Catherine A. Chesla, *Expertise in Nursing Practice: Caring, Clinical Judgment, and Ethics* (New York: Springer, 1996).

instead, to stay involved, taking failures to heart and glorying in one's successes. Such emotional involvement seems to be necessary to facilitate the switchover from detached, analytical rule following to an entirely different engaged, holistic mode of experience—from left to right hemisphere processing, one might say.

If the learner stays involved, he develops beyond competence by sharpening his perceptual ability to make refined discriminations. Among many situations, all seen as similar with respect to a plan or perspective, the expert learns to discriminate those situations requiring one reaction in order to succeed from those demanding another. That is, with enough experience in a variety of situations, all seen from the same perspective but requiring different tactical decisions, the expert, without awareness of the process, gradually decomposes this class of situations into subclasses, each of which requires a specific response. This allows the successful intuitive situational response that is characteristic of expertise.

A chess grandmaster facing a position, for example, experiences a compelling sense of the issue and the best move. In a popular kind of chess called lightning chess, the whole game has to be played in two minutes. Under such time pressure, grandmasters must make some of their moves as quickly as they can move their arms—less than a second a move—and yet they can still play master-level games. When the grandmaster is playing lightning chess, as far as he can tell, he is simply responding to the patterns on the board. At this speed he must depend entirely on perception and not at all on analysis and comparison of alternatives.

Thus, phenomenology suggests that, although many forms of expertise pass through a stage in which one needs reasons to guide action, after much involved experience, the learner develops a way of coping in which reasons play no role. After responding to an estimated million specific chess positions in the process of becoming a chess master, the master, confronted with a new position, spontaneously does something similar to what has previously worked and, lo and behold, it usually works. In general, instead of relying on rules and standards to decide on or to justify her actions, the expert immediately responds to the current concrete situation.

Recent brain imaging research confirms that amateur and expert chess players use different parts of their brain. Researchers concluded that "The distribution of focal brain activity during chess playing points to differences in the mechanisms of brain processing and functional brain organization between grandmasters and amateurs."[30]

---

[30] Ognjen Amidzic et al., "Patterns of Focal Y-Bursts in Chess Players: Grandmasters Call on Regions of the Brain Not Used So Much by Less Skilled Amateurs", *Nature*, 412 (9 Aug. 2001), 603.

To make this point clear, we need to distinguish between two kinds of rules. There are first of all *the rules of the game*. In chess, these rules include the particular moves each piece is allowed to make, the time limit placed on the game, rules against cheating, etc. There are, secondly, *tactical rules*. These heuristic rules provide guidelines for how one can best respond to each type of situation. They are acquired through lessons and coaching.

It is misleading to think that the rules of the game must be *internalized*, that is, stored in the mind. Rather, these rules are normally experienced in the background as a limit on what appears as worth doing. In this way the expert is *sensitive* to the rules of the game even if he is not following the rules consciously or unconsciously. Even if he can't remember the rules, they nonetheless govern his coping by determining what looks permissible. But he normally can be led to remember or at least acknowledge the rules when he is told them, and he knows he must conform to them or be penalized.

In the special case of games, then, we can profit from McDowell's suggestion that we think of such rules as having become second nature. But we should bear in mind that, when they function as second nature, they do not function as rules we consciously or unconsciously follow but as a landscape on the basis of which skilled coping and reasoning takes place. Only in this sense can the rules of the game be said to guide thought and action.

In the case of tactical rules, however, the master may make moves that are entirely intuitive and contrary to any preconceived plan. In such instances, when asked why he did what he did, he may be at a loss to reconstruct a reasoned account of his actions because there is none. Indeed, as we have seen, the phenomena suggest that an expert has long since abandoned general rules in the same way that bikers set aside their training wheels. Thus, when an expert is forced to give the *reasons* that led to his action, his account will necessarily be a retroactive *rationalization* that shows at best that the expert can retrieve from memory the general principles and tactical rules he once followed as a competent performer.

Consequently, if one followed the reconstructed rules articulated by an expert, one would not exhibit expertise but mere competence, and that is exactly what has happened. "Expert Systems" based on the rules so-called knowledge engineers elicited from experts were at best competent.[31] It seems that, instead of using rules they no longer remembered, as the AI researchers supposed, the experts

---

[31] Computers performed miserably at chess when they operated exclusively with heuristic rules. They couldn't play Grandmaster chess until they were powerful enough to look at a million moves a second and calculate all possible moves and responses as far as ten moves into the future, and only then use rules to evaluate the end positions. Grandmasters, in contrast, facing an unfamiliar situation, can count out and analyze only a few hundred moves.

were forced to remember rules they no longer used. Indeed, as far as anyone could tell, the experts weren't following any rules at all.[32]

So it seems clear that rules needn't play any role in *producing* skilled behavior. This is bad news for cognitivists, but McDowell is not a cognitivist. He rightly rejects the idea that skilled behavior is actually *caused* by unconscious rules. His view is much more subtle and plausible, namely, that, thanks to socialization, experts conform to reasons that can be retroactively reconstructed. After all, there must *be* one structure in common to situations that reliably solicit one type of tactical response and another to those situations that reliably solicit another. It seems one ought to, at least in principle, be able to articulate this structure in terms of reasons. But all we have a right to conclude from our phenomenology of expertise is that there must be some detectable invariant features in what J. J. Gibson calls the ambient optic array and that human beings and animals can learn to respond to them. *These features, although available to the perceptual system, needn't be available to the mind.*

We can understand this inaccessibility if we consider the way simulated neural networks can be programmed to produce reliable responses. For example, nets have been programmed to distinguish sonar echoes from mines from those from rocks. Such nets are given no rules, nor are they told what features of the signal are relevant. They are simply exposed to tens of thousands of examples and their at-first-random correct responses are reinforced.

In one very limited sense, any successfully trained multilayer neural net can be interpreted in terms of features—not everyday features but highly abstract ones. But in the case of multilayered nets that are devoted to implementing expertise, these highly abstract features are not interpretable as features that a mind could possibly experience. To construct a semantic account of what a network that has learned certain discriminations has learned, each node one level above the input nodes could, on the basis of connections to it, be interpreted as detecting when one of a certain set of input patterns is present. (Some of the patterns will be the ones used in training and some will never have been used.) If the set of input patterns that a particular node detects is given an invented name (it almost certainly won't have a name in our vocabulary), the node could be interpreted

---

[32] For example, when Air Force instructor pilots teach beginning pilots how to scan their instruments, they teach the rule that they themselves were taught, and, as far as they know, still use. At one point, however, Air Force psychologists studied the eye movements of instructors during simulated flights and found, to everyone's surprise, that the instructor pilots were not following the rule they were teaching. In fact, as far as the psychologists could determine, they weren't following any rule at all. See J. DeMaio et al., *Visual Scanning: Comparisons between Students and Instructor Pilots*, AFHRL-TR-76-10, AD-A023 634 (William Air Force Base, AZ: Flying Training Division, Air Force Human Resources Laboratory, 1976).

as detecting the highly abstract feature so named. Hence, every node one level above the input level can be characterized as a feature detector. Similarly, every node a level above these nodes can be interpreted as detecting a higher-order feature that is defined as the presence of one of a specified set of patterns among the first-level feature detectors. And so on up the hierarchy. The top features could be those in an ambient optic array that corresponded to the significance of a situation, and the net's output would then correspond to the response solicited by that situation.

Herbert Simon has estimated that an expert chess player can distinguish roughly 50,000 types of positions. This estimate presupposes the unsupported assumption that the master perceives an alphabet of chunks that he puts together by rule in order to recognize types of positions. But the speed of lightning chess suggests rather that the master isn't following rules at all. He is able to directly discriminate perhaps hundreds of thousands of types of whole positions. I say "perhaps" since there is, in principle, no way to count the types. If there were, we would have to define the types in terms of their features, but, since these would have to be very-high-order invariants in the optic array detected by high-level hidden nodes in our neural net, we, in principle, have no access to them except to see that a certain position solicits a certain move.

Phenomenologists therefore disagree with conceptualists in that phenomenologists claim that a study of expertise shows that nameable features are irrelevant to the current state of mind of the master when he acts. Granted one could, in principle, name each position or at least point to it, there is no reason to think that one could name or point to what it is about a position that makes it the type of position that requires this particular response. Abstract higher-order features detected by the hidden layers of a neural network would explain that if we could understand them. But, as we have just seen, there is no reason to believe that these higher-order features must be the sort of features we can think. *Nothing about the position need be nameable and thinkable as a reason for acting.* If this is so, expert coping isn't even *implicitly* rational in the sense of being responsive to reasons that have become habitual but could be reconstructed.

If, as Robert Brandom claims, "Sellars' principle [is] that *grasping a concept is mastering the use of a word,*"[33] then, according to Sellarsians, master chess play is nonconceptual. Yet, clearly, what is given to the chess master in his experience of the board isn't a *bare* Given. In being solicited to respond to a chess position, the

[33] Robert Brandom, *Articulating Reasons: An Introduction to Inferentialism* (Cambridge, MA: Harvard University Press, 2009), 6 (italics in original).

chess master has a take on "the layout of reality."[34] It follows that he can be mistaken. Thus, the pure perceiving of the chess master, as well as that of the *phronimos* and, indeed, the expert in any skill domain, even everyday coping, has a kind of *intentional* content; it just isn't *conceptual* content. A "bare Given" and the "thinkable" are not our only alternatives. We must accept the possibility that our ground-level coping opens up the world by opening us up to a *meaningful* Given—a Given that is *nonconceptual* but not *bare*.

How, then, should we characterize this conceptually pure yet meaningful given? Heidegger and Merleau-Ponty hold, in effect, that embodied copers directly respond to what Gibson, who was influenced by Merleau-Ponty, calls *affordances*.[35] Food affords eating, doors afford going in and out, floors afford walking on, etc. Charles Taylor describes the phenomenon:

As I navigate my way along the path up the hill, my mind totally absorbed in anticipating the difficult conversation I'm going to have at my destination, I treat the different features of the terrain as obstacles, supports, openings, invitations to tread more warily, or run freely, and so on. Even when I'm not thinking of them these things have those relevancies for me.[36]

As Taylor makes clear, responding to affordances does not require noticing them. Indeed, to best respond to affordances (whether animal or social, prelinguistic or linguistic) one must not notice them *as* affordances, but, rather, as Heidegger says, they "withdraw" and we simply "press into" them.

Note too that the affordances detected and responded to by active, involved beings are situation-specific.[37] This door does not simply afford going in and out but affords going in and out cautiously, and/or quickly, and/or silently, and/or unobtrusively, that is, in whatever way is called for by the whole situation. Or, to take another example, given our socialized second nature, in dealing with people, we are drawn to the right distance to stand from *this* specific person, in *this* light, in *this* room, with *this* background noise, and so forth. It is this necessary situational specificity of skillful coping that Aristotle and Heidegger noted in the case of the *phronimos*, and which led Heidegger to conclude that skillful coping is nonconceptual. We respond to affordances in this situation-specific

---

[34] McDowell, *Mind and World*, 26.

[35] There are cases when the affordance is relative to the *disembodied* mind. To Kasparov, but not to a merely competent player, a specific situation on the chessboard affords checkmate.

[36] Charles Taylor, "Merleau-Ponty and the Epistemological Picture", in Taylor Carman and Mark B. N. Hansen (eds), *The Cambridge Companion to Merleau-Ponty* (Cambridge: Cambridge University Press, 2005), 34.

[37] This specificity of *coping activity* corresponds to the situational specificity of perception that Sean Kelly uses to demonstrate that *perception* is non-conceptual. See Kelly, "Non-Conceptual Content".

way when we are intensely involved in what we are doing, as when negotiating a dangerous intersection, and also, as Taylor's example makes clear, when we are completely absorbed in something else. In either case, we are capable of coping concretely without *thinking* at all. Indeed, in their direct dealing with affordances, adults, infants, and animals respond alike.[38]

5. The Space of Motivations

But what room could there be for such a nonconceptual given between the space of causes and the space of reasons? It seems that either one is pushed around like a thing by meaningless physical and psychological forces, or else one's reasons, explicit or implicit, motivate one's actions. Merleau-Ponty faces this challenge by introducing a third way one can be led to cope—a way he calls *motivation.*

This is not a psychological concept for him but a perceptual one. It names the way we are directly responsive to the other-than-rational demands of our situation. In short, it is a name for the way affordances solicit one to act. As Mark Wrathall, who makes this important point, puts it:

The fundamental workings of motivations are found in the way that our environment and body work together to dispose us to particular ways of acting and experiencing. The world works by drawing on our skillful bodily dispositions.[39]

Or, as Merleau-Ponty tells us:

In perception we do not think the object and we do not think ourselves thinking it, we are given over to the object and we merge into this body which is better informed than we are about the world, and about the motives we have and the means at our disposal.[40]

My body, according to Merleau-Ponty, is drawn to get a maximal grip on its environment. As he puts it:

My body is geared into the world when my perception presents me with a spectacle as varied and as clearly articulated as possible, and when my motor intentions, as they unfold, receive the responses they expect from the world.[41]

---

[38] Because such a response is clearly possible for *animals*, it can't be conceptual in McDowell's sense of the term since, according to McDowell, animals don't have concepts.

[39] Mark A. Wrathall, "Motives, Reasons, and Causes", in Taylor Carman and Mark B. N. Hansen (eds), *The Cambridge Companion to Merleau-Ponty* (Cambridge: Cambridge University Press, 2005), 118.

[40] Merleau-Ponty, *Phenomenology of Perception*, 238.

[41] Merleau-Ponty, *Phenomenology of Perception*, 250.

Thus, perception is, in its own way, normative. As Sean Kelly puts it:

[I]t is part of my visual experience that *my body is drawn to move*, or, at any rate, that *the context should change*, in a certain way. These are inherently normative, rather than descriptive, features of visual experience. They don't represent in some objective, determinate fashion the way the world *is*, they say something about how the world *ought to be* for me to see it better.[42]

Or, more generally:

[W]e are constantly sensitive not only to what we perceive but also, and essentially, to *how well* our experience measures up to our perceptual needs and desires.[43]

More generally still: As we cope, we experience ourselves to be getting a better or worse grip on the situation. Such coping has *satisfaction conditions* but it does not have success *conditions*. Rather, it has what one might call *conditions of improvement*.[44] Its satisfaction conditions are normative rather than descriptive. True to the phenomenon of affordance and response, plus the tendency to achieve maximal grip, Merleau-Ponty is led to introduce, between the space of causes and the space of reasons, what one might call *the space of motivations*.[45]

Animals, paralinguistic infants, and everyday experts like us all live in this space. Of course, unlike infants and animals, *we* can deliberate. When a master has to deliberate in chess or in any skill domain, it's because there has been some sort of disturbance that has disrupted his intuitive response. Perhaps the situation is so unusual that no immediate response is called forth. Or several responses are solicited with equal pull.

In such cases, there are two types of deliberation available to the expert. In the first type, the expert stays involved and tests and refines his intuition. For example, if the situation does not solicit an immediate intuitive response because certain aspects of the situation are slightly, yet disturbingly, different from what would make one completely comfortable with a specific move, the master chess player contemplates the differences, looking for a move that keeps all intuitively desirable options open while reducing his sense of uneasiness. This type of deliberation yields no reasons. It is useful precisely because it clears the way for an immediate intuitive response.[46]

---

[42] Sean D. Kelly, "Seeing Things in Merleau-Ponty", in Taylor Carman and Mark B. N. Hansen (eds), *The Cambridge Companion to Merleau-Ponty* (Cambridge: Cambridge University Press, 2005), 87.

[43] Kelly, "Seeing Things in Merleau-Ponty", 97.

[44] For details, see Chapter 7, this volume.

[45] Merleau-Ponty calls the sort of intentionality definitive of the space of motivations, *motor intentionality*. Sean Kelly works out the special features of this kind of intentionality, as opposed to the conceptual kind, in his paper, "The Logic of Motor Intentionality", available at: <http://ist-socrates.berkeley.edu/~hdreyfus/188_s05/pdf/Kelly%20Logic%20of%20Motor%20Intentionality.pdf>.

[46] For more details see, Dreyfus and Dreyfus, *Mind over Machine*, 36–41.

If no response is forthcoming, however, the only alternative is a kind of rational deliberation in which one becomes detached and views the situation as an object with decontextualized features and then reasons out what to do. In chess, such analysis involves counting out the consequences of each reasonable move. In more general terms, it might mean making a list of options and their utilities and calculating which action is optimal. Such responses, however, lose the situational specificity of expertise, and so are inferior to an expert's intuitive response.

Fortunately, the expert usually does not need to calculate. If he has had enough experience and stays involved, he will find himself responding in a masterful way before he has time to think. Just as Aristotle, Heidegger, and Merleau-Ponty saw, such mastery requires a rich *perceptual* repertoire—the ability to respond to subtle differences in the appearance of perhaps hundreds of thousands of situations—but it requires no *conceptual* repertoire at all. This holds true for such refined skills as chess, jazz improvisation, sports, martial arts, etc., but equally for everyday skills such as cooking dinner, crossing a busy street, carrying on a conversation, or just getting around in the world.[47]

6. Nonconceptual Coping and the Justification of Judgments

So far we have seen that, if we understand concepts as context-free principles or rules that could be used to guide actions or at least make them intelligible, a phenomenology of expert coping shows concepts to be absent or even to get in the way of a masterful response to the specific situation. Nor can such thinkable content be reconstructed after the fact by deliberation. More basically, if concepts must be linguistic, Gibson's account of our direct pickup of affordances as high-order invariants in the optic array, and neural net considerations as to how the brain might detect such invariants, suggest that expertise does not require concepts.

---

[47] Sellarsians might counter that all coping, even the immediate response to the perceived situation in chess, is nonetheless conceptual, in that the master's play is crucially informed by an understanding of what it is to "win," to "capture" a piece, legal and illegal moves, etc. Someone who did not understand these concepts, including having the ability to use them properly in other contexts, would not be appropriately regarded as playing chess. But it is not obvious that the discrimination of positions, legal from illegal moves, etc. must be linguistic, and so conceptual by McDowell's Sellarsian standards. See John Haugeland's imaginary counterexample of super-monkeys that play chess but don't have language in John Haugeland, *Having Thought: Essays in the Metaphysics of Mind* (Cambridge, MA: Harvard University Press, 1998), 249–57. In any case, the kind of conceptuality of the rules of the game is the sort that we have seen falls legitimately under McDowell's account of second nature, but it doesn't show that there need be any *thinkable* content underlying the *execution* of the skill of playing the game that can be reconstructed in deliberation.

Indeed, the basis of expert coping may well be the sort of features that the expert could not be aware of and would not be able to think. In both cases, then, masterful action does not seem to require or even to allow placement in the space of reasons.

But these objections may seem to miss McDowell's basic point that, in so far as perception *justifies* our *judgments*, it *must be conceptual all the way out*. As McDowell puts it:

When we trace justifications back, the last thing we come to is still *a thinkable content*; not something more ultimate than that, a bare pointing to a bit of the Given.[48]

Lewis was, indeed, fundamentally mistaken in thinking that the Given had to be *ineffable* and *indubitable* in order to ground judgments, but, as we have seen, the Given needn't be understood as *bare*. It can be *pure* in the sense of nonconceptual, and yet, like affordances, still have motivational content. Conceptualists like McDowell point out, however, that the idea that any nonconceptual given, be it intuitive, practical, normative, skillful, or what have you, could make a contribution *to justification* is unintelligible. This is an important objection to the view Lewis defended but not to the phenomenologists' claim that to perform its world-disclosing function perception must be nonconceptual.

In so far as McDowell speaks of "our unproblematic openness to the world"[49] and of how "we find ourselves always already engaged with the world,"[50] he seems to agree with the phenomenologists that perception has a function more basic than justification. As Heidegger and Merleau-Ponty (as well as Wittgenstein) have argued, we can only relate to objects and make judgments about them in so far as they show up on the background of the world—and the world is not a belief system but is opened to us only through our unthinking and unthinkable engaged perception and coping.

McDowell, however, *only seems* to be in agreement with these existential phenomenologists. For McDowell, the world can only be the totality of objects, events, and states of affairs. Many of these are, indeed, directly perceivable, and we do depend on beliefs based on perception to justify our judgments about them. But this sort of openness to the world is not the most basic function of perception. We directly perceive affordances and respond to them without beliefs and justifications being involved. Moreover, these affordances are interrelated, and it is our familiarity with the whole context of affordances that gives us our ability to orient ourselves and find our way about. As Heidegger puts it:

---

[48] McDowell, *Mind and World*, 28–9 (my italics).
[49] McDowell, *Mind and World*, 155.   [50] McDowell, *Mind and World*, 134.

[W]hat is first of all "given"...is the "for writing," the "for going in and out,"..."for sitting." That is, writing, going-in-and-out, sitting, and the like are what we are *a priori* involved with. What we know when we "know our way around."[51]

Heidegger might seem to be a conceptualist himself since he continues: "My being in the world *is* nothing other than this already-operating-with-understanding."[52] But when he introduces the term "understanding," Heidegger explains (with a little help from the translator) that he means a kind of know-how:

In German we say that someone can vorstehen something—literally, stand in front of or ahead of it, that is, stand at its head, administer, manage, preside over it. This is equivalent to saying that he versteht sich darauf, understands in the sense of being skilled or expert at it, has the know-how of it.[53]

Merleau-Ponty also appeals to a nonintellectual kind of understanding:

We understand the thing as we understand a new kind of behavior, not, that is, through any intellectual operation of subsumption, but by taking up on our own account the mode of existence that the observable signs adumbrate before us.[54]

And, of course, such givens are not bare givens. As Heidegger insists:

Every act of having something in front of oneself and perceiving it is, in and of itself, a "having" something *as* something.... However, this as-structure is not necessarily related to predication. In dealing with something, I do not perform any thematical predicative. assertions.[55]

7. Where Concepts Come In

If nonconceptual perception and coping is necessary for world disclosing, and there is no way nonconceptual perceiving could ground judgments, then we must ask how the *nonconceptual given is converted into a given with conceptual content* so that perception can do its justificatory job. McDowell seems to rely on the

[51] Martin Heidegger, *Logik: Die Frage Nach Der Wahrheit* (Gesamtausgabe, 21; Frankfurt am Main: Vittorio Klostermann, 1976), 144.

[52] This disclosing function of perception we share with animals and infants. Heidegger, however, connects such understanding with our understanding of our identity. In that connection, we should note that mere coping with affordances gives animals and human beings what Heidegger calls an environment but not a world. To open a *world* in Heidegger's sense requires that the affordances that matter to us and draw us in depend not merely on our needs and previous experience, as with animals, but on what matters to us given our identities, and we are capable of changing our identities and so our world. This is an important difference between human beings and animals, but since we are focusing on the role of perception in giving us a background on the basis of which we can perceive objects and justify our beliefs about them, we needn't go into it here.

[53] Heidegger, *Basic Problems of Phenomenology*, 276.

[54] Merleau-Ponty, *Phenomenology of Perception*, 319.   [55] Heidegger, *Logik*, 144.

Myth of the Mental, the idea that pure perception is impossible so perception and coping must somehow always already be conceptual, to avoid facing this question. In his book *Body and World,* Samuel Todes, however, sees the question of how conceptual content arises from nonconceptual content as the central puzzle bequeathed to philosophers by Kant.[56] He, therefore, proposes to work out a detailed phenomenological account of how our embodied, nonconceptual perceptual and coping skills open a world, and then to suggest a possible answer to how such skills could be transformed into skills with conceptual content.

To begin with, Todes goes beyond Merleau-Ponty in showing how our world-disclosing perceptual experience is structured by the actual structure of our bodies. As we have seen, for Merleau-Ponty, the lived body is the source of the motor intentionality whereby we move to get a better and better grip on our surroundings. But Merleau-Ponty never tells us what our bodies are actually like and how their structure affects our experience. Todes notes that our body has a front/back and up/down orientation. It can move forward more easily than backward and can successfully cope only with what is in front of it. He then describes how, in order to explore features of our surrounding world and orient ourselves in it, we have to be balanced within a vertical field that we do not produce, effectively directed in a circumstantial field (toward one aspect of that field rather than another), and appropriately set to respond to the specific thing we are encountering within that field. Perceptual receptivity is thus an embodied, normative, skilled accomplishment.

Todes then works out twelve perceptual categories that correspond to Kant's conceptual categories and suggests how our nonconceptual coping categories can be transformed into the conceptual ones. But this makes all the more urgent the question: Granted that, when we are transparently responding to affordances, we do not encounter *context-independent objects* with reidentifiable *properties* about which we can then make judgments, how can our transparent coping with affordances become explicit coping with objects?

Heidegger briefly takes up the question in *Being and Time.* He points out that we have skills that enable us, step by step, to transform our perception of affordances into the perception of context-free objects, and the content of our skilled responses to perceived whole patterns into articulable conceptual content. Heidegger notes that when there is a problem with an affordance we can change our relation to it. For example, when hammering is going well the hammer is not what I focus on. The hammer simply affords hammering; the less I perceive it the better. If, however, the hammering is unusually difficult, I may experience the

---

[56] See Todes, *Body and World.*

hammer as having the *situational aspect* of being *too heavy* under these conditions. And should things go even more badly so that I have to abandon my activity, the hammer may appear as an object that has the context-free *property* of weighing five pounds.[57]

What makes us special, then, isn't that, unlike animals, we can *respond directly* to the conceptual structure of our environment; it's that, unlike animals, we can *transform* our unthinking nonconceptual engagement, and thereby encounter new, thinkable, structures. It is important to be clear that, *pace* the rationalist tradition that runs from Hegel to Brandom, these conceptual structures are not *implicit* in our involved experience any more than reasons for our actions are implicit in our expert coping, or than the detached attitude is implicit in the engaged one. Rather, according to existential phenomenologists like Heidegger, Merleau-Ponty, and Todes, analytic attention brings about a radical transformation of the affordances given to absorbed coping. Only then can we have an experience of objects with properties, about which we can form beliefs, make judgments, and justify inferences. At the same time, however, this transformation covers up the nonconceptual perception and coping that made our openness to the world possible in the first place.

This cover-up may account for the fact that McDowell does not attempt to explore the content of nonconceptual coping that opens us to the layout of reality. If he did, he might be led to shake off the Myth of the Mental and agree with the existential phenomenologists he cites approvingly that our opening a world—and much of our coping in it—need not be thinkable, but, rather, is nonlinguistic and nonconceptual. That would, indeed, be a framework for reflection that stood a chance of making traditional philosophy (including Hegelian rationalism) obsolete!

Conclusion

McDowell has taught us a lot about what is special about human experience, and he has raised the crucial question as to how perception grounds knowledge. But he has left aside how the nonconceptual perceptual and coping skills we share with animals and infants open us to a reality more basic than knowledge. Given the availability of rich descriptions of perceptual affordances and of everyday know-how, however, couldn't analytic philosophers profit from pursuing the

---

[57] Heidegger, *Being and Time*, 98–9, 412. For more details see Hubert L. Dreyfus, *Being-in-the-World: A Commentary on Heidegger's Being and Time, Division I* (Cambridge, MA: MIT Press, 1991).

question of how these nonconceptual capacities are converted into conceptual ones—how minds grow out of being-in-the-world—rather than denying the existence of the nonconceptual?

Conversely, phenomenology needs help from the analysts. Phenomenologists lack a detailed and convincing account of how rationality and language grow out of nonconceptual and nonlinguistic coping. Heidegger made a start and Todes sharpened the question and made important suggestions, but he didn't live to work out the details. The lack of any worked-out, step-by-step genesis of the conceptual categories that structure the space of reasons from the perceptual ones that structure the space of motivations might well encourage all philosophers to contribute to the task, but so far it seems to have encouraged analytic philosophers to continue their work on the upper stories of the edifice of knowledge, perfecting their rigorous, fascinating, and detailed accounts of the linguistic, conceptual, and inferential capacities that are uniquely human, while leaving the ground floor—the nonlinguistic, nonconceptual discriminations of everyday perceivers and copers such as infants, animals, and experts—to the phenomenologists.

The time is ripe to follow McDowell and others in putting aside the outmoded opposition between analytic and continental philosophy and to begin the challenging collaborative task of showing how our conceptual capacities grow out of our nonconceptual ones—how the ground floor of pure perception and receptive coping supports the conceptual upper stories of the edifice of knowledge. Why not work together to understand our grasp of reality from the ground up? Surely, that way we are more likely to succeed than trying to build from the top down.

PART III

Phenomenology and the Human Sciences

6

Holism and Hermeneutics (1980)

I

Of the many issues surrounding the new interest in hermeneutics, current debate has converged upon two:

1. Is there any difference between the natural and the human sciences?
2. If there were such a difference, what personal and political difference would it make?

In this chapter I will argue first that there is an essential difference between theoretical and practical holism and thus there is an essential difference between the natural and human sciences. I will then argue that, if one holds that there is no crucial difference between things and people, one must embrace some form of nihilism—a way of life in which all values have the same value, everything is equal, or, to put it another way, there are no meaningful differences. Richard Rorty's view, that how we treat people depends solely upon what sort of lives we happen to prefer, is one form such nihilism can take. However, if there *is* a crucial difference between self-interpreting human beings and other sorts of entities, one can counter the nihilistic possibility of what Rorty calls "conversations" between those who have opposed "preferences" with the possibility of genuine conflicts of interpretation as to the serious issues worth conversing about.

Such conflicts cannot be settled by traditional philosophical or empirical argument since traditional debates operate within a taken-for-granted understanding of what considerations can be taken seriously. In conflicts of interpretation, moreover, the question is not which view of what is important corresponds to the way things are in themselves, but rather, which is the better account of our condition, i.e. which allows a deeper appreciation of the cultural commitments we cannot help sharing because they make us what we are.

II

Let us first consider theoretical holism. This view that science involves interpretation and that interpretation is a kind of translation is generating a great deal of interest and spreading much confusion in current philosophical circles. It holds that the reason the social sciences cannot live up to the scientific objectivity of the natural sciences is that there is no such objectivity even in natural science. The very conception of objective knowledge, it is said, is a philosophical mistake left over from Descartes's rationalist interpretation of the implications of Galilean science. This critique of the accepted view of scientific method emphasizes the fact that science, like any other human cognitive activity, involves interpretation. Even natural scientists must determine what are to count as the relevant facts and what their theoretical significance is, so that there is no possibility of finding neutral uninterpreted data for deciding between competing hypotheses.

Pierre Duhem already noted in the last century that in science individual sentences are not tested against experience one by one, but only as a whole via a theory. In our time philosophers of science have worked out the implications of this view arguing that in science data are what Hanson called "theory laden." In verifying a theory we move in a circle from hypothesis to data, and data to hypothesis, without ever encountering any bare facts which could call our whole theory into question. Thus we arrive at the "anarchist" philosophy of science of Paul Feyerabend, which concludes that there is no fundamental difference between the truth of the natural and the social sciences or, indeed, between these and witchcraft since there can be no objective verification, only the confrontation of incommensurable holistic interpretations. The only difference between the natural and the social sciences, on this view, is that in natural science this battle of interpretations is repressed whereas the social sciences, for some unknown reason, have never succeeded in covering up the conflict.

If one accepts this general approach, the philosopher's job becomes one of meta-interpretation. He tries to understand these incommensurate interpretations of reality by making them commensurable. Rorty calls this "discourse about as-yet incommensurable discourse" hermeneutics, and claims that this understanding of hermeneutics "links up with the use of the term by such writers as Gadamer."[1] Dagfinn Føllesdal has pointed out that it also connects with Quine, who has argued that any attempt to understand another discourse must be like cracking a code, and with Donald Davidson, who has developed further Quine's

---

[1] Richard Rorty, *Philosophy and the Mirror of Nature* (Princeton: Princeton University Press, 1979), 343–4.

notion of "radical translation" by pointing out that in trying to make sense of another language or culture we must try to maximize agreement concerning what seems to us obviously true and false.[2] Once this project of radical translation has succeeded, the hermeneutic interpreter can understand some alien episode in his own culture, such as Ptolemaic science (Thomas Kuhn, for example, now says that his studies of Aristotelian science are hermeneutic[3]) or some other culture with a seemingly alien view of reality (as, for example, the cultural interpretations of Clifford Geertz[4]).

The important point for Rorty is that hermeneutics is always necessary whenever there is a failure of communication between competing discourses. Thus hermeneutics becomes necessary whenever there is a breakdown in understanding, whether this be between cultures or between conflicting paradigms of explanation in the natural or the social sciences. Conversely, it follows too that in any of these cases we can dispense with hermeneutics when the two competing discourses have been translated into each other or when one of them has driven out the other. In the case of the natural or social sciences, commensurability signals that a "scientific revolution" is over and the practitioners have returned to a normal shared framework.

This notion of interpretation as translation between theories leads Rorty to the conclusion that there is no important difference between the natural and the social sciences.

It might be the case that all future human societies will be (as a result, perhaps, of ubiquitous technocratic totalitarianism) humdrum variations on our own. But contemporary science (which already seems so hopeless for explaining acupuncture, the migration of butterflies, and so on) may soon come to seem as badly off as Aristotle's hylomorphism. [The important distinction] is not the line between the human and the non-human but between that portion of the field of inquiry where we feel rather uncertain that we have the right vocabulary at hand and that portion where we feel rather certain that we do. This *does*, at the moment, roughly coincide with the distinction between the fields of the Geistes and the Naturwissenschaften. But this coincidence may be *mere* coincidence.[5]

Exponents of hermeneutics as radical translation between incommensurable discourses reach these radical conclusions precisely because they treat all understanding as theoretical. From their point of view a theory is made up of the systematic interrelation of distinguishable elements. In the case of a scientific

---

[2] Dagfinn Føllesdal, "Experience and Meaning", in Samuel Guttenplan (ed.), *Mind and Language* (Oxford: Clarendon Press, 1975), 38.

[3] Thomas Kuhn, *The Essential Tension* (Chicago: University of Chicago Press, 1977), p. xiii.

[4] Clifford Geertz, *The Interpretation of Cultures* (New York: Basic Books, 1973).

[5] Rorty, *Philosophy and the Mirror of Nature*, 352.

theory these elements are related by explicit propositions stating laws; in the case of common sense, which they construe as a theory, these elements are related by conscious and unconscious posits and beliefs. Whether explicitly expressed in sentences or implicitly held as behavioral dispositions these beliefs can be regarded as hypotheses which could in principle be stated. As Quine puts it:

[H]ypotheses in various fields of inquiry may tend to receive their confirmation from different kinds of investigation, but this should in no way conflict with our seeing them all as hypotheses. We talk of framing hypotheses. Actually we inherit the main ones, growing up as we do in a going culture. The continuity of belief is due to the retention, at each particular time of most beliefs.[6]

Thus, on this view, even practical common sense is a crude scientific theory:

...science is itself a continuation of common sense. The scientist is indistinguishable from the common man in his sense of evidence, except that the scientist is more careful.[7]

On this model, understanding a person from an alien culture or understanding a radically different sort of science involves making a total theory about a total theory, i.e. making a translation into your language of the theory implied in the other person's behavior or language. This view thus treats all understanding as an *epistemological* problem, as a question of theoretical knowledge, so, on this view, there is no important difference between the knowledge sought in the social and the natural sciences.

III

On the opposed view worked out by Heidegger, *theoretical* holism with its account of interpretation as *translation* must be distinguished from what one might call *practical* holism, which thinks of interpretation as *explication*.

Practical understanding is holistic in an entirely different way from theoretical understanding. Although practical understanding—everyday coping with things and people—involves explicit beliefs and hypotheses, these can only be meaningful in specific contexts and against a background of shared practices. And just as we can learn to swim without consciously or unconsciously acquiring a theory of swimming, we acquire these social background practices by being brought up in them, not by forming beliefs and learning rules. A specific example of such a social skill is the conversational competence involved in standing the correct

---

[6] Willard V. O. Quine and J. S. Ullian, *The Web of Belief* (New York: Random House, 1978), 81.
[7] Willard V. O. Quine, *The Ways of Paradox and Other Essays* (Cambridge, MA: Harvard University Press, 1976), 233.

distance from another member of the culture depending on whether the other person is male or female, old or young, and whether the conversation involves business, courtship, friendship, etc. More generally, and more importantly, such skills embody a whole cultural interpretation of what it means to be a human being, what a material object is, and, in general, what counts as real. This is why Heidegger in *Being and Time* calls this cultural self-interpretation embodied in our practices "primordial truth." Heidegger, Merleau-Ponty, and Wittgenstein suggest that this inherited background of practices cannot be spelled out in a theory because (1) the background is so pervasive that we cannot make it an object of analysis, and (2) the practices involve skills.[8]

The first argument presupposes the second, since if it were merely the pervasiveness of one's own background which made it inaccessible to theory, it could be made an object of theoretical analysis by another culture, or, perhaps, another stage of one's own culture. For Quine and Davidson all one needs in order to understand another culture or epoch is a *theory* that maximizes agreement as to which beliefs are true and which are false. The fact that these beliefs only make sense in a practical situation against a taken-for-granted cultural background seems to them to present no special problem, since on their view the background can itself be made the explicit object of some form of theoretical detached analysis revealing further beliefs. Husserl attempted to answer Heidegger's practical holism in just this way. In *Crisis* he claims that the transcendental phenomenologist objectifies the horizon or background by "reactivating" our "sedimented" beliefs and "validities."[9] This is also the answer to practical holism implicit in any version of "cognitive science," whether artificial intelligence or information-processing psychology, which proposes to treat the background of practices as a "belief system."[10] For these various versions of theoretical holism the pervasiveness of the background makes the project of explication at worst what Husserl called an "infinite task."

The practical holist's answer to such a theoretical account of the background is twofold.

---

[8] Cultural practices obviously involve a lot more than bodily skills. For example, they include the parks, furniture, etc. which Dilthey called "objectifications of life," symbols, and the general cultural moods which Heidegger calls *befindlichkeiten* and Wittgenstein calls "cultural styles." I will focus my discussion on skills because they are a concern common to Heidegger, Wittgenstein, and Merleau-Ponty, and because the two kinds of holism can be sorted out by distinguishing their differing treatment of skills.

[9] Husserl, *Crisis of European Sciences*, §40.

[10] Roger Schank and Kenneth Colby, *Computer Models of Thought and Language* (San Francisco: W. H. Freeman, 1973).

(1) *What makes up the background is not beliefs,* either explicit or implicit, but habits and customs, embodied in the sort of subtle skills which we exhibit in our everyday interaction with things and people. Foucault calls these social strategies micro-practices. Wittgenstein notes that "[I]t is our *acting,* which lies at the bottom of the language game."[11] While one may, indeed, on reflection treat aspects of the background as specific beliefs, as for example beliefs about how far to stand from people, these ways of acting were not learned as beliefs and it is not as beliefs that they function causally in our behavior. We just do what we have been trained to do. Moreover, as practices, they have a flexibility which is lost when they are converted into propositional knowledge.

(2) If, given the distortion involved in treating skills as propositional knowledge, the theoretical holist attempts to analyze the background not as a belief system but as a set of procedures, he runs into two new problems. (*a*) If skills are to be analyzed in terms of the sort of rules people actually sometimes follow, then the cognitivist will either have to admit a skill for applying these rules, or face an infinite regress. Or, if he says that one doesn't need a rule or a skill for applying a rule, one simply does what the rule requires, then he has to answer Wittgenstein's question: why not just accept that one simply does what the situation requires, without recourse to rules at all? (*b*) If, in the light of these difficulties, the theoretical holist attempts to substitute for the ordinary sort of rule a formal, nonmental rule, as used in computer models, he faces another dead end. A formal rule must be represented as a sequence of operations. But there seem to be no basic movements or ideas to serve as the elements over which such rules would have to operate. Even though bodily skills, for example, are sometimes learned by following rules which dictate a sequence of simple movements, when the performer becomes proficient the simple movements are left behind and a single unified, flexible, purposive pattern of behavior is all that remains. It makes no sense to attempt to capture a skill by using a representation of the original elements used by beginners, since these elements are not integrated into the final skill. And no other simple elements have been proposed. No one has the slightest idea how to construct formal rules for the skills involved in swimming or speaking a language, let alone the skills embodying our understanding of what being means. It seems that the background of practices does not consist in a

---

[11] Ludwig Wittgenstein, *On Certainty* (New York: Harper & Row, 1969), 28, #204.

belief system, a system of rules, or in formalized procedures; indeed, it seems the background does not consist in representations at all.

Heidegger is the first, as far as I know, to have noted this non-cognitive precondition of all understanding, and to have seen its central importance. As he puts it in the language of *Being and Time*:

[T]he "in-order-to," the "for-the-sake-of," and the "with-which" of an involvement... resist any sort of mathematical functionalization; nor are they merely something thought, first posited in an "act of thinking." They are rather relationships in which concernful circumspection as such already dwells.[12]

To emphasize the pervasiveness of this shared background which is the foundation of everyday intelligibility and of scientific theory, Heidegger calls it primordial understanding. Whether we describe and interpret our practices as in hermeneutics, or whether we take the background for granted as in normal science and study the "objective" facts, we necessarily presuppose this background. This means that we are always already in what Heidegger calls the hermeneutic circle of understanding.

In explaining this circle Heidegger distinguishes three ways that explicit understanding involves what he calls *pre-understanding*.[13] This threefold distinction includes, but goes beyond, the insight of theoretical holism that all data are already theory laden. We can define Heidegger's three terms, for which there are no satisfactory single-term English equivalents, as follows:

1. *Vorhabe* (fore-having): The totality of cultural practices (not noticed by theoretical holism) which "have us"[14] or make us who we are, and thus determine what we find intelligible. In any science this is what Kuhn calls the "disciplinary matrix"—the skills a student acquires in becoming a scientist, which enable him to determine what are the scientifically relevant facts.

2. *Vorsicht* (fore-sight): The vocabulary or conceptual scheme we bring to any problem. At any given stage in our culture this is captured in a specific theoretical understanding of what counts as real spelled out by the philosophers. In science, *Vorsicht* is whatever is taken to be the relevant dimensions of the problem.

3. *Vorgriff*: A specific hypothesis which, within the overall theory, can be confirmed or disconfirmed by the data.

---

[12] Heidegger, *Being and Time*, 122.   [13] Heidegger, *Being and Time*, §32.
[14] This is admittedly a forced reading of *Being and Time*, but one which, I think, is true to what Heidegger is trying to get at. In a later marginal note added to his copy of *Sein and Zeit* Heidegger remarks a propos of a passage where he speaks of Dasein *having* a world where it would have been better to speak of a world being given to Dasein. "Dieser 'gebe' entspricht die 'Habe'. Da-sein 'hat' niemals Welt." Martin Heidegger, *Sein und Zeit* (Tübingen: Max Niemeyer, 1977), 441.

We can now use Heidegger's distinctions to highlight the difference between theoretical and practical holism's view of the interpretive circle. The Quinean *theoretical* circle results from what Heidegger calls *Vorsicht*, i.e. from the fact that all verification takes place within a theory, and that there is no way out of the circle of holistic hypotheses and evidence. The Heideggerian *hermeneutic* circle, on the other hand, says that this whole theoretical activity of framing and confirming hypotheses takes place not only on the background of explicit or implicit assumptions but also on a background of practices (the *Vorhabe*) which need not—and indeed cannot—be included as specific presuppositions of the theory, yet already define what could count as a confirmation. Thus all our knowledge, even our attempt to know the background, is always already shaped by what might be called our implicit ontology, an "ontology" which is in our practices as ways of behaving towards things and people, not in our minds as background assumptions which we happen to be taking for granted. Of course, this hermeneutic circle does not impose a restriction we should regret or try to overcome: without such *Vorhabe* we would have no facts and no theories at all.

Much of the confusion concerning hermeneutics in the current literature stems from the fact that Gadamer, who claims to be working out the implications of Heidegger's notion of hermeneutics, never seems to have taken a stand on Heidegger's claim that there is a level of everyday practice (the *Vorhabe*) beneath our theoretical presuppositions and assumptions (the *Vorsicht*). Gadamer often employs the right rhetoric, as when he says:

we always stand within tradition, and this is no objectifying process, i.e., we do not conceive of what tradition says as something other, something alien. It is always part of us … a recognition of ourselves which our later historical judgment would hardly see as a kind of knowledge … [15]

But at times he seems to side with cognitivists like Quine. In describing the hermeneutic pre-understanding, instead of speaking of *Vorhabe*, he speaks of *Vorurteil* (prejudice or pre-judgment), which seems for him to be an implicit belief or assumption:

The isolation of a *prejudice* clearly requires the suspension of its *validity* for us. For so long as our mind is influenced by a prejudice, we do not *know* and consider it as a *judgment*. [16]

Gadamer's claim to be expounding Heideggerian hermeneutics, when, in fact, he fails to distinguish practice and theory, leads Føllesdal, like Rorty, to assimilate *ontological* hermeneutics to Quine and Davidson's *epistemological* position:

[15] Hans-Georg Gadamer, *Truth and Method* (New York: Seabury Press, 1975), 250.
[16] Gadamer, *Truth and Method*, 266 (my italics).

Gadamer and other hermeneuticists hold that all understanding and interpretation presupposes extensive agreement concerning what is true and what is false. Similar observations have been made by Wittgenstein and many other philosophers. I have quoted several passages where Quine argues for his more limited version of the condition, namely that one should preserve agreement with regard to what one considers obvious.[17]

Incidentally this account also distorts Wittgenstein, who is much closer to Heidegger on this point (and most others) than he is to Quine. For Wittgenstein, agreement in judgments means agreement in what people *do* and *say*, not what they *believe*. As he puts it: "It is what human beings say that is true and false; and they agree in the *language* they use. That is not agreement in opinions but in form of life."[18]

According to the ontological hermeneutics of both Heidegger and Wittgenstein, when we understand another culture we come to share its *know-how and discriminations* rather than arriving at agreement concerning which *assumptions and beliefs* are true. This coordination comes about not by making a translation, or cracking a code, but by prolonged everyday interaction; the result is not a commensuration of theories but what Heidegger calls "finding a footing" and Wittgenstein refers to as "finding one's way about."

IV

One reason that the difference between Quinean and Heideggerian holism has not been noted is that both views lead to a nondeterminacy as to what is being interpreted. Føllesdal has seen that hermeneutic phenomenology entails a nondeterminacy thesis but, misled by Gadamer, he has identified this nondeterminacy with Quine's famous notion of the indeterminacy of translation. Quine's rejection of meanings, or what he calls "the idea idea," is the conclusion of an argument that in translation from one belief system to another there are no meanings for us to be right or wrong about. Likewise, the view that shared background practices embody an interpretation of what it is to be human, and in general an interpretation of what it is to be, leads to the conclusion that these practices do not have an implicit meaning to which any attempted translation must correspond. Rather, to the question: What is the meaning embodied in this practice? one can only offer an interpretation of an interpretation.

To make this different sort of nondeterminacy clear it helps to start with a discussion of aesthetics. In literary criticism, for example, if we give up the idea

---

[17] Føllesdal, "Experience and Meaning", 39.
[18] Ludwig Wittgenstein, *Philosophical Investigations* (Oxford: Blackwell, 1953), 88, #241.

that an artist's intentions determine what a work means we have to give up the idea that there is a text with a fixed meaning we can be right or wrong about. What the text means is relative to an interpretation, and interpretations change with changing background assumptions and practices.

But why must we give up appeal to the artist's intentions? One argument has been that our evidence for these intentions is simply more behavior which also must be interpreted. This is true, but it only shows that in literature as in science a theory is always underdetermined by the evidence. These difficulties are shared with natural science where they lead to what Quine has called the *underdetermination* of physics, precisely in order to distinguish it from the *indeterminacy* of translation. Similarly this argument shows only the underdetermination of literary interpretations, not their nondeterminacy.

In search of stronger arguments one could take a Freudian view that the author himself is no authority on what his intentions really are. But this again leaves us with unconscious intentions, and the implication that if we could only get at these intentions they would enable us to decide what the work really meant.

Heidegger's argument for the distinctive nondeterminacy of interpretation of works of art is different from either of these. He would point out that an artist or a thinker, just like anyone else, cannot be clear about the background practices of his life and his age, not just because there are so many of them that such explication is an infinite task, but because the background is not a set of assumptions or beliefs about which one could even in principle be clear. The artist is thus in no better position than his contemporaries to make explicit the pervasive individual and social self-interpretation his work embodies. This is what Heidegger calls the essential unthought in the work.

The greater the work of a thinker...the richer is the unthought in the work, i.e., that which through that work and through it alone, comes up as never-yet-thought.[19]

As this passage implies, this unthought is not at some unsoundable depth but right upon the surface. It can best be noticed in the case of thinkers whose intuitive grasp extends beyond that of their contemporaries (e.g. Melville in *Moby Dick*). These artists lack the language and concepts to focus what their style and choice of details are nonetheless constantly showing, and their interpretation of their own work is as limited as the comments of contemporary reviewers. A later age, in which the implications of events (in Melville's case the connection between the destruction of the whaling industry and technological objectification) have worked themselves out, can assemble and focus the author's details in

---

[19] Martin Heidegger, *Der Satz vom Grund* (Pfullingen: Gunther Neske, 1957), 123–4.

a more comprehensive interpretation. We cannot speak of *the* meaning of a work, not because we can never get at this meaning since our only evidence of the author's intentions is his behavior, but rather because there is no final determinate meaning to get at.

So, in spite of their apparent agreement, there is a crucial difference between Heidegger and Quine. For Quinean radical translation there is *nothing*, i.e. no meaning, to be right or wrong about, so any holistic translation which accounts for all the data is as good as any other; for Heideggerian hermeneutic explication there is *no thing* (fact or theory) to be right or wrong about either—as Foucault puts it, in making a similar point about Nietzsche's notion of interpretation, "if interpretation is never finished that is simply because there is nothing to interpret"—but the job of hermeneutics is still to interpret the interpretation embodied in our current practices in as comprehensive and responsible a way as possible.[20] We can, on this view, still have better or worse interpretations in literature and in the human science, but not because interpretations can be right or wrong about a meaning in itself. According to this account, better interpretations are merely those which are more liberating. For early Heidegger in *Being and Time* (as for Gadamer and Habermas) this means that a better interpretation is one that makes the interpreter more flexible and open to dialogue with other interpretations.

We shall see that Heidegger changed his view on this important point. In the later works he holds that a better interpretation is one which focuses and makes sense of more of what is at issue in a current cultural self-interpretation. But this presupposes that *something really is at issue—although*, of course, there can be no final answer as to what that something is. I will return to this important change in Heidegger's understanding of hermeneutics in the conclusion of this chapter.

V

Our distinction between theoretical and practical holism will now enable us to make a distinction between the natural and the human sciences. We have seen that current interest in the role of interpretation in all disciplines has led thinkers such as Rorty to deny that any philosophically interesting distinction can be made between types of disciplines with regard to their subject matter. Since all knowing presupposes a background of assumptions, so the story goes, no theory can correspond to things as they are in themselves, no science can be objective, and all sciences are simply either normal or abnormal. According to Rorty, when

---

[20] Michel Foucault, "Nietzsche, Freud, Marx", in Gilles Deleuze (ed.), *Nietzsche* (Cahiers de Royaumont; Paris: Editions de Minuit, 1966), 189.

the practitioners of a discipline share a taken-for-granted background of assumptions, discourse is commensurable and the discipline is normal; when the background itself is in question, discourse is incommensurable and the discipline is in crisis and needs hermeneutic help. As Rorty puts it:

there is no requirement that people should be more difficult to understand than things; it is merely that hermeneutics is only needed in the case of incommensurable discourses, and that people discourse whereas things do not. What makes the difference is not discourse vs. silence, but incommensurable discourse vs. commensurable discourse.[21]

We are now in a position to see what leads Rorty to this surprising conclusion. By thinking of understanding human discourse as a theoretical problem of making sense of behavioral facts by conjecturing other facts about beliefs and assumptions, he assimilates the understanding of the meaning of cultures, societies, and individual behavior to the understanding of meaningless physical motions. In Heideggerian terms he understands the role of hypothesis (*Vorgriff*) and conceptual scheme (*Vorsicht*) in all understanding, but he leaves out the essential role of the background of practices (*Vorhabe*) in understanding human beings.

To be clear about this special role of the background practices in the study of man we must first remember that the natural sciences too presuppose a background of techniques, shared discriminations, and a shared sense of relevance—all those skills picked up through training which Kuhn calls the "disciplinary matrix" of a science. An example would be those skills which enable modern scientists to "work-over" objects so as to fit them into a formal framework.[22] These more and more sophisticated skills and techniques serve the special purpose of enabling modern scientists to isolate properties from their context of human relevance, and then to take the meaningless properties thus isolated and relate them by strict laws. Like any skills, the practices which make natural science possible involve a kind of know-how (*Vorhabe*) which cannot be captured by strict rules. Polanyi stresses that these skills cannot be learned from textbooks but must be acquired by apprenticeship, and Kuhn adds that they are also acquired by working through exemplary problems. Moreover, these scientific skills themselves presuppose our everyday practices and discriminations so the skills themselves cannot be decontextualized like the context-free physical properties they reveal. For both these reasons (the need for examples and for

---

[21] Rorty, *Philosophy and the Mirror of Nature*, 347.

[22] According to Heidegger the objects with which science deals are produced by a special activity of refined observation which he calls *Bearbeitung*. "Every new phenomenon emerging within an area of science is refined to such a point that it fits into the normative objective coherence of the theory." Martin Heidegger, "Science and Reflection", *The Question Concerning Technology and Other Essays* (New York: Harper & Row, 1977), 167, 169.

background practices) the practices of scientists cannot be brought under the sort of explicit laws whose formulation these practices make possible. Rather, scientific practice is, according to Kuhn, "a mode of knowing that is less systematic or less analyzable than knowledge embedded in rules, laws, or criteria of identification."[23] But the important point for the natural sciences is that natural science is successful precisely to the extent that *these background practices which make science possible can be taken for granted and ignored by the science.* Thus the holistic point that *Vorhabe* is necessary even in the natural sciences does not preclude the possibility of formulating scientific theories in which the interpretative practices of the observer play no internal role.

The human sciences constantly try to copy the natural sciences' successful exclusion from their theories of any reference to the background. They hope that, by seeking a shared agreement on what is relevant and by developing shared skills of observation, etc., the background of practices of the social scientist can be taken for granted and ignored the way the background is ignored in natural science. Behaviorism in psychology and the current vogue of information-processing models in the social sciences are cases where researchers take for granted background analogies such as the computer model and are trained in shared techniques such as programming, in the hope that they can relate by rules the meaningless attributes and factors this information-processing perspective reveals. Given such formalizing techniques, normal social science might, indeed, establish itself, only, however, by leaving out the social skills which make the isolation of features or attributes possible. But such skills and the context of everyday practices they presuppose are *internal* to the human sciences, just as the laboratory skills of scientists are internal to the history and sociology of science, for *if the human sciences claim to study human activities, then the human sciences, unlike the natural sciences, must take account of those human activities which make possible their own disciplines.* If, for the sake of agreement and "objectivity," the human sciences simply ignore their nonformalizable background practices, these practices will show up in each particular human science in the form of competing schools which call attention to what has been left out. For example, in sociology ethnomethodology insists on pointing out and hermeneutically investigating the background practices of "scientific" sociology, and in linguistics formal transformational grammars have focused new interest on the nonformal aspects of semantics and pragmatics.

Thus, while in the natural sciences it is always possible and generally desirable that an unchallenged normal science which defines and resolves problems concerning the structure of the physical universe establish itself, in the social sciences

---

[23]   Kuhn, *Essential Tension*, 192.

such an unchallenged normal science would only indicate that an orthodoxy had gained control. It would mean that the basic job of exploring the background of practices and their meaning had been forgotten, and that the unique feature of human behavior, the human self-interpretation embodied in our everyday know-how (*Vorhabe*), was not being investigated but simply ignored.

Another way to put this point is that, generally speaking, the natural sciences are at their best as normal science. For them, revolution means mainly that there is a conflict of interpretations—a lack of stability and agreement—until a new orthodoxy is established. The social sciences, on the other hand, are at their best in the perpetual revolution and conflict of interpretations which inevitably arise when they are trying to account for *all* human behavior, even the pervasive background of cultural interpretation which makes action meaningful. For them, normal science would show that the disciplines involved had become conformist, complacent, and ultimately sterile.

VI

Here the social and political issues come to the fore, and Rorty is clearly aware of the apparent danger:

The fear of science, of "scientism," of "naturalism," of self-objectification, of too much knowledge turning one into a thing rather than a person, is the fear that all discourse will become normal discourse. That is, it is the fear that there will be objectively true or false answers to every question one asks, so that human worth will consist in knowing truths and human virtue be merely justified true belief.[24]

But, in spite of his belief that the social sciences are just as theoretical and objectifying as the natural sciences and just as capable of becoming normal, Rorty thinks that there is no real danger. He claims that even in a world in which objective science explained and controlled everything, people could still look at the totality of objective facts from an edifying point of view and "ask such questions as: 'What is the point?' What are we to do with ourselves now that we know the laws of our own behavior?'"[25] Rorty is clear that such edifying discourses can make no claim to being true about the world, or even to being better or worse accounts of cultural meaning, since nothing falls outside objective theory but individual feelings.

---

[24] Rorty, *Philosophy and the Mirror of Nature*, 388–9.
[25] Rorty, *Philosophy and the Mirror of Nature*, 383.

Whether [the world] seemed to point a moral to an individual would depend on that individual. It would be true or false that it so seemed, or did not seem, to him. But it would not be objectively true or false that it "really did," or did not, have a sense or a moral.[26]

Yet Rorty is confident that:

Given leisure and libraries, the conversation which Plato began will not end in self-objectification—not because aspects of the world, or of human beings escape being objects of scientific inquiry, but simply because free and leisured conversation generates abnormal discourse as the sparks fly upward.[27]

But such discourse could not be anything like serious abnormal discourse as we now understand it. As long as someone feels that something has been left out of the objective account he may be inclined to propose and defend an interpretation of what that nontheoretical residue is and what it means for human action. But if, as in Rorty's projection, all objective truth were settled, and there is no other area of serious investigation of shared phenomena, abnormal discourse could only be the expression of an individual's subjective attitude towards the facts. And once this metatruth was understood, there would be no place for disagreement about any debatable issues, and hence no need for hermeneutic efforts at commensuration. Indeed, there would be no sense in translating one discourse into another by trying to make them maximally agree on what was true and what false as proposed by Gadamer and Quine, since all discoursers would already agree on all the objective facts. All that abnormal discourse would amount to would be the expression of private fantasies, and resulting pro and con attitudes towards the facts. And all that would be left in the place of Rorty's kind of hermeneutics would be the Derridian notion of the play of discourse about discourse. This would seem to be all Rorty could mean by conversation.

Not that acknowledging with early Heidegger that the background practices can never be incorporated into a theory would be sufficient to explain why there will always be conflicts of interpretation. If, as early Heidegger claims, anxiety reveals the background practices to be meaningless, there would be reason to question the applicability to human beings of objective science, but no reason to propose and defend alternative interpretations of human practices, or to offer proposals for meaningful action. Practical holism's insight that our micro-practices cannot be objectified as beliefs, assumptions, norms, rules, stereotypes, or anything else saves us from theoretical nihilism, but since *Being and Time* can offer no way to distinguish the trivial from the important contents of the nonobjectifiable aspect

---

[26] Rorty, *Philosophy and the Mirror of Nature*, 388.
[27] Rorty, *Philosophy and the Mirror of Nature*, 389.

of the micro-practices, it lands us in practical nihilism. Holding onto anxiety can make us flexibly free of all objectification, but Heidegger can give no account of why any flexible interpretation should be taken more seriously than any other, or taken seriously at all.

VII

In conclusion, before turning to the political implications of the difference between the natural and social sciences as understood by *later* Heidegger, let us review and generalize our analysis. We have argued that in the human sciences the background is internal to the science while in the natural sciences it is external. This follows from the fact that theory succeeds by decontextualizing while the human sciences have to deal with the human context. But the importance of this difference depends on a further ontological question, whether the background can itself be treated as a belief system or a set of rules, i.e. whether there can be a theory of practice. That there can be such a theory is the unargued assumption of the view that theoretical holism is the only kind of holism.

The consequences of the acceptance of *theoretical holism* for political action is a choice between two kinds of nihilism: secular and religious. Each of these, in turn, can take two forms. Rorty's nihilism can take the form of a liberal, pragmatic naturalism which simply opts for the specific beliefs one happens to share with others about the value, loveableness, etc., of human beings. But, of course, any such values, since they are themselves merely the result of subjective preferences and pragmatic choices, could equally well be rejected. So one lets those who disagree opt for their own preferences. Or Rorty, like Derrida, can push this theoretical nihilism one step further. Although talk of meaning is mere discourse about nothing, such talk can itself become the source of enjoyment as the object of our interpretive playfulness. Derrida expresses this last stage of theoretical nihilism when he advocates with Nietzsche "the joyous affirmation of the free play of the world ... without truth, without origin, offered to an active interpretation."[28]

The religious response to this secular nihilism, which we have not had time to discuss here, tries to save seriousness in either of two ways.

(1) By pointing out that, although all our beliefs about value and meaning are in principle objectifiable and, hence, just more facts about the world, there are in fact always some beliefs so close to us that we cannot treat them as

---

[28] Jacques Derrida, "Structure, Sign, and Play in the Discourse of the Human Sciences", *The Structuralist Controversy* (Baltimore, MD: Johns Hopkins University Press, 1968), 264.

objects. This seems to be Gadamer's move. He claims that each epoch of history has pervasive shared beliefs about human beings and the meaning of Being in general which those living in that epoch cannot objectify.

(2) By Ricoeur's approach, which is the opposite of Gadamer's. Instead of finding the source of religious meaning in the ineffable depths of culture, Ricoeur finds that religious symbols point to an ineffable source above and beyond all experience. Then, in the name of this "numinous" realm, he justifies the special nature of human beings.

But this religious move in either version is still nihilistic. With Gadamer, it bases its claims that pervasive "prejudices" are unchallengeable simply on their inaccessibility to the people who hold them, which runs the risk of making a virtue of obscure, pervasive obsessions and compulsions, while with Ricoeur, the numinous is so unrelated to this world that it gives us absolutely no guidance when it comes to political action. Both views relativize *all* particular commitments. But if what makes human beings special is absolutely ineffable it makes absolutely no difference, and where action is concerned we are back to endless conversation between competing preferences.

Once we see, however, that the human practices or *Vorhabe* which give us our understanding of reality and of ourselves do not consist of representations and so cannot be treated as a theory, then this *practical holism* gives us two new possible positions: one "secular" and nihilistic, and one "religious" and safe from nihilism. These positions were held successively by Heidegger. In *Being and Time* Heidegger thought that those practices which cannot be captured as beliefs and procedures, and which thus distinguish us from computer-like objects, are nonetheless, at least in this stage of our culture, relentlessly subjectifying and objectifying. (Later Heidegger comes to see this tendency as technology; Foucault sees it as the encroachment of disciplinary society.) We can, however, early Heidegger holds, experience the fact that we are neither subjects nor objects in attacks of metaphysical anxiety. But since this experience of Nothing with a capital "N" only gets us to recognize what we are not, rather than getting us in touch with anything specific that we *are*, it gives us no motive or focus for action. In order to act at all we must return to the world of *Das Man*, and act in terms of the typified situations, roles, and goals which the disciplinary society presses upon us.

Only the "religious" alternative, sketched by later Heidegger, especially in "The Origin of the Work of Art," offers a way out of nihilism. Later Heidegger assumes the practical holism of *Being and Time*, thus avoiding both the secular and religious varieties of theoretical nihilism. He then holds open the possibility that there still exists in our micro-practices an undercurrent of a pretechnological understanding of the meaning of Being, presumably once focused in the Greek Temple. Now scattered in our inherited background practices this understanding involves nonobjectifying and nonsubjectifying ways of relating to nature, material objects, and human beings. Heidegger asks us to strengthen these practices, to "foster the saving power...in little things,"[29] and points out that artists are especially sensitive to this saving power and devoted to preserving endangered species of inherited practices. To take examples close to home, Faulkner personifies the wilderness, Pirsig speaks with respect of the quality even of technological things such as motorcycles, and Melville opposes Ishmael as mortal and preserver to Ahab as the willful mobilizer of all beings towards his arbitrary ends.

Nontechnological micro-practices, if they still exist at all, are now hard to discern, not because they are so pervasive as to be ineffable, or so numinous as to be unreachable—they were once palpably present in cultural exemplars such as the Greek Temple—but because they are dispersed by the objectifying practices which have had such success since the Enlightenment. Nor can the existence of such "saving" practices be proved by philosophical arguments. Still, only their existence and continued efficacy would account for our otherwise mysterious preference for anything rather than the disciplinary technological society.

The practical "religious" form of resistance to nihilism in late Heideggerian hermeneutics requires a two-stage strategy. First, one must deconstruct theoretical holism, and give what Heidegger in *Being and Time* calls a "concrete demonstration" that human beings and the objects they encounter are formed by cultural practices which cannot be objectified. Second, one must give an interpretation of our current cultural situation by finding a cultural paradigm (for Heidegger, the hydroelectric power station on the Rhine; for Foucault, the prison), which focuses our dominant practices, while at the same time assembling all the evidence in our micro-practices—and this of course includes our linguistic practices—that an alternative understanding of human beings once existed and still continues, although drowned out by our everyday busy concerns. Finally, having done this job, one can only hope that the micro-practices excluded by technology will find a new focus in a new paradigm.

Since this last step lies beyond our will, Heidegger has said that only a God can save us. The *first* two stages of this hermeneutic strategy, however, require our efforts. Although, as Rorty eloquently argues, philosophical debate is no longer relevant, the alternatives are not animated conversation, or silent waiting for being to speak, but rather, first, what Foucault calls genealogy, i.e. amassing and interpreting the historical details of how we got to be where we are, and second,

---

[29] Heidegger, "The Question Concerning Technology", 33.

the as-yet-unnamed hermeneutic activity devoted to interpreting and preserving the inherited understanding of what it means to be, dispersed in our everyday activities—an understanding which makes possible normal as well as abnormal disciplines and gives meaning and seriousness to our lives.[30]

[30] Earlier versions of this chapter were presented at Johns Hopkins University and the 1979 annual meeting of the American Association for the Advancement of Science. I am indebted to Paul Rabinow and Jane Rubin for their help in developing the account of nihilism which forms the conclusion of the present version.

7

The Primacy of Phenomenology over Logical Analysis (2001)

1. Introduction

When teaching at Berkeley in the 1970s, I was struck by the way that John Searle's account of intentionality resembled that given by the Husserlian branch of phenomenology.[1] I, therefore, soon found myself playing Heidegger to what I took to be Searle's Husserl. We gave several seminars together on intentionality and on what Searle came to call the background, and we read and criticized each other's papers. I thought it was a good sign for the future of American philosophy that we each respected phenomenology and analytic philosophy and drew on both traditions.

But recently, what looked like an illuminating disagreement about the phenomena has turned into a debate about the value of phenomenology, and we seem to be reproducing rather than transcending the antagonism that used to exist between our two traditions. Our fruitful discussions started hardening into polemics when I wrote "Heidegger's Critique of the Husserl/Searle Account of Intentionality,"[2] and Searle responded with a paper titled "The Limits of Phenomenology."[3] We seemed to reach the end of our dialogue when I wrote a critique of Searle's *The Construction of Social Reality* titled "Phenomenological Description versus Rational Reconstruction,"[4] and he responded with "Neither

---

[1] For a clear statement of Husserl's account of intentionality, see Dagfinn Føllesdal's classic paper, "Husserl's Notion of the Noema", 73–80. The first edition is out of print; a second edition is forthcoming.

[2] See Chapter 3, this volume. Originally published in *Social Research*, 60 (1993), 17–38.

[3] John R. Searle, "The Limits of Phenomenology", in Mark A. Wrathall and Jeff Malpas (eds), *Heidegger, Coping, and Cognitive Science: Essays in Honor of Hubert L. Dreyfus* (Cambridge, MA: MIT Press, 2000), ii. 71–92.

[4] Hubert L. Dreyfus, "Phenomenological Description versus Rational Reconstruction", *La Revue Internationale de Philosophie*, 55/217 (June 2001), 181–96.

Phenomenological Description nor Rational Reconstruction,"[5] claiming he had always been doing logical analysis, never phenomenology. For him, he said, representations are not entities in transcendental consciousness, and constitution is not a transcendental activity. In general, he considers phenomenological methods bankrupt. The logical analysis of action and of social reality reveals "causal and logical structures... beyond the reach of phenomenological analysis."[6] Thus, according to Searle, logical analysis must "go far beyond phenomenology," and the results of phenomenology are "rendered irrelevant."[7]

This chapter attempts to restart the dialogue by correcting my misunderstandings, locating what I take to be the real disagreements, and defending the relevance, indeed, the primacy, of phenomenology. I will argue that when logical analysis goes beyond phenomenology, it passes over absorbed coping—an important kind of activity—and social norms—a level of social reality whose causal structures it nonetheless presupposes.

2. Searle's Account of Action

Searle claims that for a movement to be an action it must be caused by an intention in action—a propositional representation of the action's conditions of satisfaction.[8] Drawing on Merleau-Ponty's phenomenology of everyday absorbed coping, I contested what I took to be Searle's assumption that, in *all* cases of comportment, the agent must be able to recognize in advance what would count as success.[9] Searle, I held, had correctly described intentional action, but absorbed coping does not require that the agent's movements be governed by an intention in action that represents the action's success conditions, i.e. what the agent is trying to achieve.[10] Rather, I claimed, in absorbed coping, the agent's body is led

---

[5] John R. Searle, "Neither Phenomenological Description nor Rational Reconstruction: Reply to Dreyfus", *Revue Internationale de Philosophie*, 55/216 (June 2001).

[6] Searle, "Neither Phenomenological Description".

[7] Searle, "Neither Phenomenological Description".

[8] Searle distinguishes an intention in action from a prior intention, which is an intention to act at a later time.

[9] Since I need a term to cover every sort of directed activity, I can't use "movement," which is not intentional at all, nor "action," which is usually understood to involve an explicit intention. I will, therefore, use Merleau-Ponty's term, "comportment."

[10] For Searle, the expression "intentional action" is redundant, but since I want to introduce the idea that there is another kind of comportment that I call "absorbed coping," which has intentionality but is not intentional in the strong sense that the agent must be capable of being aware of what he is trying to do, I will use "intentional action" to refer to comportment in which the agent has in mind what he is trying to achieve.

to move so as to reduce a sense of deviation from a satisfactory gestalt without the agent knowing what that satisfactory gestalt will be like in advance of achieving it. Thus, in absorbed coping, rather than a sense of *trying to achieve success,* one has a sense of *being drawn towards an equilibrium.* As Merleau-Ponty puts it: "To move one's body is to aim at things through it; it is *to allow oneself to respond to their call,* which is made upon it independently of any representation."[11]

To get the phenomenon of absorbed coping in focus, consider a tennis stroke. If one is a beginner or is off one's form, one might find oneself making an effort to keep one's eye on the ball, keep the racket perpendicular to the court, hit the ball squarely, and so forth. Even if one is an expert, under the pressure of the game, one might well be *trying* to win the point or at least to return the ball to the opponent's court. But if one is expert at the game, not bothered by the pressure to win, and things are going so well that one is absorbed in the flow, then, if one feels anything at all, one feels that one's current activity is caused *by the perceived conditions,* not by one's *volition.* Without trying, one experiences one's arm shooting out[12] and its being drawn to the optimal position, the racket forming the optimal angle with the court—an angle one need not even be aware of—all this, so as to complete the gestalt made up of the court, one's running opponent, and the oncoming ball.[13]

At this point in our debate, Searle made a move that seemed to me to confirm that he was attempting to extend the phenomenology of intentional action to all comportment. He insisted that absorbed coping was not itself a kind of intentionality, but rather that "Intentionality rises to the level of the Background abilities."[14] As Searle explained this slogan, it seemed to me to be the phenomenological claim that, in acting, the agent has to have in mind (or at least

---

[11] Merleau-Ponty, *Phenomenology of Perception,* 139; italics added.

[12] Searle claims that if I feel my arm shooting out, it is not an action. He cites Wilder Penfield's report that, when he stimulates the brain of a patient in a way that makes the patient's arm go up, the patient feels that he has not performed the movement, but that Penfield "pulled it out of him." What is missing, Searle argues, in my tennis case and in the Penfield case is the patient's sense of effort, his experience that it was his intention to raise his arm that made his arm go up. But I contend that one's arm shooting out in the tennis case feels different from the way it presumably feels when one's arm is being caused to shoot out by Penfield's electrodes. One feels in the tennis case that one's motion is relieving the tension of a deviation from an optimal gestalt, and one also feels that one could at any moment move one's arm some other way if one so desired.

[13] There is a long Zen tradition that says one must get over trying or "efforting" and just respond. This is also familiar coaching advice. The latest version is Obi Wan Kenobi's advice in the first *Star Wars* movie to the tense and straining Luke Skywalker, "Use the force, Luke."

[14] John R. Searle, "Response: The Background of Intentionality and Action", in Ernest Lepore and Robert Van Gulick (eds), *John Searle and his Critics* (Oxford: Wiley-Blackwell, 1993), 289–99, quotation on 293; italics omitted.

be able to have in mind) what he is trying to do, and that everything else required to carry out the action must be understood as nonrepresentational background capacities that cause subsidiary movements that do not themselves have conditions of satisfaction. This seemed to me to mischaracterize the phenomenon of absorbed coping, but Searle has now made clear that his claim was not meant to be a phenomenological claim at all, but a logical claim about what makes a stream of skillful bodily movements intentional.[15]

Searle's logical analysis, however, leaves me with a new problem. Since each movement involved in an action does not have its own conditions of satisfaction, it should not have intentionality; yet, as Searle points out, each subsidiary movement is done intentionally. Searle's solution is that, to be intentional, each subsidiary movement of an action must be *governed* by the relevant intention in action. As Searle puts it:

Intentionality reaches down to the bottom level of voluntary, actions. Thus, for example, the skillful skier has his Intentionality at the level of getting down the mountain. But each subsidiary movement is nonetheless an intentional movement. Each movement is governed by the Intentionality of the flow.[16]

Searle adds that "the only cause in question could be the fact that I am actually *doing it* intentionally as opposed to passively experiencing it."[17] Only in this way, according to Searle, can we explain how all the subsidiary movements involved in an action are intentional, even though only the overall action has conditions of satisfaction. But this analysis leaves unclear just how intentionality is supposed to be passed along from an intention in action that represents only the action's overall conditions of satisfaction to every movement of the flow.

---

[15] I was misled by Searle's use of examples, such as a tennis player who is paying special attention to his performance because he is behind in a tournament. Given such examples, I assumed that having an intention in action amounted either to paying close attention to each step of what one was doing, the way beginners focus on each step of their performance, or at least monitoring what one was doing, the way experts sometimes do under pressure. But, in spite of his misleading tendency to argue for his account of action by citing cases of focused, effortful action, Searle is clear that acting intentionally can be spontaneous and absent-minded, as in his example of jumping up and pacing around the room while thinking about a philosophical problem. It seems that Searle privileges the phenomenon of painstaking effort for pedagogical reasons. In such cases it is supposed to be especially clear that the agent's movements are caused by what the agent is trying to do, and so, the movements are clearly governed by what Searle calls a representation of the action's success conditions.

[16] Searle, "Response", 293. In Searle, *Intentionality: An Essay in the Philosophy of Mind*, Searle notes that "intending and intentions are just one form of Intentionality among others... [so]... to keep the distinction clear I will capitalize the technical sense of 'Intentional' and 'Intentionality'" (p. 5).

[17] Searle, *Intentionality: An Essay in the Philosophy of Mind*, 294.

Merleau-Ponty takes up precisely this problem. He calls the phenomenon of absorbed coping *motor intentionality,* and claims that it is our basic form of intentionality, missed by those who suppose that in all comportment the agent's movements must be guided by what the agent (consciously or unconsciously) is trying to achieve. According to Merleau-Ponty, in absorbed coping, the body of the performer is solicited by the situation to perform a series of movements that feel *appropriate* without the agent needing in any way to anticipate what would count as *success.* To see that normally these two kinds of satisfaction— appropriateness and success—can be separated, we need only note that, in my tennis example, I could make a return that felt just right and the ball could fail to land in the opponent's court due to an unexpected gust of wind, and, conversely, I could make a return that felt awkward and yet the ball, nonetheless, could land successfully in the opponent's court. Whatever makes the absorbed coping feel satisfactory, then, must be independent of the success achieved.

In the case of an *appropriate* tennis stroke, unlike the case of a *successful* return, there is no way to specify success in advance. Rather, my absorbed response must lower a tension without my knowing in advance how to reach equilibrium or what it would feel like to be there. Thus, besides Searle's success conditions, the phenomenologist is led to introduce what one might call *conditions of improvement.*

Once the phenomenon is clear, it also becomes clear that the intention in action need not reach down and *directly* govern the flow. Rather than a representation of the action's *success conditions* directly governing the agent's subsidiary movements, a sense of the *conditions of improvement* could take over the job as the agent felt drawn to lower the current tension. The intention in action would then be merely an *occasion* that triggered the motor intentionality of the bodily movements.

To understand motor intentionality and its kind of causality, we can begin by considering a game in which one player guides the other's search for some hidden object by saying "hot" or "cold." In that case, the performer is led by the clues without knowing where they are leading. Of course, in the hot/cold game, the player giving the clues needs to know where the hidden object is, and Merleau-Ponty admits that it seems impossible that an agent could intentionally move toward satisfaction without sensing what would count as success. Since he was clear that no account of brain function conceivable in his day could account for this phenomenon, Merleau-Ponty called it magical.[18]

---

[18] Merleau-Ponty, *Phenomenology of Perception,* 104. It's important to note that Merleau-Ponty uses "magical" in two ways. In discussing how the mind can control movement he says, "We still need to understand by what magical process the representation of a movement causes precisely that movement to be made by the body." And, he adds, "The problem can be solved provided that we cease to draw a distinction between the body as a mechanism in itself and consciousness as being for

Fortunately, Walter Freeman, a neuroscientist at Berkeley, has worked out a model of learning that can be adapted to show how the brain, operating as a dynamical system, could cause a movement that achieves satisfaction without the brain in any way representing the movement's success conditions.[19] It helps to have Freeman's model in mind when describing and defending Merleau-Ponty's surprising view that, although absorbed coping has conditions of satisfaction, these are conditions of improvement that consist in moving so as to lower a tension, not so as to achieve an already-represented success, and that, since such conditions of improvement cannot be known by the agent in advance of his feeling satisfied, they cannot be represented as a future state of success that governs or guides the agent's current movements.

According to Freeman's model of learning, after an animal has repeatedly encountered a situation in which a particular response has produced results that are useful or harmful to the animal, it forms neuron connections which, when the animal encounters stimuli from a similar situation, cause the neurons to prod-uce a burst of global activity whose energy state occupies a point in an energy landscape. A point in an energy landscape is the amount of energy it takes the whole configuration to be in that state, and the points around that point require more or less energy. A minimal energy state is called a basin of attraction, or an attractor. An energy landscape is composed of several attractors. In Freeman's model of learning, the animal's brain forms a new attractor each time the animal learns to respond to a new type of situation.

Applying Freeman's model to action, we can suppose that, through exposure to satisfactions and frustrations brought about by specific actions in a number of similar situations, the sensory-motor system forms an attractor landscape that is shaped by the possibilities for successful comportment in that type of situation. When a specific sensory input moves the system-state into the vicinity of a specific attractor, the organism is caused to move in a way that brings the system-state closer to the bottom of that basin of attraction. The tennis player's experience, in my example, of a tension drawing him to move toward a satisfactory gestalt would, on this account, be correlated with the tendency of his sensory-motor system to relax into a specific minimum energy state.

---

itself" (p. 139 n.). Here, he uses the term magical pejoratively to mean that a causal claim is based on an ontology that makes it *impossible* to account for how it could be implemented. In the case just cited, however, Merleau-Ponty uses "magical" to mean that there is no *currently conceivable* way to cash out the causal claim that absorbed coping is directed toward a goal without representing that goal.

[19] Walter J. Freeman, "The Physiology of Perception", *Scientific American*, 264 (1991), 78–85, and Walter J. Freeman and Kamil A. Grajski, "Relation of Olfactory EEG to Behavior: Factor Analysis", *Behavioral Neuroscience*, 101 (1987), 766–77.

At any given moment, the system, like the player in the "hot" and "cold" game, is in a state that is near to or far from the bottom of some specific basin. But if that were all that was going on in the person's brain, the person would be like a player who could only guess where to look next, and so at best could find what he was seeking by trial and error. But, happily, the energy landscape gives more information than just "hot" or "cold." In our hypothetical case, as soon as the experienced tennis player's perception of the situation brings his sensory-motor system under the pull of a specific attractor, his brain's relaxing into a basin of attraction is correlated with his sense of which direction of movement would make him hotter, without his knowing where the hottest point is. The system thus underlines the player's being drawn to make those movements that result in his feeling a lowering of tension—the same movements that result in his brain-state approaching the lowest accessible point in its current energy landscape, without the brain representing the lowest energy state in advance and without the player's needing to represent to himself what the final equilibrium state would be like or how to get there. As Merleau-Ponty already pictured it, the person's brain would simply be moving to lower a tension, like a soap bubble relaxing into a spherical shape without in any way representing the spherical shape toward which it was tending, and the player would simply feel drawn to complete a gestalt without knowing the shape of that gestalt in advance.[20]

The correlation can be carried further to capture the basic difference between Merleau-Ponty's and Searle's understanding of the causal role of an act of volition. An interesting feature of Freeman's model of perception is that the brain does not form conditioned responses to specific stimuli but, on the basis of experience, produces its own attractors, which are evoked and modified on the basis of further experience. Once the stimulus from the current situation has triggered a burst of neuronal activity that forms a specific attractor landscape, the attractor landscape takes over and draws the system to relax into a specific

---

[20] It is important to bear in mind that this account is only supposed to cover skillful coping in flow, not cases of deliberate action. But even thinking of all absorbed coping as moving so as to reduce a felt tension and thus *reach equilibrium* is obviously an oversimplification. Some absorbed coping, like carrying on a conversation, does not seem to be governed by a tendency to reduce tension. The Freeman/Merleau-Ponty model applies best to the basic skills we have for getting around in the world. Moreover, even when one is being drawn to reduce a tension and so tending toward equilibrium, one usually finds oneself in a new situation before one arrives at stasis, and so one is drawn toward a new equilibrium before the first equilibrium is actually reached. Thus, the agent is continually drawn toward some equilibrium state, but seldom arrives at any. In this way the Platonic/Freudian vision that people act so as to arrive at fulfillment and rest might be reconciled with the Aristotelian/Deweyan idea that the good life consists in ongoing coping. Normally, comportment on all levels might consist in a tendency to achieve equilibrium that never arrives at equilibrium but, instead, produces ongoing activity.

attractor. Thus, once the sensory input has put the system into a specific attractor landscape, it has no further job and so can, as Freeman puts it, be "thrown away" as the attractor produced by the system takes over the job of categorizing the sensory input.

If we again extend Freeman's model to comportment, we find it not only corresponds to Merleau-Ponty's tension-reduction account of motor intentionality, but also it would solve Searle's problem of explaining why the intention in action rises to the level of skill, and how, nonetheless, the subsidiary bodily movements can be intentional even though they don't have conditions of satisfaction. The brain correlate of an act of volition would put the system into a specific attractor landscape. After that, the brain correlate of the volition would no longer be causally active, but would, as it were, be thrown away as the dynamics of the attractor landscape took over as the brain correlate of the agent's movements. Thus, we don't have to suppose, with Searle, that an intention in action has to reach down and directly govern each subsidiary movement, thereby, in some mysterious way, passing its representational intentionality on to each. Instead, we can see that, on Merleau-Ponty's and Freeman's account, the intention in action would trigger absorbed coping, the movements of which would have motor rather than representational intentionality.[21]

One then has a radically different account of the intentionality of absorbed coping. For Searle, intentionality raises to the level of skill, that is, a representation of an action's success conditions somehow activates and governs intentionless background skills and capacities. To take Searle's example, an expert skier's intention in action to ski down a mountain activates and governs his background capacities as he performs the unrepresented, but nonetheless intentional, activity of shifting his weight from ski to ski, etc. On the Freeman/Merleau-Ponty account, once the volition has initiated the action, absorbed coping, with its own kind of intentionality, correlated with the causal properties of the brain as a dynamical system, takes over and carries out the task. This cashes out the metaphor of the intention in action reaching down and governing the bodily movements, and explains how each bodily movement, although not directly caused by a volition, is nonetheless intentional.

In response to my detailed phenomenological and neurological account of the difference between the intentionality of action and the intentionality of absorbed coping, Searle has clarified his position. Now, rather than attempting to assimilate absorbed coping into his account of action by what seemed to be a phenomenological

---

[21] In the phenomenological account of absorbed coping, the distinction between a prior intention and an intention in action would be unnecessary, since an act of volition would, like a prior intention, cause but not accompany absorbed coping.

claim that intentionality always rises to the level of skill, Searle holds that my attributing a phenomenological claim to him was, from the start, mistaken. He has never been doing phenomenology, but rather logical analysis. He now grants that in absorbed coping the agent need not have a representation of the end-state in order to be drawn toward it, and that the agent may find out what the final equilibrium feels like only when he gets there. And, since for Searle a propositional representation is broadly defined as any structure that can be stated in a proposition, he now claims that his technical notion of a propositional representation of conditions of satisfaction can be extended to absorbed coping. "On my account [both kinds of intentionality] are forms of Intentionality in the sense that they can succeed or fail," he says.[22]

It is not immediately clear what success and failure mean when one can only sense an improvement, but I presume that for Searle a propositional representation of the conditions of satisfaction in a case of absorbed coping would be that *this* movement lowers *this* tension. Thus, to preserve the generality of his logical analysis of action, Searle must extend his notion of the propositional representation of an action's conditions of satisfaction to cover both a general description of what one is trying to achieve (success), and a demonstrative reference to whatever the agent will sense as a reduction of tension (improvement).

In short, to analyze absorbed coping, the notion of propositional representation must be extended to cover indexicals. This may not be a problem if one is interested, as Searle is, in analyzing a broad class of phenomena, in this case all kinds of comportment, but in thus extending the notion of propositional representation, Searle obscures the issues raised by those who want to distinguish conceptual and nonconceptual forms of intentional content, and he risks giving seeming support to representationalists in cognitive psychology and neuroscience.

Here I will not go into the question whether the notion of propositional representation can successfully be extended, as Searle claims, to cover the sense of tension reduction required by absorbed coping. Rather, I will argue that, even if Searle *is* successful in defining an extended sense of propositional representation that covers all forms of comportment, such a logical analysis will necessarily miss the special character and causal priority of absorbed coping.

There are three separate issues here. I will consider them in the order of increasing importance for deciding whether phenomenology or logical analysis has a more adequate account of the causality involved in comportment.

(1) Whether, in the case of actions initiated by an intention in action, the intention in action need be the direct cause of the bodily movements?

---

[22] Searle, "Response", 294.

(2) Whether there could be absorbed coping not initiated by an intention in action?

(3) Whether all action is dependent on a background of absorbed coping?

(1) Searle's logical analysis convincingly shows that the bodily movements that make up an action must be caused by an intention in action. But there is an important difference between Searle's logical conclusions and Merleau-Ponty's phenomenological ones. Searle assumes that there is only one kind of intentional causality, and that, therefore, the intention in action that causes the bodily movements must reach down and govern them directly, whereas Merleau-Ponty would contend that the intention in action is only an occasional cause that merely initiates the absorbed coping that carries out the action. On this account, the causal relations between the intention in action and the absorbed coping are more complex than the account of propositional representations activating background mechanisms suggested by Searle's logical analysis. The bodily movements that make up an *action* must, indeed, be initiated by an intention in action with success conditions, but carrying out such actions normally depends on the contribution of *absorbed coping* with its conditions of improvement. *It thus turns out that, where intentional action is concerned, each form of intentionality requires the other.*

(2) Once we see that the role of the intention in action is simply to trigger absorbed coping, the question arises whether one always needs an intention in action to initiate absorbed coping. Phenomenology then reveals that there are many comportments that do not have success conditions but only conditions of improvement. For example, the distance one stands from one's fellows in any particular culture depends on being socialized into what feels appropriate. Sometimes, this sense of standing the appropriate distance is a part of an action with success conditions, as when someone is trying to have a conversation and so stands the appropriate distance so as to have one. But sometimes, as when several people find themselves together in an elevator and each simply moves to the distance from the others that feels comfortable, no intention in action seems to be required to initiate the bodily movements involved. In general, we don't have intentions for comporting ourselves in socially acceptable ways.

Freeman's and Merleau-Ponty's accounts might seem to leave unexplained how such cases of coping can take place without being initiated by an intention in action. But each has a suggestion as to what might be going on. Merleau-Ponty notes that motor intentionality is continuously in play so that the flow of coping is only rarely initiated from scratch. Freeman has a similar idea. For him, the body is continually moving toward equilibrium, but before it can arrive at a stable state some new movement is required, and the body falls under the sway of another attractor. *Thus, existential phenomenologists and avant-garde neuroscience agree that, normally, absorbed coping does not need to be initiated by an intention in action, and so is more basic than intentional action.*

(3) In general, when intentional action occurs, it is only possible on the background of ongoing absorbed coping—what Wittgenstein calls finding one's way about in the world. Indeed, as Heidegger argues at length in *Being and Time*, absorbed coping produces the intelligibility and familiarity on the basis of which intentional action is possible.[23] *Thus, in the last phenomenological analysis, absorbed coping is the background condition of the possibility of all forms of comportment.*

The above dependencies of intentional action upon absorbed coping are covered up when the notion of propositional representation, developed to give a logical analysis of intentional action, is stretched to cover the phenomenon of absorbed coping. Only phenomenology can reveal the two different types of comportment; further, only phenomenology can reveal that, of the two, absorbed coping is more primordial.

3. The Construction of Social Reality

Again, I will begin with what I took to be Searle's Husserlian position, then explain how my interpretation, while seemingly supported by the text, turned out to be a misunderstanding, once Searle clarified his position. I will argue that phenomenology, nonetheless, turns out to be necessary in order to distinguish the way a tension-reduction kind of collective intentionality *produces social norms* from the way a conventionally representational kind of collective intentionality *constitutes institutional facts*. Finally, I will discuss the dependency relations between these two types of collective intentionality.

Searle's basic idea is that, to *constitute institutional* facts, human beings must *impose* status functions on *natural* facts that have no intrinsic social function. Searle tells us: "the form of the constitutive rule [is] '[a natural fact] X counts as [an institutional fact] Y in [context] C.'"[24] To see that Searle seems to hold a Husserlian view of institutional facts, we need only ask just how the imposition of a status function is to be understood. Specifically, how are we to construe Searle's formula that the X term must come to *count as* having function Y?

---

[23] For the detailed argument, see ch. 5 of Dreyfus, *Being-in-the-World*, 88–107.
[24] John R. Searle, *The Construction of Social Reality* (New York: Free Press, 1995), 43–4.

Like Husserl and Heidegger, Searle begins with a description of everyday phenomena from within the everyday practical world:

As far as our normal experiences of the inanimate parts of the world are concerned, we do not experience things *as* material objects, much less as collections of molecules. Rather, we experience a world of chairs and tables, houses and cars, lecture halls, pictures, streets, gardens, houses, and so forth.[25]

But then, like Husserl but unlike Heidegger, Searle switches to a detached logical stance and tells us: "The important thing to see at this point is that functions are never intrinsic to the physics of any phenomenon but are *assigned* from *outside* by conscious observers and users."[26]

When I first read this sentence I took it to be the claim that we "conscious observers and users" actually "assign" functions to brute stuff from "outside." It thus sounded to me like Husserl's claim in *Logical Investigations* that, for there to be language, the subject has to assign meaning to otherwise meaningless noises and squiggles, and like the further claim in *Ideas* that, in perception, the transcendental subject has to take meaningless sensory input as some sort of object in order to be able to experience objects at all. Since Searle was discussing the functions of tables and chairs, he sounded to me exactly as if he were making Husserl's claim in *Cartesian Meditations* that mere physical things are encountered first and then are given meaning as cultural objects: "An existent mere physical thing (when we disregard all the ... 'cultural' characteristics that make it knowable as, for example, a hammer ...) is given beforehand."[27]

I therefore set out to follow Heidegger in showing that such a claim was bad phenomenology. As Heidegger points out, we normally are not detached minds or transcendental subjects confronting meaningless physical things to which we assign functions. Rather, we are from the start socialized into a world in which we cope with equipment. Searle seems to agree when he says:

God could not see screwdrivers, cars, bathtubs, etc., because intrinsically speaking there are no such things. Rather, God would see *us treating* certain objects as screwdrivers, cars, bathtubs, etc. But ... our standpoint [is] the standpoint of beings who are not gods but are inside the world.[28]

However, given his claim that functions are assigned from *outside*, Searle sounded to me not like Heidegger, but like Husserl, describing the "natural standpoint" only to claim he could bracket it.

It seemed to me that both the external, logical, godlike claim that, for there to be a social world, the brute facts in nature must somehow acquire meaning, and

---

[25] Searle, *Construction of Social Reality*, 14.   [26] Searle, *Construction of Social Reality*, 14.
[27] Husserl, *Cartesian Meditations*, 78.
[28] Searle, *Construction of Social Reality*, 12; italics added.

the internal phenomenological description of human beings as always-already-in a meaningful world, were correct but in tension, and, like Heidegger and Merleau-Ponty, I was sure that trouble would arise if the external, logical conditions that describe the constitution of institutional facts were invoked to explain the existence of our involved experience of an already meaningful world.

The problem comes up in an acute way when Searle asks how "the child... learns to treat the sounds that come out of her own and others' mouths as standing for, or meaning something."[29] The very question belies the phenomenon. Developmental psychologists have found evidence that the human fetus already responds differently to the mother's speech from the way it responds to other sounds. This research suggests that there is no sense in asking *from the child's point of view* how she *learns* to take as meaningful the acoustic blasts coming out of people's mouths. It seems that meaningfulness does not have to be learned. Rather, the talking that comes out of people's mouths is always already experienced by the child as meaningful, although, of course, the child has to learn the meaning.

In order to provide a theoretical explanation of language, one can, nonetheless, take an external perspective from outside the world of linguistic meaning and ask what makes language possible. One can then ask:

(1) The *logical* question (that Merleau-Ponty calls the question concerning the conditions of possibility): What *constitutive conditions must be satisfied* for the sounds coming out of people's mouths to count as language?
(2) The *ontological* question: What *must be added* to mere noises for them to be experienced as language?
(3) The *scientific* question: How does the brain transform acoustic blasts into what the subject experiences as meaningful words?[30]

But neither from the external nor from the involved point of view is there any place for the question: How does the child learn to impose meaning on meaningless noises? Normally, in the world as it actually exists, the participant just hears meaningful words and there is no justification for, in Merleau-Ponty's terms, taking the *logical conditions of possibility* as *conditions of existence*. There is no justification, that is, for taking the logical conditions of constitution as somehow producing the phenomena. According to Merleau-Ponty, this is the

---

[29] Searle, *Construction of Social Reality*, 73.

[30] One might wonder how, short of adopting our modern ontology, one could even pose these questions. It just turns out, however, that anyone, even an Aristotelian or Christian, can turn the words coming out of his or her mouth into meaningless noises simply by repeating the same word over and over. Of course, only a modern would think that the acoustic blast thus revealed could be fundamental.

mistake which leads thinkers like Husserl to invent a transcendental activity of assigning or imposing meaning that purports to explain how a subject who starts by experiencing meaningless squiggles or noises comes to experience them as meaningful words.

With Husserl's transcendental phenomenology and Searle's claim that the child *learns* to impose linguistic meaning on meaningless noises in mind, I could not help but think, when Searle says in explaining the constitution of institutional facts, that "functions are... *assigned* from *outside* by *conscious* observers and users," that he was echoing Husserl's claim that this assigning is something transcendental consciousness actually does. But Searle has now made clear that he never intended to make this Husserlian move. In his account of the constitution of social facts, as in his theory of action, he has from the start been working out a *logical analysis*.

Seen in this light, Searle's analysis exhibits a seductive structural parallel between the logic of action and the constitution of institutional facts. In the case of action, a *movement* X is an *action* Y if and only if it is caused by a representation of its conditions of satisfaction; likewise, a *bare fact* X counts as an *institutional fact* Y if and only if it is represented as counting as Y. This claim can be granted both by phenomenologists and by logical analysts—i.e. those who consider a representation to be a mental entity, as phenomenologists do, or merely a logical structure, as Searle does. But, just as existential phenomenology shows that intentional action is a special case of everyday comportment, and that *absorbed coping* has its own form of directedness, so it shows that institutional facts are a special case of social facts and that *social norms* have their own form of social status. So we must be prepared for trouble when we try to generalize Searle's logical account of institutional facts to social norms.

I hope to show that, in so far as Searle's analytical approach to institutional facts has the same structure as his approach to action, it suffers from the same neglect of important phenomenological distinctions. Just as he takes the causal role of propositional representations in intentional action as his paradigm and then, when forced to acknowledge absorbed coping, generalizes his logical analysis of action to *all* comportment, even absorbed coping, so, in his book on social reality, Searle takes institutional facts as his subject matter and ignores other ways that human beings add norms to nature.

In both cases, the logical analysis covers up an important distinction. Absorbed coping turns out to be *occasioned* by trying, but the skilled activity itself is *caused*, not by trying, but by a response to a gestalt tension that cannot be represented in a context-free way. And, as we shall now see, an *institutional fact is*, indeed, *constituted* by the imposition of a status function on a natural fact by represent- ing that fact as having that status. But institutional facts turn out to be dependent on *social norms* that are *produced* by a response to a gestalt tension that need not be symbolically represented or even representable.

Searle's way of stating his project covers up the distinction I am trying to bring out. He says: "I have already stipulated that any fact involving collective intentionality is a social fact. Thus, for example, hyenas hunting a lion and Congress passing legislation are both cases of social facts. Institutional facts, it will turn out, are a special subclass of social facts."[31]

Note that Searle begins by broadly defining social facts as any cases that involve collective intentionality. He then says he will not deal with the animal cases but only with the constitution of institutional facts. This dichotomy hides precisely the kind of social fact that I want to focus on as basic. I have been calling it a *social norm*. A social norm is a kind of social fact that is not found among animals but is not an institutional fact either. I thus propose to distinguish *three* kinds of social fact:

(1) *Social behavior.* Animals exhibit social behavior. For example, hyenas hunt as a pack and apes follow the lead of the strongest male. But as Searle points out, such social facts, while collectively *recognized*, are not *constituted* by a collective intentionally assigning to something natural a new status and function that *has no basis in nature*. Thus, while animals *exhibit* social behavior, they do not *constitute* institutional facts. Hunting in packs is just naturally more effective than hunting alone, and the alpha male is normally the strongest male.[32]

(2) *Social norms.* Social norms do not have a basis in nature. They are not based on natural functions, nor do they hold for the whole species. Rather, like proper pronunciation, they are learned by members of a group being socialized into a sense of what is collectively considered appropriate and inappropriate.[33] For example, gender and social class are produced and perpetuated by the members of a group being socialized into the appropriate way for those with a certain sex or those in a certain economic class to comport themselves. Likewise, a particular person could come to be a leader because people found it appropriate to follow that person's advice, imitate his style of speaking, etc., no matter how strong or smart that person was. This is presumably the way charismatic leaders are created.

---

[31] Searle, *Construction of Social Reality*, 38.

[32] There are ambiguous cases, of course, such as the fact that women are both *naturally* weaker than men and that, in most societies, they are also constituted as *socially* weaker.

[33] Animals can learn new functions—using a stick to get termites out of their holes, for example—and such techniques can, *if useful*, be passed on to the subsequent generations. But social norms are not discovered to be useful; instead, they are felt as appropriate.

Note that each such leader will gain his followers in his own way, and that there are no general rules for what counts as a charismatic leader.

(3) *Institutional facts.* In this case, some *type of* brute fact X *counts as* an institutional fact Y because it has been assigned a function by collective intentionality. At this level, someone would count as a leader because he went through a certain process such as coronation or election and swearing in. Followers must be able to recognize that what makes their leader a leader is not any natural or supernatural fact about him, but the collective agreement that assigns to a certain type of person the status of leader. Such a status carries with it a system of rights and obligations and thus is the basis of deontic power.

I will now argue, first, that, if Searle were to try to include social norms in his general theory of social reality, as he has reluctantly come to try to include absorbed coping in his theory of action, the notion of propositional representation he uses in analyzing the constitution of institutional facts would have to be extended in a way that would cover up the special nature of social norms. Second, I will argue that, since Searle sets out to "describe the elementary construction of social facts and the logical structure of *the development of institutional facts from simpler forms of social facts*,"[34] he needs an analysis of social norms that he cannot provide. As Merleau-Ponty would put it, Searle's analysis of the conditions of possibility of institutional facts is incomplete because it cannot account for their conditions of existence.

We have seen that, in his logical analysis of action, Searle wishes to extend his claim—i.e. that the bodily movements making up an action must be caused by a propositional representation of that action's success conditions—to cover absorbed coping. But we have also seen that he can do so only by introducing a minimal version of propositional representation according to which an agent, moving toward a sense of equilibrium, can be said to represent his comportment's success conditions—that this tension be reduced—even though the agent could not have in mind what that reduction would be like before achieving it.[35] Now we will see that, just as in the case of action Searle can only account for absorbed coping with its conditions of improvement by extending his logical notion of propositional representation to include indexicals, so here, to account for social norms, Searle would have to extend his account of constitution to

---

[34] Searle, *Construction of Social Reality*, 31; italics added.
[35] Nor could the agent describe in advance which tension would be reduced until it was reduced. The agent could only sense that the tension of the overall situation would somehow be reduced and that that would happen by reducing some part of the overall tension.

include the "assigning" of a social status, not just to *types* of facts, but to *instances* of facts that could not be described apart from their actual situated production.

It seems plausible that, taking institutional facts as the paradigm case, as Searle claims, "there can be no prelinguistic way of formulating the content of the agreement [on the value of the Y term] because there is no prelinguistic *natural* phenomenon there."[36] But phenomenological description shows that, in the case of social norms, the shift from the brute level to the value level need not be represented linguistically by the agents involved. Indeed, there need be no brute level. For those raised in a culture, a prelinguistic sense of tension can create a sense of the appropriateness and inappropriateness of a social activity without the mediation of linguistic representations. This sense of appropriateness does not involve the imposition of a type of status function on an independently recognizable and describable type of bare fact. Just as a child does not need to learn to *give* the meaningless noises coming out of people's mouths *meaning*, because in the child's world the sounds people make are already meaningful, so in the social world, social norms need not be *constituted* as are institutional facts. All that is needed to *produce* a social norm is collective agreement in judgments in the Wittgensteinian sense, i.e. the tensions and tension-resolutions that people socialized into a culture feel in specific social situations must be coordinated.

To see how this works, we can return to the phenomenon of standing the appropriate distance from others. A child learns such a social norm from her parents without the parents even sensing they are inducting her into the practice. Simply, if the child stands too close or too far away, the parent feels a tension and corrects the impropriety by backing away or moving closer. The child then ends up feeling comfortable in each specific situation only when standing the culturally appropriate distance away. Thus, from the phenomenological point of view, a certain *type of physical distance* doesn't *count as* the appropriate *type of social* distance; in each specific situation a person is just drawn to the comfortable and therefore appropriate place.[37]

But this would be an objection to Searle only if he were claiming to give a logical analysis of social norms, whereas he is clear that he is only attempting to give a logical analysis of how institutional facts are constituted. But if logical analysis goes "far beyond phenomenological analysis" so that the results of

---

[36] Searle, *Construction of Social Reality*, 69; italics added.

[37] The distance can feel wrong if one is in a strange culture or in a strange situation on one's own—if, for example, the other person has a cold or there is a loud air hammer nearby. But normally if it feels appropriate to one and to one's interlocutor, it *is* appropriate. In each specific situation, the appropriate distance is simply the distance at which those skilled in the culture's distance-standing practices and involved in that situation feel comfortable.

phenomenological analysis are "rendered irrelevant," Searle cannot simply ignore social norms. He will have to apply his logical apparatus to them. But, just as the logical requirements for a bodily movement's being an action have to be extended almost beyond recognition in order to apply to absorbed coping, the logical requirements for the constitution of institutional facts do not apply without radical modification to social norms.

To see this, we need only note that Searle claims that *natural facts* must be *constituted* as institutional facts by *symbolically representing* them, which seems to mean collectively recognizing their social status since, as natural facts, they have no social status. But, as our phenomenology has already revealed, the appropriateness of certain comportments is produced by socialization without there needing to be any linguistically describable status assigned to a brute fact. For example, in the case of distance standing, the agent need not be sensitive to a *class* of *physical distances* in a certain *type of situation* that is constituted as the appropriate distance; the agent need only be skillfully moving to lower a tension.

In general, Searle's constitutive rule need not apply to social norms. In the case of social norms, there need be no *type* of bare X that, under codifiable conditions, has a symbolically represented Y characteristic imposed upon it, the way a collective agreement concerning a certain *type* of cellulose with certain *types* of ink stains on it can be turned into legal tender by expressing the agreement in a rule. Indeed, what makes a certain practice appropriate is often so situationally determined that it may be impossible to specify a set of physical features that define the X term and to specify in a general way the specific status and function of the Y term. There need be no rule that can be codified.[38]

Of course, these arguments do not prevent the defender of the logic of the constitution of institutional facts such as Searle from extending his analysis to the constitution of social norms, but to do so he would have to weaken his account of constitution by changing the type of propositional representation involved from descriptive to demonstrative. The extended sort of representation could not be a symbolic representation of a *type* of fact X as having a certain *type* of status S in a certain *type* of context C, but rather would have to be a representation of a specific token X counting as having a specific status Y in a specific context C. One can, indeed, say from an external logical point of view that, in a particular

---

[38] I've made the argument that skills such as distance standing are so contextual that they cannot be captured in rules in Dreyfus and Dreyfus, *Mind over Machine*. Pierre Bourdieu and Wittgenstein make similar points. Moreover, although it is not necessary for my argument, it is interesting to note that social norms such as distance standing and gender do not have a single function or even a set of functions, the way institutional facts such as property, leadership, and money do.

situation, a specific objective physical distance is thus constituted as an appropriate social distance. But this is a very attenuated sense of constitution.

In sum, one can give a *phenomenological description* of the *conditions of existence* of social norms, but to give a *logical analysis* of their *conditions of possibility* one would have to extend the sense of symbolic representation from descriptive to indexical. As in the case of the generalization of the logical analysis of intentional acting to absorbed coping, such a move to an indexical saves the generality of the logical account of non-natural social facts, but only at the expense of covering up an important phenomenological distinction—the difference between context-free propositional intentionality and the context-determined sort of intentionality that Merleau-Ponty calls motor intentionality.

But Searle might well ask: Why should we care about social norms such as distance standing when the locus of deontic power in society is institutional facts? The answer is that, just as coping skills underlie and make possible intentional action, the social skills that produce and sustain social norms underlie and make possible social institutions. According to the phenomenologist, in the analysis of social reality, as in the case of comportment, the logical analyst has the dependencies upside down. Our sense of what is appropriate sets up the power relations that, in turn, give institutions the powers codified as rights and obligations.

Social institutions such as class and gender—which are surely important cases of power relations—depend for their stability and efficacy upon certain norms being accepted as natural, and this acceptance, in turn, depends on people's socialization into a sense of the appropriateness of certain styles of behavior. As Bourdieu, drawing on Merleau-Ponty, points out, the basis of power lies not in social institutions but in "the imperceptible cues of body *hexis*."[39] Certain forms of address and marks of respect as well as different styles of eye contact, intervention in conversation, deferential or defiant posture, and so forth are sensed as appropriate by members of each gender or class. These norms determine who commands and who obeys.

Given his commitment to the logical analysis of institutional facts as the source of deontic power, however, Searle is led to claim, for example, that the submissive attitude of women "*expresses* [rather than produces] their lack of power."[40] But this claim is ambiguous. In so far as women are naturally physically weaker than men, a cringing attitude in the presence of men may well express this lack of power, but the power we are interested in here is the institutional power

---

[39] Pierre Bourdieu, *Outline of a Theory of Practice*, tr. Richard Nice (Cambridge: Cambridge University Press, 1977), 82.
[40] Conversation between Searle and the author, 14 July 1999.

produced by collective intentionality. In such cases, according to Bourdieu, the prelinguistic bodily understanding that he calls our *habitus* continually "reactivates the sense objectified in institutions."[41] It is, after all, what feels appropriate for men and women to do that gets stabilized as a system of rough gender rules. And it is for the most part such "rules" that are subsequently codified as men's and women's rights and obligations.

Even institutional facts that are, indeed, constituted can, and normally do, evolve out of social norms. So, for example, although money is constituted, as Searle argues, by imposing a type of function on a type of object, the practice of using money grows out of and makes sense in terms of the practice of barter. Before a medium of exchange can exist there have to be practices of exchanging things. But in barter-exchanges the physical objects exchanged are not assigned a value by collective intentionality; rather, what something can be exchanged for depends on its actual and expected use-value and a shared sense of what is appropriate in the specific bargaining situation. Money comes into existence when barter develops into people's using some specific material thing—first in important trading situations, and then in all situations—as a medium of exchange. Searle avoids discussing the conditions of the existence of money by seeming to grant that the institution of money evolves, but then he passes over the pre-institutional stages of this evolution to begin his logical analysis at a stage where collective intentionality already accepts a type of X as having a type of function Y. Thus he says:

> Money gradually evolves in ways that we are not aware of. It is not the case that one fine day we all decided to count bits of paper as money; rather, the form that the collective intentionality takes is that we begin to accept... *promissory notes as media of exchange*, and we continue collectively to accept them.... One way to impose a function on an object is just to start using the object to perform that function.[42]

Searle's commitment to logical analysis leads him to overlook the social norms already involved in using something as a medium of exchange. In general, he blurs the distinction between two different kinds of collective intentionality— productive and constitutive—and so passes over the important developmental role social norms play in making possible the constitution of institutional facts.

Even in the case of highly codified institutions such as property, the institution must draw on the social norms out of which it evolved if it is to make sense to people and so be accepted and perpetuated. Our sense of the appropriate ways of using things, letting others use them, or excluding others from using them underlies our practices for dealing with property and, in the end, underlies the

---

[41] Bourdieu, *Logic of Practice*, 67.
[42] Searle, *Construction of Social Reality*, 126; italics added.

laws spelling out property relations in terms of rights and duties. Indeed, it is this underlying practical sense of the "spirit" of our institutions that allows judges to extend the laws codifying our practices to new cases.

In the last phenomenological analysis, then, the deontic powers that fascinate Searle draw their force from those norms of appropriateness whose difference from and priority over institutional facts is covered up by Searle's logical analysis.

4. An Alternative Ontology

We have now seen that Searle's logical analysis of comportment and of social facts is based on an analysis of the intentionality of an important subclass of each of these domains: in the case of comportment, *intentional action*, i.e. consciously (or unconsciously) trying to do something, and in the case of social facts, *institutional facts*, i.e. facts that set up rights and obligations. In these special cases, the actions and institutional facts analyzed are *made possible* (caused and constituted, respectively) by their being propositionally *represented as* actions and institutional facts. But there is another sort of comportment that I've called absorbed coping and another sort of social fact that I've called social norms that are too specific and contextual to be analyzed using the usual philosophical understanding of propositional representation.

We have also seen that Searle can extend the usual characterization of the sort of propositional representations that are the logical conditions for a movement's being an action and of a natural fact's counting as an institutional fact, so as to cover both absorbed coping and social norms. In so doing, however, he covers over an important logical and phenomenological distinction—the distinction between the actions and institutions that are *constituted* by a *representation* of their *context-free* conditions of possibility, and the absorbed coping and social norms *produced* by their *concrete situational* conditions of existence.

This distinction may not be important if one is simply interested in a general logical analysis of the role of all forms of representation in all forms of intentional constitution, but it becomes crucial if one is interested, as Searle is, in the causal powers of the mind and of institutions. Then logical analysis, by covering up the distinction between absorbed coping and social norms, on the one hand, and action and institutional facts, on the other, will necessarily cover up the way the former underlie the latter.

Such an analysis thereby reveals the need for a richer ontology than the Cartesian ontology of individual subjects, on the one hand, and natural objects, on the other. That, thanks to human beings, a meaningful world somehow devolves upon a meaningless universe is a contemporary given, accepted by analytic philosophers and phenomenologists alike. So, phenomenologists do not object in principle to the logical analyst's attempt to construct an account of how, given our modern set of ontological primitives—mental representations and brute facts—actions and institutional facts are possible.

Existential phenomenologists, such as Heidegger and Merleau-Ponty, however, stress the way human beings are always already in the world, and so object to *transcendental* phenomenologists, such as Husserl, who claim that, to make intelligible the possibility of a meaningful world, meaning must be brought into the meaningless universe from outside, as it were, by meaning-giving minds. We have now seen why they would also object to a logical account such as Searle's which claimed to account for *all* forms of comportment and *all* forms of social facts by generalizing and formalizing transcendental constitution.

Existential phenomenologists such as Merleau-Ponty claim that, to do justice to the unique character of absorbed coping and social norms, we should adopt a richer ontology than the Cartesian one of minds and nature assumed by Husserl and Searle. According to Merleau-Ponty, the absorbed coping and social norms that underlie action and institutions can't be understood as constituted by the imposition of the intentional on the physical. Rather, absorbed coping and social norms have what Merleau-Ponty calls a third kind of being—a kind of being that is neither natural nor constituted, but is produced by the embodied intentionality that is always already present in the world of involved, active, social beings.[43]

---

[43] I would like to thank Jerry Wakefield for first formulating Merleau-Ponty's account of action in terms of tension reduction. See our paper, Hubert L. Dreyfus and Jerry Wakefield, "Intentionality and the Phenomenology of Action", in Ernest Lepore and Robert Van Gulick (eds), *John Searle and his Critics* (Cambridge: Basil Blackwell, 1991), 259–70. I also thank Mark Wrathall for his helpful comments and especially Sean Kelly, whose criticisms and suggestions in response to many drafts of this chapter have transformed and improved it so much that it barely resembles the original version.

8

From Depth Psychology to Breadth Psychology

A Phenomenological Approach to Psychopathology (1988)

Hubert L. Dreyfus and Jerome Wakefield

Philosophical accounts of the nature of the mind are useful to psychologists because they suggest the form that explanations of mental phenomena should take.[1] By the same token, underlying philosophical conceptions can limit the flexibility of a field in its search for explanations of new or previously ignored phenomena and may have to be adjusted as the concerns of the field evolve. We believe that a change of focus in the field of psychoanalysis since Freud's day, from neurotic symptoms to character styles and personality disorders, has led to a situation where the original philosophy of mind underlying Freud's thinking is currently not very useful in moving the field forward. In fact, some features of that philosophy have simply been jettisoned without explicit discussion in much subsequent theorizing about ego development, object relations theory, and characterology. In this chapter, we will first make explicit some strands of the philosophy of mind that influenced Freud, considering some of its strengths and weaknesses as a guide to clinical theorizing. Then we will set out some features of an alternative approach to mental phenomena suggested by recent hermeneutic philosophers, similarly examining the implications of this view for theories of psychopathology and therapy, and contrast this view with Freud's. We believe this alternative view is worth exploring because it may provide a more useful way of understanding global character styles and disorders than has so far

---

[1] Both authors contributed equally to this chapter and to their rejoinder to Joel Kovel. Names are in alphabetical order.

been provided within the traditional view. In his psychological theorizing, Freud generally presupposed a traditional conception of the mind that we shall call the *epistemological* view of mind. Epistemology is the theory of knowledge, and we call Freud's view epistemological because it was originally developed by Descartes to explain how a subject can have knowledge of objects outside itself.

The epistemological conception of mind is roughly that the mind consists of a set of ideas, analogous to images or descriptions, that represent the outside world and may correspond or fail to correspond to what is actually out there in the world. The mind is a set of representations, and through these representations the person knows and relates to the world.

This view of the mind reached its culmination in Franz Brentano's notion of intentionality. According to Brentano, what is unique about mental states such as perception, memory, desire, belief, and fear is that they are all "of" something or "about" something. That is, you can't simply remember or desire or believe, you must remember or desire or believe something; your mental state must contain a specific idea or content that directs it at some feature of the world. Brentano claimed that it is this directedness or aboutness, called by him *intentionality*, which is characteristic of the mind and nothing else.

One student who followed Brentano's courses in Vienna was Sigmund Freud. He accepted the intentionalist conception of mind as a set of mental states directed toward objects by means of representations. However, the entire tradition from Descartes to Brentano had maintained that all intentional states must be conscious, whereas Freud learned from his work with hypnosis that not every mental representation was immediately accessible to reflection. Thus Freud was led to introduce the notion of an unconscious that, just like the conscious mind, was directed toward objects by means of representations, but whose representations were not directly accessible to the conscious subject. Even unconscious instinctual impulses, according to Freud, must be directed via unconscious ideas. For example, libidinal energy has its effect on our behavior by cathecting a specific representation or idea of some object, which we then desire for sexual gratification.

The epistemological conception of mind, joined with the idea that some mental contents can be unconscious, led to Freud's epistemological conceptions of pathology and therapy. Freud accounts for pathology by hypothesizing that representations that are deprived of consciousness remain causally active but are not integrated into the web of conscious mental states, and so manifest themselves to consciousness as symptoms. Thus the epistemological account of mind when used to account for pathology becomes a depth psychology concerned with representations buried in the unconscious. Corresponding to these epistemological views of mind and pathology, there is an epistemological conception of the therapeutic process. In depth psychology the basic problem is that some mental contents are unconscious, and not properly integrated into the ego's overall set of representations. Therapy thus consists of helping the patient to uncover the hidden contents and to reintegrate them into his overall mental system. Since the patient has strong motivations for keeping these contents hidden, the therapist must contend with the patient's resistance to allowing the contents to emerge.

As is well known, Freud's clinical focus was on neurotic symptomatology. His central insight was that such symptoms, as well as many other seemingly meaningless behaviors, could be understood as meaningful actions. Given this approach, the epistemological framework was well suited to Freud's theoretical endeavors. Once Freud came to see symptoms as meaningful actions, his epistemological view gave him a simple implicit framework for constructing explanations by hypothesizing underlying representational states analogous to the beliefs and desires that on the epistemological model explain ordinary action.

But not all versions of psychoanalysis are committed to understanding all psychological phenomena in terms of specific mental contents. From Wilhelm Reich's classic work on character analysis down to the current focus within ego psychology and object relations theory on neurotic styles and character pathology, there is a long and currently active psychoanalytic tradition that focuses on overall styles of behavior and experience. Theoreticians of character styles usually end up implicitly deviating from the representational approach to explanation because the epistemological view—for reasons to be explained later—does not provide an illuminating framework for explaining such styles in the way it does for symptoms. In short, reducing character and style to the effects of specific beliefs, desires, schemata, and other representational states just doesn't seem to be a useful strategy. Despite this, the idea that representations must mediate between subject and action has seldom been explicitly questioned in the psychoanalytic literature, and alternatives to the epistemological explanatory framework have not been systematically explored. The remainder of this chapter will be an attempt to distill a nonrepresentational approach to the explanation of pathology from the works of recent hermeneutic philosophers as a step toward developing an alternative possible framework for current practice.

Recently, philosophers such as Martin Heidegger and Maurice Merleau-Ponty, reacting against the Cartesian tradition, have developed an alternative model of the mind's relation to reality. This account is so radical that, strictly speaking, these philosophers do not refer to the mind at all. Rather they prefer to speak of the way that the whole human being is related to the world. Indeed, even "relation" is misleading, since it suggests the coming together of two separate entities—human being and world—whereas these philosophers see mind and world as inseparable. So they are finally driven to replace the epistemological relation of subject and object with a way of being they call "being-in-the-world," in which human being is a kind of space in which coping with certain kinds of beings becomes possible. Since ontology is the study of that which determines entities as entities, this approach to the mind is called *ontological.*

The ontological view does not deny that human beings sometimes have mental states by which their minds are directed towards objects. Rather, the ontologists assert that mental states presuppose a context in which objects can show up and make sense, so that the context both opens up and limits the kinds of objects that can be represented or can be dealt with directly. According to Heidegger, this context is provided by social practices. The shared practices into which we are socialized provide a background understanding of what counts as objects, what counts as human beings, and ultimately what counts as real, on the basis of which we can direct our actions towards particular things and people. Heidegger calls this background understanding of what it means to be, which is embodied in the tools, language, and institutions of a society and in each person growing up in that society, but not represented in that person's mind, an understanding of Being. This understanding of Being creates what Heidegger calls a *clearing* (*Lichtung*) in which entities can then show up for us.

The clearing is on the side neither of the subject nor of the object—it is not a set of implicit and explicit beliefs nor a set of facts—rather it contains both and makes their relation possible. It is a context that both opens up and limits the kinds of objects we can deal with—or, as Heidegger puts it, what things can show up for us *as,* for example, *as* a hammer, or *as* a person.

Merleau-Ponty, following Heidegger, compares this clearing to the illumination in a room. The illumination allows us to perceive objects, but is not itself an object toward which the eye can be directed. He argues that this clearing is correlated with our bodily skills and thus with the bodily stance we take toward people and things. Each person not only incorporates his culture, but also his subculture and the understanding of human beings and of objects that is his family's variation of the current social practices. Finally, each person has his or her own embodied understanding of what counts as real, which is, of course, not private but is a variation on the shared public world.

The ontological view leads to an alternative account of the unconscious, of psychopathology, and therapy. Merleau-Ponty claims that pathology occurs when some aspect of a person's relationship to particular objects in the world merges into the context on the basis of which objects are encountered. When this happens the person's world or clearing becomes restricted and rigid. The person suffers from a lack of possibilities that he cannot understand and over which he has no control. To highlight the contrast between Freud and Merleau-Ponty, this ontological account of psychopathology as the expanding of content into context might be called *breadth* psychology.

On this ontological view, pathology occurs when a particular way a person relates to some people or some objects becomes a way of relating to all people and all objects, so that it becomes the form or style of all relationships. That is, some aspect of the epistemological relation of a subject to other persons and objects, which should take place in the clearing, becomes a dimension of the clearing itself. Merleau-Ponty calls this shift *generalization*, and uses this idea to give an alternative account of repression:

Repression...consists in the subject's entering upon a certain course of action—a love affair, a career, a piece of work—in his encountering on this course some barrier, and, since he has the strength neither to surmount the obstacle nor to abandon the enterprise, he remains imprisoned in the attempt and uses up his strength indefinitely renewing it....Time in its passage does not carry away with it these impossible projects; it does not close up on traumatic experience; the subject remains open to the same impossible future, if not in his explicit thoughts, then in his actual being.[2]

Merleau-Ponty's prose is famous for its literary polish but hardly for its simplicity and clarity. He is saying that in a neurotic reaction to frustration and conflict the subject gets stuck in a certain way of having a clearing or sense of being, and so repeats his "solution" endlessly, thus generalizing it and taking it out of time.

This is, of course, a new version of the unconscious. Merleau-Ponty uses as an example of such a generalized unconscious the case of someone who relates to each person as if the issue were one of determining who is inferior and who is superior. In Merleau-Ponty's terms, inferior/superior, once an issue in the clearing, has become a dimension of the clearing. Merleau-Ponty uses the notion of context—this time called *atmosphere*—to explain why such a self-defeating stance is outside of the sufferer's awareness and control: "An inferiority complex...means that I have committed myself to inferiority, that I have made it my abode, that this past, though not a fate, has at least a specific weight and is not a set of events over there, at a distance from me, but the atmosphere of my present."[3]

Once such a way of taking people becomes a dimension of the background of all experience, a person is unlikely to experience anything that could cause him to change his one-sided way of relating to other people. Thus Merleau-Ponty arrives at an account of the static character of neurotic time, parallel to, but totally different from, Freud's notion of the timelessness of the unconscious:

[2] Merleau-Ponty, *Phenomenology of Perception*, 83.
[3] Merleau-Ponty, *Phenomenology of Perception*, 442.

One present among all presents thus acquires an exceptional value; it displaces the others and deprives them of their value as authentic presents. We continue to be the person who once entered on this adolescent affair, or the one who once lived in this parental universe. New perceptions, new emotions even, replace the old ones, but this process of renewal touches only the content of our experience and not its structure. Impersonal time continues its course, but personal time is arrested... This fixation does not merge into memory; it even *excludes memory* in so far as the latter spreads out in front of us... whereas this past which remains our true present does not leave us but *remains constantly hidden behind our gaze instead of being displayed before it.* The traumatic experience does not survive as a *representation* in the mode of objective consciousness and as a "dated" moment; it is of its essence to survive *only as a manner* of *being with a certain degree of generality.*[4]

So far we have seen that Merleau-Ponty claims that if a child is faced with a particularly painful conflict, the specific pattern already in place in the child's life gets generalized and becomes a dimension of the background upon which, from then on, persons and events show up. Merleau-Ponty does not tell us just why a conflict leads to the sort of ontological generalization that constitutes a character disorder, but using some ideas from Heidegger we can construct an account of how and why such a change might occur. To begin with, conflicts lead to strong emotions. Heidegger classifies emotions and moods as forms of what he calls *attunement (Befindlichkeit)*, and he notes that attunements in his sense have an ontological capacity, i.e. they can color a whole world.[5]

Moods, for example, are always total. When one is in an elated mood everything is encountered as colorful and challenging, and, conversely, in depression everything shows up as drab and uninteresting. Emotions, unlike moods, are not always general. They can be quite specific, such as fear of a particular event, or anger at a particular person. Indeed, they normally are directed toward something specific that concerns some specific aspect of a person in some specific way. But emotions can flare up and come to color the child's whole world like a mood, as when a child's anger at how his father is treating him becomes anger at how his father *always* treats him, and even rage at how *everyone* has always treated him.

Now if we apply these ideas to the process of ontological generalization, we can see why emotion plays a central role. When the issues set up by the family lead to a crisis, the emotional reaction of the child not only magnifies and intensifies the crisis, but actually totalizes it, so that it engulfs the child's whole world.[6]

---

[4] Merleau-Ponty, *Phenomenology of Perception*, 83.

[5] Heidegger, *Being and Time*, §§29 and 32.

[6] Silvan S. Tomkins, "Script Theory: Differential Magnifications of Affects", in H. E. Howe Jr. and R. A. Dienstbier (eds), *Nebraska Symposium on Motivation, 1978* (26; Lincoln, NE: University of Nebraska Press, 1979), develops a similar idea but he only speaks of affects as amplifying and generalizing but not as totalizing.

Ordinarily, the emotion then subsides and the meaning it has carried out to the limits of the world again comes to be directed at the appropriate object in the world. But if, for any reason, the emotion is arrested in its course, then the local issue remains totalized and becomes an ontological dimension, or to put it in a way in keeping with Merleau-Ponty's emphasis on the body as correlative with the world, the body remains frozen in a certain stance which then distorts everything that shows up in its clearing.

On the hermeneutic account, a child comes to encounter all significant figures as superior, for example, not because the representations of specific threatening others make him anxious and are therefore repressed and return in disguised form as symptoms. An unconscious belief that he is inferior would not adequately account for the pervasive style of his behavior nor his imperviousness to counter-arguments. A belief, or schema, is inadequate to account for a style of behavior because such mental representations do not explain how the person who has them behaves with the appropriate style in each particular case.[7] To see why a belief or schema cannot account for a style, take a concrete example. If our patient simply believes he is inferior or has a rule, e.g. whenever asked to do something claim he is not adequate for the job, he would not know just how to apply the rule to anomalous situations such as when his wife asks him to take out the garbage or when his boss congratulates him on work he has done. Yet it is clear that he will exhibit his unique style of inferiority behavior in each of these situations and indefinitely many others. According to Merleau-Ponty's account, the child's anger or shame about inferiority is sedimented into his posture and other body-sets, which structure his world so that all significant persons show up as dominating and lead him to respond in a similar way to each new situation. We do not claim to know how a human body picks up a style of behavior, but it does seem clear that a cognitivist account in terms of beliefs and rules cannot explain precisely the unity of style across many types of situation that need explaining.

Even after an issue *in* the world, e.g. who is superior, has become one of the dimensions of the clearing, however, a person's world is not completely static and one-dimensional. There are still other dimensions people can show up on, e.g. as sexually attractive. To understand the last step to the closed world of pathology requires explication of one last ontological notion from Heidegger and Merleau-Ponty. Heidegger, in his later work, introduces the idea of a particular event in the clearing or Open, which focuses and stabilizes the cultural meanings already

---

[7] See Michael A. Westerman, "Meaning and Psychotherapy: A Reconceptualization of the Value and Limitations of Insight-Oriented, Behavioral, and Strategic Approaches", American Psychological Association Convention (Montreal, 1980).

in the public practices. As Heidegger puts it: "There must always be some being in this Open ... in which the openness takes its stand and attains its constancy."[8] He gives as an example the Greek temple that opens up and organizes a multi-dimensional world by highlighting crucial issues that then become the locus of conflicts of interpretation and the starting point of history. Heidegger's notion of an event that gives constancy to a cultural clearing might be called a cultural paradigm, for it has much in common with Thomas Kuhn's notion of a scientific paradigm, a particular experiment or explanation that serves as a model of good science and organizes the activities of researchers in a scientific community. Søren Kierkegaard emphasizes that a lover or a cause to which one is committed can serve the same function in an individual's life.[9]

In his last book Merleau-Ponty introduces a similar idea concerning the role of particular objects or events in an individual's life. "It is necessary to have the ontological capacity ... to take *a* being as a representative of Being.... The fixation of 'character' [takes place] by investment of the openness of Being in an entity—and, henceforth, takes place *through this entity*. Any entity can be *accentuated* as an emblem of Being."[10] The emblem, as Merleau-Ponty calls the paradigmatic object, has the effect of reorganizing the background or clearing in which all contents appear. Thus, even though it is an object we actually confront, it performs the same function as the clearing.

Heidegger and Merleau-Ponty have noticed two closely related but antithetical kinds of ontological entities. Heidegger's notion of an event that gives constancy to a cultural clearing might be called a *positive paradigm*. Merleau-Ponty, on the other hand, is suggesting that there can also be negative paradigms—objects, persons, or events that focus a world not in opening it up but by closing it down, thus substituting timelessness for history.

As opposed to a positive paradigm, which determines what is important in a shared, many-dimensional reality and so sets up conflicts of interpretation, the neurotic paradigm is a telling example that shows the hopeless way things are once and for all. A neurotic paradigm totalizes the world in advance so that all anomalies are either ignored or assumed to be assimilable to the reigning account. A healthy paradigm, on the other hand, allows anomalies to be revealed that can then be focused on as possibilities containing a truth that can challenge the old theory and may become central in a new one.

---

[8] Martin Heidegger, "The Origin of the Work of Art", *Poetry, Language, Thought* (New York: Harper & Row, 1971), 61.

[9] Søren Kierkegaard, *Fear and Trembling* (Princeton: Princeton University Press, 1983).

[10] Maurice Merleau-Ponty, *The Visible and the Invisible* (Chicago: Northwestern University Press, 1968), 270.

If psychopathology is the result of generalizing an issue until it becomes a dimension of experience and then focusing this dimension so that it colors all the others, then the cure must begin by showing the patient that his way of being-in-the-world has acquired a pervasive coloring. This is not to say that the patient must be given a new frame. The patient's problem is not merely that he has a disabling frame and needs a freer one. His problem is that a normal and sensible occasional issue, like the question of superiority, has become a frame. Any other specific issue that was treated as a frame would be just as disabling. So the problem for therapy is not changing frames, but putting some issue that has become a frame back into the patient's picture.

The patient cannot see that his clearing has a fixed and narrow content because he has nothing to contrast it with. So what can the therapist do? The therapist may try to lead the patient to experience the world before it became one-dimensional by being focused by an emblematic event, or, even further back, to remember how things showed up before a specific issue in the family became one of the dimensions of his clearing. Of course, any ordinary memory will show the past as already colored by the current clearing, but perhaps there can be a kind of spontaneous recall, especially in dreams, in which past events are experienced as they were originally, not as they have been retroactively interpreted.

To get the patient to see he has a pervasive interpretation, the analyst can call attention to the pervasive and inappropriate style of the patient's behavior by making it difficult for the patient to fit the therapist into his world and calling attention to the anomalies that arise when he tries. Thus transference would be conceptualized differently in these two pure cases. Rather than following Freud in using transference primarily in dealing with specific resistances, one would work with transference, as most current therapists do anyway, as an occasion for showing the patient the inappropriate coloring or style of his world by pointing out that he is reacting to the therapist in a typical but inappropriate way. The therapist thus uses the fact that he inevitably becomes an emblematic focus for the one dimension through which the neurotic sees everything in his world to call attention to this dimension.

Even if the patient were thus led by contrast with the past to recognize the coloring of his present clearing, however, he would be likely to insist that at a certain time in the past he simply found out how things really are. Then the therapeutic strategy for turning the ontological back into the epistemological must undermine the patient's current sense of reality that the style or pattern of his life makes manifest. This is accomplished by working with the patient to piece together an account of how the patient's narrow version of reality developed through a series of accidental events, misunderstandings, and frozen emotions.

Pointing out cognitive contradictions in the patient's view of reality will also help overcome the patient's conviction that reality must be the way he sees it.

Simultaneously the patient must be led to see the connection between his view of reality and his pain. The therapist thus tries to get the patient to see that what he takes to be unchangeable reality is really simply his particular and quirky story, and that this understanding has a high price. This "genealogy" will tend to undermine the patient's conviction that his way of seeing things is the way things are and have to be.

Also, since an issue in the world becomes a dimension when it is totalized by an emotion that is not allowed to subside in the normal way, the emotion that has been stuck in world expansion must be worked through so that the issue it has ontologized can shrink down to size. Only then will the patient be able to see the struggle for, say, superiority, only where it is appropriate—rather than as the central dimension of all human interactions.

Finally, resistance will be considered differently on the two views. Whereas Freud considered resistance to be the interpersonal manifestation of the patient's attempts to hide certain mental contents, and thus part of the pathological process, an ontological approach emphasizes that the patient is simply defending what to him is the real meaning of his experience. In other words resistance displays not merely pathology, but a form of integrity.

These techniques are not new to psychotherapy. The ontological view does not change what counts as pathology nor does it cast doubt on what have been successful ways of treating it. Rather, it conceptualizes both the pathology and the treatment in a new way. The issue that, as a dimension, has come to govern all possible ways of acting for the patient must once again become an object for him so that he can confront and deal with it freely as one issue among others in his world.

There are differences between the practices dictated by the two conceptualizations in their pure forms, however. These differences are not obvious in actual therapy since new ideas have entered therapy since Freud, and even Freud saw and did many things his model did not adequately explain. Nonetheless, one who thinks of neurosis as a pattern of behavior that has become generalized into an ontological dimension will tend to focus on character pathologies rather than symptoms. Furthermore, if Merleau-Ponty is right that a rigid reality is correlated with a rigid body stance, some kind of body work may be called for. Thus the kind of pathology that is taken as paradigmatic and the kind of therapy practiced begins to sound more like the Reich of *Character Analysis* than like Freud of the Dora case.[11]

---

[11] Wilhelm Reich, *Character Analysis (Part 1)* (New York: Simon & Schuster, 1972).

The idea of an ontological form of therapy based on Heidegger's work is not new. Both Ludwig Binswanger and Medard Boss are well-known existential or hermeneutic therapists. Both understand psychopathology as a distortion of the human clearing that makes it narrow and rigid. Binswanger distinguishes my world from *the* world and thinks of therapy as adjusting my world to the world. He was concerned with the style of a person's world. Thus, for example, he was not interested in the content of dreams but in the personal way of structuring space and time that dreams revealed. Binswanger also was concerned with constructing a narrative that captured the developing pattern of a person's life, but he was interested in the narrative as a way of clarifying and rendering consistent a patient's way of being-in-the-world, not as a way of undermining a patient's sense of reality. Thus, in "The Case of Ellen West," Binswanger tells how he helped his patient see that her desires were hopelessly contradictory, and so gave her the courage and insight to confront the nature of her own being-in-the-world (which in turn led her to commit suicide). In contrast, Medard Boss in his "Daseinanalysis" was committed to healing the patient by opening up his or her constricted world. He used the transference as a way of providing the love absent in a patient's childhood so as to enable the patient to develop a self that could open itself to more styles of relationship. Both Binswanger and Boss, however, get their basic conceptions from early Heidegger so they have no sense of the role of paradigms—introduced by later Heidegger—nor of the lived body introduced by Merleau-Ponty. Having only the idea of an empty clearing as in early Heidegger, both see psychopathology as a constriction of the patient's world, but neither sees this narrowing as the result of content becoming context by being focused in a paradigm and/or sedimented in a specific body stance correlated with specific expectations.

It is now time to consider briefly the relative merits of the epistemological and ontological views as conceptualizations of neurotic and character pathologies. Let us first take a look at a simple, very circumscribed symptom. In his *Introductory Lectures on Psychoanalysis*, Freud describes a man who, at odds with his wife, cannot find a book she gave him as a gift. When the couple are reconciled once more, he finds the book without difficulty. According to Freud a specific memory had been repressed.

Now, Merleau-Ponty holds that we never reject a specific memory in such a case. Rather, repression is always directed against a region of our experience, which includes a whole class of memories. Moreover, it is not the number of forgotten memories, but why the forgetting occurs at all that distinguishes Merleau-Ponty's view from Freud's. About Freud's example, Merleau-Ponty says, "Everything connected with his wife had ceased to exist for him, he had shut it out from his life, and at one stroke, broken the circuit of all actions relating to her, and thus placed himself on the hither side of all knowledge and ignorance, assertion and negation, in so far as these were voluntary."[12]

Merleau-Ponty is saying, somewhat hyberbolically, that this man had not merely shut out a group of memories, but he had shut out a space of possible relations with his wife, a dimension of experience. His coldness to her had become part of his background, and he now saw his wife differently, in fact was no longer capable of seeing or responding to her in a range of ways that had earlier been available to him. She has ceased to exist as the same sort of being she was before, for the man's space of possible actions, the "circuit" of actions, as Merleau-Ponty puts it, has been radically altered. This collapse of space of possibilities when we come to see someone differently suggests what Merleau-Ponty has in mind when he says that the man is now on the "hither side of knowledge and ignorance!" The man's coldness began as a choice, a response to specific events within a relationship that contained many possibilities. But the coldness generalized so that open and warm feelings toward his wife are no longer a potential in his world. It is no longer the case that he could be warm or cold, but chooses to be cold. Rather, his field of possible choices has actually narrowed.

But how does the collapse of a set of possibilities for feeling and action toward his wife explain the man's inability to remember where he put his wife's gift? Merleau-Ponty's answer is, "In hysteria and repression, we may well overlook something although we know of it, because our memories and our body, instead of presenting themselves to us in singular and determinate conscious acts, are enveloped in generality.... [M]emories are expressly grasped and recognized by us only in so far as they adhere generally to that area of our body and our life to which they are relevant."[13] In other words, generalization of some issue into the background provides a new context or ground in which certain memories may not easily emerge. Generalization, then, sets bounds not only to the immediate availability of objects but to the availability of the past. The man's generalized issue with his wife has created a context where the memory of the gift does not easily come to mind.

Merleau-Ponty's account has the advantage that it attempts to explain how the symptom resulted from more general background issues. As a result it provides a built-in partial answer to the problem of the "choice of symptom" that has puzzled analytic theoreticians since Freud. On the other hand, Merleau-Ponty's explanation seems excessively convoluted, and goes far beyond the facts given in

[12] Merleau-Ponty, *Phenomenology of Perception*, 162.
[13] Merleau-Ponty, *Phenomenology of Perception*, 162.

Freud's case vignette. In fact, the patient's wife did not "cease to exist" for him, and the degree of his shutting her out is unclear. There is no report of the loss of other memories concerned with her; in fact, it is the isolated nature of the amnesia that makes it so striking. In all, Freud's case does seem like one best explained at least initially as the repression of a specific memory. A deeper explanation might require some of Merleau-Ponty's machinery, especially if we wanted to explore why this man is the sort of man who would respond to marital disharmony in the way he did, but the epistemological level of explanation seems to have a rightful place here as the simplest explanation covering the known facts. In the case of other symptoms, the facts might warrant the opposite conclusion.

We turn now to the domain of character disorders. Character formation has always been a problematic area for traditional psychoanalytic explanation. A major impetus for dealing with character has been the desire to explain symptom choice, but once character is acknowledged to be involved, and in need of explanation itself, the overall explanatory situation seems to become worse rather than better. As David Shapiro says, "The view of symptomatic behavior as a reflection of how individuals characteristically think and see things is in certain ways not only different from but actually contrary to the traditional dynamic view."[14]

Freud himself appears to have been quite dissatisfied with his own attempts to give the representationalist mechanics of character formation. The classic position is stated in Freud's *Three Essays on Sexuality*: "What we describe as a person's 'character' is built up to a considerable extent from the material of sexual excitations and is composed of instincts that have been fixed since childhood, of constructions achieved by means of sublimation, and of other constructions."[15] Yet character traits are so global that it seems hard to imagine their derivation from specific mental contents. Even in his most explicit attempts to account for traits, Freud acknowledged this essential mystery. In "Character and Anal Eroticism," he argues that an entire constellation of traits, including orderliness, stinginess, and obstinacy, derive from fixations in the anal stage of psychosexual development through the mechanisms of reaction formation and sublimation. Yet he acknowledges that "the intrinsic necessity for this connection is not clear, of course, even to myself,"[16] and that his explanations leave a residue of unintelligibility to the connection. When he confronts the relationship between character and symptom in his paper, "The Disposition to Obsessional

[14] David Shapiro, *Autonomy and Rigid Character* (New York: Basic Books, 1981), 3–4.
[15] Sigmund Freud, *Three Essays on the Theory of Sexuality*, ed. James Strachey (Complete Psychological Works of Sigmund Freud, 7; London: Hogarth, 1905), 238.
[16] Sigmund Freud, *Character and Anal Erotism*, ed. James Strachey (Complete Psychological Works of Sigmund Freud, 9; London: Hogarth Press, 1908), 172.

Neurosis," he insists that "in the field of the development of *character* we are bound to meet with the same instinctual forces which we have found at work in the neuroses," and at the same time recognizes that "a sharp theoretical distinction between the two is necessitated by the single fact that the failure of repression and the return of the repressed . . . are absent in the formation of character."[17] But psychoanalysis is a process for exploiting failures of repression to bring forth the repressed, so Freud is forced to admit: "The processes of the formation of character are more obscure and less accessible to analysis than neurotic ones."[18]

Later, in *The Ego and the Id*, Freud suggests identification as a central mechanism of character formation, along with sublimation. He describes identification as an alteration of the ego in which an object that has been lost is somehow replaced by a representation in the ego. This is as near as the representational view can get to the notion of an emblem. But without the notion of a clearing, how this process works, and especially how it brings about global stylistic changes in behavior, cannot be explained. Instead Freud admits: "The exact nature of this substitution is as yet unknown to us."[19] Indeed, the two mechanisms Freud most often cites as possibly leading from specific representational states to global character traits, identification and sublimation, have in common that their natures are extremely vague and obscure compared to other defense strategies.

We feel that Freud's tentativeness was well-founded, and that there are intrinsic difficulties in explaining global character styles in terms of the workings of specific representational states. We cannot go through the entire argument here, nor is there likely to be a knockdown argument that complex webs of beliefs and desires, impulses, and defenses could never explain character. Again, it is a matter of plausibility and the smoothness of fit between theory and data. Character traits are notoriously difficult to change through the usual means of cognitive or depth approaches. They are not merely ego-syntonic, which might be explained by rationalization or very smoothly working defensive structures, but they are experienced as part of the essence and identity of the self. Rather than a person's style getting its meaning from specific mental contents, our intuition is that the direction of meaning—and hence of interpretation—should go the other way, with the global style giving meaning to the specific contents.

---

[17] Sigmund Freud, *The Disposition to Obsessional Neurosis: A Contribution to the Problem of Choice of Neurosis*, ed. James Strachey (Complete Psychological Works of Sigmund Freud, 12; London: Hogarth, 1913), 323.

[18] Freud, *Disposition to Obsessional Neurosis*, 323.

[19] Sigmund Freud, *The Ego and the Id*, ed. James Strachey (Complete Psychological Works of Sigmund Freud, 19; London: Hogarth, 1923), 29.

Contrary to the awkwardness of the epistemological approach, Merleau-Ponty's ontological view directly accounts for the extreme globalness, ego-syntonicity, and relative intractability to therapeutic efforts of character pathology. The context, or background, in which representational states appear will automatically have global implications for all areas of functioning, for it will determine the possible kinds of representations that can appear. Ontological generalization by its nature affects the whole of ego functioning at once. It is ego-syntonic because it is the structure of the ego, its source is not external hidden impulses nor particular introjects. And it is difficult to change in part because there is no easy target, such as an unconscious idea, to try to change. It is no less than the global structure of the patient's world, which is everywhere at once, that therapist and patient must attempt to alter.

Indeed, it is hard to see how therapy could succeed if every aspect of the patient's life had been infected by his one-dimensional view. For therapeutic, genealogical reconstruction of the arbitrariness of the patient's sense of reality then would be seen by the patient merely as showing the strange and idiosyncratic route he followed in arriving at the truth. Fortunately, however, this need not be his response. When a patient's world becomes totalized and one-dimensional, other ways of behaving from earlier days endure. These marginal stances, interpretations, and practices endure precisely because they are too fragmentary and trivial to be seen as important. The therapist must recover and focus the lost possibilities. Here transference has a positive role. Merleau-Ponty seems to be getting at this positive function of transference—the therapist as a positive paradigm—when he writes: "Psychoanalytical treatment does not bring about its cure by producing direct awareness of the past, but ... by binding the subject to his doctor through new existential relationships. ... It is a matter of reliving this or that as significant, and this the patient succeeds in doing only by seeing his past in the perspective of his co-existence with the doctor."[20] Other ways of encountering things and people, which were once possible for the patient and are still present in his body and behavior but are dispersed, can be drawn together in the patient's relation to the therapist. The therapist can thus become for the patient a provisional paradigm that focuses and stabilizes an open and multidimensional world.

[20] Merleau-Ponty, *Phenomenology of Perception*, 445.

9

What is Moral Maturity?

Towards a Phenomenology
of Ethical Expertise (1992)

Hubert L. Dreyfus and Stuart E. Dreyfus

Phenomenology has a great deal to contribute to the contemporary confrontation between those who demand a *detached* critical *morality* based on *principles* that tells us what is *right* and those who defend an *ethics* based on *involvement in a tradition* that defines what is *good*.[1] This new debate between *Moralität* and *Sittlichkeit* has produced two camps which can be identified with Jürgen Habermas and John Rawls on the one hand, and Bernard Williams and Charles Taylor on the other. The same polarity appears in feminism where the Kohlberg scale, which defines the highest stage of moral maturity as the ability to stand outside the situation and justify one's actions in terms of universal moral principles, is attacked by Carol Gilligan in the name of an intuitive response to the concrete situation.

What one chooses to investigate as the relevant phenomena will prejudice from the start where one stands on these important issues. If one adopts the traditional philosophical approach one will focus on the rationality of moral judgments. For example, on the first page of his classic text, *The Moral Judgment of the Child*, Jean Piaget explicitly restricts ethics to judgments. He states at the start that "It is the moral judgment that we propose to investigate, not moral behavior..."[2] Maurice Mandelbaum in his book, *The Phenomenology of Moral Experience*, a recent but unsuccessful attempt to introduce phenomenology into current ethical debate, makes the same move:

---

[1] We would like to thank Drew Cross, David Greenbaum, Wayne Martin, Charles Spinosa, Charles Taylor and Kailey Vernallis for their helpful comments.

[2] Jean Piaget, *The Moral Judgment of the Child* (Glencoe, IL: Free Press, 1935), p. vii.

The phenomenological approach's... essential methodological conviction is that a solution to any of the problems of ethics must be educed from, and verified by, a careful and direct examination of individual moral judgments.[3]

Moreover, Mandelbaum does not seem to realize that he has already made a fateful exclusion. He claims that: "Such an approach... aims to discover the generic characteristics of *all* moral experience."[4]

But why equate moral experience with judgment, rather than with ethical comportment? Mandelbaum's answer to this question is symptomatic of the intellectualist prejudice embodied in this approach. He first gives a perceptive nod to spontaneous ethical comportment:

I sense the embarrassment of a person, and turn the conversation aside; I see a child in danger and catch hold of its hand; I hear a crash and become alert to help.[5]

He then notes:

Actions such as these (of which our daily lives are in no small measure composed) do not... seem to spring from the self: in such cases I am reacting directly and spontaneously to what confronts me.... [I]t is appropriate to speak of "reactions" and "responses," for in them a sense of initiative or feeling of responsibility is present... [W]e can only say that we acted as we did because the situation extorted that from us.[6]

Mandelbaum next contrasts this unthinking and egoless response to the situation with deliberate action in which one experiences the causal power of the "I."

In "willed" action, on the other hand, the source of action is the self. I act in a specific manner because I wish, or will, to do so... the "I" is experienced as being responsible for willed action.[7]

He continues:

To give a phenomenological account of this sense of responsibility is not difficult. It is grounded in the fact that every willed action aims at and espouses an envisioned goal. When we envision a goal which transcends what is immediately given, and when we set ourselves to realizing that goal, we feel the action to be ours.

And focusing on willed or deliberate action and its goal, we arrive at rationality. In willed actions... we can give a *reason*: we acted as we did because we aimed to achieve a particular goal. [W]hen asked to explain our action, we feel no hesitation in attributing it to the value of the goal which we aimed to achieve.[8]

---

[3]   Maurice Mandelbaum, *The Phenomenology of Moral Experience* (New York: Free Press, 1955), 31.
[4]   Mandelbaum, *Phenomenology of Moral Experience*, 36; our italics.
[5]   Mandelbaum, *Phenomenology of Moral Experience*, 48.
[6]   Mandelbaum, *Phenomenology of Moral Experience*, 48–9.
[7]   Mandelbaum, *Phenomenology of Moral Experience*, 48.
[8]   Mandelbaum, *Phenomenology of Moral Experience*, 48–9.

Thus the phenomenology of moral experience comes to focus on judgment and justification. Granted that one aspect of the moral life and most of moral philosophy has been concerned with choice, responsibility, and justification, we should, nonetheless, take seriously what Mandelbaum sees and immediately dismisses, viz., that most of our everyday ethical comportment consists in unreflective, egoless responses to the current interpersonal situation. Why not begin on the level of this spontaneous coping?

Several methodological precautions must, then, be borne in mind in attempting a phenomenology of the ethical life.

1. We should begin by describing our everyday ongoing ethical coping.
2. We should determine under which conditions deliberation and choice appear.
3. We should beware of making the typical philosophical mistake of reading the structure of deliberation and choice back into our account of everyday coping.

Since our everyday ethical skills seem to have been passed over and even covered up by moral philosophy, we had better begin with some morally neutral area of expertise and delineate its structure. To this end we will lay out a phenomenological description of five stages in the development of expertise, using driving and chess as examples. Only then will we turn to the much more difficult questions of the nature of ethical expertise, the place and character of moral judgments, and the stages of moral maturity.

1. A Phenomenology of Skill Acquisition

Stage 1: Novice

Normally, the instruction process begins with the instructor decomposing the task environment into context-free features which the beginner can recognize without benefit of experience. The beginner is then given rules for determining actions on the basis of these features, like a computer following a program. The student automobile driver learns to recognize such interpretation-free features as speed (indicated by his speedometer). Timing of gear shifts is specified in terms of speed. The novice chess player learns a numerical value for each type of piece regardless of its position, and the rule: "Always exchange if the total value of pieces captured exceeds the value of pieces lost." But such rigid rules often fail to work. A loaded car stalls on a hill; a beginner in chess falls for every sacrifice.

Stage 2: Advanced Beginner

As the novice gains experience actually coping with real situations, he begins to note, or an instructor points out, perspicuous examples of meaningful additional components of the situation. After seeing a sufficient number of examples, the student learns to recognize them. Instructional *maxims* now can refer to these new *situational aspects*. We use the terms *maxims* and *aspects* here to differentiate this form of instruction from the first, where strict *rules* were given as to how to respond to context-free *features*. Since maxims are phrased in terms of aspects they already presuppose experience in the skill domain.

The advanced beginner driver uses (situational) engine sounds as well as (nonsituational) speed. He learns the maxim: shift up when the motor sounds like it is racing and down when it sounds like it is straining. No number of words can take the place of a few choice examples of racing and straining sounds.

Similarly, with experience, the chess student begins to recognize such situational aspects of positions as a weakened king's side or a strong pawn structure, despite the lack of precise definitional rules. He is then given maxims to follow, such as attack a weakened king side.

Stage 3: Competence

With increasing experience, the number of features and aspects to be taken account of becomes overwhelming. To cope with this information explosion, the performer learns to adopt a hierarchical view of decision-making. By first choosing a plan, goal, or perspective which organizes the situation and by then examining only the small set of features and aspects that he has learned are relevant given that plan, the performer can simplify and improve his performance.

A competent driver leaving the freeway on a curved off-ramp may, after taking into account speed, surface condition, criticality of time, etc., decide he is going too fast. He then has to decide whether to let up on the accelerator, remove his foot altogether, or step on the brake. He is relieved when he gets through the curve without mishap and shaken if he begins to go into a skid.

The class-A chess player, here classed as competent, may decide after studying a position that his opponent has weakened his king's defenses so that an attack against the king is a viable goal. If the attack is chosen, features involving weaknesses in his own position created by the attack are ignored, as are losses of pieces inessential to the attack. Removing pieces defending the enemy king becomes salient. Successful plans induce euphoria and mistakes are felt in the pit of the stomach.

In both of these cases, we find a common pattern: detached planning, conscious assessment of elements that are salient with respect to the plan, and an analytical rule-guided choice of action, followed by an emotionally involved experience of the outcome. The experience is emotional because choosing a plan, goal, or perspective is no simple matter for the competent performer. Nobody gives him any rules for how to choose a perspective, so he has to make up various rules which he then adopts or discards in various situations depending on how they work out. This procedure is frustrating, however, since each rule works on some occasions and fails on others, and no set of objective features and aspects correlates strongly with these successes and failures. Nonetheless, the choice is unavoidable. Familiar situations begin to be accompanied by emotions such as hope, fear, etc., but the competent performer strives to suppress these feelings during his detached choice of perspective.

Stage 4: Proficiency

As soon as the competent performer stops reflecting on problematic situations as a detached observer, and stops looking for principles to guide his actions, the gripping, holistic experiences from the competent stage become the basis of the next advance in skill.

Having experienced many emotion-laden situations, chosen plans in each, and having obtained vivid, emotional demonstrations of the adequacy or inadequacy of the plan, the performer involved in the world of the skill "notices," or "is struck by," a certain plan, goal, or perspective. No longer is the spell of involvement broken by detached conscious planning.

Since there are generally far fewer "ways of seeing" than "ways of acting," however, after understanding without conscious effort what is going on, the proficient performer will still have to think about what to do. During this thinking, elements that present themselves as salient are assessed and combined by rule and maxim to produce decisions.

On the basis of prior experience, a proficient driver fearfully approaching a curve on a rainy day may sense that he is traveling too fast. Then, on the basis of such salient elements as visibility, angle of road bank, criticalness of time, etc., he decides whether to let up on the gas, take his foot off the gas, or to step on the brake. (These factors were used by the *competent* driver to *decide that* he was speeding.)

The proficient chess player, who is classed a master, can recognize a large repertoire of types of positions. Experiencing a situation as a field of conflicting forces and seeing almost immediately the sense of a position, he sets about calculating the move that best achieves his goal. He may, for example, know that he should attack, but he must deliberate about how best to do so.

Stage 5: Expertise

The proficient performer, immersed in the world of skillful activity, *sees* what needs to be done, but must *decide* how to do it. With enough experience with a variety of situations, all seen from the same perspective but requiring different tactical decisions, the proficient performer seems gradually to decompose this class of situations into subclasses, each of which shares the same decision, single action, or tactic. This allows an immediate intuitive response to each situation.

The expert driver, generally without any attention, not only knows by feel and familiarity when an action such as slowing down is required; he knows how to perform the action without calculating and comparing alternatives. He shifts gears when appropriate with no awareness of his acts. On the off-ramp his foot just lifts off the accelerator. What must be done, simply is done.

The expert chess player, classed as an international master or grandmaster, in most situations experiences a compelling sense of the issue and the best move. Excellent chess players can play at the rate of 5–10 seconds a move and even faster without any serious degradation in performance. At this speed they must depend almost entirely on intuition and hardly at all on analysis and comparison of alternatives. We recently performed an experiment in which an international master, Julio Kaplan, was required rapidly to add numbers presented to him audibly at the rate of about one number per second, while at the same time playing five-second-a-move chess against a slightly weaker, but master-level, player. Even with his analytical mind completely occupied by adding numbers, Kaplan more than held his own against the master in a series of games. Deprived of the time necessary to solve problems or construct plans, Kaplan still produced fluid and strategic play.

It seems that beginners make judgments using strict rules and features, but that with talent and a great deal of involved experience the beginner develops into an expert who sees intuitively what to do without applying rules and making judgments at all. The intellectualist tradition has given an accurate description of the beginner and the expert facing an unfamiliar situation, but normally an expert does not *solve problems*. He does not *reason*. He does not even act deliberately. Rather, he spontaneously does what has normally worked and, naturally, it normally works.

We are all experts at many tasks, and our everyday coping skills usually function smoothly and transparently so as to free us to be aware of other aspects of our lives where we are not so skillful. That is why philosophers overlooked them for 2,500 years, until pragmatism and phenomenology came along.

John Dewey introduced the distinction between knowing how and knowing that to call attention to just such thoughtless mastery of the everyday:

We may...be said to *know how* by means of our habits...We walk and read aloud, we get off and on street cars, we dress and undress, and do a thousand useful acts without thinking of them. We know something, namely, how to do them...[I]f we choose to call [this] knowledge...then other things also called knowledge, knowledge *of* and *about* things, knowledge *that* things are thus and so, knowledge that involves reflection and conscious appreciation, remains of a different sort...[9]

We should try to impress on ourselves what a huge amount of our lives—working, getting around, talking, eating, driving, and responding to the needs of others—manifests know-how, and what a small part is spent in the deliberate, effortful, subject/object mode which requires knowing that. Yet deliberate action, and its extreme form, deliberation, are the ways of acting we tend to notice, and so are the only ones that have been studied in detail by philosophers.

2. Implications of the Phenomenology of Expertise for Ethical Experience

The rest of this chapter is based on a conditional: *If* the skill model we have proposed is correct, then, in so far as ethical comportment is a form of expertise, we should expect it to exhibit a developmental structure similar to that which we have described. On analogy with chess and driving it would seem that the budding ethical expert would learn at least some of the ethics of his community by following strict rules, would then go on to apply contextualized maxims, and, in the highest stage, would leave rules and principles behind and develop more and more refined spontaneous ethical responses.

To take a greatly oversimplified and dramatic example, a child at some point might learn the rule: never lie. Faced with the dilemma posed by Kant—an avowed killer asking the whereabouts of the child's friend—the child might tell the truth. After experiencing regret and guilt over the death of the friend, however, the child would move toward the realization that the rule, "Never lie," like the rule, "Shift at ten miles per hour," needs to be contextualized, and would seek maxims to turn to in different typical situations. Such a maxim might be: "Never lie except when someone might be seriously hurt by telling the truth." Of course, this maxim too would, under some circumstances, lead to regret. Finally,

[9] John Dewey, *Human Nature and Conduct: An Introduction to Social Psychology* (London: George Allen & Unwin, 1922), 177–8.

with enough experience, the ethical expert would learn to tell the truth or lie, depending upon the situation, without appeal to rules and maxims.[10]

Since we are assuming that such a spontaneous response exhibits ethical expertise, the parallel with chess and driving expertise raises two difficult questions: (1) What is *ethical* expertise? and (2) How does one learn it? In driving and chess there is a clear criterion of expertise. In chess one either wins or loses, in driving one makes it around a curve or skids off the road. But what, one may well ask, counts as success or failure in ethics? It seems that in ethics what counts as expert performance is doing what those who already are accepted as ethical experts do and approve. Aristotle tells us: "What is best is not evident except to the good man."[11] This is circular but not viciously so.

Learning exhibits the same circularity. To become an expert in any area of expertise one has to be able to respond to the same types of situations as similar as do those who are already expert. For example, to play master-level chess one has to respond to the same similarities as masters. This basic ability is what one calls having talent in a given domain. In addition, the learner must experience the appropriate satisfaction or regret at the outcome of his response. To become an expert driver one should feel fear not elation as one skids around a curve. Likewise, to acquire ethical expertise one must have the talent to respond to those ethical situations as similar that ethical experts respond to as similar, and one must have the sensibility to experience the socially appropriate sense of satisfaction or regret at the outcome of one's action.[12]

Aristotle was the first to see that expert ethical comportment is spontaneous, and Dewey repeats his insight:

As Aristotle pointed out...it takes a fine and well-grounded character to *react immediately* with the right approvals and condemnations.[13]

But the tradition leads even the most careful to pass over ongoing coping. Thus even Dewey privileges problem solving. In *Theory of the Moral Life* he tells us:

---

[10] This is not to deny that, as in driving, a great deal of background skill picked up by imitation and by trial and error is required before one can learn by testing rules.

[11] *Nicomachean Ethics* 1144a34.

[12] It is easy to see that if one enjoyed skidding one could never become an accepted member of the everyday driving community (although one might well become an expert stunt driver). Similarly, without a shared ethical sensibility to what is laudable and what condemnable one would go on doing what the experts in the community found inappropriate, develop bad habits, and become what Aristotle calls an unjust person.

[13] John Dewey, *Theory of the Moral Life* (New York: Holt, Rinehart & Winston, 1960), 131; our italics.

[E]ven the good man can trust for enlightenment to his direct responses... only in *simpler* situations, in those which are already upon the whole familiar. The better he is, the more likely he is to be perplexed as to what to do in *novel, complicated situations.*[14]

This, according to Dewey, arouses deliberation:

We hesitate, and then hesitation becomes deliberation... A preference emerges which is intentional and which is based on consciousness of the values which deliberation has brought into view.[15]

Dewey seems here to be equating the simple with the familiar and the novel with the complicated. But if our analogy with the chess grandmaster can be trusted, Dewey, on this interpretation of the passage, is making a traditional mistake. True, ethical persons can trust their practical wisdom only in familiar situations, but why should these be only the "simple situations"? The chess grandmaster does, indeed, have a more refined set of discriminations which makes him or her sensitive to differences that fail to affect a merely proficient performer, but this same refined set of distinctions, based on a wider range of familiar situations, is precisely what allows the expert to respond spontaneously to *complex* situations without deliberation. As ethical skills increase one would expect the expert to encounter fewer and fewer breakdowns. Indeed, phenomenological description suggests that, the greater the experience, the rarer the need for deliberation. The basketball star, Larry Bird, to switch to sports for a moment, is sensitive to more threats and opportunities than his teammates, but this does not mean that he has to deliberate more often. Indeed, he says just the opposite:

[A lot of the] things I do on the court are just reactions to situations... I don't think about... the things I'm trying to do... A lot of times, I've passed the basketball and not realized I've passed it until a moment or so later.[16]

But the mistaken idea that when the situation becomes complex an agent must deliberate—articulate his or her principles and draw conclusions as to how to act— only becomes dangerous when the philosopher reads the structure of deliberation back into the spontaneous response. This intellectualizes the phenomenon. One will then assume that intentional content—what John Searle calls an intention in action, and Kant calls the maxim of the act—underlies all moral comportment.

Even Aristotle, whom Heidegger lauded as "the last of the great philosophers who had eyes to see and, what is still more decisive, the energy and tenacity to continue to force inquiry back to the phenomena,"[17] seems, in this area, to be

---

[14] Dewey, *Theory of the Moral Life*, 131.   [15] Dewey, *Theory of the Moral Life*, 149.
[16] Quoted in Levine, *Bird.*   [17] Heidegger, *Basic Problems of Phenomenology*, 232.

corrupted by intellectualism. Like a good phenomenologist dedicated to "saving the phenomena," Aristotle stays close to normal everyday experience and sees the immediate, intuitive response precisely as characteristic of an expert. "Know-how (*technê*) does not deliberate" he tells us in the *Physics* (2.8). But when it comes to ethics, he sometimes seems to overlook skillful coping for intentional content. In the *Nicomachean Ethics* he tells us that to act justly or temperately the agent "must choose the acts, and choose them *for their own* sakes."[18] "Choice" here could be given a non-intellectualist reading as meaning responding to the situation by doing one thing rather than another. But that still leaves the troubling claim that the action must be done for the right reason—"for its own sake." It seems that according to Aristotle we must know what the agent thought he was doing— what he was aiming at. This is like saying that good chess players, drivers, and basketball players should be praised or blamed not for their brilliant intuitive responses, but only for what they were trying to do. We must be prepared to face the disturbing fact that a person may be responsible for an action he was not intending to perform, and that therefore there may be no intentional content which determines under what aspect we are to judge the action. We can only tell if a person is courageous, for example, by seeing his spontaneous response in many different situations.

In most contexts Aristotle can be interpreted as having understood this, but many commentators seem to go out of their way to emphasize Aristotle's intellectualism. Alasdair MacIntyre, who is willing to correct Aristotle where necessary, tells us that, according to Aristotle: "The genuinely virtuous agent... acts on the basis of a true and rational judgment."[19] Indeed, in MacIntyre's account of the virtuous life, the moral agent is reduced to a competent performer deliberately choosing among maxims:

In practical *reasoning* the possession of [an adequate sense of the tradition to which one belongs]... appears in the kind of capacity for *judgment* which the agent possesses in knowing how to *select* among the relevant stack of *maxims* and how to *apply them* in particular situations.[20]

Perhaps MacIntyre accepts this view, which would seem to undermine his own position, because he has not understood the nature of intuitive skills. It may be no coincidence that his description of chess expertise sees it as "a certain highly particular kind of analytical skill."[21]

[18] Aristotle, *Nicomachean Ethics*, tr. William David Ross (Oxford: Clarendon Press, 1908), 2.4 (our italics).

[19] Alasdair MacIntyre, *After Virtue* (Notre Dame, IN: University of Notre Dame Press, 1981), 140.

[20] MacIntyre, *After Virtue*, 207–8; our italics.   [21] MacIntyre, *After Virtue*, 175–6.

We have shown so far that the level of everyday intuitive ethical expertise, which Aristotle saw was formed by the sort of daily practice that produces good character, has, from Aristotle himself to Dewey, from Mandelbaum to MacIntyre, been passed over by philosophers, or if recognized distorted by reading back into it the mental content found in deliberation. It would be a mistake, however, to become so carried away with the wonder of spontaneous coping as to deny an important place to deliberative judgment. One should not conclude from the pervasiveness of egoless, situation-governed comportment that thought is always disruptive and inferior. Getting deliberation right is half of what phenomenology has to contribute to the study of ethical expertise.

Expert deliberation is not inferior to intuition, but neither is it a self-sufficient mental activity that can dispense with intuition. It is *based upon* intuition. The intellectualist account of self-sufficient cognition fails to distinguish the *involved* deliberation of an intuitive expert facing a *familiar* but problematic situation from the *detached* deliberation of an expert facing a *novel* situation in which he has no intuition and so, like a beginner, must resort to abstract principles. A chess master confronted with a chess problem, constructed precisely so as not to resemble a position that would show up in a normal game, is reduced to using analysis. Likewise, an ethical expert when confronted with cases of "life-boat morality" may have to fall back on ethical principles. But since *principles* are unable to produce expert behavior, it should be no surprise if falling back on them produces inferior responses. The resulting decisions are necessarily crude since they have not been refined by the experience of the results of a variety of intuitive responses to emotion-laden situations and the learning that comes from subsequent satisfaction and regret. Therefore, in familiar but problematic situations, rather than standing back and applying abstract principles, the expert deliberates about the appropriateness of his *intuitions*. Common as this form of deliberation is, little has been written about such buttressing of intuitive understanding, probably because detached, principle-based, deliberation is often incorrectly seen as the only alternative to intuition.

Let us turn again to the phenomenon. Sometimes, but not often, an intuitive decision-maker finds himself torn between two equally compelling decisions. Presumably this occurs when the current situation lies near the boundary between two discriminable types of situations, each with its own associated action. Occasionally one can compromise between these actions, but often they are incompatible. Only a modified understanding of the current situation can break the tie, so the decision-maker will delay if possible and seek more information. If a decision-maker can afford the time, the decision will be put off until something is learned that leaves only one action intuitively compelling. As Dewey puts it:

[T]he only way out [of perplexity] is through examination, inquiry, turning things over in [the] mind till something presents itself, perhaps after prolonged mental fermentation, to which [the good man] can directly react.[22]

Even when an intuitive decision seems obvious, it may not be the best. Dewey cautions:

[An expert] is set in his ways, and his immediate appreciations travel in the grooves laid down by his unconsciously formed habits. Hence the spontaneous "intuitions" of value have to be entertained subject to correction, to confirmation and revision, by personal observation of consequences and cross-questioning of their quality and scope.[23]

Aware that his current clear perception may well be the result of a chain of perspectives with one or more questionable links and so might harbor the dangers of tunnel vision, the wise intuitive decision-maker will attempt to dislodge his current understanding. He will do so by attempting to re-experience the chain of events that led him to see things the way he does, and at each stage he will intentionally focus upon elements not originally seen as important to see if there is an alternative intuitive interpretation. If current understanding cannot be dislodged in this way, the wise decision-maker will enter into dialogue with those who have reached different conclusions. Each will recount a narrative that leads to seeing the current situation in his way and so as demanding his response. Each will try to see things the other's way. This may result in one or the other changing his mind and therefore in final agreement. But, since various experts have different past experiences, there is no reason why they should finally agree. In cases of ethical disagreement, the most that can be claimed is that, given the shared *Sittlichkeit* underlying their expertise, two experts, even when they do not agree, should be able to understand and appreciate each other's decisions. This is as near as expert ethical judgments can or need come to impartiality and universality.

3. Current Relevance

But, one might well ask, so what? Transparent, spontaneous, ethical coping might, indeed, occur, but why not begin our philosophical analysis where the tradition has always begun—where there is something interesting to describe, viz., moral judgments, validity claims, and justification? Still, before passing over

---

[22] Dewey, *Theory of the Moral Life*, 131.   [23] Dewey, *Theory of the Moral Life*, 132.

everyday coping as philosophically irrelevant, we should remember that getting the story right about action and mind had huge consequences for the pretensions of a new discipline that calls itself cognitive science. Concentrating on representations, rules, reasoning, and problem solving, cognitivists passed over but presupposed a more basic level of coping, and this blindness is now resulting in what more and more researchers are coming to recognize as the degeneration of their research program.[24] So it behooves us to ask: Does the passing over of ethical expertise have equally important practical implications?

We believe it does. The phenomenology of expertise allows us to sharpen up and take sides in an important contemporary debate. The debate centers on the ethical implications of Lawrence Kohlberg's Piagetian model of moral development. Kohlberg holds that the development of the capacity for moral judgment follows an invariant pattern. He distinguishes three levels: a Preconventional Level on which the agent tries to satisfy his needs and avoid punishment; a Conventional Level, during a first stage of which the agent conforms to stereotypical images of majority behavior, and at a second stage follows fixed rules and seeks to retain the given social order; and a Postconventional and Principled Level. The highest stage of this highest level is characterized as follows:

> Regarding what is right, Stage 6 is guided by universal ethical principles... These are not merely values that are recognized, but are also principles used to generate particular decisions.[25]

Jürgen Habermas has taken up Kohlberg's findings and modified them on the basis of his own discourse ethics, adding a seventh stage—acting upon universal procedural principles that make possible arriving at rational agreement through dialogue.

Habermas sees Kohlberg's work as evidence that moral consciousness begins with involved ethical comportment, but that the highest stages of moral consciousness require the willingness and the ability to "consider moral questions from the hypothetical and disinterested perspective."[26] Thus, according to Habermas, Kohlberg's research lends empirical support to his modified, but still recognizable, Kantian view that the highest level of moral maturity consists in judging actions according to abstract, universal principles. He tells us that "The normative reference point of the developmental path that Kohlberg analyzes

---

[24] See Chapter 10, this volume.   [25] See Chapter 10, this volume.
[26] Jürgen Habermas, "A Reply to my Critics", in John B. Thompson and David Held (eds), *Habermas: Critical Debates* (Cambridge, MA: MIT Press, 1982), 253.

empirically is a principled morality in which we can recognize the main features of discourse ethics."[27]

It follows for Habermas that our Western European morality of abstract justice is developmentally superior to the ethics of any culture lacking universal principles. Furthermore, when the Kohlberg developmental scale is tested in empirical studies of the moral judgments of young men and women, it turns out that men are generally more morally mature than women.

In her book, *In a Different Voice*, Carol Gilligan contests this second result, claiming that the data on which it is based incorporate a male bias. She rests her objection on her analyses of responses to a moral dilemma used in Kohlberg's studies. She explains as follows:

The dilemma... was one in the series devised by Kohlberg to measure moral development in adolescence by presenting a conflict between moral norms and exploring the logic of its resolution... [A] man named Heinz considers whether or not to steal a drug which he cannot afford to buy, in order to save the life of his wife... [T]he description of the dilemma... is followed by the question, "Should Heinz steal the drug?"[28]

Kohlberg found that morally mature men, i.e. those who have reached stage 6, tended to answer that Heinz should steal the drug because the right to life is more basic than the right to private property. Women, however, seemed unable to deal with the dilemma in a mature, logical way. Here is Gilligan's analysis of a typical case:

Seeing in the dilemma not a math problem... but a narrative of relationships that extends over time, Amy envisions the wife's continuing need for her husband and the husband's continuing concern for his wife and seeks to respond to the druggist's need in a way that would sustain rather than sever connection...

Seen in this light, her understanding of morality as arising from the *recognition* of relationship, her *belief* in communication as the mode of conflict resolution, and her *conviction* that the solution to the dilemma will follow from its compelling *representation* seem far from naive or cognitively immature.[29]

The first point to note in responding to these interesting observations is that many women are "unable to verbalize or explain the rationale"[30] for their moral

[27] Jürgen Habermas, *Moral Consciousness and Communicative Action*, tr. Christian Lenhardt and Shierry Weber (Cambridge, MA: MIT Press, 2001), 150.
[28] Carol Gilligan, *In a Different Voice: Psychological Theory and Women's Development* (Cambridge, MA: Harvard University Press, 1982), 27.
[29] Gilligan, *In a Different Voice*, 27–30. The cognitivist vocabulary we have italicized should warn us that, in spite of her critique, Gilligan may well have uncritically taken over the cognitivist assumptions underlying Kohlberg's research.
[30] Gilligan, *In a Different Voice*, 49.

responses; they stay involved in the situation and trust their intuition. Many men, on the other hand, when faced with a moral problem, attempt to step back and articulate their principles as a way of deciding what to do. Yet as we have seen, principles can never capture the know-how an expert acquires by dealing with, and seeing the outcome of, a large number of concrete situations. Thus, when faced with a dilemma, the expert does not seek principles but, rather, reflects on and tries to sharpen his or her spontaneous intuitions by getting more information until one decision emerges as obvious. Gilligan finds the same phenomenon in her subjects' deliberations:

The proclivity of women to reconstruct hypothetical dilemmas in terms of the real, *to request or to supply missing information* about the nature of the people and the places where they live, shifts their judgment away from the hierarchical ordering of principles and the formal procedures of decision making.[31]

Gilligan, however, undermines what is radical and fascinating in her discoveries when she seeks her subjects' *solutions* to *problems*, and tries to help them articulate the *principles* underlying these solutions. "Amy's moral *judgment is grounded in* the belief that, 'if somebody has something that would keep somebody alive, then it's not right not to give it to them,'"[32] she tells us. Yet, if the phenomenology of skillful coping we have presented is right, principles and theories serve only for early stages of learning; no principles or theory "ground" an expert ethical response, any more than in chess there is a theory or rule that explains a master-level move.

As we would expect, Gilligan's intuitive subjects respond to philosophical questions concerning the principles justifying their actions with tautologies and banalities, e.g. that they try to act in such a way as to make the world a better place in which to live. They might as well say that their highest moral principle is "do something good." If Gilligan had not tried to get her intuitive subjects to formulate their principles for dealing with problems, but had rather investigated how frequently they *had* problems and how they deliberated about their spontaneous ethical comportment when they did, she might well have found evidence that moral maturity results in having fewer problems and, when problems do arise, being able to act without detaching oneself from the concrete situation, thereby retaining one's ethical intuitions.

The second, and more important, point to consider is that Gilligan correctly detects in Amy's responses to the Heinz dilemma an entirely different approach

---

[31] Gilligan, *In a Different Voice*, 100–1; our italics.
[32] Gilligan, *In a Different Voice*, 28; our italics.

198 PHENOMENOLOGY AND THE HUMAN SCIENCES

to the ethical life than acting on universal principles. This is the different voice she is concerned to hear and to elaborate in her book. In answering her critics she makes clear that it is not the central point of her work that these two voices are gendered.

The title of my book was deliberate, it reads, "in a *different* voice," not "in *a woman's* voice."...I caution the reader that "this association is not absolute, and the contrasts between male and female voices are presented here to highlight a distinction between two modes of thought...rather than to represent a generalization about either sex."[33]

She calls the two voices "the justice and care perspectives."[34] On one description to be good is to be *principled*, on the other, it is to be *unprincipled*, i.e. without principles.

Although Gilligan does not make the point, it should be obvious to philosophers that we inherit the justice tradition from the Greeks, especially Socrates and Plato. It presupposes that two situations can be the same in the relevant moral respects, and requires principles which treat the same types of situation in the same way. The principle of universalizability thus becomes, with Kant, definitive of the moral. All of us feel the pull of this philosophical position when we seek to be fair, and when we seek universal principles guaranteeing justice and fairness as the basis of our social and political decisions. Moreover, we must resort to universal principles when we seek to justify what we do as right, rather than simply doing what the wisest in our culture have shown us is appropriate.

The other voice carries the early Christian message that, as St. Paul put it, "the law is fulfilled," so that henceforth to each situation we should respond with love. Proponents of this view sense that no two situations, and no two people, are ever exactly alike. Even a single individual is constantly changing because, as one acquires experience, one's responses become constantly more refined. Thus there is no final answer as to what the appropriate response in a particular situation should be. Since two abstractly identical situations will elicit different responses, caring comportment will look like injustice to the philosopher but will look like

---

[33] Carol Gilligan, "On In a Different Voice: An Interdisciplinary Forum", *Signs: Journal of Women in Culture and Society*, 11/2 (1986), 327.

[34] Gilligan, "On In a Different Voice", 330. For an early intuition that the two voices are, indeed, gendered, at least in our culture, see Nietzsche in *Human All Too Human*:

Can women be just at all if they are so used to loving, to feeling immediately pro or con? For this reason they are also less often partial to causes, more often to people; but if to a cause, they immediately become partisan, therefore ruining its pure, innocent effect....What would be more rare than a woman who really knew what science is? (tr. R. J. Hollingdale, Cambridge: Cambridge University Press, 1986, §416).

compassion or mercy to the Christian. We feel the pull of these Christian caring practices when we respond intuitively to the needs of those around us.

It is important to be clear, however, as Gilligan is not, that the care perspective does not entail any particular way of acting—for example, that one should promote intimate human relationships. The Christian command to love one's neighbor does not dictate how that love should be expressed. Caring in its purest form is not ordinary loving; it is doing spontaneously whatever the situation demands. As we have seen, even if two situations were identical in every respect, two ethical experts with different histories would not necessarily respond in the same way. Each person must simply respond as well as he or she can to each unique situation with nothing but experience-based intuition as guide. Heidegger captures this ethical skill in his notion of *authentic care* as a response to the *unique*, as opposed to the *general*, situation.[35] Authentic caring in this sense is common to *agape* and *phronesis*.

Responding to the general situation occurs when one follows ethical maxims and gives the standard acceptable response. This would correspond to the last stage of Kohlberg's Conventional Level. For Kohlberg and Habermas, on the next Level the learner seeks principled justification. On our model, however, reaching the Postconventional Level would amount to acting with authentic care. When an individual becomes a master of the *Sittlichkeit* he or she no longer tries to do what *one* normally does, but rather responds to the unique situation out of a fund of experience in the culture.

This gets us back to the debate over which is more mature, acting upon rational judgments of rightness, or intuitively doing what the culture deems good. On the one hand, we have Kohlberg's Stage 6 and Habermas's Stage 7, both of which define moral maturity in terms of the ability to detach oneself from the concrete ethical situation and to act on abstract, universal, moral principles. On the other hand, we have Gilligan (with John Murphy, who views the "transition to maturity as a shift from 'the moral environment to the ethical, from the formal to the existential'"[36]). According to this view the mature subject accepts "contextual relativism."[37] Murphy and Gilligan state the issue as follows:

There are...people who are fully formal in their logical thinking and fully principled in their moral judgments; and yet...are not fully mature in their moral understanding.

---

[35] Heidegger, *Being and Time*, 346.

[36] William Graves Perry, *Forms of Intellectual and Ethical Development in the College Years: A Scheme* (New York: Holt, Rinehart & Winston, 1968), 205, as quoted in John M. Murphy and Carol Gilligan, "Moral Development in Late Adolescence and Adulthood: A Critique and Reconstruction of Kohlberg's Theory", *Human Development*, 23 (1980), 79.

[37] Murphy and Gilligan, "Moral Development", 79.

Conversely, those people whose thinking becomes more relativistic in the sense of being more open to the contextual properties of moral judgments and moral dilemmas frequently fail to be scored at the highest stages of Kohlberg's sequence. Instead, the relativising of their thinking over time is construed as regression or moral equivocation, rather than as a developmental advance.[38]

Habermas recognizes that "the controversy [raised by Gilligan] has drawn attention to problems which, in the language of the philosophical tradition, pertain to the relation of *morality* to ethical life (*Sittlichkeit*)."[39] He, of course, continues to contend that rational morality is developmentally superior to *Sittlichkeit*. And, indeed, if, like Habermas, one thinks of morality exclusively in terms of *judgments* which are generated by *principles*, the ability to stand back from personal involvement in the situation so as to insure reciprocity and universality becomes a sign of maturity. But if being good means being able to learn from experience and use what one has learned so as to respond more appropriately to the demands of others in the concrete situation, the highest form of ethical comportment consists in being able to stay involved and to refine one's intuitions. Habermas needs to supply an argument why the development of ethical expertise should follow a different course than the development of expertise in other domains. Otherwise, it looks like we should follow Murphy and Gilligan in recognizing that at the Postconventional Level the learner accepts his intuitive responses, thus reaching a stage of maturity that leaves behind the rules of conventional morality for a new contextualization.

It is important to see that all this in no way shows that questioning the justice or rightness of aspects of our *Sittlichkeit* is illegitimate or immature. But the demand for fairness and justice in social decision-making and for a rational critique of ethical judgments has to exhibit its own developmental stages and requires an independent source of justification. Our skill model is meant neither to contribute to finding grounds for such rightness claims nor to call into question Habermas's important contribution in this area. What we are arguing here is that, even if there are claims on us as rational moral agents, acting on such claims cannot be shown to be superior to involved ethical comportment by asserting that such claims are the outcome of a development that makes explicit the abstract rationality implicit in context-dependent ethical comportment. Like any skill, ethical comportment has its *telos* in involved intuitive expertise.

---

[38] Murphy and Gilligan, "Moral Development", 80. (Again note the cognitivist vocabulary: thinking, judgment, dilemmas.)

[39] Habermas, *Moral Consciousness and Communicative Action*, 223.

When one measures Gilligan's two types of morality—her two voices—against a phenomenology of expertise, the traditional Western and male belief in the superiority of critical detachment to intuitive involvement is reversed. If, in the name of a cognitivist account of development, one puts ethics and morality on one single developmental scale, the claims of justice, which require judging that two situations are equivalent so as to be able to apply universal principles, look like regression to a competent understanding of the ethical domain, while the caring response to the unique situation stands out as mature practical wisdom.[40] In this case the phenomenology of expertise would not be just an academic corrective to Aristotle, Kant, Piaget, and Habermas. It would be a step towards righting a wrong to involvement, intuition, and care that traditional philosophy, by passing over skillful coping, has maintained for 2,500 years.

---

[40] If one accepts the view of expertise presented here, one must accept the superiority of the involved caring self. But our skill model does not support Gilligan's Piagetian claim that the *development* of the self requires crises. Skill learning, and that would seem to be any skill learning, requires learning from *mistakes* but not necessarily from *crises*. A crisis would occur when one had to alter one's criterion for what counted as success. Aristotle surely thought that in his culture, the men at least could develop character without going through crises. The idea of the necessity of moral crises for development goes with an intellectualist view of theory change that may well be true for science but which has nothing to do with selves. This is not to deny that in our pluralistic culture, and especially for those who are given contradictory and distorting roles to play, crises may be necessary. It may well be that women are led into traps concerning success and need crises to get out of them. Thus Gilligan may well be right that crises in *fact* play a crucial role in modern Western women's moral development, even if they are not *necessary*.

PART IV

Embodied Coping and Artificial Intelligence

10

Making a Mind versus Modeling the Brain

Artificial Intelligence Back at a Branchpoint (1988)

Hubert L. Dreyfus and Stuart E. Dreyfus

[N]othing seems more possible to me than that people some day will come to the definite opinion that there is no copy in the...nervous system which corresponds to a particular thought, or a particular idea, or memory.[1]

(Ludwig Wittgenstein, 1948)

[I]nformation is not stored anywhere in particular. Rather, it is stored everywhere. Information is better thought of as "evoked" than "found."[2]

(David Rumelhart and Donald Norman, 1981)

In the early 1950s, as calculating machines were coming into their own, a few pioneer thinkers began to realize that digital computers could be more than number crunchers. At that point two opposed visions of what computers could be, each with its correlated research program, emerged and struggled for recognition. One faction saw computers as a system for manipulating mental symbols; the other, as a medium for modeling the brain. One sought to use computers to instantiate a formal representation of the world; the other, to simulate the interactions of neurons. One took problem solving as its paradigm of intelligence;

---

[1] Ludwig Wittgenstein, *Last Writings on the Philosophy of Psychology* (1; Chicago: Chicago University Press, 1982), i. 504 (66e). (Translation corrected.)

[2] David E. Rumelhart and Donald A. Norman, "A Comparison of Models", in Geoffrey Hinton and James Anderson (eds), *Parallel Models of Associative Memory* (Hillsdale, NJ: Lawrence Erlbaum Associates, 1981), 3.

the other, learning. One utilized logic; the other, statistics. One school was the heir to the rationalist, reductionist tradition in philosophy; the other viewed itself as idealized, holistic neuroscience.

The rallying cry of the first group was that both minds and digital computers are physical symbol systems. By 1955 Allen Newell and Herbert Simon, working at the Rand Corporation, had concluded that strings of bits manipulated by a digital computer could stand for anything—numbers, of course, but also features of the real world. Moreover, programs could be used as rules to represent relations between these symbols, so that the system could infer further facts about the represented objects and their relations. As Newell put it recently in his account of the history of issues in AI:

The digital-computer field defined computers as machines that manipulated numbers. The great thing was, adherents said, that everything could be encoded into numbers, even instructions. In contrast, the scientists in AI saw computers as machines that manipulated symbols. The great thing was, they said, that everything could be encoded into symbols, even numbers.[3]

This way of looking at computers became the basis of a way of looking at minds. Newell and Simon hypothesized that the human brain and the digital computer, while totally different in structure and mechanism, had at a certain level of abstraction a common functional description. At this level both the human brain and the appropriately programmed digital computer could be seen as two different instantiations of a single species of device—a device that generated intelligent behavior by manipulating symbols by means of formal rules. Newell and Simon stated their view as a hypothesis:

The Physical Symbol System Hypothesis. A physical symbol system has the necessary and sufficient means for general intelligent action.

By "necessary" we mean that any system that exhibits general intelligence will prove upon analysis to be a physical symbol system. By "sufficient" we mean that any physical symbol system of sufficient size can be organized further to exhibit general intelligence.[4]

Newell and Simon trace the roots of their hypothesis back to Gottlob Frege, Bertrand Russell, and Alfred North Whitehead,[5] but Frege and company were of course themselves heirs to a long, atomistic, rationalist tradition. Descartes had already assumed that all understanding consisted of forming and manipulating

---

[3] Allen Newell, "Intellectual Issues in the History of Artificial Intelligence", in F. Machlup and U. Mansfield (eds), *The Study of Information: Interdisciplinary Messages* (New York: Wiley, 1983), 196.

[4] Allen Newell and Herbert Simon, "Computer Science as Empirical Inquiry: Symbols and Search", in John Haugeland (ed.), *Mind Design* (Cambridge, MA: MIT Press, 1981), 41.

[5] Newell and Simon, "Computer Science", 42.

appropriate representations, that these representations could be analyzed into primitive elements (*naturas simplices*), and that all phenomena could be understood as complex combinations of these simple elements. Moreover, at the same time, Hobbes had implicitly assumed that the elements were formal components related by purely syntactic operations, so that reasoning could be reduced to calculation. "When a man *reasons,* he does nothing else but conceive a sum total from addition of parcels," Hobbes wrote, "for REASON...is nothing but reckoning...."[6] Finally, Leibniz, working out the classical idea of mathesis—the formalization of everything—sought support to develop a universal symbol system so that "we can assign to every object its determined characteristic number."[7] According to Leibniz, in understanding we analyze concepts into more simple elements. In order to avoid a regress to simpler and simpler elements, there must be ultimate simples in terms of which all complex concepts can be understood. Moreover, if concepts are to apply to the world, there must be simple features that these elements represent. Leibniz envisaged "a kind of alphabet of human thoughts"[8] whose "characters must show, when they are used in demonstrations, some kind of connection, grouping and order which are also found in the objects."[9]

Ludwig Wittgenstein, drawing on Frege and Russell, stated in his *Tractatus Logico-Philosophicus* the pure form of this syntactic, representational view of the relation of the mind to reality. He defined the world as the totality of logically independent atomic facts:

1.1.   The world is the totality of facts, not of things.

Facts in turn, he held, could be exhaustively analyzed into primitive objects.

2.01.   An atomic fact is a combination of objects.
2.0124.   If all objects are given, then *thereby* all atomic facts are given.

These facts, their constituents, and their logical relations, Wittgenstein claimed, were represented in the mind.

2.1.   We make to ourselves pictures of facts.
2.15.   That the elements of the picture are combined with one another in a definite way, represents that the things are so combined with one another.[10]

---

[6] Thomas Hobbes, *Leviathan* (New York: Library of Liberal Arts, 1958), 45.

[7] Gottfried Wilhelm Leibniz, *Leibniz: Selections*, ed. Philip P. Weiner (New York: Scribner, 1951), 18.

[8] Leibniz, *Selections*, 20.   [9] Leibniz, *Selections*, 10.

[10] Ludwig Wittgenstein, *Tractatus Logico-Philosophicus* (London: Routledge & Kegan Paul, 1960).

AI can be thought of as the attempt to find the primitive elements and logical relations in the subject (man or computer) that mirror the primitive objects and their relations that make up the world. Newell and Simon's physical symbol system hypothesis in effect turns the Wittgensteinian vision (which is itself the culmination of the classical rationalist philosophical tradition) into an empirical claim and bases a research program on it.

The opposed intuition, that we should set about creating artificial intelligence by modeling the brain rather than the mind's symbolic representation of the world, drew its inspiration not from philosophy but from what was soon to be called neuroscience. It was directly inspired by the work of D. O. Hebb, who in 1949 suggested that a mass of neurons could learn that, when neuron A and neuron B were simultaneously excited, excitation increased the strength of the connection between them.[11]

This lead was followed by Frank Rosenblatt, who reasoned that, since intelligent behavior based on our representation of the world was likely to be hard to formalize, AI should instead attempt to automate the procedures by which a network of neurons learns to discriminate patterns and respond appropriately. As Rosenblatt put it:

The implicit assumption [of the symbol-manipulating research program] is that it is relatively easy to specify the behavior that we want the system to perform, and that the challenge is then to design a device or mechanism which will effectively carry out this behavior.... [I]t is both easier and more profitable to axiomatize the *physical system* and then investigate this system analytically to determine its behavior, than to axiomatize the *behavior* and then design a physical system by techniques of logical synthesis.[12]

Another way to put the difference between the two research programs is that those seeking symbolic representations were looking for a formal structure that would give the computer the ability to solve a certain class of problems or discriminate certain types of patterns. Rosenblatt, on the other hand, wanted to build a physical device, or to simulate such a device on a digital computer, that could then generate its own abilities:

Many of the models which we have heard discussed are concerned with the question of what logical structure a system must have if it is to exhibit some property, X. This is essentially a question about a static system....

---

[11] Donald O. Hebb, *The Organization of Behavior* (New York: Wiley, 1949).
[12] Frank Rosenblatt, "Strategic Approaches to the Study of Brain Models", in H. Von Foerster (ed.), *Principles of Self-Organization* (Elmsford, NY: Pergamon Press, 1962), 386.

An alternative way of looking at the question is: what kind of a system can *evolve* property X? I think we can show in a number of interesting cases that the second question can be solved without having an answer to the first.[13]

Both approaches met with immediate and startling success. By 1956 Newell and Simon had succeeded in programming a computer using symbolic representations to solve simple puzzles and prove theorems in the propositional calculus. On the basis of these early impressive results it looked as if the physical symbol system hypothesis was about to be confirmed, and Newell and Simon were understandably euphoric. Simon announced:

It is not my aim to surprise or shock you.... But the simplest way I can summarize is to say that there are now in the world machines that think, that learn and that create. Moreover, their ability to do these things is going to increase rapidly until—in a visible future—the range of problems they can handle will be coextensive with the range to which the human mind has been applied.[14]

He and Newell explained:

[W]e now have the elements of a theory of heuristic (as contrasted with algorithmic) problem solving; and we can use this theory both to understand human heuristic processes and to simulate such processes with digital computers. Intuition, insight, and learning are no longer exclusive possessions of humans: any large high-speed computer can be programmed to exhibit them also.[15]

Rosenblatt put his ideas to work in a type of device that he called a perceptron.[16] By 1956 Rosenblatt was able to train a perceptron to classify certain types of

---

[13] Rosenblatt, "Strategic Approaches", 387.

[14] Herbert Simon and Allen Newell, "Heuristic Problem Solving: The Next Advance in Operations Research", *Operations Research*, 6 (Jan.–Feb. 1958), 6.

[15] Simon and Newell, "Heuristic Problem Solving", 6. Heuristic rules are rules that when used by human beings are said to be based on experience or judgment. Such rules frequently lead to plausible solutions to problems or increase the efficiency of a problem-solving procedure. Whereas algorithms guarantee a correct solution (if there is one) in a finite time, heuristics only increase the likelihood of finding a plausible solution.

[16] David E. Rumelhart, James L. McClelland, and PDP Research Group, *Parallel Distributed Processing: Explorations in the Microstructure of Cognition* (Cambridge, MA: MIT Press, 1986), 111, describe the perceptron as follows:

> Such machines consist of what is generally called a *retina*, an array of binary inputs sometimes taken to be arranged in a two-dimensional spatial layout; a set of *predicates*, a set of binary threshold units with fixed connections to a subset of units in the retina such that each predicate computes some local function over the subset of units to which it is connected; and one or more decision units, with modifiable connections to the predicates.

They contrast the way a parallel distributed processing (PDP) model like the perceptron stores information with the way information is stored by symbolic representation:

patterns as similar and to separate these from other patterns that were dissimilar. By 1959 he too was jubilant and felt his approach had been vindicated:

It seems clear that the...perceptron introduces a new kind of information processing automaton: For the first time, we have a machine which is capable of having original ideas. As an analogue of the biological brain, the perceptron, more precisely, the theory of statistical separability, seems to come closer to meeting the requirements of a functional explanation of the nervous system than any system previously proposed....As concept, it would seem that the perceptron has established, beyond doubt, the feasibility and principle of non-human systems which may embody human cognitive functions....The future of information processing devices which operate on statistical, rather than logical, principles seems to be clearly indicated.[17]

In the early 1960s both approaches looked equally promising, and both made themselves equally vulnerable by making exaggerated claims. Yet the results of the internal war between the two research programs were surprisingly asymmetrical. By 1970 the brain simulation research, which had its paradigm in the perceptron, was reduced to a few lonely, underfunded efforts, while those who proposed using digital computers as symbol manipulators had undisputed control of the resources, graduate programs, journals, and symposia that constitute a flourishing research program.

Reconstructing how this change came about is complicated by the myth of manifest destiny that any ongoing research program generates. Thus, it looks to the victors as if symbolic information processing won out because it was on the right track, while the neural network or connectionist approach lost because it simply didn't work. But this account of the history of the field is a retrospective

In most models, knowledge is stored as a static copy of a pattern. Retrieval amounts to finding the pattern in long-term memory and copying it into a buffer or working memory. There is no real difference between the stored representation in long-term memory and the active representation in working memory. In PDP models, though, this is not the case. In these models, the patterns themselves are not stored. Rather, what is stored is the *connection strengths* between units that allow these patterns to be re-created. (p. 31)

[K]nowledge about any individual pattern is not stored in the connections of a special unit reserved for that pattern, but is distributed over the connections among a large number of processing units. (p. 33)

This new notion of representation led directly to Rosenblatt's idea that such machines should be able to acquire their ability through learning rather than by being programmed with features and rules:

[I]f the knowledge is [in] the strengths of the connections, learning must be a matter of finding the right connection strengths so that the right patterns of activation will be produced under the right circumstances. This is an extremely important property of this class of models, for it opens up the possibility that an information processing mechanism could learn, as a result of tuning its connections, to capture the interdependencies between activations that it is exposed to in the course of processing. (p. 32)

[17] Frank Rosenblatt, *Mechanisation of Thought Processes: Proceedings of a Symposium Held at the National Physical Laboratory* (London: Her Majesty's Stationery Office, 1958), i. 449.

illusion. Both research programs had ideas worth exploring, and both had deep, unrecognized problems.

Each position had its detractors, and what they said was essentially the same: each approach had shown that it could solve certain easy problems but that there was no reason to think either group could extrapolate its methods to real-world complexity. Indeed, there was evidence that, as problems got more complex, the computation required by both approaches would grow exponentially and so would soon become intractable. In 1969 Marvin Minsky and Seymour Papert said of Rosenblatt's perceptron:

> Rosenblatt's schemes quickly took root, and soon there were perhaps as many as a hundred groups, large and small, experimenting with the model....
>
> The results of these hundreds of projects and experiments were generally disappointing, and the explanations inconclusive. The machines usually work quite well on very simple problems but deteriorate very rapidly as the tasks assigned to them get harder.[18]

Three years later, Sir James Lighthill, after reviewing work using heuristic programs such as Simon's and Minsky's, reached a strikingly similar negative conclusion:

> Most workers in AI research and in related fields confess to a pronounced feeling of disappointment in what has been achieved in the past 25 years. Workers entered the field around 1950, and even around 1960, with high hopes that are very far from having been realized in 1972. In no part of the field have the discoveries made so far produced the major impact that was then promised....
>
> [O]ne rather general cause for the disappointments that have been experienced: failure to recognize the implications of the 'combinatorial explosion'. This is a general obstacle to the construction of a...system on a large knowledge base which results from the explosive growth of any combinatorial expression, representing numbers of possible ways of grouping elements of the knowledge base according to particular rules, as the base's size increases.[19]

As David Rumelhart and David Zipser have succinctly summed it up: "Combinatorial explosion catches you sooner or later, although sometimes in different ways in parallel than in serial."[20] Both sides had, as Jerry Fodor once put it, walked into a game of three-dimensional chess, thinking it was tick-tack-toe. Why then, so early in the game, with so little known and so much to learn, did

---

[18] Marvin Minsky and Seymour Papert, *Perceptrons: An Introduction to Computational Geometry* (Cambridge, MA: MIT Press, 1969), 19.

[19] James Lighthill, "Artificial Intelligence: A General Survey", *Artificial Intelligence: A Paper Symposium* (London: Science Research Council, 1973), 3–18.

[20] Rumelhart et al., *Parallel Distributed Processing*, 158.

one team of researchers triumph at the total expense of the other? Why, at this crucial branchpoint, did the symbolic representation project become the only game in town?

Everyone who knows the history of the field will be able to point to the proximal cause. About 1965, Minsky and Papert, who were running a laboratory at MIT dedicated to the symbol-manipulation approach and therefore competing for support with the perceptron projects, began circulating drafts of a book attacking the idea of the perceptron. In the book they made clear their scientific position:

Perceptrons have been widely publicized as "pattern recognition" or "learning" machines and as such have been discussed in a large number of books, journal articles, and voluminous "reports." Most of this writing ... is without scientific value.[21]

But their attack was also a philosophical crusade. They rightly saw that traditional reliance on reduction to logical primitives was being challenged by a new holism:

Both of the present authors (first independently and later together) became involved with a somewhat therapeutic compulsion: to dispel what we feared to be the first shadows of a "holistic" or "Gestalt" misconception that would threaten to haunt the fields of engineering and artificial intelligence as it had earlier haunted biology and psychology.[22]

They were quite right. Artificial neural nets may, but need not, allow an interpretation of their hidden nodes[23] in terms of features a human being could recognize and use to solve the problem. While neural network modeling itself is committed to neither view, it can be demonstrated that association does not *require* that the hidden nodes be interpretable. Holists like Rosenblatt happily assumed that individual nodes or patterns of nodes were not picking out fixed features of the domain.

Minsky and Papert were so intent on eliminating all competition, and so secure in the atomistic tradition that runs from Descartes to early Wittgenstein, that their book suggests much more than it actually demonstrates. They set out to analyze the capacity of a one-layer perceptron,[24] while completely ignoring in the mathematical portion of their book Rosenblatt's chapters on multilayer machines

---

[21] Minsky and Papert, *Perceptrons*, 4.   [22] Minsky and Papert, *Perceptrons*, 19.

[23] Hidden nodes are nodes that neither directly detect the input to the net nor constitute its output. They are, however, either directly or indirectly linked by connections with adjustable strengths to the nodes detecting the input and those constituting the output.

[24] A one-layer network has no hidden nodes, while multilayer networks do contain hidden nodes.

and his proof of the convergence of a probabilistic learning algorithm based on back propagations[25] of errors.[26] According to Rumelhart and McClelland,

Minsky and Papert set out to show which functions can and cannot be computed by [one-layer] machines. They demonstrated, in particular, that such perceptrons are unable to calculate such mathematical functions as parity (whether an odd or even number of points are on the retina) or the topological function of connectedness (whether all points that are on are connected to all other points that are on either directly or via other points that are also on) without making use of absurdly large numbers of predicates. The analysis is extremely elegant and demonstrates the importance of a mathematical approach to analyzing computational systems.[27]

But the implications of the analysis are quite limited. Rumelhart and McClelland continue:

Essentially... although Minsky and Papert were exactly correct in their analysis of the *one-layer perceptron*, the theorems don't apply to systems which are even a little more complex. In particular, it doesn't apply to multilayer systems nor to systems that allow feedback loops.[28]

Yet in the conclusion to *Perceptrons*, when Minsky and Papert ask themselves the question, have you considered perceptrons with many layers? they give the impression, while rhetorically leaving the question open, of having settled it:

Well, we have considered Gamba machines, which could be described as "two layers of perceptron." We have not found (by thinking or by studying the literature) any other really interesting class of multilayered machine, at least none whose principles seem to have a significant relation to those of the perceptron.... [W]e consider it to be an important research problem to elucidate (or reject) our intuitive judgment that the extension is sterile.[29]

Their attack on gestalt thinking in AI succeeded beyond their wildest dreams. Only an unappreciated few, among them Stephen Grossberg, James A. Anderson,

---

[25] Back propagation of errors requires recursively computing, starting with the output nodes, the effects of changing the strengths of connections on the difference between the desired output and the output produced by an input. The weights are then adjusted during learning to reduce the difference.

[26] Frank Rosenblatt, *Principles of Neurodynamics, Perceptrons and the Theory of Brain Mechanisms* (Washington, DC: Spartan Books, 1962), 292. See also:

> The addition of a fourth layer of signal transmission units, or cross-coupling the A-units of a three-layer perceptron, permits the solution of generalization problems, over arbitrary transformation groups. (p. 576)

> In back-coupled perceptrons, selective attention to familiar objects in a complex field can occur. It is also possible for such a perceptron to attend selectively to objects which move differentially relative to their background. (p. 576)

[27] Rumelhart et al., *Parallel Distributed Processing*, 111.

[28] Rumelhart et al., *Parallel Distributed Processing*, 112.

[29] Minsky and Papert, *Perceptrons*, 231–2.

and Teuvo Kohonen, took up the "important research problem." Indeed, almost everyone in AI assumed that neural nets had been laid to rest forever. Rumelhart and McClelland note:

Minsky and Papert's analysis of the limitations of the one-layer perceptron, coupled with some of the early successes of the symbolic processing approach in artificial intelligence, was enough to suggest to a large number of workers in the field that there was no future in perceptron-like computational devices for artificial intelligence and cognitive psychology.[30]

But why was it enough? Both approaches had produced some promising work and some unfounded promises.[31] It was too early to close accounts on either approach. Yet something in Minsky and Papert's book struck a responsive chord. It seemed AI workers shared the quasi-religious philosophical prejudice against holism that motivated the attack. One can see the power of the tradition, for example, in Newell and Simon's article on physical symbol systems. The article begins with the scientific hypothesis that the mind and the computer are intelligent by virtue of manipulating discrete symbols, but it ends with a revelation: "The study of logic and computers has revealed to us that intelligence resides in physical-symbol systems."[32]

Holism could not compete with such intense philosophical convictions. Rosenblatt was discredited along with the hundreds of less responsible network research groups that his work had encouraged. His research money dried up, and he had trouble getting his work published. By 1970, as far as AI was concerned, neural nets were dead. In his history of AI, Newell says the issue of symbols versus numbers "is certainly not alive now and has not been for a long time."[33] Rosenblatt is not even mentioned in John Haugeland's or Margaret Boden's histories of the AI field.[34]

---

[30] Rumelhart et al., *Parallel Distributed Processing*, 112.

[31] For an evaluation of the symbolic representation approach's actual successes up to 1978, see Dreyfus, *What Computers Still Can't Do*.

[32] Newell and Simon, "Computer Science as Empirical Inquiry", 197.

[33] Newell, "Intellectual Issues in the History of Artificial Intelligence", 10.

[34] John Haugeland, *Artificial Intelligence: The Very Idea* (Cambridge, MA: MIT Press, 1985), and Margaret Boden, *Artificial Intelligence and Natural Man* (New York: Basic Books, 1977). Work on neural nets was continued in a marginal way in psychology and neuroscience. James A. Anderson at Brown University continued to defend a net model in psychology, although he had to live off other researchers' grants, and Stephen Grossberg worked out an elegant mathematical implementation of elementary cognitive capacities. For Anderson's position see James A. Anderson, "Neural Models with Cognitive Implications", in D. Laberse and S. J. Samuels (eds), *Basic Processing in Reading* (Hillsdale, NJ: Lawrence Erlbaum Associates, 1978). For examples of Grossberg's work during the dark ages, see his book, Stephen Grossberg, *Studies of Mind and Brain: Neural Principles of Learning, Perception, Development, Cognition and Motor Control* (Boston: Reidel Press, 1982). Kohonen's early work is reported in Teuvo Kohonen, *Associative Memory: A System-Theoretical Approach*

But blaming the rout of the connectionists on an anti-holistic prejudice is too simple. There was a deeper way philosophical assumptions influenced intuition and led to an overestimation of the importance of the early symbol-processing results. The way it looked at the time was that the perceptron people had to do an immense amount of mathematical analysis and calculating to solve even the most simple problems of pattern recognition, such as discriminating horizontal from vertical lines in various parts of the receptive field, while the symbol-manipulating approach had relatively effortlessly solved hard problems in cognition, such as proving theorems in logic and solving combinatorial puzzles. Even more important, it seemed that, given the computing power available at the time, the neural net researchers could do only speculative neuroscience and psychology, while the simple programs of symbolic representationalists were on their way to being useful. Behind this way of sizing up the situation was the assumption that thinking and pattern recognition are two distinct domains and that thinking is the more important of the two. As we shall see later in our discussion of the commonsense knowledge problem, to look at things this way is to ignore both the preeminent role of pattern discrimination in human expertise and also the background of commonsense understanding that is presupposed in everyday real-world thinking. Taking account of this background may well require pattern recognition.

This thought brings us back to the philosophical tradition. It was not just Descartes and his descendants who stood behind symbolic information processing, but all of Western philosophy. According to Heidegger, traditional philosophy is defined from the start by its focusing on facts in the world while "passing over" the world as such.[35] This means that philosophy has from the start systematically ignored or distorted the everyday context of human activity.[36] The branch of the philosophical tradition that descends from Socrates through Plato, Descartes, Leibniz, and Kant to conventional AI takes it for granted, in

---

(Berlin: Springer-Verlag, 1977). At MIT Minsky continued to lecture on neural nets and to assign theses investigating their logical properties. But, according to Papert, Minsky did so only because nets had interesting mathematical properties, whereas nothing interesting could be proved concerning the properties of symbol systems. Moreover, many AI researchers assumed that since Turing machines were symbol manipulators and Turing had proved that Turing machines could compute anything, he had proved that all intelligibility could be captured by logic. On this view a holistic (and in those days statistical) approach needed justification, while the symbolic AI approach did not. This confidence, however, was based on confusing the uninterpreted symbols of a Turing machine (zeros and ones) with the semantically interpreted symbols of AI.

[35] Heidegger, *Being and Time*, §§14–21; Dreyfus, *Being-in-the-World*.

[36] According to Heidegger, Aristotle came closer than any other philosopher to understanding the importance of everyday activity, but even he succumbed to the distortion of the phenomenon of the everyday world implicit in common sense.

addition, that understanding a domain consists in having a *theory* of that domain. A theory formulates the relationships among objective, *context-free* elements (simples, primitives, features, attributes, factors, data points, cues, etc.) in terms of abstract principles (covering laws, rules, programs, etc.).

Plato held that in theoretical domains, such as mathematics and perhaps ethics, thinkers apply explicit, context-free rules or theories they have learned in another life, outside the everyday world. Once learned, such theories function in this world by controlling the thinker's mind, whether he or she is conscious of them or not. Plato's account did not apply to everyday skills but only to domains in which there is a priori knowledge. The success of theory in the natural sciences, however, reinforced the idea that in any orderly domain there must be some set of context-free elements and some abstract relations among those elements that account for the order of that domain and for man's ability to act intelligently in it. Thus, Leibniz boldly generalized the rationalist account to all forms of intelligent activity, even everyday practice:

[T]he most important observations and turns of skill in all sorts of trades and professions are as yet unwritten. This fact is proved by experience when passing from theory to practice we desire to accomplish something. *Of course, we can also write up this practice, since it is at bottom just another theory more complex and particular.*[37]

The symbolic information-processing approach gains its assurance from this transfer to all domains of methods that have been developed by philosophers and that are successful in the natural sciences. Since, in this view, any domain must be formalizable, the way to do AI in any area is obviously to find the context-free elements and principles and to base a formal, symbolic representation on this theoretical analysis. In this vein Terry Winograd describes his AI work in terms borrowed from physical science:

We are concerned with developing a formalism, or "representation," with which to describe...knowledge. We seek the "atoms" and "particles" of which it is built, and the "forces" that act on it.[38]

No doubt theories about the universe are often built up gradually by modeling relatively simple and isolated systems and then making the model gradually more complex and integrating it with models of other domains. This is possible because all the phenomena are presumably the result of the lawlike relations between what Papert and Minsky call "structural primitives." Since no one *argues*

[37] Leibniz, *Selections*, 48 (italics added).
[38] Terry Winograd, "Artificial Intelligence and Language Comprehension", *Artificial Intelligence and Language Comprehension* (Washington, DC: National Institute of Education, 1976), 9.

for atomistic reduction in AI, it seems that AI workers just implicitly *assume* that the abstraction of elements from their everyday context, which defines philosophy and works in natural science, must also work in AI. This assumption may well account for the way the physical symbol system hypothesis so quickly turned into a revelation and for the ease with which Papert and Minsky's book triumphed over the holism of the perceptron.

Teaching philosophy at MIT in the mid-1960s, one of us—Hubert—was soon drawn into the debate over the possibility of AI. It was obvious that researchers such as Newell, Simon, and Minsky were the heirs to the philosophical tradition. But given the conclusions of the later Wittgenstein and the early Heidegger, that did not seem to be a good omen for the reductionist research program. Both these thinkers had called into question the very tradition on which symbolic information processing was based. Both were holists, both were struck by the importance of everyday practices, and both held that one could not have a theory of the everyday world.

It is one of the ironies of intellectual history that Wittgenstein's devastating attack on his own *Tractatus*, his *Philosophical Investigations*,[39] was published in 1953, just as AI took over the abstract, atomistic tradition he was attacking. After writing the *Tractatus*, Wittgenstein spent years doing what he called phenomenology[40]—looking in vain for the atomic facts and basic objects his theory required. He ended by abandoning his *Tractatus* and all rationalistic philosophy. He argued that the analysis of everyday situations into facts and rules (which is where most traditional philosophers and AI researchers think theory must begin) is itself only meaningful in some context and for some purpose. Thus, the elements chosen already reflect the goals and purposes for which they are carved out. When we try to find the ultimate context-free, purpose-free elements, as we must if we are going to find the primitive symbols to feed a computer, we are in effect trying to free aspects of our experience of just that pragmatic organization which makes it possible to use them intelligently in coping with everyday problems.

In the *Philosophical Investigations* Wittgenstein directly criticized the logical atomism of the *Tractatus*:

"What lies behind the idea that names really signify simples"?—Socrates says in the *Theaetetus*: "If I make no mistake, I have heard some people say this: there is no definition of the primary elements—so to speak—out of which we and everything else are composed.... But just as what consists of these primary elements is itself complex, so

---

[39] Wittgenstein, *Philosophical Investigations*.
[40] Ludwig Wittgenstein, *Philosophical Remarks* (Chicago: University of Chicago Press, 1975).

the names of the elements become descriptive language by being compounded together." Both Russell's "individuals" and my "objects" (*Tractatus Logico-Philosophicus*) were such primary elements. But what are the simple constituent parts of which reality is composed? ... It makes no sense at all to speak absolutely of the "simple parts of a chair."[41]

Already, in the 1920s, Martin Heidegger had reacted in a similar way against his mentor, Edmund Husserl, who regarded himself as the culmination of the Cartesian tradition and was therefore the grandfather of AI.[42] Husserl argued that an act of consciousness, or noesis, does not on its own grasp an object; rather, the act has intentionality (directedness) only by virtue of an "abstract form," or meaning, in the noema correlated with the act.[43]

This meaning, or symbolic representation, as conceived by Husserl, is a complex entity that has a difficult job to perform. In *Ideas Pertaining to a Pure Phenomenology*,[44] Husserl bravely tried to explain how the noema gets the job done. Reference is provided by "predicate-senses," which, like Fregean *Sinne*, just have the remarkable property of picking out objects' atomic properties. These predicates are combined into complex "descriptions" of complex objects, as in Russell's theory of descriptions. For Husserl, who was close to Kant on this point, the noema contains a hierarchy of strict rules. Since Husserl thought of intelligence as a context-determined, goal-directed activity, the mental representation of any type of object had to provide a context, or a "horizon" of expectations or "predelineations" for structuring the incoming data: "a rule governing *possible* other consciousness of [the object] as identical—possible, as exemplifying essentially predelineated types."[45] The noema must contain a rule describing all the features that can be expected with certainty in exploring a certain type of object— features that remain "inviolably the same: as long as the objectivity remains intended as *this* one and of this kind."[46] The rule must also prescribe predelineations of properties that are possible, but not necessary, features of this type of

[41] Wittgenstein, *Philosophical Investigations*, 21.

[42] See Hubert Dreyfus (ed.), *Husserl, Intentionality and Cognitive Science* (Cambridge, MA: MIT Press, 1984).

[43] "Der Sinn ... so wie wir ihn bestimmt haben, ist nicht ein konkretes Wesen im Gesamtbestande des Noema, sondern eine Art ihm einwohnender abstrackter Form." See Husserl, *Ideen* (1950). For evidence that Husserl held that the noema accounts for the intentionality of mental activity, see Hubert L. Dreyfus, "Husserl's Perceptual Noema", in Hubert L. Dreyfus (ed.), *Husserl, Intentionality and Cognitive Science* (Cambridge, MA: MIT Press, 1984).

[44] Edmund Husserl, *Ideas Pertaining to a Pure Phenomenology and to a Phenomenological Philosophy*, tr. F. Kersten (The Hague: Martinus Nijhoff, 1982).

[45] Husserl, *Cartesian Meditations*, 45.

[46] Husserl, *Cartesian Meditations*, 53.

object: "Instead of a completely determined sense, there is always, therefore, a *frame of empty sense...* "[47]

In 1973 Marvin Minsky proposed a new data structure, remarkably similar to Husserl's, for representing everyday knowledge:

A *frame* is a data-structure for representing a stereotyped situation, like being in a certain kind of living room, or going to a child's birthday party....

We can think of a frame as a network of nodes and relations. The top levels of a frame are fixed, and represent things that are always true about the supposed situation. The lower levels have many *terminals—slots* that must be filled by specific instances or data. Each terminal can specify conditions its assignments must meet...

Much of the phenomenological power of the theory hinges on the inclusion of expectations and other kinds of presumptions. *A frame's terminals are normally already filled with "default" assignments.*[48]

In Minsky's model of a frame, the "top level" is a developed version of what, in Husserl's terminology, remains "inviolably the same" in the representation, and Husserl's predelineations have become "default assignments"—additional features that can normally be expected. The result is a step forward in AI techniques from a passive model of information processing to one that tries to take account of the interactions between a knower and the world. The task of AI thus converges with the task of transcendental phenomenology. Both must try in everyday domains to find frames constructed from a set of primitive predicates and their formal relations.

Heidegger, before Wittgenstein, carried out, in response to Husserl, a phenomenological description of the everyday world and everyday objects like chairs and hammers. Like Wittgenstein, he found that the everyday world could not be represented by a set of context-free elements. It was Heidegger who forced Husserl to face precisely this problem by pointing out that there are other ways of "encountering" things than relating to them as objects defined by a set of predicates. When we use a piece of equipment like a hammer, Heidegger said, we actualize a skill (which need not be represented in the mind) in the context of a socially organized nexus of equipment, purposes, and human roles (which need not be represented as a set of facts). This context, or world, and our everyday ways of skillful coping in it, which Heidegger called "circumspection," are not something we *think* but part of our socialization, which forms the way we *are*. Heidegger concluded:

---

[47] Husserl, *Cartesian Meditations*, 51.
[48] Marvin Minsky, "A Framework for Representing Knowledge", in John Haugeland (ed.), *Mind Design* (Cambridge, MA: MIT Press, 1981), 96.

The context ... can be taken formally in the sense of a system of relations. But ... [t]he phenomenal content of these "relations" and "relata" ... is such that they resist any sort of mathematical functionalization; nor are they merely something thought, first posited in an "act of thinking". They are rather relationships in which concernful circumspection as such already dwells.[49]

This defines the splitting of the ways between Husserl and AI on the one hand and Heidegger and the later Wittgenstein on the other. The crucial question becomes: Can there be a theory of the everyday world as rationalist philosophers have always held? Or is the commonsense background rather a combination of skills, practices, discriminations, and so on, which are not intentional states and so, a fortiori, do not have any representational content to be explicated in terms of elements and rules?

By making a move that was soon to become familiar in AI circles, Husserl tried to avoid the problem Heidegger posed. Husserl claimed that the world, the background of significance, the everyday context, was merely a very complex system of facts correlated with a complex system of beliefs, which, since they have truth conditions, he called validities. One could, in principle, he held, suspend one's dwelling in the world and achieve a detached description of the human belief system. One could thus complete the task that had been implicit in philosophy since Socrates: one could make explicit the beliefs and principles underlying all intelligent behavior. As Husserl put it:

[E]ven the background ... of which we are always concurrently conscious but which is momentarily irrelevant and remains completely unnoticed, still functions according to its implicit validities.[50]

Since he firmly believed that the shared background could be made explicit as a belief system, Husserl was ahead of his time in raising the question of the possibility of AI. After discussing the possibility that a formal axiomatic system might describe experience and pointing out that such a system of axioms and primitives—at least as we know it in geometry—could not describe everyday shapes such as "scalloped" and "lens-shaped," Husserl left open the question whether these everyday concepts could nonetheless be formalized. (This was like raising and leaving open the AI question whether one can axiomatize common-sense physics.) Taking up Leibniz's dream of a mathesis of all experience, Husserl added:

---

[49] Heidegger, *Being and Time*, 121–2.   [50] Husserl, *Crisis of European Sciences*, 149.

The pressing question is . . . whether there could not be . . . an idealizing procedure that substitutes pure and strict ideals for intuited data and that would . . . serve . . . as the basic medium for a mathesis of experience.[51]

But, as Heidegger predicted, the task of writing out a complete theoretical account of everyday life turned out to be much harder than initially expected. Husserl's project ran into serious trouble, and there are signs that Minsky's has too. During twenty-five years of trying to spell out the components of the subject's representation of everyday objects, Husserl found that he had to include more and more of the subject's commonsense understanding of the everyday world:

To be sure, even the tasks that present themselves when we take single types of objects as restricted clues prove to be extremely complicated and always lead to extensive disciplines when we penetrate more deeply. That is the case, for example, with . . . spatial objects (to say nothing of a Nature) as such, of psycho-physical being and humanity as such, culture as such.[52]

He spoke of the noema's "huge concreteness"[53] and of its "tremendous complication,"[54] and he sadly concluded at the age of 75 that he was a perpetual beginner and that phenomenology was an "infinite task."[55]

There are hints in his paper "A Framework for Representing Knowledge" that Minsky has embarked on the same "infinite task" that eventually overwhelmed Husserl:

Just constructing a knowledge base is a major intellectual research problem. . . . We still know far too little about the contents and structure of common-sense knowledge. A "minimal" common-sense system must "know" something about cause-effect, time, purpose, locality, process, and types of knowledge. . . . We need a serious epistemological research effort in this area.[56]

To a student of contemporary philosophy, Minsky's naïveté and faith are astonishing. Husserl's phenomenology *was* just such a research effort. Indeed, philosophers from Socrates through Leibniz to early Wittgenstein carried on serious epistemological research in this area for two thousand years without notable success.

---

[51] Husserl, *Ideen* (1971), iii. 134.   [52] Husserl, *Cartesian Meditations*, 54–5.

[53] Edmund Husserl, *Formal and Transcendental Logic*, tr. D. Cairns (The Hague: Martinus Nijhoff, 1969), 244.

[54] Husserl, *Formal and Transcendental Logic*, 246.

[55] Husserl, *Crisis of European Sciences*, 291.

[56] Minsky, "Framework for Representing Knowledge", 124.

In the light of Wittgenstein's reversal and Heidegger's devastating critique of Husserl, one of us—Hubert—predicted trouble for symbolic information processing. As Newell notes in his history of AI, this warning was ignored:

Dreyfus's central intellectual objection ... is that the analysis of the context of human action into discrete elements is doomed to failure. This objection is grounded in phenomenological philosophy. Unfortunately, this appears to be a nonissue as far as AI is concerned. The answers, refutations, and analyses that have been forthcoming to Dreyfus's writings have simply not engaged this issue—which indeed would be a novel issue if it were to come to the fore.[57]

The trouble was, indeed, not long in coming to the fore, as the everyday world took its revenge on AI as it had on traditional philosophy. As we see it, the research program launched by Newell and Simon has gone through three ten-year stages. From 1955 to 1965 two research themes, representation and search, dominated the field then called "cognitive simulation." Newell and Simon showed, for example, how a computer could solve a class of problems with the general heuristic search principle known as means–end analysis—namely, to use any available operation that reduces the distance between the description of the current situation and the description of the goal. They then abstracted this heuristic technique and incorporated it into their General Problem Solver (GPS).

The second stage (1965–75), led by Marvin Minsky and Seymour Papert at MIT, was concerned with what facts and rules to represent. The idea was to develop methods for dealing systematically with knowledge in isolated domains called "micro-worlds." Famous programs written around 1970 at MIT include Terry Winograd's SHRDLU, which could obey commands given in a subset of natural language about a simplified "blocks-world," Thomas Evan's analogy problem program, David Waltz's scene analysis program, and Patrick Winston's program, which could learn concepts from examples.

The hope was that the restricted and isolated micro-worlds could be gradually made more realistic and combined so as to approach real-world understanding. But researchers confused two domains, which, following Heidegger, we shall distinguish as "universe" and "world." A set of interrelated facts may constitute a *universe*, like the physical universe, but it does not constitute a *world*. The latter, like the world of business, the world of theater, or the world of the physicist, is an organized body of objects, purposes, skills, and practices on the basis of which human activities have meaning or make sense. To see the difference, one can contrast the *meaningless* physical universe with the *meaningful* world of the

---

[57] Newell, "Intellectual Issues in the History of Artificial Intelligence", 222–3.

discipline of physics. The world of physics, the business world, and the theater world make sense only against a background of common human concerns. They are local elaborations of the one commonsense world we all share. That is, subworlds are not related like isolable physical systems to the larger systems they *compose* but rather are local elaborations of a whole that they *presuppose*. Micro-worlds are not worlds but isolated meaningless domains, and it has gradually become clear that there is no way they could be combined and extended to arrive at the world of everyday life.

In its third stage, roughly from 1975 to the present (1988), AI has been wrestling with what has come to be called the commonsense knowledge problem. The representation of knowledge was always a central problem for work in AI, but the two earlier periods—cognitive simulation and micro-worlds—were characterized by an attempt to avoid the problem of commonsense knowledge by seeing how much could be done with as little knowledge as possible. By the mid-1970s, however, the issue had to be faced. Various data structures, such as Minsky's frames and Roger Schank's scripts, have been tried without success. The commonsense knowledge problem has kept AI from even beginning to fulfill Simon's prediction of twenty years ago that "within twenty years machines will be capable of doing any work a man can do."[58]

Indeed, the commonsense knowledge problem has blocked all progress in theoretical AI for the past decade. Winograd was one of the first to see the limitations of SHRDLU and all script and frame attempts to extend the micro-worlds approach. Having "lost faith" in AI, he now teaches Heidegger in his computer science course at Stanford and points out "the difficulty of formalizing the commonsense background that determines which scripts, goals and strategies are relevant and how they interact."[59]

What sustains AI in this impasse is the conviction that the commonsense knowledge problem must be solvable, since human beings have obviously solved it. But human beings may not normally use commonsense *knowledge* at all. As Heidegger and Wittgenstein pointed out, what commonsense *understanding* amounts to might well be *everyday know-how*. By "know-how" we do not mean procedural rules but knowing what to do in a vast number of special cases.[60] For example, commonsense physics has turned out to be extremely

[58] Herbert Simon, *The Shape of Automation for Men and Management* (New York: Harper & Row, 1965), 96.

[59] Terry Winograd, "Computer Software for Working with Language", *Scientific American* (Sept. 1984), 142.

[60] This account of skill is spelled out and defended in Hubert L. Dreyfus and Stuart E. Dreyfus, *Mind over Machine* (New York: Simon & Schuster, 2000).

hard to spell out in a set of facts and rules. When one tries, one either requires more common sense to understand the facts and rules one finds or else one produces formulas of such complexity that it seems highly unlikely they are in a child's mind.

Doing theoretical physics also requires background skills that may not be formalizable, but the domain itself can be described by abstract laws that make no reference to these background skills. AI researchers mistakenly conclude that commonsense physics too must be expressible as a set of abstract principles. But it just may be that the problem of finding a *theory* of commonsense physics is insoluble because the domain has no theoretical structure. By playing with all sorts of liquids and solids every day for several years, a child may simply learn to discriminate prototypical cases of solids, liquids, and so on and learn typical skilled responses to their typical behavior in typical circumstances. The same might well be the case for the social world. If background understanding is indeed a skill and if skills are based on whole patterns and not on rules, we would expect symbolic representations to fail to capture our commonsense understanding.

In the light of this impasse, classical, symbol-based AI appears more and more to be a perfect example of what Imre Lakatos has called a degenerating research program.[61] As we have seen, AI began auspiciously with Newell and Simon's work at Rand and by the late 1960s turned into a flourishing research program. Minsky predicted that "within a generation the problem of creating 'artificial intelligence' will be substantially solved."[62] Then, rather suddenly, the field ran into unexpected difficulties. It turned out to be much harder than one expected to formulate a theory of common sense. It was not, as Minsky had hoped, just a question of cataloguing a few hundred thousand facts. The commonsense knowledge problem became the center of concern. Minsky's mood changed completely in five years. He told a reporter that "the AI problem is one of the hardest science has ever undertaken."[63]

The rationalist tradition had finally been put to an empirical test, and it had failed. The idea of producing a formal, atomistic theory of the everyday commonsense world and of representing that theory in a symbol manipulator had run into just the difficulties Heidegger and Wittgenstein had discovered. Frank Rosenblatt's intuition that it would be hopelessly difficult to formalize the world and thus to give a formal specification of intelligent behavior had been

---

[61] Imre Lakatos, *Philosophical Papers*, ed. J. Worrall (Cambridge: Cambridge University Press, 1978).

[62] Marvin Minsky, *Computation: Finite and Infinite Machines* (New York: Prentice-Hall, 1977), 2.

[63] Gina Kolata, "How Can Computers Get Common Sense?", *Science*, 217 (24 Sept. 1982), 1237.

vindicated. His repressed research program (using the computer to instantiate a holistic model of an idealized brain), which had never really been refuted, became again a live option.

In journalistic accounts of the history of AI, Rosenblatt is vilified by anonymous detractors as a snake-oil salesman:

Present-day researchers remember that Rosenblatt was given to steady and extravagant statements about the performance of his machine. "He was a press agent's dream," one scientist says, "a real medicine man. To hear him tell it, the Perceptron was capable of fantastic things. And maybe it was. But you couldn't prove it by the work Frank did."[64]

In fact, he was much clearer about the capacities and limitations of the various types of perceptrons than Simon and Minsky were about their symbolic programs.[65] Now he is being rehabilitated. David Rumelhart, Geoffrey Hinton, and James McClelland reflect this new appreciation of his pioneering work:

---

[64] Pamela McCorduck, *Machines Who Think* (San Francisco: W. H. Freeman, 1979), 87.

[65] Some typical quotations from Rosenblatt's *Principles of Neurodynamics*:

In a learning experiment, a perceptron is typically exposed to a sequence of patterns containing representatives of each type or class which is to be distinguished, and the appropriate choice of a response is "reinforced" according to some rule for memory modification. The perceptron is then presented with a test stimulus, and the probability of giving the appropriate response for the class of the stimulus is ascertained.... If the test stimulus activates a set of sensory elements which are entirely distinct from those which were activated in previous exposures to stimuli of the same class, the experiment is a test of "pure generalization." The simplest of perceptrons...have no capability for pure generalization, but can be shown to perform quite respectably in discrimination experiments particularly if the test stimulus is nearly identical to one of the patterns previously experienced. (p. 68)

Perceptrons considered to date show little resemblance to human subjects in their figure-detection capabilities, and gestalt-organizing tendencies. (p. 71)

The recognition of sequences in rudimentary form is well within the capability of suitably organized perceptrons, but the problem of figural organization and segmentation presents problems which are just as serious here as in the case of static pattern perception. (p. 72)

In a simple perceptron, patterns are recognized before "relations"; indeed, abstract relations, such as "A is above B" or "the triangle is inside the circle" are never abstracted as such, but can only be acquired by means of a sort of exhaustive rote-learning procedure, in which every case in which the relation holds is taught to the perceptron individually. (p. 73)

A network consisting of less than three layers of signal transmission units, or a network consisting exclusively of linear elements connected in series, is incapable of learning to discriminate classes of patterns in an isotropic environment (where any pattern can occur in all possible retinal locations, without boundary effects). (p. 575)

A number of speculative models which are likely to be capable of learning sequential programs, analysis of speech into phonemes, and learning substantive "meanings" for nouns and verbs with simple sensory referents have been presented in the preceding chapters. Such systems represent the upper limits of abstract behavior in perceptrons considered to date. They are handicapped by a lack of a satisfactory "temporary

Rosenblatt's work was very controversial at the time, and the specific models he proposed were not up to all the hopes he had for them. But his vision of the human information processing system as a dynamic, interactive, self-organizing system lies at the core of the PDP approach.[66]

The studies of perceptrons...clearly anticipated many of the results in use today. The critique of perceptrons by Minsky and Papert was widely misinterpreted as destroying their credibility, whereas the work simply showed limitations on the power of the most limited class of perceptron-like mechanisms, and said nothing about more powerful, multiple layer models.[67]

Frustrated AI researchers, tired of clinging to a research program that Jerry Lettvin characterized in the early 1980s as "the only straw afloat," flocked to the new paradigm. Rumelhart and McClelland's book *Parallel Distributed Processing* sold 6,000 copies the day it went onto the market, and 30,000 are now in print. As Paul Smolensky put it:

In the past half-decade the connectionist approach to cognitive modeling has grown from an obscure cult claiming a few true believers to a movement so vigorous that recent meetings of the Cognitive Science Society have begun to look like connectionist pep rallies.[68]

If multilayered networks succeed in fulfilling their promise, researchers will have to give up the conviction of Descartes, Husserl, and early Wittgenstein that the only way to produce intelligent behavior is to mirror the world with a formal theory in the mind. Worse, one may have to give up the more basic intuition at the source of philosophy that there must be a theory of every aspect of reality—that is, there must be elements and principles in terms of which one can account for the intelligibility of any domain. Neural networks may show that Heidegger, later Wittgenstein, and Rosenblatt were right in thinking that we behave intelligently in the world without having a theory of that world. If a theory is not *necessary* to explain intelligent

---

memory," by an inability to perceive abstract topological relations in a simple fashion, and by an inability to isolate meaningful figural entities, or objects, except under special conditions. (p. 577)

The applications most likely to be realizable with the kinds of perceptrons described in this volume include character recognition and "reading machines," speech recognition (for distinct, clearly separated words), and extremely limited capabilities for pictorial recognition, or the recognition of objects against simple backgrounds. "Perception" in a broader sense may be potentially within the grasp of the descendants of our present models, but a great deal of fundamental knowledge must be obtained before a sufficiently sophisticated design can be prescribed to permit a perceptron to compete with a man under normal environmental conditions. (p. 583)

[66] Rumelhart, McClelland, and Group, *Parallel Distributed Processing*, i. 45.
[67] Rumelhart, McClelland, and Group, *Parallel Distributed Processing*, ii. 535.
[68] Paul Smolensky, "On the Proper Treatment of Connectionism", *Behavioral and Brain Sciences*, 11/1 (Mar. 1988), 1–23.

behavior, we have to be prepared to raise the question whether in everyday domains such a theoretical explanation is even *possible*.

Neural net modelers, influenced by symbol-manipulating AI, are expending considerable effort, once their nets have been trained to perform a task, in trying to find the features represented by individual nodes and sets of nodes. Results thus far are equivocal. Consider Hinton's network for learning concepts by means of distributed representations.[69] The network can be trained to encode relationships in a domain that human beings conceptualize in terms of features, without the network being given the features that human beings use. Hinton produces examples of cases in which some nodes in the trained network can be interpreted as corresponding to the features that human beings pick out, although these nodes only roughly correspond to those features. Most nodes, however, cannot be interpreted semantically at all. A feature used in a symbolic representation is either present or not. In the net, however, although certain nodes are more active when a certain feature is present in the domain, the amount of activity not only varies with the presence or absence of this feature but is affected by the presence or absence of other features as well.

Hinton has picked a domain—family relationships—that is constructed by human beings precisely in terms of the features that human beings normally notice, such as generation and nationality. Hinton then analyzes those cases in which, starting with certain random initial-connection strengths, some nodes can, after learning, be interpreted as representing those features. Calculations using Hinton's model show, however, that even his net seems to learn its associations for some random initial-connection strengths without any obvious use of these everyday features.

In one very limited sense, any successfully trained multilayer net can be interpreted in terms of features—not everyday features but what we shall call highly abstract features. Consider the simple case of layers of binary units activated by feed-forward, but not lateral or feedback, connections. To construct such an account from a network that has learned certain associations, each node one level above the input nodes could, on the basis of the connections to it, be interpreted as detecting when one of a certain set of input patterns is present. (Some of the patterns will be the ones used in training, and some will never have been used.) If the set of input patterns that a particular node detects is given an invented name (it almost certainly won't have a name in our vocabulary), the node could be interpreted as detecting the highly abstract feature so named.

[69] Geoffrey Hinton, "Learning Distributed Representations of Concepts", *Proceedings of the Eighth Annual Conference of the Cognitive Science Society* (Amherst, MA: Cognitive Science Society, 1986), 1–12.

Hence, every node one level above the input level could be characterized as a feature detector. Similarly, every node a level above those nodes could be interpreted as detecting a higher-order feature, defined as the presence of one of a specified set of patterns among the first level of feature detectors. And so on up the hierarchy.

The fact that intelligence, defined as the knowledge of a certain set of associations appropriate to a domain, can always be accounted for in terms of relations among a number of highly abstract features of a skill domain does not, however, preserve the rationalist intuition that these explanatory features must capture the essential structure of the domain so that one could base a theory on them. If the net were taught one more association of an input–output pair (where the input prior to training produced an output different from the one to be learned), the interpretation of at least some of the nodes would have to be changed. So the features that some of the nodes picked out before the last instance of training would turn out not to have been invariant structural features of the domain.

Once one has abandoned the philosophical approach of classical AI and accepted the atheoretical claim of neural net modeling, one question remains: How much of everyday intelligence can such a network be expected to capture? Classical AI researchers are quick to point out—as Rosenblatt already noted— that neural net modelers have so far had difficulty dealing with stepwise problem solving. Connectionists respond that they are confident that they will solve that problem in time. This response, however, reminds one too much of the way that the symbol manipulators in the 1960s responded to the criticism that their programs were poor at the perception of patterns. The old struggle continues between intellectualists, who think that because they can do context-free logic they have a handle on everyday cognition but are poor at understanding perception, and gestaltists, who have the rudiments of an account of perception but no account of everyday cognition.[70] One might think, using the metaphor of the right and the left brain, that perhaps the brain or the mind uses each strategy when appropriate. The problem would then be how to combine the strategies. One cannot just switch back and forth for, as Heidegger and the gestaltists saw, the pragmatic background plays a crucial role in determining relevance, even in everyday logic and problem solving, and experts in any field, even logic, grasp operations in terms of their functional similarities.

[70] For a recent influential account of perception that denies the need for mental representation, see James J. Gibson, *The Ecological Approach to Visual Perception* (Boston: Houghton Mifflin, 1979). Gibson and Rosenblatt collaborated on a research paper for the US Air Force in 1955; see James J. Gibson, Paul Olum, and Frank Rosenblatt, "Parallax and Perspective during Aircraft Landing", *American Journal of Psychology*, 68 (1955), 372–85.

It is even premature to consider combining the two approaches, since so far neither has accomplished enough to be on solid ground. Neural network modeling may simply be getting a deserved chance to fail, as did the symbolic approach.

Still, there is an important difference to bear in mind as each research program struggles on. The physical symbol system approach seems to be failing because it is simply false to assume that there must be a theory of every domain. Neural network modeling, however, is not committed to this or any other philosophical assumption. Nevertheless, building an interactive net sufficiently similar to the one our brain has evolved may be just too hard. Indeed, the commonsense knowledge problem, which has blocked the progress of symbolic representation techniques for fifteen years, may be looming on the neural net horizon, although researchers may not yet recognize it. All neural net modelers agree that for a net to be intelligent it must be able to generalize; that is, given sufficient examples of inputs associated with one particular output, it should associate further inputs of the same type with that same output. The question arises, however: What counts as the same type? The designer of the net has in mind a specific definition of the type required for a reasonable generalization and counts it a success if the net generalizes to other instances of this type. But when the net produces an unexpected association, can one say it has failed to generalize? One could equally well say that the net has all along been acting on a different definition of the type in question and that that difference has just been revealed. (All the "continue this sequence" questions found on intelligence tests really have more than one possible answer, but most human beings share a sense of what is simple and reasonable and therefore acceptable.)

Neural network modelers attempt to avoid this ambiguity and make the net produce "reasonable" generalizations by considering only a prespecified allowable family of generalizations—that is, allowable transformations that will count as acceptable generalizations (the hypothesis space). These modelers then attempt to design the architecture of their nets so that they transform inputs into outputs only in ways that are in the hypothesis space. Generalization will then be possible only on the designer's terms. While a few examples will be insufficient to identify uniquely the appropriate member of the hypothesis space, after enough examples only one hypothesis will account for all the examples. The net will then have learned the appropriate generalization principle. That is, all further input will produce what, from the designer's point of view, is the appropriate output.

The problem here is that the designer has determined, by means of the architecture of the net, that certain possible generalizations will never be found.

This is all well and good for toy problems in which there is no question of what constitutes a reasonable generalization, but in real-world situations a large part of human intelligence consists in generalizing in ways that are appropriate to a context. If the designer restricts the net to a predefined class of appropriate responses, the net will be exhibiting the intelligence built into it by the designer for that context but will not have the common sense that would enable it to adapt to other contexts, as a truly human intelligence would.

Perhaps a net must share size, architecture, and initial-connection configuration with the human brain if it is to share our sense of appropriate generalization. If it is to learn from its own "experiences" to make associations that are humanlike rather than be taught to make associations that have been specified by its trainer, a net must also share our sense of appropriateness of output, and this means it must share our needs, desires, and emotions and have a humanlike body with appropriate physical movements, abilities, and vulnerability to injury.

If Heidegger and Wittgenstein are right, human beings are much more holistic than neural nets. Intelligence has to be motivated by purposes in the organism and goals picked up by the organism from an ongoing culture. If the minimum unit of analysis is that of a whole organism geared into a whole cultural world, neural nets as well as symbolically programmed computers still have a very long way to go.

11

Merleau-Ponty and Recent Cognitive Science (2004)

In opposition to mainline cognitive science, which assumes that intelligent behavior must be based on representations in the mind or brain, Merleau-Ponty holds that the most basic sort of intelligent behavior, skillful coping, can and must be understood without recourse to any type of representation. He marshals convincing phenomenological evidence that higher primates and human beings learn to act skillfully without acquiring *mental* representations of the skill domain and of their goals. He also saw that no brain model available at the time he wrote could explain how this was possible. I argue that now, however, there *are* models of brain function that show how skills could be acquired and exercised without mind or brain representations.

1. The Failure of Representationalist Models of the Mind

The cognitivist, Merleau-Ponty's intellectualist opponent, holds that, as the learner improves through practice, he abstracts and interiorizes more and more sophisticated rules.[1] There is no phenomenological or empirical evidence that convincingly supports this view, however, and, as Merleau-Ponty points out, the flexibility, transferability, and situational sensitivity of skills make the intellectualist account implausible. Merleau-Ponty's most telling argument is that the intellectualist cannot explain how the organism could possibly use features of the current situation to determine which rule or concept should be applied.

---

[1] As I use the term "cognitivism," it is synonymous with Merleau-Ponty's term "intellectualism." For the cognitivist, like the intellectualist, even perception is a kind of thinking based on unconscious inferences and rule following. "Cognitive *science*," however, as I use the term, is the discipline that seeks to understand the mind or brain in whatever way turns out to work.

There are just too many features, so the selection of the relevant features requires that one has already subsumed the situation under the relevant concept.

In response to the difficulties of intellectualism, the empiricist claims that skills are acquired by the learner storing the memories of past situations as cases paired with successful responses. This approach is now known as case-based learning.[2] Case-based learning has not been successful, however, because as Merleau-Ponty saw, it faces the same problem that defeated the intellectualist. How can an organism classify cases so that the relevant case can be retrieved, even when, as is almost always the case, the organism finds itself in a situation that is not exactly like any of the stored cases? Cases would have to be classified by features and, to be associated with a similar already stored case, a new situation would have to be recognized as having the appropriate defining features. As Merleau-Ponty again points out, however, there are too many ways in which situations are similar for the learner to consider all features in seeking those matching an already stored case. Thus, learners need to restrict themselves to the possibly relevant features, but which features these are can only be determined once the current situation has been understood as similar to an already stored case. As Merleau-Ponty puts it, "An impression can never by itself be associated with another impression. Nor has it the power to arouse others. It does so only provided that it is already *understood*" (25/17/20).[3]

Merleau-Ponty has turned out to be right. Neither computer programs abstracting more and more sophisticated rules nor those classifying and storing more and more cases have produced intelligent behavior. To understand how this problem of finding the relevant representations can be avoided, we need to lay out more fully than Merleau-Ponty did how one's relation to the world is transformed as one acquires a skill.[4]

---

[2] See e.g. Roger C. Schank, *What We Learn When We Learn by Doing*, Technical Report, 60 (Evanston, IL: Northwestern University, Institute for Learning Sciences, 1995).

[3] Parenthetical references in this chapter are to *The Phenomenology of Perception*. The first number refers to the French-language edition: Maurice Merleau-Ponty, *Phénoménologie de la perception* (Paris: Librairie Gallimard, 1945). The next two numbers refer to the two different editions of the English-language translation by Colin Smith: Merleau-Ponty, *Phenomenology of Perception*, and Maurice Merleau-Ponty, *The Phenomenology of Perception* (Reprint edn; London: Routledge Classics, 2002).

[4] Although the French have a word for skill *(habilité)*, Merleau-Ponty prefers to use the word *habitude* to stress the fact that we *have* our skills, that they are embodied (203/174/202). The English edition correctly translates *"habitude"* as "habit," but the *Oxford English Dictionary* says "habit" refers primarily to "a settled disposition or tendency to act in a certain way, especially one acquired by frequent repetition of the same act until it becomes almost or quite involuntary." This rigid behavior is exactly what Merleau-Ponty is trying to distinguish from the flexible and situation-sensitive skills that make up *l'habitude* (see 166/142/164ff.). So, wherever the translation says "habit," I substitute "skill." For a more detailed account of skill acquisition, see Dreyfus and Dreyfus, *Mind over Machine*.

2. A Phenomenological Account of Skill Acquisition

Like a computer, beginners, who have no experience in a specific skill domain, must rely on *rules* and predetermined relevant *features*. For example, a learner driver may be given the rule "shift at ten miles per hour." A more advanced beginner can be led to notice *prototypes* such as typical engine sounds and can then be given the *maxims* such as "shift down when the motor sounds like it's straining." Merleau-Ponty does not discuss these early stages of skill acquisition, except as they appear in pathological cases, such as that of Schneider, who cannot acquire new skills but must in each case reason out what to do like a rule-following computer.

Part of Schneider's problem may well be that he lacks the capacity for emotional involvement, for to progress to more flexible and context-sensitive comportment, the learner must give up the detached rule-following or case-associating stance for a more involved relation to the skill domain. To learn to cope in any complex skill domain, the learner must adopt a perspective or goal so that features of the situation show up as more or less relevant and then act on this interpretation of the situation so as to find out which goals lead to success and which to failure. If the learner takes to heart his successes and failures, the resulting positive and negative emotional experiences seem to strengthen the neural connections that result in successful responses and inhibit those that produce unsuccessful ones, so that the learner's representations of rules and prototypical cases are gradually replaced by situational discriminations.[5] Then, in any given situation, rather than having to figure out which perspective to take or goal to pursue, the learner finds that *the situation directly shows up perspectivally,* but at this stage, which we might call mere proficiency, the learner still needs to *figure out* what to do.

If, however, the learner stays involved and dwells on her successes and failures, such involved experience will gradually turn the proficient performer into an expert. That is, starting with a variety of features, some of which are taken to be relevant to classifying a situation as requiring a specific response, with further experience the brain of the performer comes to recognize immediately the general situation, and the performer can then calculate consciously an appropriate response. Finally, with sufficient experience, the brain gradually decomposes each class of situations into subclasses, each of which elicits the type of response appropriate in that type of situation. No representation of rules, features, or cases

---

[5] If the learner resists involvement, he or she will remain merely competent. Patricia Benner has described this phenomenon in the training of nurses in Benner, *From Novice to Expert*, 164.

is required.[6] An example of such a classification skill would be a radiologist's reading of X-ray pictures. To take a more extreme case, a chess grandmaster, when shown a position that could occur in an actual game, almost immediately experiences a compelling sense of the current issue and spontaneously makes the appropriate move. Experientially, as one becomes an expert, the world's solicitations to act take the place of representations as a way of storing and accessing what one has learned.

3. The Intentional Arc and Simulated Neural Networks

The preceding sketch of a phenomenology of skillful coping makes clear that skills are acquired by dealing repeatedly with situations that then gradually come to show up as requiring more and more selective responses. This feedback loop between the learner and the perceptual world is what Merleau-Ponty calls the "intentional arc." He says, "the life of consciousness—cognitive life, the life of desire or perceptual life—is subtended by an 'intentional arc,' which projects round about us our past, our future, our human setting" (158/136/157).[7] Merleau-Ponty refers to this feedback structure as a dialectical or circular relation of milieu and action: "the relations between the organism and its milieu are not relations of linear causality but of circular causality."[8]

The notion of a dialectic of milieu and action is meant to capture the idea that, in learning, past experience is projected back into the perceptual world of the learner and shows up as affordances or solicitations to further action. As Merleau-Ponty puts it, a "person's projects polarize the world, bringing magically to view a host of signs which guide action, as notices in a museum guide the visitor" (130/112/129).[9] On this account, the best "representation" of our practical understanding of the world turns out to be the world itself.

---

[6] For the sake of simplicity, I am here describing the change from proficient to expert in the acquisition of skills that do not require continuous adaptation over time. I deal with sequential skills in section 3.

[7] Merleau-Ponty stresses that the intentional arc is tied up with the involved way in which the organism projects its activity into the future and, we should add, learns from the results. Thus, he concludes that Schneider's detached, robotic behavior comes from a weakening of the intentional arc, "which gives way in the patient, and which, in the normal subject, endows experience with its degree of vitality and fruitfulness" (184/157/182).

[8] Maurice Merleau-Ponty, *La Structure du comportement* (Paris: Presses Universitaires de France, 1942), 13/Merleau-Ponty, *Structure of Behavior*, 15.

[9] It's important to note that Merleau-Ponty uses "magical" in two ways. Here "magically" means without needing to understand how we do it. But, in discussing how the mind can control movement, he says, "We still need to understand by what magical process the representation of a movement causes precisely that movement to be made by the body." He adds, "The problem can be solved provided that we cease to draw a distinction between the body as a mechanism in itself and

Merleau-Ponty argues persuasively that no representationalist model of mind or brain function can account for the way past learning is manifest in present experience so as to guide future action. Until recently, however, opponents of such a nonrepresentationalist view, such as Herbert Simon, could argue that intellectualist or associationist models must somehow explain skilled behavior because there was no way to understand how else it could be produced. Merleau-Ponty's response that the perception–action loop is "magical" did not help to win over his opponents.

Fortunately, however, there are now models of what might be going on in the brain of an active perceiver forming an intentional arc that do not introduce brain representations. Such models are called simulated neural networks. Simulated neurons are generally called nodes. Networks consist of a layer of input nodes, connected to a layer of output nodes by way of a number of intermediate nodes called hidden nodes. The simulated strengths of synaptic connection between neurons are called weights. The output of a neuron is called its activation. Running such a net means specifying the activations of the input neurons and then calculating the activation of the nodes connected to them using a formula involving the weights on these connections, and so on, until the activation of the output nodes is calculated.

Consider the case in which a net is to be trained, by a supervisor or by the environment, to respond appropriately to a number of different patterns. Each time the net associates an input pattern with an output response, the weights on the connections between the nodes are changed according to an algorithm that adjusts the weight on each connection in such a way as to cause the net to respond more appropriately the next time the same input occurs. The training is complete when each pattern used in the training evokes what the trainer has defined as the appropriate response.

In a network trained using such a sequence of input, output, adjustment of connection weights, and then new input, the current weights on the connections between the nodes correspond to what the net has already learned through prior training using a large number of inputs. The net with the current weighted connections is thus able to classify the current inputs and respond differentially to them. This corresponds to the discrimination ability that, according to Merleau-Ponty, the skilled organism brings to a situation, on the basis of which the situation solicits a specific response.

---

consciousness as being for itself" (163n/139n/160n). Here he is using the term "magical" pejoratively to mean that a causal claim is based on an ontology that makes it *impossible* to account for how that claim could be implemented.

It is precisely the advantage of simulated neural networks that past experience with a large number of cases, rather than being stored as memories, modifies the weights between the simulated neurons, which in turn determine the response. New inputs thus produce outputs based on past experience without the net needing to represent its past experience as cases or rules for determining further actions. Simulated neural networks are thus able to avoid the problem posed by Merleau-Ponty concerning how to find the *relevant* rule to apply or how to associate the current input to the *relevant* past impression. For by changing neural connection weights and activation on the basis of past experience without remembering or in any way storing past cases, nets dispense with remembered cases altogether and so, too, with the problem of how to retrieve the appropriate one. The neural-net model thus suggests a nonrepresentational, and yet non-magical, brain basis of the intentional arc.

A fundamental problem of similarity recognition, however, reappears in any such disembodied model of neural-net learning. When a net is trained by being given inputs paired with appropriate responses, the net can only be said to have learned to respond appropriately when it responds appropriately to *new* inputs similar to, but different from, those used in training it. Otherwise, it could be regarded as merely having learned all the specific pairs used in the training. In one way, this is not a problem. Because of the way nets work, they always respond when given a new input by producing an output. If, however, the response is to be judged *appropriate* by human beings, the net must respond to the current input not merely in some arbitrary way. The net must respond to the *same similarities* to which human beings respond. But everything is similar to everything else and different from everything else in an indefinitely large number of ways. We just do not notice it. Thus, the insoluble problem of a disembodied mind responding to what is relevant in the input, which Merleau-Ponty notes concerning case retrieval and rule application, leads neural-network modelers to the basic problem of *generalization*.

Neural-network modelers agree that an intelligent network must be able to generalize. For a given classification task, given sufficient examples of inputs associated with one particular type of output, it should learn to associate further inputs of the same type with that same type of output. But what counts as the same type? The network's designer usually has in mind a specific type required for a reasonable generalization and counts it a success if the net generalizes to other instances of this type. When the net produces an unexpected association, however, can one say it has failed to generalize? One could equally well say that the net had all along been acting on a different definition of the type in question and that this difference has just been revealed. One might think of this unexpected response as showing an alien sort of intelligence, but if a neural net did not respond to the same types of situations as similar that human beings do, it would not be able to learn our skills, could not find its way about in our world, and would seem to us to be hopelessly stupid.

How, then, do human beings learn to generalize like other human beings so that they acquire the skills required to get along in the human world? Merleau-Ponty would no doubt hold that the fact that we all have similar bodies is essential to understanding how we generalize. There are at least two ways the human body constrains the space of possible generalizations. The first is due to the brain; the second is due to how our lived body copes with things.

First, the possible responses to a given input are constrained by brain architecture. This innate structure accounts for phenomena such as the perceptual constants and similarities the Gestalt psychologists investigated. These are given from the start by the perceptual system as if they had always already been learned. Merleau-Ponty calls them "a past that has never been a present" (280/242/282).

This alone, however, would not be enough to constrain the generalization space so that, in a classification situation, all human beings would respond in the same way to the same set of inputs. It turns out, however, that in a net with a large number of connections with adjustable weights, not only the training cases but also the order and frequency of the cases determine the particular weights and, therefore, how a net will generalize. The training cases, as well as their order and frequency, are normally selected by the trainer. If, however, the net were to be set up to learn by itself, that is, if its connection strengths were arranged so as to adjust themselves on the basis of the input–output pairs that the net encountered in the world, then the order and frequency of the inputs would depend on the interaction of the structure of the embodied network and the structure of the world. For example, if the net controlled a robot with a body like a human body, things nearby that afforded reaching would be noticed early and often. Such body-dependent order and frequency would provide a second constraint on generalization.[10] Thus, while the generalization problem is inevitable for disembodied neural-net models, the problem might be solved for embodied organisms that share certain constraints on how they are able to cope.[11] As Merleau-Ponty

---

[10] For a worked-out account of human body structure and how it is correlative with the structure of the human world, see Todes, *Body and World*.

[11] Giving robots bodies is a much more complicated problem than it first appeared to be. At the Massachusetts Institute of Technology (MIT) in the 1970s, researchers tried building a shoulder, arm, wrist, and hand, all guided by a television camera, which were collectively to be able to pick up blocks. Merleau-Ponty would have been pessimistic as to the success of the project. He had already pointed out in *Phenomenology of Perception* that the objective body is in objective space; therefore, to move such a body, one would have to calculate how to get its hand from one objective location to

says, "Although our body does not impose definite instincts upon us from birth, as it does upon animals, it does at least give to our life the form of generality" (171/146/169).

Of course, the body-dependence of shared generalizations puts disembodied neural networks at a serious disadvantage when it comes to learning to cope in the human world. Nothing is more alien to our form of life than a network with no varying degrees of access, no up–down, front–back orientation, no preferred way of moving, such as moving forward more easily than backward, and no emotional response to its failures and successes. The odds are overwhelming against such a disembodied net generalizing the way we do, and so learning to classify situations and affordances as we do. It should therefore come as no surprise that such classification models have succeeded only in domains cut off from everyday embodied experience, such as discriminating between sonar signals reflected from a mine and those reflected from a rock.[12]

another, which in turn involved locating the shoulder, arm, wrist, hand, and fingers and moving them in a coordinated way, whereas our bodies are given to us directly in phenomenal space, in which we can directly move our limbs to a location relative to our body. He says e.g. "if I am ordered to touch my ear or my knee, I move my hand to my ear or my knee by the shortest route, without having to think of the initial position of my hand, or that of my ear, or the path between them" (169/144/167).

As Merleau-Ponty would have expected, the MIT researchers found that the robot arm had so many degrees of freedom that they could not solve the problem of how to coordinate, in objective space, the movements of all the components. Now, however, neural nets promise a solution that does not use rules to determine how to move each joint in objective space. See the suggestion of how reaching and grasping could be solved as a problem of dealing with multiple simultaneous constraints in Rumelhart et al., *Parallel Distributed Processing*, i. 4–6.

For a more worked-out proposal using attractor theory to explain a kind of skillful coping, see Hon C. Kwan et al., "Network Relaxation as Biological Computation", *Behavioral and Brain Sciences*, 14/2 (June 1991), 354–6. H. C. Kwan et al., "Network Relaxation as Biological Computation." As Sean Kelly explains,

> On the conceptualization of movement generation suggested by Borrett and Kwan, a movement is conceived as the behavioral correlate of the evolution or relaxation of a recurrent neural network toward a fixed point attractor. Thus, the initial conditions of the network represent the initial position of the limb, the relaxation of the network toward the attractor state represents the movement of the limb, and the final state of the network at the fixed point attractor represents the position of the limb at its desired endpoint.
>
> The initial conditions of the model, like the initial intention to grasp, is sufficient to ensure, in normal circumstances, that the limb will reach the appropriate endpoint in the appropriate way. In this sense we can say that the neural-net model of limb movement reproduces the central phenomenological features of grasping behavior since, as with grasping, the model is from the outset "magically at its completion."
> Sean D. Kelly, "Grasping at Straws: Motor Intentionality and the Cognitive Science of Skilled Behavior", in Mark A. Wrathall and Jeff Malpas (eds), *Heidegger, Coping, and Cognitive Science* (Cambridge, MA: MIT Press, 2000).

[12] R. Paul Gorman and Terrence J. Sejnowski, "Learned Classification of Sonar Targets Using a Massively Parallel Network", *IEEE Transactions on Acoustics, Speech, and Signal Processing*, 36/7 (July 1988), 1135–40.

4. Maximum Grip

The capacity of an embodied agent to feed back what it has learned into the way the world shows up—the intentional arc—is only the first half of Merleau-Ponty's story. His most important contribution is his description of a dynamic version of the dialectic of milieu and action. He gives an example from sports:

> For the player in action the football field is … pervaded with lines of force (the "yard lines"; those which demarcate the "penalty area") and articulated in sectors (for example, the "openings" between the adversaries) which call for a certain mode of action and which initiate and guide the action as if the player were unaware of it. The field itself is not given to him, but present as the immanent term of his practical intentions; the player becomes one with it and feels the direction of the "goal," for example, just as immediately as the vertical and the horizontal planes of his own body. … At this moment consciousness is nothing other than the dialectic of milieu and action. Each maneuver undertaken by the player modifies the character of the field and establishes in it new lines of force in which the action in turn unfolds and is accomplished, again altering the phenomenal field.[13]

This kind of skillful response to a temporally unfolding situation is, of course, also exhibited by expert drivers and has been studied in chess players. Excellent chess players can play at the rate of 5 to 10 seconds a move and even faster without any serious degradation in performance; Simon has estimated that an expert chess player remembers roughly 50,000 types of position.[14] This is, of course, a case-based model that, as anyone who understands Merleau-Ponty would expect, has not produced expert chess play.[15] Rather, a careful description of the phenomenon suggests that, while beginners learn to distinguish specific patterns and follow rules for how to respond to them, the chess master, by playing thousands of games, has refined his dispositions to respond appropriately to each situation, and these changing dispositions to respond are correlated with changing lines of force on the board, which in turn solicit appropriate responses. So there is no need for the expert to *remember* or in any way store a repertoire of 50,000 typical positions. Still, the number of types of pattern on the chessboard

---

[13] Merleau-Ponty, *Structure du comportement*, 182–3/Merleau-Ponty, *Structure of Behavior*, 168–9.

[14] Herbert A. Simon, *Models of Thought* (New Haven, CT: Yale University Press, 1979), 386–403.

[15] Deep Blue might seem to be an exception to this claim, but actually it confirms it. This program, which defeated the world chess champion, is not an expert system operating with rules and cases. Rather, Deep Blue uses brute force to look at a billion moves a second and so can look at *all* moves approximately seven moves into the future. Except for a crude evaluation function that selects which beginning move ends in the best situation seven moves down the line, Deep Blue is no more intelligent than an adding machine.

the master has learned to respond to differentially must no doubt be as large as Simon estimates.[16]

In general, once an expert has learned to cope successfully, at each stage in a sequential, goal-directed activity, either he senses that he is doing as well as possible at that stage, or he senses a tension that tells him he is deviating from an optimal gestalt and feels drawn to make a next move that, thanks to his previous learning, is likely to be accompanied by less tension. As experts in getting around in the world, we are all constantly drawn to what Merleau-Ponty thinks of as a maximal grip on our situation. As Merleau-Ponty puts it:

For each object, as for each picture in an art gallery, there is an optimum distance from which it requires to be seen, a direction viewed from which it vouchsafes most of itself: at a shorter or greater distance we have merely a perception blurred through excess or deficiency. We therefore tend towards the maximum of visibility, and seek a better focus as with a microscope. (348/302/352)

Paintings are interesting special cases in which we are still learning, so that we have to experiment with each painting, making trial-and-error movements that oscillate around the optimum, in order to find the best grip, whereas, in everyday experience, once we have learned to cope with a certain type of object, we are normally drawn directly to the optimal coping point: "my body is geared onto the world when my perception presents me with a spectacle as varied and as clearly articulated as possible, and when my motor intentions, as they unfold, receive the responses they expect from the world" (289–90/250/292). According to Merleau-Ponty, finite, involved, embodied coping beings are constantly "motivated" to move so as to achieve the best possible grip on the world.

Merleau-Ponty is clear that, for this movement toward maximal grip to take place, one does not need a representation of a goal. Rather, acting is experienced as a steady flow of skillful activity in response to one's sense of the situation. Part

---

[16] That amateur and expert chess players use different parts of the brain has been confirmed by recent magnetic resonance imaging research. See Amidzic et al., "Patterns of Focal Y-Bursts in Chess Players," who report the following: "We use a new technique of magnetic imaging to compare focal bursts of y-band activity in amateur and professional chess players during matches. We find that this activity is most evident in the medial temporal lobe in amateur players, which is consistent with the interpretation that their mental acuity is focused on analysing unusual new moves during the game. In contrast, highly skilled chess grandmasters have more y-bursts in the frontal and parietal cortices, indicating that they are retrieving chunks from expert memory by recruiting circuits outside the medial temporal lobe." It should be noted that the claim that these MRI results support Simon's assumption that experts "are retrieving chunks [i.e. representations of typical chess positions] from memory" is in no way supported by this research. What the research does suggest is the researchers' weaker claim that "These marked differences in the distribution of focal brain activity during chess playing point to differences in the mechanisms of brain processing and functional brain organization between grandmasters and amateurs."

of that experience is a sense of whether or not coping is going well. When one senses a deviation from the optimal body—environment gestalt—one's activity tends to take one closer to an optimal body–environment relationship that relieves the "tension." As Merleau-Ponty puts it, "our body is not an object for an 'I think,' it is a grouping of lived-through meanings that moves toward its equilibrium" (179/153/177).

Skilled drivers or master-level chess players not only can sense at each stage how well they are doing, they also sense whether their actions are making their current situation better or worse. That is, the learners' past involved experience of their successes and failures results in a reliable sense that things are going well or that they are deviating from a satisfactory gestalt—a gestalt that need not be represented in their brain or mind. Learners are simply drawn to respond in a way that is likely to lower their sense of tension or disequilibrium. Thus, skillful coping does not require any representation of a *goal*. It can be *purposive* without the agent entertaining a *purpose*. As Merleau-Ponty puts it, "to move one's body is to aim at things through it; it is to allow oneself to respond to their call, which is made upon it independently of any representation" (161/139/160–1).[17]

To distinguish this body-based intentionality from the representational intentionality presupposed by cognitivism, Merleau-Ponty calls the body's response to the ongoing situation "motor intentionality" (128/110/127). This term describes the way an organism is sensitive to conditions of *improvement* without needing to represent its goal, that is, the action's conditions of *satisfaction*.[18]

5. Reinforcement Learning

So far, we have seen that artificial neural networks are normally taught appropriate responses to situations by immediate feedback, that is, the researcher (or the situation itself) determines what counts as success and "rewards" the net when it makes a right association and "corrects" it when it makes a wrong one. This is a useful model of the formation of an intentional arc in the early stages of skill acquisition in which the beginner's brain is, for example, learning to classify inputs such as motor sounds so as to make an appropriate response. Most

---

[17] To help convince us that no representation of the final gestalt is needed for the skilled performer to move toward it, Merleau-Ponty uses the analogy of a soap bubble. The bubble starts as a deformed film. The bits of soap respond to local forces according to laws that happen to work so as to dispose the entire system to end up as a sphere, but the spherical result does not play a causal role in producing the bubble.

[18] For a detailed account of the difference between propositional *conditions of satisfaction* and nonpropositional *conditions of improvement*, see Hubert L. Dreyfus, "The Primacy of Phenomenology over Logical Analysis," Chapter 7, this volume.

learning, however, is not of this static and passive sort. Normally, the learner has to make a series of decisions that lead to a reward in the future. How is it possible to learn to make the right decision at an early stage without immediate feedback as to whether that decision increases or decreases the chance of a future reward many steps later? This would seem to be an even more magical capacity than that exhibited by the intentional arc.

We can find a clue in Merleau-Ponty's account of the tendency toward getting a maximal grip. As we have just seen, Merleau-Ponty's phenomenological account of the movement of the organism toward getting a maximal grip need not involve a representation of the goal, but only a sense of whether one's motor intentions, as they unfold, are affecting one's skillful performance as one expects. Researchers have recently developed a technique called *actor–critic reinforcement learning*, which makes use of an idea similar to Merleau-Ponty's, namely, that in learning a skill, a learner only needs to have a sense of how things are going at each stage of the action. Reinforcement learning techniques enable neural-net models to develop a reliable evaluation of how things are going from feedback based on the long-term successes or failures of their current actions.[19] Yet how, one may well ask, can the model evaluate how well it is doing without representing its goal and its current relation to it? How else could the far-off goal determine how the net evaluated its current action?

To understand the answer offered by the reinforcement learning model, we need first to recall that the frequency of electrical impulses produced by a neuron is called its "activation." Next we need to note that, unlike in the classification models discussed in section 3, in reinforcement learning models, at each moment the *change in activation* of a particular node is a function of its *current activation*, together with its inputs from the other nodes connected directly to it, the activation of which in turn depends on the activation of still other nodes and the weights on their connections to that node.

Now, consider the case in which a net is to be trained to act appropriately at each step in a sequence of steps and to do so for a large number of such sequences. The input activation provided by the environment plus the current activation level of the nodes determined by all prior inputs and actions in a particular sequence is called a situation. (The current activation of a network at each moment during a sequence of actions can be said to correspond to the anticipation, or perspective, that, according to Merleau-Ponty, the skilled organism brings to the situation.) Each situation produces an activation of the output nodes.

[19] See Richard S. Sutton and Andrew G. Barto, *Reinforcement Learning: An Introduction* (Cambridge, MA: MIT Press, 1998).

Given a situation during a training sequence, the simulated learner gradually learns to generate two outputs—one, of course, is the action that, in that situation, will produce the expectation of maximal reward, while at each moment the second output represents the prospect of future reward—all without needing to represent its goal.[20] This second output, according to the reinforcement learning model, is the key to learning a skill. It is also something skilled performers experience, as reflected in Merleau-Ponty's talk of the tension produced by actions that deviate from what in the past has led to an optimal grip. On the basis of how, in a sequence of actions, the current action affected the previously estimated prospect of reward, the network refines both its estimate of the prospect of reward and its choice of action.

There are more or less rewarding sequences, so the net's learning takes place, in each situation, by random explorations (small changes) in the action that its prior results have taught it, thereby finding out how this change would affect the prospect of reward. An action that improves the prospect of reward is then reinforced, and the value representing the prospect of reward is simultaneously increased. At each step, when the model makes a random variation that is less than optimal, the estimate of the prospect of reward goes down, and when the model improves its response, the estimated reward goes up. As the learning progresses, the actions represented in the model approach the optimal, and the anticipation of future reward becomes more accurate. Gradually the size of the random explorations necessary for learning is reduced to zero. A skill has been acquired when no experimental action improves the critic's estimate of future reward.

Thus, in *learning*, according to the model, the significance of the reward for the organism plays a crucial role. After the learning has established the most rewarding behavior, however, all the organism needs, according to the model, is the feedback at each stage, based on past experience, that the prospect of future reward is either increasing, decreasing, or remaining constant. At the end of the training, the organism represented in the model will act in such a way that the prospect of reward is optimal and stays constant.

The reward function has the interesting property that the behavior of the organism is, as the modelers say, "myopic."[21] The network simply reacts to the report of how it is doing in the current situation. It can be myopic and yet

---

[20] The numerical value representing the prospect of reward in the reinforcement learning model represents the organism's sense of how well it is doing. The organism itself, however, need not represent how it is doing. It simply feels the flow directly or feels drawn to modify its behavior.

[21] In Merleau-Ponty's example of the soap bubble, the bits are myopic with respect to the sphere they end up producing.

successful thanks to learning the prospect of reward. No representation of the goal is required in the model. The numerical value representing the prospect of future reward corresponds to the organism's sense of tension in getting further away from the optimal, or its sense that things are going as well as could be expected, which Merleau-Ponty describes as a sense of equilibrium. This tension, this sense of how things are going, is not just a sense of pleasure or pain, comfort or discomfort. It is a normative sensitivity to one's current situation as better or worse, relative to the optimal (ongoing) state. It is a sense of rightness and wrongness, success and failure, as ongoing processes, not as final goals. Thus, according to Merleau-Ponty, the organism's behavior is not simply *caused* by a feeling of how things are going, nor does the organism *infer* from the feeling what it should do next; rather, the feeling of how things are going *motivates* its behavior.[22]

The model really works. For example, a simulated neural net has learned to play backgammon at world-champion level after playing millions of games with itself, yet it does not "remember" any game or position, it has not abstracted any rules, nor does it represent its goal. It has acquired its skill simply by the weight changes made by the program, so that, when its current board position is the input, the output of the neural net, after a considerable number of games, approximates the maximal reward to the moving player. The program then chooses the move that yields the board position with the minimal reward for the opponent.[23]

We have just seen that, on this model, learning is controlled by trial-and-error variations that are tested on the basis of what, in the long run, is rewarding for the organism. Merleau-Ponty's description of learning a skill makes the same point. The organism, he tells us, "builds up aptitudes [skills], that is, the general power of responding to situations of a certain type by means of varied reactions which have nothing in common but the meaning.... Situation and reaction ... are two moments of a circular process."[24]

[22] Likewise, in the reinforcement learning model, the prospect-of-reward value represents a state of the brain that is not just a state of pleasure or pain, comfort or discomfort, but is a measure of the *significance* of the results of previous actions for the organism. This sensitivity to significance comes as near as any brain models we have to instantiating nonrepresentational intentionality.

[23] Gerald J. Tesauro, "TD-Gammon, a Self-Teaching Backgammon Program, Achieves Master-Level Play", *Neural Computation*, 6/2 (1994), 215–19. Unlike the way a net learns according to the reinforcement learning model, the backgammon program learns only the prospect of reward, not optimal actions, because the rule that restricts legal moves in backgammon enables the program to examine *all* legal moves in each position and choose the best one based on the prospect of reward. A full-fledged actor–critic account of skill learning can be found in Rajarshi Das and Sreerupa Das, "Catching a Baseball: A Reinforcement Learning Perspective Using a Neural Network", *Proceedings of 12th National Conference on Artificial Intelligence* (Seattle, WA: AAAI, 1994).

[24] Merleau-Ponty, *Structure du comportement*, 140/Merleau-Ponty, *Structure of Behavior*, 130. In the reinforcement learning model, the reward is thought of as that which satisfies a need of the organism, whereas for Merleau-Ponty it seems that, although the organism must of course have

Thus, the important insight of the reinforcement learning model is that, once learned, skilled behavior is sensitive to an end that is significant for the organism, and that this significance, encapsulated in the learned prospect of reward, directs every step of the organism's activity without being represented in the organism's mind or brain. Thus, Merleau-Ponty's claim that the representationalist accounts of our most basic and pervasive forms of learning and skillful action are mistaken, and that a different account is required, can be defended not only on phenomenological grounds, but on neuroscientific grounds as well.

6. Merleau-Ponty's Relation to Neuroscience

One important question remains. Granted that recent models of the role of the brain in learning and in skillful activity have features that are isomorphic with Merleau-Ponty's account of learning and coping without brain or mental representations, would Merleau-Ponty regard this development as support for his phenomenological account of perception and action?

Given his claim that the skilled organism is solicited by its environment to respond to its situation in a way that approaches an optimal gestalt, it might seem obvious that Merleau-Ponty would be happy with any brain model that attempted to generalize the Gestaltists' hypothesis that the structure of the perceptual field is isomorphic with field effects in the brain.[25]

Merleau-Ponty, however, rejects the Gestaltists' hypothesis for at least three related reasons. First, given that, according to him, the whole organism is geared

---

specific needs and satisfy them, ongoing coping is an end in itself. Thus, he says, "the preferred behavior is the one that permits the easiest and most adapted action: for example, the most exact spatial designations, the finest sensory discriminations. Thus each organism, in the presence of a given milieu, has its optimal conditions of activity and its proper manner of realizing equilibrium." Merleau-Ponty, *Structure du comportement*, 160–1/Merleau-Ponty, *Structure of Behavior*, 148. It seems that what we are trying to do in our motor-intentional behavior, according to Merleau-Ponty, is not merely achieve some specific goal, but maintain the feedback we expect as we act. For example, we try to stay in the groove when playing jazz, and in the flow in sports. The tension between these two accounts of what human beings are ultimately aiming at, whether it is a goal or an ongoing activity, is reflected in Merleau-Ponty's example of the movement toward maximal grip as the tendency to achieve the goal of getting the best view of a picture in an art gallery. As Todes puts it, we are constantly involved in making our indeterminate situation more determinate (see Todes, *Body and World*, ch. 4). Perhaps the best way to think about the relation between the goal-directed aspect of skilled comportment and what Merleau-Ponty refers to as the tendency toward a "maximum sharpness of perception and action" (290/250/292) is to note that ongoing coping forms the background necessary for any specific goal-directed activity.

[25] The Gestaltists sought to show e.g. that unstable figures such as the Necker cube flipped from one stable form to another when the correlated brain field became saturated and weakened and the brain switched to a fresh organization.

into the whole world, even if one had an account of perceptual experiences in terms of local fields in the brain, one would find no isolable classes of events in the world correlated with isolable classes of events in the brain. For this reason, Merleau-Ponty rejected any causal account of the brain basis of phenomena when such an account claimed to explain the phenomena by psychophysical laws.[26]

Second, given his rejection of the possibility of psychophysical laws, Merleau-Ponty rejects any form of reductionism or eliminativism—the view he would call "naturalism." Presumably, he would even reject any form of mind–brain identity because he is sure that "perception is not an event of nature."[27]

Third, contra the Gestaltists, Merleau-Ponty held that any account of the working of the brain in terms of *internal* forces and equilibria missed the most important feature of comportment, namely, that the organism does not respond to the stimuli impinging on its sense organs but determines and responds to the *significance* of the situation for the organism. Thus, the organism's sense of tending toward equilibrium is not just the result of gestalt fields *in* the brain tending toward a least energy configuration, like a soap bubble tending toward a spherical shape. Rather, the minimum whole reaching equilibrium must be the organism involved in the world. According to Merleau-Ponty,

The privileged state, the invariant, can no longer be defined as the result of reciprocal actions which actually unfold in the system.... [I]f one tried to hold with Kohler that preferred behavior is that involving the least expenditure of energy ... it is too clear that the organism is not a machine governed according to a principle of *absolute* economy. For the most part preferred behavior is the simplest and most economical *with respect to the task in which the organism finds itself engaged*; and its fundamental forms of activity and the character of its possible action are presupposed in the definition of the structures which will be the simplest *for* it, preferred *in* it.... This signifies that the organism itself measures the action of things upon it and itself delimits its milieu by a circular process that is without analogy in the physical world.[28]

Merleau-Ponty's important point, then, is that any acceptable explanation of the brain activity underlying and giving rise to our comportment requires that the organism be actively involved in seeking a grip on the world and that it constantly receive feedback as to its successes and failures, which guide and refine its tendency to move toward a maximal grip on its environment. The brain basis

[26] This is similar to the view Donald Davidson calls "anomalous monism"; see Davidson, "Actions, Reasons, and Causes", *Actions and Events* (Oxford: Oxford University Press, 1980).

[27] Merleau-Ponty, *Structure du comportement*, 157/Merleau-Ponty, *Structure of Behavior*, 145.

[28] Merleau-Ponty, *Structure du comportement*, 158–61/Merleau-Ponty, *Structure of Behavior*, 146–8.

of comportment, therefore, cannot be an equilibrium formed in the brain alone, but a tendency toward equilibrium of the active organism in the situation that reflects the meaning of that situation for the organism.

7. Conclusion

It seems clear that the neural-net models discussed here meet all of Merleau-Ponty's requirements. They offer a circular model of brain function according to which the brain picks up what is significant to the organism in the world, while denying psychophysical laws and so without reducing meaningful comportment and perception to brain functions. They could thus be the basis of the sort of organism–world relation Merleau-Ponty describes:

physical stimuli act upon the organism only by eliciting a global response which will vary qualitatively when the stimuli vary quantitatively; with respect to the organism they play the role of occasions rather than of cause; the reaction depends on their vital significance rather than on the material properties of the stimuli. Hence, between the variables upon which conduct actually depends and this conduct itself there appears a relation of meaning, an intrinsic relation. One cannot assign a moment in which the world acts on the organism, since the very effect of this "action" expresses the internal law of the organism.[29]

It would be satisfying to think that Merleau-Ponty would happily embrace some such model, but there are passages in *Phenomenology of Perception* in which Merleau-Ponty seems to foreclose the possibility of *any* account of brain function that could in any way be the basis of motor intentionality. He states categorically, "How significance and intentionality could come to dwell in molecular edifices or

---

[29] Merleau-Ponty, *Structure du comportement*, 174/Merleau-Ponty, *Structure of Behavior*, 161. Walter Freeman has worked out a different model of how the brain learns to classify experiences according to what they mean to the organism. His model uses chaotic attractors. See Freeman, "The Physiology of Perception." Such an approach could be adapted to show how the brain, operating as a dynamical system, could cause a series of movements that achieve a goal without the brain in any way representing that goal in advance of achieving it. See H. L. Dreyfus, "The Primacy of Phenomenology over Logical Analysis," Chapter 7, this volume. In addition, Freeman, like Merleau-Ponty, is opposed to linear transmission models of brain activity. He argues that they face what is called the binding problem, the problem about how activity in one part of the brain communicates its results to just those other parts where the results are relevant. He proposes that the attractors formed in acquiring a skill are like local storm patterns in that they communicate with other areas of the brain not by linear transmission, but by setting up overall field effects that are selectively picked up by the parts of the brain attuned to the relevant patterns. Merleau-Ponty seems to anticipate an attractor view like Freeman's when he says, "It is necessary only to accept the fact that the physicochemical actions of which the organism is in a certain manner composed, instead of unfolding in parallel and independent sequences (as the anatomical spirit would have it), instead of intermingling in a totality in which everything would depend on everything and in which no cleavage would be possible, are constituted, following Hegel's expression, in 'clusters' or in relatively stable 'vortices.'" Merleau-Ponty, *Structure du comportement*, 166/Merleau-Ponty, *Structure of Behavior*, 153.

248 EMBODIED COPING AND ARTIFICIAL INTELLIGENCE

masses of cells is something which can never be made comprehensible, and here Cartesianism is right" (403/351/409).

One would think that it is an empirical question whether and how brain activity underlies motor intentionality and that the conviction that a naturalized account *must be possible* (as Koffka[30] and John Searle, for example, maintain) or that it is inconceivable (as Merleau-Ponty contends in the preceding passage and as thinkers such as Thomas Nagel sometimes suggest) both go beyond what we have a right to claim. For the time being, one thing we can surely do is to follow Merleau-Ponty in rejecting the atomistic causal accounts offered by his contemporaries and by current mainstream neuroscience, while investigating with open minds the latest holistic and representationless brain models of learning and skillful coping that correct just what Merleau-Ponty found inadequate in the brain models that his contemporaries accepted.[31]

[30] Merleau-Ponty quotes Koffka as saying, "I admit that in our *ultimate* explanations, we can have but *one* universe of discourse and that it must be the one about which physics has taught us so much." Kurt Koffka, *Principles of Gestalt Psychology* (New York: Harcourt, Brace, 1935), 48; Merleau-Ponty, *Structure du comportement*, 144/Merleau-Ponty, *Structure of Behavior*, 133.

[31] I thank Stuart Dreyfus for the account of skill acquisition used in this chapter. I'm also indebted to him for helping me understand how the reinforcement learning model of brain function supports Merleau-Ponty's phenomenology of representation-free coping.

12

Why Heideggerian AI Failed and How Fixing it Would Require Making it More Heideggerian (2007)

1. Symbolic AI as a Degenerating Research Program

When I was teaching at MIT in the 1960s, students from the Artificial Intelligence Laboratory would come to my Heidegger course and say in effect: "You philosophers have been reflecting in your armchairs for over 2,000 years and you still don't understand intelligence. We in the AI Lab have taken over and are succeeding where you philosophers have failed." But in 1963, when I was invited to evaluate the work of Alan Newell and Herbert Simon on physical symbol systems, I found to my surprise that, far from replacing philosophy, these pioneering researchers had learned a lot, directly and indirectly, from us philosophers: e.g. Hobbes's claim that reasoning was calculating, Descartes's mental representations, Leibniz's idea of a "universal characteristic" (a set of primitives in which all knowledge could be expressed), Kant's claim that concepts were rules, Frege's formalization of such rules, and Wittgenstein's postulation of logical atoms in his *Tractatus*. In short, without realizing it, AI researchers were hard at work turning rationalist philosophy into a research program.

But I began to suspect that the insights formulated in existentialist armchairs, especially Heidegger's and Merleau-Ponty's, were bad news for those working in AI laboratories—that, by combining representationalism, conceptualism, formalism, and logical atomism into a research program, AI researchers had condemned their enterprise to reenact a failure. Using Heidegger as a guide, I began looking for signs that the whole AI research program was degenerating. I was particularly struck by the fact that, among other troubles, researchers were running up against the problem of representing significance and relevance—a problem that Heidegger saw was implicit in Descartes's understanding of the world as a set of meaningless facts to which the mind assigned values, which John Searle now calls function predicates.

Heidegger warned that values are just more meaningless facts. To say a hammer has the function, hammering, leaves out the defining relation of hammers to nails and other equipment, to the point of building things, to the skill required in actually using a hammer, etc.—all of which Heidegger called "readiness-to-hand"— so attributing functions to brute facts couldn't capture the meaningful organization of the everyday world and so missed the way of being of equipment. "By taking refuge in 'value'-characteristics," Heidegger said, "we are ... far from even catching a glimpse of being as readiness-to-hand."[1]

Head of MIT's AI Lab, Marvin Minsky, unaware of Heidegger's critique, was convinced that representing a few million facts about objects, including their functions, would solve what had come to be called the commonsense knowledge problem. It seemed to me, however, that the real problem wasn't storing millions of facts; it was knowing which facts were relevant in any given situation. One version of this relevance problem is called the "frame problem." If the computer is running a representation of the current state of the world and something in the world changes, how does the program determine which of its represented facts can be assumed to have stayed the same, and which might have to be updated?

As Michael Wheeler puts it in *Reconstructing the Cognitive World*:

Given a dynamically changing world, how is a nonmagical system ... to take account of those state changes in that world ... that matter, and those unchanged states in that world that matter, while ignoring those that do not? And how is that system to retrieve and (if necessary) to revise, out of all the beliefs that it possesses, just those beliefs that are relevant in some particular context of action?[2]

Minsky suggested as a solution that AI programmers could use descriptions of typical situations like going to a birthday party to list and organize those, and only those, facts that were normally relevant. He suggested a structure of essential features and default assignments—a structure Husserl had already proposed and called a "frame."[3]

---

[1] Heidegger, *Being and Time*, 132–3.

[2] Michael Wheeler, *Reconstructing the Cognitive World: The Next Step* (Cambridge, MA: MIT Press, 2005), 179.

[3] Edmund Husserl, *Experience and Judgment* (Evanston, IL: Northwestern University Press, 1973), 38. Roger Schank proposed what he called "scripts." He tells us: "A script is a structure that describes appropriate sequences of events in a particular context. A script is made up of slots and requirements about what can fill those slots. The structure is an interconnected whole, and what is in one slot affects what can be in another. A script is a predetermined, stereotyped sequence of actions that defines a well-known situation" (Roger C. Schank and Robert P. Abelson, *Scripts, Plans, Goals and Understanding: An Inquiry into Human Knowledge Structures* (Hillsdale, NJ: Lawrence Erlbaum, 1977), 41; as cited in John Preston and Mark Bishop (eds), *Views into the Chinese Room: New Essays on Searle and Artificial Intelligence* (Oxford: Clarendon Press, 2002), 17).

But a system of frames isn't *in* a situation, so in order to identify the possibly relevant facts in the current situation one would need a frame for recognizing that situation, etc. It thus seemed to me obvious that any AI program using frames was going to be caught in a regress of frames for recognizing relevant frames for recognizing relevant facts, and that, therefore, the commonsense knowledge storage and retrieval problem wasn't just a *problem*; it was a sign that something was seriously wrong with the whole approach.

Unfortunately, what has always distinguished AI research from a science is its failure to face up to, and learn from, its failures. To avoid the relevance problem, AI programmers in the 1960s and early 1970s limited their programs to what they called 'micro-worlds'—artificial situations in which the small number of features that were possibly relevant was determined beforehand. It was assumed that the techniques used to construct these micro-worlds could be made more realistic and generalized to cover commonsense knowledge—but there were no successful follow-ups, and the frame problem remains unsolved.

John Haugeland argues that symbolic AI has failed and refers to it as "Good Old Fashioned AI" (GOFAI). That name has been widely accepted as capturing symbolic AI's current status. Michael Wheeler goes further, arguing that a new paradigm is already taking shape: "A Heideggerian cognitive science is . . . emerging right now, in the laboratories and offices around the world where embodied-embedded thinking is under active investigation and development."[4]

Wheeler's well-informed book could not have been more timely since there are now at least three versions of supposedly Heideggerian AI that might be thought of as articulating a new paradigm for the field: Rodney Brooks's behaviorist approach at MIT, Phil Agre's pragmatist model, and Walter Freeman's dynamic neural model. All three approaches accept Heidegger's critique of Cartesian internalist representationalism and, instead, embrace John Haugeland's slogan that cognition is "embedded and embodied."[5]

2. Heideggerian AI, Stage One: Eliminating Representations by Building Behavior-Based Robots

Winograd notes the irony in the MIT AI Lab's becoming a cradle of "Heideggerian AI" after its initial hostility to my presentation of these ideas.[6] Here's how it

[4] Wheeler, *Reconstructing the Cognitive World*, 285.

[5] John Haugeland, "Mind Embodied and Embedded", *Having Thought: Essays in the Metaphysics of Mind* (Cambridge, MA: Harvard University Press, 1998), 207–37.

[6] Terry Winograd, "Heidegger and the Design of Computer Systems", *Applied Heidegger* (Berkeley, CA: University of California Press, 1989), as cited in Dreyfus, *What Computers Still Can't Do*, p. xxxi.

happened. In March 1986, the MIT AI Lab under its new director, Patrick Winston, reversed Minsky's attitude toward me and allowed, if not encouraged, several graduate students to invite me to give a talk I called "Why AI Researchers Should Study *Being and Time*." There I repeated the Heideggerian message of my *What Computers Can't Do*: "The meaningful objects... among which we live are not a *model* of the world stored in our mind or brain; *they are the world itself*."[7]

The year of my talk, Rodney Brooks published a paper criticizing the GOFAI robots that used representations of the world and problem-solving techniques to plan their movements. He reported that, based on the idea that "the best model of the world is the world itself," he had "developed a different approach in which a mobile robot uses the world itself as its own representation—continually referring to its sensors rather than to an internal world model."[8] Looking back at the frame problem, he says: "And why could my simulated robot handle it? Because it was using the world as its own model. It never referred to an internal description of the world that would quickly get out of date if anything in the real world moved."[9] Although he doesn't acknowledge the influence of Heidegger directly (and even denies it[10]), Brooks gives me credit for "being right about many issues such as the way in which people operate in the world [that] is intimately coupled to the existence of their body."[11]

Brooks's approach is an important advance, but his robots respond only to *fixed features* of the environment, not to context or changing significance. They are like ants, and Brooks aptly calls them "animats." Brooks thinks he does not need to worry about learning, putting it off as a concern of possible future research. But by operating in a fixed world and responding only to the small set of possibly relevant features that their receptors can pick up, Brooks's animats beg the question of changing relevance and so finesse rather than solve the frame problem.

Merleau-Ponty's work, on the contrary, offers a nonrepresentational account of the way the body and the world are coupled that suggests a way of avoiding the frame problem. What the learner acquires through experience is not *represented* at all but is *presented* to the learner as more and more finely discriminated situations and, if the situation does not clearly solicit a single response or if the response does not produce a satisfactory result, the learner is led to further refine

---

[7] Dreyfus, *What Computers Can't Do*, 265–6.
[8] Rodney A. Brooks, "Intelligence without Representation", in John Haugeland (ed.), *Mind Design II: Philosophy, Psychology, and Artificial Intelligence* (Cambridge, MA: MIT Press, 1997), 416.
[9] Brooks, *Flesh and Machines*, 42.
[10] Brooks, "Intelligence without Representation", 415.
[11] Brooks, *Flesh and Machines*, 168.

his discriminations, which, in turn, solicit more refined responses. For example, what we have learned from our experience of finding our way around in a city is sedimented in how that city *looks* to us. Merleau-Ponty calls this feedback loop between the embodied agent and the perceptual world the "intentional arc."[12]

Brooks comes close to a basic insight spelled out by Merleau-Ponty in *The Structure of Behavior*, namely, that intelligence is founded on and presupposes the more basic way of coping we share with animals: "The 'simple' things concerning perception and mobility in a dynamic environment... are a necessary basis for 'higher-level' intellect... Therefore, I proposed looking at simpler animals as a bottom-up model for building intelligence."[13] Surprisingly, the modesty Brooks exhibited in choosing to first construct simple insect-like devices did not deter Brooks and Daniel Dennett from deciding to leap ahead and "[embark] on a longterm project to design and build a humanoid robot, Cog, whose cognitive talents will include speech, eye-coordinated manipulation of objects, and a host of self-protective, self-regulatory and self-exploring activities."[14]

Of course, the "longterm project" was short-lived. Cog failed to achieve any of its goals and is already in a museum.[15] But, as far as I know, neither Dennett nor anyone connected with the project has published an account of the failure and asked what mistaken assumptions underlay their absurd optimism. In a personal communication, Dennett blamed the failure on a lack of graduate students and claimed "Progress was being made on all the goals, but slower than had been anticipated." If progress was actually being made the graduate students wouldn't have left, or others would have continued to work on the project. Clearly some specific assumptions must have been mistaken, but all we find in Dennett's assessment is the implicit assumption that human intelligence is on a continuum with insect intelligence, and that therefore adding a bit of complexity to what has already been done with animats counts as progress toward humanoid intelligence. At the beginning of AI research, Yehoshua Bar-Hillel called this way of thinking the first-step fallacy, and my brother at RAND quipped, "it's like claiming that the first monkey that climbed a tree was making progress towards flight to the moon."

In contrast to Dennett's assessment, Brooks is prepared to entertain the possibility that he is barking up the wrong tree, making the sober comment that:

---

[12] Merleau-Ponty, *Phenomenology of Perception*, 136.

[13] Brooks, "Intelligence without Representation", 418.

[14] Daniel C. Dennett, "The Practical Requirements for Making a Conscious Robot", *Philosophical Transactions of the Royal Society*, 349/1689 (15 Oct. 1994), 133.

[15] Although you couldn't tell it from the Cog webpage: <http://www.ai.mit.edu/projects/human oid-robotics-group/cog/cog.html>.

Perhaps there is a way of looking at biological systems that will illuminate an inherent necessity in some aspect of the interactions of their parts that is completely missing from our artificial systems...perhaps at this point we simply do not *get it*, and that there is some fundamental change necessary in our thinking in order that we might build artificial systems that have the levels of intelligence, emotional interactions, long term stability and autonomy, and general robustness that we might expect of biological systems.[16]

Heidegger and Merleau-Ponty would say that, in spite of the breakthrough of giving up internal symbolic representations, Brooks, indeed, doesn't get it—that what AI researchers have to face and understand is not only why our everyday coping couldn't be understood in terms of inferences from symbolic representations, as Minsky's intellectualist approach assumed, but also why it can't be understood in terms of responses caused by fixed features of the environment, as in Brooks's empiricist approach. AI researchers need to consider the possibility that embodied beings like us take as input energy from the physical universe and respond in such a way as to open themselves to a world organized in terms of their needs, interests, and bodily capacities, without their *minds* needing to impose meaning on a meaningless given, as Minsky's frames require, nor their *brains* converting stimulus input into reflex responses, as in Brooks's animats.

Later I'll suggest that Walter Freeman's neurodynamics offers a radically new basis for a Heideggerian/Merleau-Pontyan approach to human intelligence—an approach compatible with physics and grounded in the neuroscience of perception and action. But first we need to examine another approach to AI contemporaneous with Brooks's that actually calls itself Heideggerian.

3. Heideggerian AI, Stage Two: Programming the Ready-to-Hand

In my talk at the MIT AI Lab, I introduced Heidegger's nonrepresentational account of the relation of Dasein (human being) and the world. I also explained that Heidegger distinguished two modes of being: the *readiness-to-hand* of equipment when we are involved in using it, and the *presence-at-hand* of objects when we contemplate them. Out of that explanation, and the lively discussion that followed, grew the second type of Heideggerian AI—the first to acknowledge its lineage.

This new approach took the form of Phil Agre's and David Chapman's program, Pengi, which guided a virtual agent playing a computer game called

---

[16] Rodney A. Brooks, "From Earwigs to Humans", *Robotics and Autonomous Systems*, 20 (1997), 301.

Pengo, in which the player and penguins kick large and deadly blocks of ice at each other.[17] Agre's approach, called "interactionism," was more self-consciously Heideggerian than Brooks's in that Agre tried explicitly to capture "Heidegger's phenomenological analysis of routine activity."[18]

Agre's interesting new idea is that the world of the game in which the Pengi agent acts is made up, not of present-at-hand objects with properties, but of possibilities for action that trigger appropriate responses from the agent. To program this situated approach Agre used what he called "deictic representations." He tells us: "This proposal is based on a rough analogy with Heidegger's analysis of everyday intentionality in Division I of *Being and Time*, with objective intentionality corresponding to the present-at-hand and deictic intentionality corresponding to the ready-to-hand."[19] And he explains: "[Deictic representations] designate, not a particular object in the world, but rather a role that an object might play in a certain time-extended pattern of interaction between an agent and its environment. Different objects might occupy this role at different times, but the agent will treat all of them in the same way."[20]

Looking back on my talk at MIT and re-reading Agre's book, I now see that, in a way, Agre understood Heidegger's account of readiness-to-hand better than I did at the time. I thought of the ready-to-hand as a special class of *entities*, viz., equipment, whereas the Pengi program treats what the agent responds to purely as *functions*. For Heidegger and Agre the ready-to-hand is not a *what* but a *for-what*.[21]

As Agre saw, Heidegger wants to get at something more basic than simply a class of objects defined by their use. At his best, Heidegger would, I think, deny that a hammer in a drawer has readiness-to-hand as its way of being. Rather, he sees that, *for the user*, equipment is a solicitation to act, not an entity with a function feature. Heidegger also notes that to observe a hammer or to observe

---

[17] Philip E. Agre, *The Dynamic Structure of Everyday Life*, Technical Report, 1085 (Cambridge, MA: MIT Artificial Intelligence Lab, 1988), Ch. Al, part Ala, p. 9.

[18] Philip E. Agre, *Computation and Human Experience* (Cambridge: Cambridge University Press, 1997), 5.

[19] Agre, *Computation and Human Experience*, 332.

[20] Agre, *Computation and Human Experience*, 251.

[21] Heidegger himself is unclear about the status of the ready-to-hand. When he is stressing the holism of equipmental relations, he thinks of the ready-to-hand as equipment, and of equipment as things like lamps, tables, doors, and rooms that have a place in a whole nexus of other equipment. Furthermore, he holds that breakdown reveals that these interdefined pieces of equipment are made of present-at-hand stuff that was there all along. See Heidegger, *Being and Time*, 97. At one point Heidegger even goes so far as to include the ready-to-hand under the same categories that characterize the present-at-hand: "We call 'categories'—characteristics of being for entities whose character is not that of Dasein.... Any entity is either a 'who' (existence) or a *what* (present-at-hand in the broadest sense)." Heidegger, *Being and Time*, 71; italics added.

ourselves hammering undermines our skillful coping. We can and do observe our surroundings while we cope, and sometimes, if we are learning, monitoring our performance as we learn improves our performance in the long run, but, in the short run, such attention interferes with our performance.

Heidegger struggles to describe the special, and he claims, basic, way of being he calls the ready-to-hand. The Gestaltists would later talk of "solicitations." In *Phenomenology of Perception*, Merleau-Ponty speaks of "motivations," and later, of "the flesh." All these terms point at what is not objectifiable—a situation's way of drawing one into it. Indeed, in his 1925 course, *Logic: The Question of Truth*, Heidegger describes our most basic experience of what he later calls "pressing into possibilities" not as dealing with the desk, the door, the lamp, the chair and so forth, but as directly responding to a "what for":

> What is first of all "given"...is the "for writing," the "for going in and out," the "for illuminating," the "for sitting." That is, writing, going-in-and-out, sitting, and the like are what we are a priori involved with. What we know when we "know our way around" and what we learn are these "for-what's."[22]

It's clear here, unlike what some people take Heidegger to suggest in *Being and Time*, that this basic experience has no as-structure. That is, when absorbed in coping, I can be described *objectively* as using the door *as* a door, but I'm not *experiencing* the door *as* a door. In coping at my best, I'm not experiencing *the door* at all but simply pressing into the possibility of going out. The important thing to realize is that, when we are pressing into possibilities, there is no experience of an *entity* doing the soliciting; just the solicitation. Such solicitations disclose the world on the basis of which we sometimes do step back and perceive things *as* things.

But Agre's Heideggerian AI did not try to program this experiential aspect of being drawn in by an affordance. Rather, with his deictic representations, Agre *objectified* both the functions and their situational relevance for the agent. In Pengi, when a virtual ice cube defined by its function is close to the virtual player, a rule dictates the response (e.g. kick it). No skill is involved and no learning takes place.

So Agre had something right that I was missing—the transparency of the ready-to-hand—but he nonetheless fell short of being fully Heideggerian. For Heidegger the ready-to-hand is not a fixed function, encountered in a predefined type of situation that triggers a predetermined response that either succeeds or

---

[22] Heidegger, *Logik*, 144; Martin Heidegger, *Logic: The Question of Truth*, tr. Thomas Sheehan (Studies in Continental Thought; Bloomington, IN: Indiana University Press, 2010), 121.

fails. Rather, as we have begun to see and will soon see further, readiness-to-hand is experienced as a solicitation that calls forth a flexible response to the *significance* of the current situation—a response which is experienced as either improving the situation or making it worse.

Moreover, although he proposed to program Heidegger's account of everyday routine activities, Agre doesn't even try to account for how our experience feeds back and changes our sense of the significance of the next situation and what is relevant in *it*. In putting his virtual agent in a virtual world where all possible relevance is determined beforehand, Agre doesn't account for how we learn to respond to new relevancies, and so, like Brooks, he finesses rather than solves the frame problem. Thus, sadly, his Heideggerian AI turned out to be a dead end. Happily, however, Agre never claimed he was making progress towards building a human being.

4. Pseudo Heideggerian AI: Situated Cognition and the Embedded, Embodied, Extended Mind

Wheeler, in *Reconstructing the Cognitivist World*, praises me for putting the confrontation between Cartesian and Heideggerian ontologies to the test in the empirical realm. Wheeler claims, however, that I only made negative predictions about the viability of GOFAI and cognitive science research programs. The time has come, he says, for a positive Heideggerian approach and that the emerging embodied-embedded paradigm in the field is a thoroughly Heideggerian one.

As if taking up from where Agre left off with his objectified version of the ready-to-hand, Wheeler tells us: "Our global project requires a defense of action-oriented representation.... action-oriented representation may be interpreted as the subagential reflection of online practical problem solving, as conceived by the Heideggerian phenomenologist. Embodied-embedded cognitive science is implicitly a Heideggerian venture."[23] He further notes: "As part of its promise, this nascent, Heideggerian paradigm would need to indicate that it might plausibly be able either to solve or to dissolve the frame problem."[24] And he suggests: "The good news for the reoriented Heideggerian is that the kind of evidence called for here may already exist in the work of recent *embodied-embedded cognitive science*" (p. 188). He concludes:

[23] Wheeler, *Reconstructing the Cognitive World*, 222–3.
[24] Wheeler, *Reconstructing the Cognitive World*, 187.

Let's be clear about the general relationships at work here. Dreyfus is right that the philosophical impasse between a Cartesian and a Heideggerian metaphysics can be resolved empirically via cognitive science. However, he looks for resolution in the wrong place. For it is not any alleged empirical failure on the part of orthodox cognitive science, but rather the concrete empirical success of a cognitive science with Heideggerian credentials, that, if sustained and deepened, would ultimately vindicate a Heideggerian position in cognitive theory.[25]

I agree it is time for a positive account of how Heideggerian AI and an underlying Heideggerian neuroscience could solve the frame problem, but I think Wheeler is the one looking in the wrong place. Merely in supposing that Heidegger is concerned with subagential *problem solving* and action-oriented *representations*, Wheeler's project reflects not a step beyond Agre but a regression to pre-Brooks GOFAI. Heidegger, indeed, claims that skillful coping is basic, but he is also clear that all coping takes place on the background of coping he calls "being-in-the-world" which doesn't involve any form of representation at all.[26]

Wheeler's cognitivist misreading of Heidegger leads to an overestimation of the importance of Clark and Chalmers's[27] attempt to free us from the Cartesian idea that the mind is essentially inner by pointing out that in thinking we sometimes make use of external artifacts like pencil, paper, and computers. Unfortunately, this argument for the extended mind preserves the Cartesian assumption that our basic way of relating to the world is by using representations such as beliefs and memories, be they in the mind or in notebooks in the world. In effect, while Brooks and Agre dispense with representations where coping is concerned, all Clark, Chalmers, and Wheeler give us as a supposedly radical new Heideggerian approach to the human way of being in the world is the observation that memories and beliefs are not necessarily *inner* entities and that, therefore, *thinking bridges the distinction between inner and outer representations.*[28]

Heidegger's important insight is not that, when we solve problems, we sometimes make use of representational equipment outside our bodies, but that *being-in-the-world* is more basic than *thinking* and solving problems; it is not representational at all. That is, when we are coping at our best, we are drawn in by solicitations and respond directly to them, so that the distinction between us and our equipment vanishes. As Heidegger sums it up: "I *live* in the

---

[25] Wheeler, *Reconstructing the Cognitive World*, 188–9.

[26] Merleau-Ponty says the same: "[T]o move one's body is to aim at things through it; it is to allow oneself to respond to their call, which is made upon it independently of any representation" (*Phenomenology of Perception*, 139).

[27] Andy Clark and David J. Chalmers, "The Extended Mind", *Analysis*, 58 (1998), 7–19.

[28] According to Heidegger, intentional content isn't in the mind, nor in some third realm (as it is for Husserl), *nor in the world*; it isn't anywhere. It's a way of being-towards.

understanding of writing, illuminating, going-in-and-out, and the like. More precisely: as Dasein I am—in speaking, going, and understanding—an act of understanding dealing-with. My being in the world *is* nothing other than this already-operating-with-understanding in this mode of being."[29]

Heidegger's and Merleau-Ponty's understanding of embedded-embodied coping, therefore, is not that the *mind* is sometimes *extended into the world* but rather that, in our most basic way of being—i.e. as skillful copers—we are not minds at all but *one with the world*. Heidegger sticks to the phenomenon, when he says that, in its most basic way of being, "Dasein is its world existingly."[30] (To make sense of this slogan, it's important to be clear that Heidegger distinguishes the human *world* from the physical *universe*.)

When you stop thinking that mind is what characterizes us most basically but, rather, that most basically we are absorbed copers, the inner–outer distinction becomes problematic. There's no easily askable question about where the absorbed coping is—in me or in the world. Thus, for a Heideggerian all forms of *cognitivist* externalism presuppose a more basic *existentialist* externalism where even to speak of "externalism" is misleading since such talk presupposes a contrast with the internal. Compared to this genuinely Heideggerian view, extended-mind externalism is contrived, trivial, and irrelevant.

5. What Motivates Embedded-Embodied Coping?

But why is Dasein called to cope at all? According to Heidegger, we are constantly solicited to improve our familiarity with the world: "Caring takes the form of a looking around and seeing, and as this circumspective caring it is at the same time anxiously concerned about developing its circumspection, that is, about *securing and expanding its familiarity* with the objects of its dealings."[31] This pragmatic perspective is developed by Merleau-Ponty, and by Samuel Todes.[32]

---

[29] Heidegger, *Logik*, 146. It's important to realize that when he introduces the term "understanding," Heidegger explains that he means a kind of know-how. Heidegger, *Basic Problems of Phenomenology*, 276.

[30] Heidegger, *Being and Time*, 416.

[31] Martin Heidegger, "Phenomenological Interpretations in Connection with Aristotle", in John Van Buren (ed.), *Supplements: From the Earliest Essays to Being and Time and Beyond* (Albany, NY: State University of New York Press, 2002), 115. This way of putting the source of *significance* covers both animals and people. By the time he published *Being and Time*, however, Heidegger was interested exclusively in the special kind of significance found in the world opened up by human beings who are defined by the stand they take on their own being. We might call this *meaning*. In this chapter I'm putting the question of uniquely human meaning aside to concentrate on the sort of *significance* we share with animals.

[32] Todes, *Body and World*.

These heirs to Heidegger's account of familiarity and coping describe how an organism, animal or human, interacts with what is objectively speaking the meaningless physical universe in such a way as to experience it as an environment organized in terms of what that organism needs in order to find its way around. All such coping beings are motivated to get a more and more refined and secure sense of their environment and of the specific objects of their dealings. According to Merleau-Ponty: "My body is geared into the world when my perception presents me with a spectacle as varied and as clearly articulated as possible."[33]

In short, in our skilled activity we are drawn to move so as to achieve a better and better grip on our situation. For this movement towards maximal grip to take place, one doesn't need a mental representation of one's goal nor any subagential problem solving as would a GOFAI robot. Rather, acting is experienced as a steady flow of skillful activity in response to one's sense of the situation. When one's situation deviates from some optimal body-environment gestalt, one's activity takes one closer to that optimum and thereby relieves the "tension" of the deviation. One does not need to know what that optimum is in order to move towards it. One's body is simply solicited by the situation to lower the tension. As Merleau-Ponty puts it: "Our body is not an object for an 'I think', it is a grouping of lived-through meanings that moves towards its equilibrium."[34]

6. Modeling Situated Coping as a Dynamical System

Describing the phenomenon of everyday coping as being "geared into" the world and moving towards "equilibrium" suggests a *dynamic* relation between the coper and the environment. Timothy van Gelder calls this dynamic relation "coupling," explaining its importance as follows:

The post-Cartesian agent manages to cope with the world without necessarily representing it. A dynamical approach suggests how this might be possible by showing how the internal operation of a system interacting with an external world can be so subtle and complex as to *defy* description in representational terms—how, in other words, cognition can *transcend* representation.[35]

Van Gelder shares with Brooks the idea that thought is grounded in a more basic relation of agent and world. As van Gelder puts it: "Cognition can, in sophisticated cases, involve representation and sequential processing; but such

---

[33] Merleau-Ponty, *Phenomenology of Perception*, 250, translation modified.

[34] Merleau-Ponty, *Phenomenology of Perception*, 153.

[35] Tim van Gelder, "Dynamics and Cognition", in John Haugeland (ed.), *Mind Design II* (Cambridge, MA: MIT Press, 1997), 448.

phenomena are best understood as emerging from a dynamical substrate, rather than as constituting the basic level of cognitive performance."[36] This dynamical substrate is precisely the subagential causal basis of the skillful coping first described by Heidegger and worked out in detail by Merleau-Ponty.

Van Gelder importantly contrasts the rich interactive temporality of real-time online coupling of coper and world with the austere step-by-step temporality of thought. Wheeler helpfully explains:

Whilst the computational architectures proposed within computational cognitive science require that inner events happen in the right order, and (in theory) fast enough to get a job done, there are, in general, no constraints on how long each operation within the overall cognitive process takes, or on how long the gaps between the individual operations are. Moreover, the transition events that characterize those inner operations are not related in any systematic way to the real-time dynamics of either neural biochemical processes, non-neural bodily events, or environmental phenomena (dynamics which surely involve rates and rhythms).[37]

Computation is thus paradigmatically austere. Wheeler adds: "Turing machine computing is digital, deterministic, discrete, effective (in the technical sense that behavior is always the result of an algorithmically specified finite number of operations), and temporally austere (in that time is reduced to mere sequence)."[38]

Ironically, Wheeler's highlighting the contrast between rich and austere temporality enables us to see clearly that his appeal to extended minds as a Heideggerian response to Cartesianism leaves out the essential embodied embedding. Clark and Chalmers's examples of extended minds dealing with representations are clearly a case of computational austerity—no rates and rhythms are involved. Wheeler is aware of this possible objection to his backing of both the *dynamical systems* model and the *extended mind* approach. He asks: "What about the apparent clash between continuous reciprocal causation and action orientated representations? On the face of it this clash is a worry for our emerging cognitive science."[39] But instead of facing up to the incompatibility of these two opposed models of ground-level intelligence, Wheeler suggests that we must somehow combine them and that "this is the biggest of the many challenges that lie ahead."[40]

---

[36] Van Gelder, "Dynamics and Cognition", 439.
[37] Michael Wheeler, "Change in the Rules: Computers, Dynamical Systems, and Searle", in John Preston and Mark Bishop (eds), *Views into the Chinese Room: New Essays on Searle and Artificial Intelligence* (Oxford: Clarendon Press, 2002), 345.
[38] Wheeler, "Change in the Rules", 344–5.
[39] Wheeler, *Reconstructing the Cognitive World*, 280.
[40] Wheeler, *Reconstructing the Cognitive World*, 280.

Wheeler's ambivalence as to which model is more basic, the representational or the dynamic, undermines his Heideggerian approach. For, as Wheeler himself sees, the Heideggerian claim is that action-oriented coping, as long as it is involved (online, Wheeler would say), is not representational at all and does not involve any problem solving, and that all representational problem solving takes place later offline.[41] Showing in detail how the representational un-ready-to-hand in all its forms is derived from the nonrepresentational ready-to-hand is exactly the Heideggerian project. It requires a basic choice of ontology, phenomenology, and brain model, between a cognitivist model that gives a basic role to representations, and a dynamical model like Merleau-Ponty's and van Gelder's that denies a basic role to any sort of representation—even action-oriented ones—and gives a primordial place to equilibrium and in general to rich coupling.

Ultimately, we have to choose which sort of AI and which sort of neuroscience to back, and so we are led to the questions: could the brain in its causal support of our active coping instantiate a richly coupled dynamical system, and is there any evidence it actually does so? If so, could this coupling be modeled on a digital computer to give us Heideggerian AI?

7. Walter Freeman's Heideggerian/ Merleau-Pontyan Neurodynamics

We have seen that our experience of the everyday world is organized in terms of significance and relevance and that this significance can't be constructed by giving meaning to brute facts—both because we don't experience brute facts and, even if we did, no value predicate could do the job of giving them situational significance. Yet all that the organism can receive as input is mere physical energy. How can such senseless physical stimulation be experienced directly as significant? If we can't answer this question, the phenomenological observation that the world is its own best representation, and that the significance we find in our world is constantly enriched by our experience in it, seems to require that the brain be what Dennett derisively calls "wonder tissue."

---

[41] I'm oversimplifying here. Wheeler does note that Heidegger has an account of online, involved problem solving that Heidegger calls dealing with the "un-ready-to-hand." But while for Heidegger and for Wheeler coping at its best deals directly with the ready-to-hand with no place for representations of any sort, for Heidegger but not for Wheeler *all* un-ready-to-hand coping takes place on the background of an even more basic nonrepresentational holistic coping which allows copers to orient themselves in the world. As we shall see, it is this basic coping, not any kind of problem solving, agential or subagential, that enables Heideggerian AI to avoid the frame problem.

Fortunately, there is at least one model of how the brain could provide the causal basis for the intentional arc. Walter Freeman, a founding figure in neuroscience and the first to take seriously the idea of the brain as a nonlinear dynamical system, has worked out an account of how the brain of an active animal can find and augment significance in its world. On the basis of years of work on olfaction, vision, touch, and hearing in alert and moving rabbits, Freeman proposes a model of rabbit learning based on the coupling of the brain and the environment. To bring out the relevance of Freeman's account to our phenomenological investigation, I propose to map Freeman's neurodynamic model onto the phenomena we have already noted in the work of Merleau-Ponty.

7.1. Involved action–perception: Merleau-Ponty's being-absorbed-in-the-world (être au monde)—his version of Heidegger's in-der-Welt-Sein

The organism normally actively seeks to improve its current situation. Thus, according to Freeman's model, when hungry, frightened, disoriented, etc., the rabbit sniffs around until it falls upon food, a hiding place, or whatever else it senses it needs. The animal's neural connections are then strengthened to the extent that reflects the extent to which the result satisfied the animal's current need. In Freeman's neurodynamic model, the input to the rabbit's olfactory bulb modifies the bulb's neuron connections according to the Hebbian rule that neurons that fire together wire together.

7.2. Holism

The change is much more radical than adding a new mechanical response. The next time the rabbit is in a similar state of seeking and encounters a similar smell, the entire bulb goes into a state of global chaotic activity. Freeman tells us:

Experiments show clearly that every neuron in the [olfactory] bulb participates in generating each olfactory perception. In other words, the salient information about the stimulus is carried in some distinctive pattern of *bulb wide activity*, not in a small subset of feature-detecting neurons that are excited only by, say, foxlike scents.[42]

7.3. Direct perception of significance

After each sniff, the rabbit's bulb exhibits a distribution of energy states. The bulb then tends toward minimum energy the way a ball tends to roll towards the bottom of a container, no matter where it starts from within the container. Each

---

[42] Freeman, "Physiology of Perception", 79; italics added.

possible minimal energy state is called an "attractor." The brain states that tend towards a particular attractor are called its "basin of attraction."[43]

The rabbit's brain forms a new basin of attraction for each new significant input. Thus, the significance of past experience is preserved in the set of basins of attraction. The set of basins of attraction that an animal has learned forms what is called an "attractor landscape," and "The state space of the cortex can therefore be said to comprise an attractor landscape with several adjoining basins of attraction, one for each class of learned stimuli."[44]

Freeman argues that each new attractor does not *represent*, say, a carrot, or the smell of carrot, or even what to do with a carrot. Rather, the brain's current state is the result of the sum of the animal's past experiences with carrots, and this state is directly coupled with or resonates to the affordance offered by the current carrot. What in the physical input is directly picked up and resonated to when the rabbit sniffs, then, is the affords-eating. Freeman tells us "The macroscopic bulbar patterns [do] not relate to the stimulus directly but instead to the significance of the stimulus."[45]

7.4. The stimulus is not further processed or acted upon (Merleau-Ponty: we normally have no experience of sense data)

Since on Freeman's account the bulb responds directly to the contextual significance of the current input, after activating a specific attractor landscape the stimulus has no further job to perform. So the stimulus need not be processed into a representation of the current situation, on the basis of which the brain then has to infer what to do. As Freeman explains:

The new pattern is selected, not imposed, by the stimulus. It is determined by prior experience with this class of stimulus. The pattern expresses the nature of the class and its significance for the subject rather than the particular event. The identities of the particular neurons in the receptor class that are activated are irrelevant and are not retained.... Having played its role in setting the initial conditions, the sense-dependent activity is washed away.[46]

---

[43] Just how Hebbian learning is translated into an attractor is not something Freeman claims to know in detail. He simply notes: "The attractors are not shaped by the stimuli directly, but by previous experience with those stimuli...and neuromodulators as well as sensory input. Together these modify the synaptic connectivity within the neuropil and thereby also the attractor landscape." Freeman, *How the Brain Makes up its Mind*, 62.

[44] Freeman, *How the Brain Makes up its Mind*, 62. Quotations from Freeman's books have been reviewed by him to correspond to his latest vocabulary and way of thinking about the phenomena.

[45] Walter J. Freeman, *Societies of Brains: A Study in the Neuroscience of Love and Hate* (Hillsdale, NJ: Lawrence Erlbaum Associates, 1995), 59.

[46] Freeman, *Societies of Brains*, 66-7.

7.5. The perception–action loop

The brain's movement towards the bottom of a particular perceptual basin of attraction underlies the perceiver's perception of the significance of a particular experience. For example, if a carrot affords eating the rabbit is directly readied to eat the carrot, or perhaps readied to carry off the carrot depending on which attractor is currently activated. Freeman tells us: "The same global states that embody the significance provide... the patterns that make choices between available options and that guide the motor systems into sequential movements of intentional behavior."[47]

The animal must take account of how things are going and either continue on a promising path, or, if the overall action is not going as well as anticipated, the brain self-organizes so the attractor system jumps to another attractor. Either this causes the animal to act in such a way as to increase its sense of impending reward, or the brain will shift attractors again, until it lands in one that improves its sense of impending reward.[48] The attractors can change like switching from frame to frame in a movie film with each further sniff or with each shift of attention. If the rabbit achieves what it is seeking, a report of its success is fed back to reset the sensitivity of the olfactory bulb. And the cycle is repeated.

7.6. Optimal grip

The animal's movements are presumably experienced by the animal as its being drawn toward getting an optimal perceptual take on what is currently significant, and, where appropriate, an actual optimal bodily grip on it. Minimum tension is correlated with achieving an optimal grip.[49]

---

[47] Freeman, *How the Brain Makes up its Mind*, 114.

[48] In this connection Freeman speaks of "expectations" and a brain function he calls "preafference," but I suspect that this is bad phenomenology leading to dubious neurospeculation. Once the stimulus has been classified by selecting an attractor that says eat this now, the problem for the brain is just how this eating is to be done. Online coping needs a stimuli-driven feedback policy dictating how to move rapidly over the terrain and approach and eat the carrot. Here, an actor–critic version of temporal difference reinforcement learning (TDRL) is needed to augment the Freeman model. According to TDRL, learning the appropriate movements in the current situation requires learning the expected final award as well as the movements. These two functions are learned slowly through repeated experiences. Then the brain can monitor directly whether the expectation of reward is being met as the rabbit approaches the carrot to eat it. There need be no expectation of a goal state. If the expected final reward suddenly decreases due e.g. to the current inaccessibility of the carrot, the relevant part of the brain prompts the olfactory bulb to switch to a new attractor or perspective on the situation that dictates a different learned action, say dragging the carrot with *its* expected reward. Only after a skill is thus acquired can the current stimuli, plus the past history of responding to related stimuli now wired into cell assemblies, produce the rapid responses required for ongoing skillful coping.

[49] If it seems that much of the time we don't experience any such pull toward the optimal, Merleau-Ponty would no doubt respond that the sensitivity to deviation is nonetheless guiding one's

Freeman sees his account of the brain dynamics underlying perception and action as structurally isomorphic with Merleau-Ponty's:

Merleau-Ponty concludes that we are moved to action by disequilibrium between the self and the world. In dynamic terms, the disequilibrium ... puts the brain onto ... a pathway through a chain of preferred states, which are learned basins of attraction. The penultimate result is not an equilibrium in the chemical sense, which is a dead state, but a descent for a time into the basin of an attractor, giving an awareness of closure.[50]

Thus, according to Freeman, in governing action the brain normally moves from one basin of attraction to another, descending into each basin for a time without coming to rest in any of them. If so, Merleau-Ponty's talk of *reaching* equilibrium or maximal grip is misleading. But Merleau-Pontyans should be happy to improve their phenomenological description on the basis of Freeman's model. Normally, the coper moves *towards* a maximal grip but, instead of coming to rest when the maximal grip is achieved, the coupled coper, without coming to rest, is drawn to move on in response to the call of another affordance that solicits her to take up the same task from another angle, or to turn to the next task that grows out of the current one.

7.7. Experience feeds back into the look of the world (Merleau-Ponty's intentional arc)

Freeman claims his read-out from the rabbit's brain shows that each learning experience that is significant in a new way sets up a new attractor and rearranges all the other attractor basins in the landscape:

I have observed that brain activity patterns are constantly dissolving, reforming and changing, particularly in relation to one another. When an animal learns to respond to a new odor, there is a shift in all other patterns, even if they are not directly involved with the learning. There are no fixed representations, as there are in [GOFAI] computers; there are only significances.[51]

And he adds elsewhere:

I conclude that context dependence is an essential property of the cerebral memory system, in which each new experience must change all of the existing store by some

---

coping, just as an airport radio beacon doesn't give a warning signal unless the plane strays off course, and then, let us suppose, the plane gets a signal whose intensity corresponds to how far off course it is and the intensity of the signal diminishes as it approaches getting back on course. The silence that accompanies being on course doesn't mean the beacon isn't continually guiding the plane, likewise in the case of the absence of tension felt in perception.

[50] Freeman, *How the Brain Makes up its Mind*, 121.
[51] Freeman, *How the Brain Makes up its Mind*, 22.

small amount, in order that a new entry be incorporated and fully deployed in the existing body of experience. This property contrasts with memory stores in computers...in which each item is positioned by an address or a branch of a search tree. There, each item has a compartment, and new items don't change the old ones. Our data indicate that in brains the store has no boundaries or compartments...Each new state transition...initiates the construction of a local pattern that impinges on and modifies the whole intentional structure.[52]

The whole constantly updated pattern of attractors is correlated with the agent's experience of the changing significance of things in the world. Merleau-Ponty likewise concludes that, thanks to the intentional arc, no two experiences of the world are ever exactly alike.

The important point is that Freeman offers a model of learning which is not an associationist model according to which, as one learns, one adds more and more fixed connections, nor a cognitivist model based on offline representations of objective facts about the world that enable offline inferences as to which facts to expect next, and what they mean. Rather, Freeman's model instantiates a genuine intentional arc according to which there are no linear causal connections nor a fixed library of data, but where, each time a new significance is encountered, the whole perceptual world of the animal changes so that significance as directly displayed is contextual, global, and continually enriched.

7.8. Circular causality

Such systems are self-organizing. Freeman explains:

Macroscopic ensembles exist in many materials, at many scales in space and time, ranging from...weather systems such as hurricanes and tornadoes, even to galaxies. In each case, the behavior of the microscopic elements or particles is constrained by the embedding ensemble, and microscopic behavior cannot be understood except with reference to the macroscopic patterns of activity.[53]

Thus, the cortical field controls the neurons that create the field. In Freeman's terms, in this sort of circular causality the overall activity "enslaves" the elements. As he emphasizes:

Having attained through dendritic and axonal growth a certain density of anatomical connections, the neurons cease to act individually and start participating as part of a group, to which each contributes and from which each accepts direction...The activity level is now determined by the population, not by the individuals. This is the first building block of neurodynamics.[54]

---

[52] Freeman, *Societies of Brains*, 99.
[53] Freeman, *How the Brain Makes up its Mind*, 52.
[54] Freeman, *How the Brain Makes up its Mind*, 53.

Given the way the whole brain can be tuned by past experience to influence individual neuron activity, Freeman can claim: "Measurements of the electrical activity of brains show that dynamical states of Neuroactivity emerge like vortices in a weather system, triggered by physical energies impinging onto sensory receptors.... These dynamical states determine the structures of intentional actions."[55] Merleau-Ponty seems to anticipate Freeman's neurodynamics when he says: "It is necessary only to accept the fact that the physico-chemical actions of which the organism is in a certain manner composed, instead of unfolding in parallel and independent sequences, are constituted ... in relatively stable 'vortices'."[56]

In its dynamic coupling with the environment the brain tends towards equilibrium but continually (discontinuously) switching from one attractor basin to another. The discreteness of these global state transitions from one attractor basin to another makes it possible to model the brain's activity on a computer. Freeman notes that: "At macroscopic levels each perceptual pattern of Neuroactivity is discrete, because it is marked by state transitions when it is formed and ended ... I conclude that brains don't use numbers as symbols, but they do use discrete events in time and space, so we can represent them ... by numbers in order to model brain states with digital computers."[57] That is, the computer can model the input and the series of discrete transitions from basin to basin they trigger in the brain, thereby modeling how, on the basis of past experiences of success or failure, physical input acquires significance for the organism. When one actually programs such a model of the brain as a dynamic physical system, one has an explanation of how the brain does what Merleau-Ponty thinks the brain must be doing, and, since Merleau-Ponty is working out of Heidegger's ontology, one has developed Freeman's neurodynamics into Heideggerian AI.

Freeman has actually programmed his model of the brain as a dynamic physical system, and so claims to have shown what the brain is doing to provide the material substrate for Heidegger's and Merleau-Ponty's phenomenological account of everyday perception and action. This may well be the new paradigm for the cognitive sciences that Wheeler proposes to present in his book but which he fails to find. It would show how the emerging embodied-embedded approach could be a step towards a genuinely existential AI. Although, as we shall see, it would still be a very long way from programming human intelligence. Meanwhile, the job of phenomenologists is to get clear concerning the phenomena that

[55] Freeman, *Societies of Brains*, 111.
[56] Merleau-Ponty, *Structure of Behavior*, 153.
[57] Freeman, *Societies of Brains*, 105.

must be explained. That would include an account of how human beings, unlike the so-called Heideggerian computer models we have discussed, don't just ignore the frame problem nor solve it, but show why it doesn't occur.

Time will tell whether Freeman's Merleau-Pontyan model is on the right track for explaining how the brain finds and feeds back significance into the meaningless physical universe. Only then will we find out if one can actually produce intelligent behavior by programming a model of the physical state transitions taking place in the brain. That would be the positive Heideggerian contribution to the cognitive sciences that Wheeler proposes to present but fails to find. It would show how the emerging embodied-embedded approach, when fully understood, could, indeed, be a step towards a genuinely Heideggerian AI. Meanwhile, the job of phenomenologists is to get clear concerning the phenomena that need to be explained. That includes an account of how *we*, unlike classical representational computer models, avoid the frame problem.

8. How Would Heideggerian AI Dissolve the Frame Problem?

As we have seen, Wheeler rightly thinks that the simplest test of the viability of any proposed AI program is whether it can solve the frame problem. We've also seen that the two current supposedly Heideggerian approaches to AI avoid the frame problem. Brooks's empiricist/behaviorist approach in which the environment directly causes responses avoids it by leaving out significance and learning altogether, while Agre's action-oriented approach, which includes only a small fixed set of possibly relevant responses, fails to face the problem of changing relevance.

Wheeler's approach, however, by introducing flexible action-oriented *representations*, like any representational approach, has to face the frame problem head on. To see why, we need only slightly revise his statement of the problem (quoted earlier), substituting "representation" for "belief": "Given a dynamically changing world, how is a nonmagical system . . . to retrieve and (if necessary) to revise, out of all the *representations* that it possesses, just those *representations* that are relevant in some particular context of action?"[58] Wheeler's frame problem, then, is to explain how his allegedly Heideggerian system can determine in some systematic way which of the action-oriented representations it contains or can generate are relevant in any current situation, and to keep track of how this

---

[58] Wheeler, *Reconstructing the Cognitive World*, 179.

relevance changes with changes in the situation. Not surprisingly, in the concluding chapter of his book where Wheeler returns to the frame problem to test his proposed Heideggerian AI, he offers no solution or dissolution of the problem. Rather he asks us to "give some credence to [his] informed intuitions."[59]

I agree with Wheeler's general intuition, which I take to be on the scent of Freeman's account of rabbit olfaction, viz., that nonrepresentational causal coupling must play a crucial role. But I take issue with his conclusion that:

In extreme cases the neural contribution will be nonrepresentational in character. In other cases, representations will be active partners alongside certain additional factors, but those representations will be action oriented in character, and so will realize the same content-sparse, action-specific, egocentric, context-dependent profile that Heideggerian phenomenology reveals to be distinctive of online representational states at the agential level.[60]

All representational states are part of the problem. Therefore, Wheeler, as I understand him, cannot give an explanation of how online dynamic coupling will dissolve the online frame problem. Nor does it help to bring in, as Wheeler does, action-oriented representations and the extended mind. Any attempt to solve the frame problem by giving any role to any sort of representational states, even online ones, has so far proved to be a dead end. It looks like nonrepresentational neural activity can't be understood to be the "extreme case" that Wheeler claims it is. Rather, such activity must be, as Heidegger, Merleau-Ponty, and Freeman claim, our basic way of responding directly to relevance in the everyday world so that the frame problem does not arise.

Heidegger and Merleau-Ponty argue that, thanks to our embodied coping and the intentional arc it makes possible, our skill in directly sensing and responding to relevant changes in the world is constantly improved. In coping in a particular context, say a classroom, we learn to ignore most of what is in the room, but, if it gets too warm, the windows solicit us to open them. We ignore the chalk dust in the corners and chalk marks on the desks but we attend to the chalk marks on the blackboard. We take for granted that what we write on the board doesn't affect the windows, even if we write "open windows," and what we do with the windows doesn't affect what's on the board. And as we constantly refine this background know-how, the things in the room and its layout take on more and more significance. In general, given our experience in the world, whenever there is a change in the current context we respond to it only if in the past it has turned out to be significant, and when we sense a significant change we treat everything else as unchanged except what our familiarity with the world suggests might also have

---

[59] Wheeler, *Reconstructing the Cognitive World*, 279.
[60] Wheeler, *Reconstructing the Cognitive World*, 276.

changed and so needs to be checked out. Thus a local version of the frame problem does not arise.

But the frame problem reasserts itself when we need to change contexts. How do we sense when a situation on the margin of our current activity has become relevant to our current tasks? Merleau-Ponty has a suggestion. When speaking of one's attention being drawn by an affordance on the margin of one's current experience, Merleau-Ponty uses the term "summons" to describe the influence of the affordance on the perceiver: "To see an object is either to have it on the fringe of the visual field and be able to concentrate on it, or else respond to this *summons* by actually concentrating on it."[61] Thus, for example, as one faces the front of a house, one's body is already being *summoned* (not just *prepared*) to go around the house to get a better look at its back.[62]

Merleau-Ponty's treatment of what Husserl calls the *inner* horizon of the perceptual object, e.g. its insides and back, applies equally to our experience of a situation's *outer* horizon of other potential situations. As I cope with a familiar task in a specific situation, other situations that have in the past been relevant are *right now* present on the horizon of my experience, summoning my attention as potentially (not merely possibly) relevant to the current situation. If Freeman is right, the attraction of familiar-but-not-currently-fully-present aspects of what is currently ready-to-hand (inner horizon) as well as the attraction of potentially relevant other familiar situations on the outer horizon of the current situation might well be correlated with the fact that our brains are not simply in one attractor basin at a time but are influenced by other attractor basins in the same landscape, and by other attractor landscapes.

According to Freeman, what makes us open to the horizonal influences of other attractors instead of our being stuck in the current attractor is that the whole system of attractor landscapes collapses and is rebuilt with each new rabbit sniff, or in our case, presumably with each shift in our attention. And once one correlates Freeman's neurodynamic account with Merleau-Ponty's description of the way the intentional arc feeds back our past experience into the way the world appears ever more familiar to us and solicits from us ever more appropriate responses to its changing significance, the frame problem of how we can deal with changing relevance by seeing what will change and what will stay the same no longer seems unsolvable.

But there is a generalization of the problem of relevance, and thus of the frame problem, that seems intractable. In *What Computers Can't Do* I gave as an

---

[61] Merleau-Ponty, *Phenomenology of Perception*, 67; italics added.
[62] Kelly, "Seeing Things in Merleau-Ponty".

example how, in placing a racing bet, we can usually restrict ourselves to such facts as the horse's age, jockey, past performance, and competition, but there are always other factors such as whether the horse is allergic to goldenrod or whether the jockey has just had a fight with the owner, which may in some cases be decisive. Human handicappers are capable of recognizing the relevance of such facts when they come across them.[63] But since anything in experience can be relevant to anything else, such an ability seems magical.

Jerry Fodor follows up on my pessimistic remark:

The problem is to get the structure of an entire belief system to bear on individual occasions of belief fixation. We have, to put it bluntly, no computational formalisms that show us how to do this, and we have no idea how such formalisms might be developed...If someone—a Dreyfus, for example—were to ask us why we should even suppose that the digital computer is a plausible mechanism for the simulation of global cognitive processes, the answering silence would be deafening.[64]

However, once we give up computational cognitivism, and see ourselves instead as basically coupled copers, we can see how the frame problem can be dissolved by an appeal to existential phenomenology and neurodynamics. In the light of how learning our way around in the world modifies our brain so that relevance is directly experienced in the way tasks summon us, even the general problem raised by the fact that anything in our experience could in principle be related to anything else no longer seems a mystery.

9. Conclusion

It would be satisfying if we could now conclude that, with the help of Merleau-Ponty and Freeman, we can fix what is wrong with current allegedly Heideggerian AI by making it more Heideggerian. There is, however, a big remaining problem. Merleau-Ponty's and Freeman's account of how we directly pick up significance and improve our sensitivity to relevance depends on our responding to what is significant for *us* given our needs, body size, ways of moving, and so forth, not to mention our personal and cultural self-interpretation. Thus, to program Heideggerian AI, we would not only need a model of the brain functioning underlying coupled coping such as Freeman's, but we would also need—and here's the rub—a model of our particular way of being embedded and embodied such that what we experience is significant for us in the particular way that it is. That is, we would have to include in our program a model of a body very much like ours with our

---

[63] Dreyfus, *What Computers Still Can't Do*, 258.
[64] Fodor, *Modularity of Mind*, 128–9.

needs, desires, pleasures, pains, ways of moving, cultural background, etc. If we can't make our brain model responsive to the significance in the environment as it shows up specifically for human beings, the project of developing an embedded and embodied Heideggerian AI can't get off the ground.

So, according to the view I have been presenting, even if the Heideggerian/ Merleau-Pontyan approach to AI suggested by Freeman is ontologically sound in a way that GOFAI and the subsequent supposedly Heideggerian models proposed by Brooks, Agre, and Wheeler are not, a neurodynamic computer model would still have to be given a detailed description of our body and motivations like ours if things were to count as significant for it so that it could learn to act intelligently in our world. The idea of super-computers containing detailed models of human bodies and brains may seem to make sense in the wild imaginations of a Ray Kurzweil or Bill Joy, but they haven't a chance of being realized in the real world.

Bibliography

Agre, Philip E. (1988), *The Dynamic Structure of Everyday Life*, Technical Report, 1085 (Cambridge, MA: MIT Artificial Intelligence Lab).

Agre, Philip E. (1997), *Computation and Human Experience* (Cambridge: Cambridge University Press).

Amidzic, Ognjen, et al. (2001), "Patterns of Focal Y-Bursts in Chess Players: Grandmasters Call on Regions of the Brain Not Used So Much by Less Skilled Amateurs", *Nature*, 412 (9 Aug.), 603.

Anderson, James A. (1978), "Neural Models with Cognitive Implications", in D. LaBerse and S. J. Samuels (eds), *Basic Processing in Reading* (Hillsdale, NJ: Lawrence Erlbaum Associates), 27–90.

Aristotle (1908), *The Nicomachean Ethics*, tr. William David Ross (Oxford: Clarendon Press).

Aristotle (1955), *The Ethics of Aristotle*, tr. J. A. K. Thomson (Harmondsworth: Penguin).

Barnett, G. Octo (1982), "The Computer and Clinical Judgment", *New England Journal of Medicine,* 307(8), 493.

Barr, Avron, and Feigenbaum, Edward A. (1981), *The Handbook of Artificial Intelligence* (Los Altos, CA: Wm. Kaufmann), i.

Benner, Patricia (1984), *From Novice to Expert: Excellence and Power in Clinical Nursing Practice* (Reading, MA: Addison-Wesley).

Benner, Patricia A., Tanner, Cristine A., and Chesla, Catherine A. (1996), *Expertise in Nursing Practice: Caring, Clinical Judgment, and Ethics* (New York: Springer).

Berliner, Hans (1980), "Computer Backgammon", *Scientific American* (June), 64–72.

Boden, Margaret (1977), *Artificial Intelligence and Natural Man* (New York: Basic Books).

Bourdieu, Pierre (1977), *Outline of a Theory of Practice*, tr. Richard Nice (Cambridge: Cambridge University Press).

Bourdieu, Pierre (1980), *The Logic of Practice* (Stanford, CA: Stanford University Press).

Brandom, Robert (2009), *Articulating Reasons: An Introduction to Inferentialism* (Cambridge, MA: Harvard University Press).

Brooks, Rodney A. (1997), "Intelligence without Representation", in John Haugeland (ed.), *Mind Design II: Philosophy, Psychology, and Artificial Intelligence* (Cambridge, MA: MIT Press), 395–420.

Brooks, Rodney A. (1997), "From Earwigs to Humans", *Robotics and Autonomous Systems,* 20, 291–304.

Brooks, Rodney A. (2002), *Flesh and Machines: How Robots Will Change Us* (New York: Vintage Books).

Cairns, Dorton (1968), "An Approach to Phenomenology", in Marvin Farber (ed.), *Philosophical Essays in Memory of Edmund Husserl* (Cambridge, MA: Harvard University Press), 3–18.

Chisholm, Roderick (1957), *Perceiving: A Philosophical Study* (Ithaca, NY: Cornell University Press).

Clark, Andy, and Chalmers, David J. (1998), "The Extended Mind", *Analysis*, 58, 7–19.

Coleman, Daniel (1979), "Holographic Memory: An Interview with Karl Pribram", *Psychology Today*, 12(9), 80.

Das, Rajarshi, and Das, Sreerupa (1994), "Catching a Baseball: A Reinforcement Learning Perspective Using a Neural Network", *Proceedings of 12th National Conference on Artificial Intelligence* (Seattle, WA: AAAI), 3–19.

Davidson, Donald (1980), "Actions, Reasons, and Causes", *Essays on Actions and Events* (Oxford: Oxford University Press).

DeMaio, J., Parkinson, S., Leshowitz, B., Crosby, J., and Thorp, J. A. (1976), *Visual Scanning: Comparisons between Students and Instructor Pilots*, AFHRL-TR-76-10, AD-A023 634 (William Air Force Base, AZ: Flying Training Division, Air Force Human Resources Laboratory).

Dennett, Daniel C. (1994), "The Practical Requirements for Making a Conscious Robot", *Philosophical Transactions of the Royal Society*, 349 (1689), 133–46.

Derrida, Jacques (1967), "La Forme et le vouloir-dire", *Revue Internationale de Philosophie*, 81, 277–99.

Derrida, Jacques (1970), "Structure, Sign, and Play in the Discourse of the Human Sciences", in Richard Macksey and Eugenio Donato (eds), *The Structuralist Controversy* (Baltimore, MD: Johns Hopkins University Press), 247–65.

Dewey, John (1922), *Human Nature and Conduct: An Introduction to Social Psychology* (London: George Allen & Unwin).

Dewey, John (1960), *Theory of the Moral Life* (New York: Holt, Rinehart & Winston).

Dreyfus, Hubert L. (1963), *Husserl's Phenomenology of Perception: From Transcendental to Existential Phenomenology* (Cambridge, MA: Harvard University Press).

Dreyfus, Hubert (1972), *What Computers Can't Do: A Critique of Artificial Reason* (New York: Harper & Row).

Dreyfus, Hubert (ed.) (1982), *Husserl, Intentionality and Cognitive Science* (Cambridge, MA: MIT Press).

Dreyfus, Hubert (1984), "Husserl's Perceptual Noema", in Hubert L. Dreyfus (ed.), *Husserl, Intentionality and Cognitive Science*. (Cambridge, MA: MIT Press), 97–123.

Dreyfus, Hubert (1991), *Being-in-the-World: A Commentary on Heidegger's* Being and Time, *Division I* (Cambridge, MA: MIT Press).

Dreyfus, Hubert (1992), *What Computers Still Can't Do* (Cambridge, MA: MIT Press).

Dreyfus, Hubert (2000), "Teaching between Skill and Philosophy by a Philosopher of Skills", *Journal of Nordic Educational Research*, 20(2), 107–16.

Dreyfus, Hubert (2000), "A Merleau-Pontian Critique of Husserl's and Searle's Representationalist Accounts of Action", *Proceedings of the Aristotelian Society*, 100, 287–302.

Dreyfus, Hubert (2001), "Phenomenological Description versus Rational Reconstruction", *La Revue Internationale de Philosophie*, 55 (217), 181–96.

Dreyfus, Hubert L., and Dreyfus, Stuart (1988), *Mind over Machine* (New York: Free Press).

Dreyfus, Hubert L., and Dreyfus, Stuart E. (2000), *Mind over Machine* (New York: Simon & Schuster).

Dreyfus, Hubert L., and Wakefield, Jerry (1991), "Intentionality and the Phenomenology of Action", in Ernest LePore and Robert Van Gulick (eds), *John Searle and his Critics* (Cambridge: Basil Blackwell), 259–70.

Duda, Richard O., and Gashnig, John G. (1981), "Knowledge-Based Expert Systems Come of Age", *Byte* (Sept.), 254.

Duda, Richard O., and Shortliffe, Edward H. (1983), "Expert Systems Research", *Science*, 220/4594, 266.

Feigenbaum, Edward, and McCorduck, Pamela (1983), *The Fifth Generation: Artificial Intelligence and Japan's Computer Challenge to the World* (Reading, MA: Addison-Wesley).

Firth, Roderick (1949), "Sense Data and the Percept Theory", *Mind*, 58(232), 434–65.

Fodor, Jerry A. (1983), *The Modularity of Mind* (Cambridge, MA: Bradford/MIT Press).

Føllesdal, Dagfinn (1969), "Husserl's Notion of the Noema", *Journal of Philosophy*, 66 (20), 681–7.

Føllesdal, Dagfinn (1975), "Meaning and Experience", in Samuel Guttenplan (ed.), *Mind and Language* (Oxford: Clarendon Press), 25–44.

Føllesdal, Dagfinn (1979), "Husserl and Heidegger on the Role of Actions in the Constitution of the World", in E. Saarinen, R. Hilpinen, I. Niiniluoto, and M. B. Provence Hintikka (eds), *Essays in Honour of Jaakko Hintikka* (Dordrecht: D. Reidel), 365–78.

Foucault, Michel (1966), "Nietzsche, Freud, Marx", in Gilles Deleuze (ed.), *Nietzsche* (Cahiers de Royaumont; Paris: Editions de Minuit), 183–220.

Freeman, Walter J. (1991), "The Physiology of Perception", *Scientific American*, 264, 78–85.

Freeman, Walter J. (1995), *Societies of Brains: A Study in the Neuroscience of Love and Hate* (Hillsdale, NJ: Lawrence Erlbaum Associates).

Freeman, Walter J. (2001), *How the Brain Makes up its Mind* (New York: Columbia University Press).

Freeman, Walter J., and Grajski, Kamil A. (1987), "Relation of Olfactory EEG to Behavior: Factor Analysis", *Behavioral Neuroscience*, 101, 766–77.

Frege, Gottlob (1960), *Translations from the Philosophical Writings of Gottlob Frege* (Oxford: Blackwell).

Freud, Sigmund (1905), *Three Essays on the Theory of Sexuality*, ed. James Strachey (Standard Edition, Complete Psychological Works of Sigmund Freud, 7; London: Hogarth).

Freud, Sigmund (1908), *Character and Anal Erotism*, ed. James Strachey (Standard Edition, Complete Psychological Works of Sigmund Freud, 9; London: Hogarth Press).

Freud, Sigmund (1913), *The Disposition to Obsessional Neurosis: A Contribution to the Problem of Choice of Neurosis*, ed. James Strachey (Standard Edition, Complete Psychological Works of Sigmund Freud, 12; London: Hogarth).

Freud, Sigmund (1923), *The Ego and the Id*, ed. James Strachey (Standard Edition, Complete Psychological Works of Sigmund Freud, 19; London: Hogarth).

Gadamer, Hans-Georg (1975), *Truth and Method* (New York: Seabury Press).

Geertz, Clifford (1973), *The Interpretation of Cultures* (New York: Basic Books).

Gelder, Tim van (1997), "Dynamics and Cognition", in John Haugeland (ed.), *Mind Design II* (Cambridge, MA: MIT Press), 421–50.

Gibson, James J. (1979), *The Ecological Approach to Visual Perception* (Boston: Houghton Mifflin).

Gibson, James J., Olum, Paul, and Rosenblatt, Frank (1955), "Parallax and Perspective during Aircraft Landing", *American Journal of Psychology*, 68, 372–85.

Gilligan, Carol (1982), *In a Different Voice: Psychological Theory and Women's Development* (Cambridge, MA: Harvard University Press).

Gilligan, Carol (1986), "On In a Different Voice: An Interdisciplinary Forum", *Signs: Journal of Women in Culture and Society*, 11(2), 327.

Gorman, R. Paul, and Sejnowski, Terrence J. (1988), "Learned Classification of Sonar Targets Using a Massively Parallel Network", *IEEE Transactions on Acoustics, Speech, and Signal Processing*, 36(7), 1135–40.

Grice, Paul (1965), "The Causal Theory of Perception", in Robert Swartz (ed.), *Perceiving, Sensing, and Knowing* (New York: Anchor Books), 438–72.

Grossberg, Stephen (1982), *Studies of Mind and Brain: Neural Principles of Learning, Perception, Development, Cognition and Motor Control* (Boston: Reidel Press).

Gurwitsch, Aron (1964), *The Field of Consciousness* (Pittsburgh: Duquesne University Press).

Gurwitsch, Aron (1965), "The Phenomenology of Perception: Perceptual Implications", in James Edie (ed.), *An Invitation to Phenomenology* (Chicago: Quadrangle Books), 17–20.

Gurwitsch, Aron (1966), *Studies in Phenomenology and Psychology* (Evanston, IL: Northwestern University Press).

Gurwitsch, Aron (1967), "Husserl's Theory of Intentionality of Consciousness in Historical Perspective", *Phenomenology and Existentialism* (Baltimore, MD: Johns Hopkins University Press), 25–57.

Gurwitsch, Aron (1970), "Towards a Theory of Intentionality", *Philosophy and Phenomenological Research*, 27, 345–67.

Gurwitsch, Aron (1974), "Perceptual Coherence as the Foundation of the Judgement of Predication", in Aron Gurwitsch and Lester Embree (eds), *Phenomenology and the Theory of Science* (Evanston, IL: Northwestern University Press), 241–68.

Gurwitsch, Aron (1979), *Human Encounters in the Social World* (Pittsburgh: Duquesne University Press).

Habermas, Jürgen (1982), "A Reply to my Critics", in John B. Thompson and David Held (eds), *Habermas: Critical Debates* (Cambridge, MA: MIT Press), 219–83.

Habermas, Jürgen (2001), *Moral Consciousness and Communicative Action*, tr. Christian Lenhardt and Shierry Weber (Cambridge, MA: MIT Press).

Haugeland, John (1985), *Artificial Intelligence: The Very Idea* (Cambridge, MA: MIT Press).

Haugeland, John (1998), *Having Thought: Essays in the Metaphysics of Mind* (Cambridge, MA: Harvard University Press).

Haugeland, John (1998), "Mind Embodied and Embedded", *Having Thought: Essays in the Metaphysics of Mind* (Cambridge, MA: Harvard University Press), 207–37.

Hebb, Donald O. (1949), *The Organization of Behavior* (New York: Wiley).

Heidegger, Martin (1957), *Der Satz vom Grund* (Pfullingen: Gunther Neske).

Heidegger, Martin (1962), *Being and Time*, tr. John Macquarrie and Edward Robinson (New York: Harper & Row).

Heidegger, Martin (1971), "The Origin of the Work of Art", *Poetry, Language, Thought* (New York: Harper & Row), 15–86.

Heidegger, Martin (1976), *Logik: Die Frage nach der Wahrheit* (Gesamtausgabe, 21; Frankfurt am Main: Vittorio Klostermann).

Heidegger, Martin (1977), "The Question Concerning Technology", *The Question Concerning Technology and Other Essays* (New York: Harper & Row), 3–35.

Heidegger, Martin (1977), *Sein und Zeit* (Tübingen: Niemeyer).

Heidegger, Martin (1977), "Science and Reflection", *The Question Concerning Technology and Other Essays* (New York: Harper & Row), 155–82.

Heidegger, Martin (1982), *Basic Problems of Phenomenology*, tr. Albert Hofstadter (Bloomington, IN: Indiana University Press).

Heidegger, Martin (1984), *The Metaphysical Foundation of Logic* (Bloomington, IN: Indiana University Press).

Heidegger, Martin (1985), *The History of the Concept of Time* (Bloomington, IN: Indiana University Press).

Heidegger, Martin (1997), *Plato's Sophist*, tr. Richard Rojcewicz and André Schuwer (Bloomington, IN: Indiana University Press).

Heidegger, Martin (2002), "Phenomenological Interpretations in Connection with Aristotle", in *Supplements: From the Earliest Essays to Being and Time and Beyond*, ed. John Van Buren (Albany, NY: State University of New York Press), 111–46.

Heidegger, Martin (2010), *Logic: The Question of Truth*, tr. Thomas Sheehan (Studies in Continental Thought; Bloomington, IN: Indiana University Press).

Hinton, Geoffrey (1986), "Learning Distributed Representations of Concepts", *Proceedings of the Eighth Annual Conference of the Cognitive Science Society* (Amherst, MA: Cognitive Science Society), 1–12.

Hobbes, Thomas (1958), *Leviathan* (New York: Library of Liberal Arts).

Husserl, Edmund (1948), *Erfahrung und Urteil* (Hamburg: Claassen & Govert).

Husserl, Edmund (1950), *Ideen zur einer reinen Phänomenologie und phänomenologischen Philosophie* (Husserliana, 3; The Hague: Martinus Nijhoff).

Husserl, Edmund (1960), *Cartesian Meditations*, tr. Dorion Cairns (The Hague: Martinus Nijhoff).

Husserl, Edmund (1962), *Phänomenologische Psychologie* (Husserliana; The Hague: Martinus Nijhoff).

Husserl, Edmund (1969), *Formal and Transcendental Logic*, tr. D. Cairns (The Hague: Martinus Nijhoff).

Husserl, Edmund (1970), *Logical Investigations*, tr. J. N. Findlay (New York: Humanities Press).

Husserl, Edmund (1970), *The Crisis of European Sciences and Transcendental Phenomenology* (Evanston, IL: Northwestern University Press).

Husserl, Edmund (1971), *Ideen zur einer reinen Phänomenologie und phänomenologischen Philosophie*, iii. *Die Phänomenologie und die Fundamente der Wissenschaften*, ed. Marly Biemel (Husserliana, 5; The Hague: Martinus Nijhoff).

Husserl, Edmund (1973), *Experience and Judgment* (Evanston, IL: Northwestern University Press).

Husserl, Edmund (1982), *Ideas Pertaining to a Pure Phenomenology and to a Phenomenological Philosophy*, tr. F. Kersten (The Hague: Martinus Nijhoff).

Kelly, Sean D. (1999), "What Do We See (When We Do)?", *Philosophical Topics*, 27(2), 107–28.

Kelly, Sean D. (2000), "Grasping at Straws: Motor Intentionality and the Cognitive Science of Skilled Behavior", in Mark A. Wrathall and Jeff Malpas (eds), *Heidegger, Coping, and Cognitive Science* (Cambridge, MA: MIT Press), 161–77.

Kelly, Sean D. (2001), "Demonstrative Concepts and Experience", *Philosophical Review*, 110(3), 397–420.

Kelly, Sean D. (2001), "The Non-Conceptual Content of Perceptual Experience: Situation Dependence and Fineness of Grain", *Philosophy and Phenomenological Research*, 62(3), 601–8.

Kelly, Sean D. (2005), "Seeing Things in Merleau-Ponty", in Taylor Carman and Mark B. N. Hansen (eds), *The Cambridge Companion to Merleau-Ponty* (Cambridge: Cambridge University Press), 74–110.

Kierkegaard, Søren (1983), *Fear and Trembling* (Princeton: Princeton University Press).

Koffka, Kurt (1935), *Principles of Gestalt Psychology* (New York: Harcourt, Brace).

Kohonen, Teuvo (1977), *Associative Memory: A System-Theoretical Approach* (Berlin: Springer-Verlag).

Kolata, Gina (1982), "How Can Computers Get Common Sense?", *Science*, 217 (24 Sept.), 1237–8.

Kuhn, Thomas (1977), *The Essential Tension* (Chicago: University of Chicago Press).

Kwan, Hon C., Yeap, Tet H., Barrett, Donald, and Jiang, Bai C. (1991), "Network Relaxation as Biological Computation", *Behavioral and Brain Sciences*, 14(2), 354–6.

Lakatos, Imre (1978), *Philosophical Papers*, ed. J. Worrall (Cambridge: Cambridge University Press).

Lee, Dembart (1984), "Man Is Still Master: King of Chess Computers Humbled by Wily Human", *Los Angeles Times*, 12 May.

Leibniz, Gottfried Wilhelm (1951), *Leibniz: Selections*, ed. Philip P. Weiner (New York: Scribner).

Levine, Lee Daniel (1988), *Bird: The Making of an American Sports Legend* (New York: McGraw-Hill).

Lighthill, James (1973), "Artificial Intelligence: A General Survey", *Artificial Intelligence: A Paper Symposium* (London: Science Research Council), 3–18.

MacIntyre, Alasdair (1981), *After Virtue* (Notre Dame, IN: University of Notre Dame Press).

McCorduck, Pamela (1979), *Machines Who Think* (San Francisco: W. H. Freeman).

McDowell, John (1994), *Mind and World* (Cambridge, MA: Harvard University Press).

McDowell, John (1998), "Virtue and Reason", *Mind, Value, and Reality* (Cambridge, MA: Harvard University Press), 50–73.

Mandelbaum, Maurice (1955), *The Phenomenology of Moral Experience* (New York: Free Press).

Merleau-Ponty, Maurice (1942), *La Structure du comportement* (Paris: Presses Universitaires de France).

Merleau-Ponty, Maurice (1945), *Phénoménologie de la perception* (Paris: Librairie Gallimard).

Merleau-Ponty, Maurice (1962), *Phenomenology of Perception*, tr. Colin Smith (New York: Humanities Press).

Merleau-Ponty, Maurice (1964), "Cézanne's Doubt", *Sense and Nonsense* (Chicago: Northwestern University Press), 9–25.

Merleau-Ponty, Maurice (1964), "The Film and the New Psychology", *Sense and Nonsense* (Chicago: Northwestern University Press).

Merleau-Ponty, Maurice (1966), *The Structure of Behavior*, tr. A. L. Fisher (2nd edn; Boston: Beacon Press).

Merleau-Ponty, Maurice (1968), *The Visible and the Invisible* (Chicago: Northwestern University Press).

Merleau-Ponty, Maurice (1979), *The Phenomenology of Perception* (London: Routledge & Kegan Paul).

Merleau-Ponty, Maurice (2002), *The Phenomenology of Perception* (Reprint edn; London: Routledge Classics).

Miller, Randolph A., Jr., Pople, Harry E., and Myers, Jack D. (1982), "INTERNIST-I, an Experimental Computer-Based Diagnostic Consultant for General Internal Medicine", *New England Journal of Medicine*, 307(8), 494.

Minsky, Marvin (1977), *Computation: Finite and Infinite Machines* (New York: Prentice-Hall).

Minsky, Marvin (1981), "A Framework for Representing Knowledge", in John Haugeland (ed.), *Mind Design* (Cambridge, MA: MIT Press), 95–128.

Minsky, Marvin, and Papert, Seymour (1969), *Perceptrons: An Introduction to Computational Geometry* (Cambridge, MA: MIT Press).

Murphy, John M., and Gilligan, Carol (1980), "Moral Development in Late Adolescence and Adulthood: A Critique and Reconstruction of Kohlberg's Theory", *Human Development*, 23, 77–104.

Newell, Allen (1983), "Intellectual Issues in the History of Artificial Intelligence", in F. Machlup and U. Mansfield (eds), *The Study of Information: Interdisciplinary Messages* (New York: Wiley), 187–227.

Newell, Allen, and Simon, Herbert (1981), "Computer Science as Empirical Inquiry: Symbols and Search", in John Haugeland (ed.), *Mind Design* (Cambridge, MA: MIT Press), 35–66.

Nietzsche, Friedrich (1986), *Human, All Too Human*, tr. R. J. Hollingdale (Cambridge: Cambridge University Press).

Okrent, Mark (1988), *Heidegger's Pragmatism* (Ithaca, NY: Cornell University Press).

Perry, William Graves (1968), *Forms of Intellectual and Ethical Development in the College Years: A Scheme* (New York: Holt, Rinehart & Winston).

Piaget, Jean (1935), *The Moral Judgment of the Child* (Glencoe, IL: Free Press).

Preston, John, and Bishop, Mark (eds) (2002), *Views into the Chinese Room: New Essays on Searle and Artificial Intelligence* (Oxford: Clarendon Press).

Quine, Willard V. O. (1976), *The Ways of Paradox and Other Essays* (Cambridge, MA: Harvard University Press).

Quine, Willard V. O., and Ullian, J. S. (1978), *The Web of Belief* (New York: Random House).

Reich, Wilhelm (1972), *Character Analysis (Part 1)* (New York: Simon & Schuster).

Rorty, Richard (1979), *Philosophy and the Mirror of Nature* (Princeton: Princeton University Press).

Rosenblatt, Frank (1958), *Mechanisation of Thought Processes: Proceedings of a Symposium Held at the National Physical Laboratory* (London: Her Majesty's Stationery Office).

Rosenblatt, Frank (1962), "Strategic Approaches to the Study of Brain Models", in H. von Foerster (ed.), *Principles of Self-Organization* (Elmsford, NY: Pergamon Press), 385–96.

Rosenblatt, Frank (1962), *Principles of Neurodynamics, Perceptrons and the Theory of Brain Mechanisms* (Washington, DC: Spartan Books).

Rumelhart, David E., and Norman, Donald A. (1981), "A Comparison of Models", in Geoffrey Hinton and James Anderson (eds), *Parallel Models of Associative Memory* (Hillsdale, NJ: Lawrence Erlbaum Associates), 1–7.

Rumelhart, David E., McClelland, James L., and Group, PDP Research (1986), *Parallel Distributed Processing: Explorations in the Microstructure of Cognition* (Cambridge, MA: MIT Press), i.

Schank, Roger, and Colby, Kenneth (1973), *Computer Models of Thought and Language* (San Francisco: W. H. Freeman).

Schank, Roger C. (1995), *What We Learn When We Learn by Doing*, Technical Report, 60 (Evanston, IL: Northwestern University, Institute for Learning Sciences).

Schank, Roger C., and Abelson, Robert P. (1977), *Scripts, Plans, Goals and Understanding: An Inquiry into Human Knowledge Structures* (Hillsdale, NJ: Lawrence Erlbaum).

Schutz, Alfred (1962), *Collected Papers* (The Hague: Martinus Nijhoff).

Searle, John (1983), *Intentionality: An Essay in the Philosophy of Mind* (Cambridge: Cambridge University Press).

Searle, John R. (1993), "Response: The Background of Intentionality and Action", in Ernest LePore and Robert Van Gulick (eds), *John Searle and his Critics* (Oxford: Wiley-Blackwell), 289–300.

Searle, John R. (1995), *The Construction of Social Reality* (New York: Free Press).

Searle, John R. (2000), "The Limits of Phenomenology", in Mark A. Wrathall and Jeff Malpas (eds), *Heidegger, Coping, and Cognitive Science: Essays in Honor of Hubert L. Dreyfus* (Cambridge, MA: MIT Press), ii. 71–92.

Searle, John R. (2001), "Neither Phenomenological Description Nor Rational Reconstruction: Reply to Dreyfus", *Revue Internationale de Philosophie*, 55(216), 277–95.

Shapiro, David (1981), *Autonomy and Rigid Character* (New York: Basic Books).

Simon, Herbert (1965), *The Shape of Automation for Men and Management* (New York: Harper & Row).

Simon, Herbert A. (1979), *Models of Thought* (New Haven, CT: Yale University Press).

Simon, Herbert, and Newell, Allen (1958), "Heuristic Problem Solving: The Next Advance in Operations Research", *Operations Research*, 6, 1–10.

Smolensky, Paul (1988), "On the Proper Treatment of Connectionism", *Behavioral and Brain Sciences*, 11(1), 1–23.

Sutton, Richard S., and Barto, Andrew G. (1998), *Reinforcement Learning: An Introduction* (Cambridge, MA: MIT Press).

Taylor, Charles (2005), "Merleau-Ponty and the Epistemological Picture", in Taylor Carman and Mark B. N. Hansen (eds), *The Cambridge Companion to Merleau-Ponty* (Cambridge: Cambridge University Press), 26–49.

Tesauro, Gerald J. (1994), "TD-Gammon, a Self-Teaching Backgammon Program, Achieves Master-Level Play", *Neural Computation*, 6(2), 215–19.

Todes, Samuel (1966), "Comparative Phenomenology of Perception and Imagination", *Journal of Existentialism* (Spring and Fall), 6, 253–68.

Todes, Samuel J. (1969), "Sensuous Abstraction and the Abstract Sense of Reality", in James M. Edie (ed.), *New Essays in Phenomenology* (Chicago: Quadrangle Books), 15–23.

Todes, Samuel (2001), *Body and World* (Cambridge, MA: MIT Press).

Tomkins, Silvan S. (1979), "Script Theory: Differential Magnifications of Affects", in H. E. Howe Jr. and R. A. Dienstbier (eds), *Nebraska Symposium on Motivation, 1978* (26; Lincoln, NE: University of Nebraska Press), 201–36.

Wakefield, Jerry, and Dreyfus, Hubert L. (1990), "Intentionality and the Phenomenology of Action", in Ernest LePore and Robert Van Gulick (eds), *John Searle and his Critics* (Cambridge: Basil Blackwell), 259–70.

Westerman, Michael A. (1980), "Meaning and Psychotherapy: A Reconceptualization of the Value and Limitations of Insight-Oriented, Behavioral, and Strategic Approaches", American Psychological Association Convention (Montreal).

Wheeler, Michael (2002), "Change in the Rules: Computers, Dynamical Systems, and Searle", in John Preston and Mark Bishop (eds), *Views into the Chinese Room: New Essays on Searle and Artificial Intelligence* (Oxford: Clarendon Press), 338–59.

Wheeler, Michael (2005), *Reconstructing the Cognitive World: The Next Step* (Cambridge, MA: MIT Press).

Winograd, Terry (1976), "Artificial Intelligence and Language Comprehension", *Artificial Intelligence and Language Comprehension* (Washington, DC: National Institute of Education), 1–26.

Winograd, Terry (1984), "Computer Software for Working with Language", *Scientific American* (Sept.), 142.

Winograd, Terry (1995), "Heidegger and the Design of Computer Systems", in A. Feenberg and A. Hannay (eds), *Technology and the Politics of Knowledge* (Bloomington, IN: Indiana University Press), 108–27.

Wittgenstein, Ludwig (1953), *Philosophical Investigations* (Oxford: Blackwell).

Wittgenstein, Ludwig (1960), *Tractatus Logico-Philosophicus* (London: Routledge & Kegan Paul).

Wittgenstein, Ludwig (1969), *On Certainty* (New York: Harper & Row).

Wittgenstein, Ludwig (1975), *Philosophical Remarks* (Chicago: University of Chicago Press).

Wittgenstein, Ludwig (1982), *Last Writings on the Philosophy of Psychology* (Chicago: Chicago University Press), i.

Wrathall, Mark A. (2005), "Motives, Reasons, and Causes", in Taylor Carman and
Mark B. N. Hansen (eds), *The Cambridge Companion to Merleau-Ponty* (Cambridge:
Cambridge University Press), 111–28.

Yu, Victor L., et al. (1979), "Antimicrobial Selection by a Computer", *Journal of the
American Medical Association*, 242(12), 1279–82.

Index

Printed and bound by CPI Group (UK) Ltd, Croydon, CR0 4YY